NABOKOV: THE MAN AND HIS WORK

THE
UNIVERSITY
OF
WISCONSIN
PRESS,
MADISON
MILWAUKEE
AND
LONDON
1967

STUDIES
EDITED
BY
L. S. DEMBO

NABOKOV
THE
MAN
AND
HIS
WORK

Published by
The University of Wisconsin Press
Madison, Milwaukee, and London
U.S.A.: Box 1379
Madison, Wisconsin 53701
U.K.: 26–28 Hallam Street
London W.1
Copyright © 1967 by the
Regents of the University of Wisconsin
All Rights Reserved
Printed in
the United States of America
by NAPCO, Inc.
Milwaukee, Wisconsin
Library of Congress
Catalog Card Number 67-26625

TO JOHN J. ENCK

PREFACE

This collection of essays is, with the exception of articles on *The Real Life of Sebastian Knight* by Charles Nicol and on *Pnin* by Ambrose Gordon, Jr., a reprint of the Spring, 1967, issue of *Wisconsin Studies in Contemporary Literature*. Conceived by John J. Enck before his premature death in March, 1966, the number was intended to help provide a long overdue recognition of Nabokov's genius. I shared Mr. Enck's enthusiasm for the project and in bringing it to fruition I can only hope that I have done justice to his original inspiration. Although the issue was double-sized, it was not possible to include discussions of all Nabokov's major writing. Nonetheless, the range is broad and many of the essays are meticulously detailed; thus the reader will gain, I believe, an insight into the significance of Nabokov's work as a whole as well as an appreciation of the complexities of several individual pieces. I must also express my indebtedness to Donald Sheehan, managing editor of *WSCL*, whose expert assistance made my own efforts more a pleasure than a labor.

L.S.D.

Madison
Summer, 1967

CONTENTS

NABOKOV: THE MAN AND HIS WORK

VLADIMIR NABOKOV, AN INTRODUCTION

L. S. Dembo

During the past forty years Vladimir Nabokov has published over a dozen novels, several collections of short stories, a number of plays, two volumes of poetry, a memoir, and a study of Gogol. He has also rendered into English some Russian poems, the chief one being Pushkin's verse-narrative, *Eugene Onegin*, to which Nabokov added over two volumes of notes and commentary. Five of the novels, representing his major work since the early nineteen-forties, were written originally in English; of the nine Russian novels, published between 1926 and 1938, all but three have been translated, either by Nabokov himself, his son, or other persons working closely with him.[1] The true character of this achievement, of which the linguistic feat is only a part, is but gradually being recognized, and the following essays will, it is hoped, hasten that recognition. With much of his work either available to or written for the English-speaking reader, there is no reason for Nabokov's reputation to rest on *Lolita* alone, just as there is no reason for not viewing this novel in its true perspective, as an expression of a consistent, subtle artistic vision rather than as an exotic tour de force.

Alfred Appel attempts to establish "the rightful context" of *Lolita* by tracing its intricate system of word-play and determining the relationship of this system to the "parodic" structure. Word-play, a favorite device of Nabokov, is, he finds, no less the narrator's primary artistic defense against the horror of his activities and the "terror of everyday life." Related to this view is Simon Karlinsky's formulation of a general principle of Nabokov's writing: "the hero

---

[1] See the Selected Bibliography.

uses his imagination to devise a reality of his own, which he seeks to impose on a central reality. The question of which reality is *real*, that of the hero or that of the environment, is usually left open. What matters is which of the two realities is the more relevant one for the artistic conception of the story." In *Lolita* there are at least three levels of reality: the world as it is (Lolita as an ordinary teenager), the world as a phenomenon of the mind of the narrator, Humbert Humbert (Lolita as a nymphet or butterfly), and finally the verbal world of hidden semantic cross-connections by which Humbert seeks to transform his sexual-aesthetic experience into "pure" art.

Nabokov's concern with artistic or pseudo-artistic perception and its consequences appears in both his serio-comic and wholly serious work. As Mr. Karlinsky implies, most of Nabokov's heroes are solipsists or at least subjectivists; and the greater their imaginative capacity, the more suspect is their sanity. *The Eye* (1930),[2] discussed at length by Andrew Field, presents a typically paradoxical situation. The narrator is a lonely, disoriented young émigré who shoots himself after being beaten by the jealous husband of his mistress. Whether he survives his wounds and becomes involved with a group of fellow exiles literally, or whether he has succeeded in killing himself and is merely experiencing a "post mortem" vision of his own making, is left to the reader to decide. Thus he tells us, "I progressed from the incomprehensible sensation of tight bandages to the idea of a hospital, and, at once obedient to my will, a spectral hospital ward materialized around me. . . . What a mighty thing was human thought, that it could hurtle on beyond death! Heaven knows how much longer it would pulsate and create images after my defunct brain had long since ceased to be of any use." (p. 31) In any case, the speaker describes himself as "a cold, insistent, tireless eye" observing self-generated images, the various persons of the émigré group. He speaks, detachedly, of one Smurov, a mysterious member of the group, who appears in a different light to each of the other members: "all these people I met were not live beings but only chance mirrors for Smurov." (p. 99) He has resolved to "dig up the true Smurov, being already aware that his image was influenced by the climatic conditions prevailing in various souls—that within a cold soul he assumed one aspect but in a glowing one had a different coloration." (p. 64) As Nabokov explains in the introduction, Smurov exists only in the minds of the members of the group, just

---

[2] Phaedra, New York, 1955.

as the members of the group exist only in the mind of the narrator. When the speaker finally discovers that Smurov is himself, the circle is complete. What is important, however, is not the exact locus of reality, but the process of perception itself: "I have realized that the only happiness in this world is to observe, to spy, to watch, to scrutinize oneself and others, to be nothing but a big, slightly vitreous, somewhat bloodshot, unblinking eye. . . . Oh, to shout it so that all of you believe me at last, you cruel, smug people. . . ." (pp. 113–114) Whether this is the outcry of a madman or a "pure" artist or both it is impossible to say.

Exotic perception recurs throughout *Speak, Memory* (1951; published in England as *Conclusive Evidence*)[3] in terms of the "white," rather than the "black," magic of bizarre optical experiences. Characteristic of this memoir, which views the past through various prisms or by means of a slide projector, is a child's-eye description of the landscape seen from a dining-car: "as the meal progressed toward its fatal last course, one would keep catching the car in the act of being recklessly sheathed, lurching waiters and all, in the landscape, while the landscape itself went through a complex system of motion, the daytime moon stubbornly keeping abreast of one's plate, the distant meadows opening fanwise, the near trees sweeping upon invisible swings toward the track, a parallel rail line all at once committing suicide by anastomosis, a bank of nictitating grass rising, rising, rising, until the little witness of mixed velocities was made to disgorge his portion of *omelette aux confitures de fraises*." (p. 96) For all its levity, this passage describes a mode of viewing that is, in a sense, the purely optical counterpart to that in *The Eye*: a moving world is regarded by a stationary perceiver. (One will also notice that while it is a child who is doing the perceiving, it is an adult who is doing the describing—a basic technique in the memoir.) Although this particular episode had unpleasant results, analogous optical experiences provided a joy that could be felt only by the artist. *Speak, Memory* concludes with a scene in which the author and his family approach the dock where a ship that will carry them to America is tied up: "There in front of us, where a row of broken houses stood between us and the harbor, and where the eye encountered all sorts of stratagems, such as pale-blue and pink underwear cakewalking on a clothes-line, or a lady's bicycle and striped cat oddly sharing a rudimentary balcony of cast iron, it was most satisfy-

---

[3] The Universal Library, Grosset and Dunlap, New York, 1951.

ing to make out among the jumbled angles of roofs and walls, a
splendid ship's funnel, showing from behind the clothesline as something in a scrambled picture—Find What the Sailor Has Hidden—
that the finder cannot unsee once it has been seen." (p. 240) That
funnel was, of course, to have its literary incarnation in the cryptograms and word-play of *Lolita* and *Pale Fire*, just as it had incar-
nations in the chess patterns of *The Defense* and the criminal
machinations of *Despair*.

Most of Nabokov's fiction deals with hypersensitive vision and
the insanity or suicide in which it culminates. *Laughter in the Dark*
(1936; *Camera Obscura* in England)[4] is the story of an art critic
whose infatuation with a teen-aged trollop is both sexual and aesthetic—a reaction against his drab, bourgeois existence. Albinus,
who has neither the wit nor the acuteness of Humbert Humbert, is
thoroughly duped because of his trusting nature; when he becomes
blinded in an automobile accident, he is even more vulnerable to
his mistress' and her actual lover's deceptions. On discovering the
truth, he attempts to murder the girl and is himself murdered.
Although this novel has been called a parody of the conventional
triangle, and while it is at least obvious that all the characters are
actors in a melodrama, Albinus' story remains that of a man whose
obsession blinded him spiritually long before it did physically. Nabokov is only incidentally interested in the moral consequences of
Albinus' behavior; his actual concern is with depicting a particular
kind of sensibility.

If the man who has eyes only for physical beauty inhabits a dark
room removed from the world of responsibility (Albinus does not
even attend the funeral of his daughter for fear it will reunite him
with his wife), the man who has eyes only for chess patterns is
the complete solipsist. As Nabokov writes in *Speak, Memory*, *The
Defense* (1930)[5] is about "a champion chess player who goes mad
when chess combinations pervade the actual pattern of his existence."
(p. 217) He later declares that composing chess problems is like the
"writing of one of those incredible novels where the author, in a
fit of lucid madness, has set himself certain unique rules that he
observes, certain nightmare obstacles that he surmounts, with the
zest of a deity building a live world from the most unlikely ingredients. . . ." (p. 220) The chess world is, then, an art world and it

---

4 Bobbs-Merrill, Indianapolis and New York, 1938.
5 Popular Library, New York, 1964.

possesses similar joys and terrors. Like the narrator of *The Eye*, Luzhin, the hero, seeks to live in a world of his own creation: "He was wide-awake and his mind worked clearly, purged of all dross and aware that everything apart from chess was only an enchanting dream. . . . Real life, chess life, was orderly, clear-cut, and rich in adventure, and Luzhin noted with pride how easy it was for him to reign in this life, and the way everything obeyed his will and bowed to his schemes." (p. 132) One refinement of this solipsistic absorption with an abstract world is to eliminate even the chessmen as visible, physical objects. By playing blind, Luzhin is no longer distracted by the "crude mortal shell" of the pieces and he is able to sense "exquisite, invisible" forces "in their original purity." (p. 89) The disembodied eye, however, is beyond love or compassion, and Luzhin's wife is helpless to save him from insanity.

Whether the solipsist controls the abstract mental world in which he is involved or whether that world finally controls him is the question upon which such insanity is based. Terror as well as joy is a part of the chessplayer's vision: "he had seen something unbearably awesome, the full horror of the abysmal depths of chess. He glanced at the chessboard and his brain wilted from hitherto unprecedented weariness. But the chessmen were pitiless, they held and absorbed him. There was horror in this, but in this also was the sole harmony, for what else exists in the world besides chess? Fog, the unknown, non-being. . . ." (p. 137) "Chess weariness" leads Luzhin to a reaction against the game, but paradoxically, this reaction only raises his enslavement to a new dimension. He becomes increasingly taken with the notion that "just as some combination, known from chess problems, can be indistinctly repeated on the board in actual play—so now the consecutive repetition of a familiar pattern was becoming noticeable in his present life." (p. 212) As to be expected, he is initially delighted with the idea of a pattern, but, as with the game itself, he gradually becomes terrified: "how elegantly and how flexibly, move by move, the images of his childhood had been repeated (country house . . . town . . . school . . . aunt), but he still did not quite understand why this combinational repetition inspired his soul with such dread." (pp. 212–213) It is against the play of this invisible opponent (fate) that Luzhin attempts to work out a "defense."

Needless to say, the problem here involves domination by "necessity" and Luzhin finds an Existential answer: one achieves freedom by "voluntarily committing some absurd unexpected act that would be outside the systematic order of life, thus confusing the sequence of moves planned by his opponent." (p. 241) He interprets a suspected plot by his former agent, to have him return to the game professionally, as the culminating "combinational repetition." "The key was found. The aim of the attack was plain. By an implacable repetition of moves it was leading once more to that same passion [chess] which would destroy the dream of life. Devastation, horror, madness." (p. 244) He meets this ultimate attack with an ultimate defense. The question remains, however, whether by committing suicide Luzhin has won or lost, escaped his fate or fallen victim to it. He has died in what his chess-obsessed mind takes to be a real-life game so that he will not have to die from playing the actual game. Whatever the case, he has remained a chessplayer, and a solipsist, to the end.

Despair (1937)[6] is a serio-comic work in which the artistic impulse expresses itself in the desire to commit a perfect crime by killing one's double. (Claire Rosenfield discusses the psychology of the double and its artistic implications in her full analysis of the novel and Patricia Merivale uses the criminal theme as one point of comparison between Nabokov and the Argentine writer, Jorge Luis Borges. Nabokov, incidentally, expresses an admiration for Borges' work in the Interview.) Struck by the resemblance to himself of a vagrant he has come upon while on a business trip, Hermann, the narrator, a restless and increasingly less successful émigré merchant living in Berlin, plots to murder him, convinced that the world will think that he himself has been killed. He attempts to deceive his wife about the actual circumstances of the proposed murder and arranges to meet her in Switzerland as soon as she collects the insurance money. The wit of the novel lies in Hermann's attitude toward his machinations, for it gradually becomes clear that the resemblance is wholly subjective. Hermann, who flees to a resort in southern France after the slaying to await the fruition of his "art," discovers from the newspapers that he has fooled no one. Here is his interpretation of his failure: "Not only taking for granted, with strange prejudication, that the dead man could not be I; not only failing to observe our resemblance, but, as it were, a priori, excluding its possibility (for people do not see what they are loath to see), the police gave a brilliant example of logic when they expressed their surprise at my having hoped to deceive the world simply by dressing up in

[6] G. P. Putnam's Sons, New York, 1966.

my clothes an individual who was not in the least like me. The imbecility and blatant unfairness of such reasoning are highly comic. The next logical step was to make me mentally deficient; they even went so far as to suppose I was not quite sane. . . ." (p. 201) The ironies in this passage scarcely need be pointed out: the police are, of course, quite right.

Frustrated by the "imbecility" of the world, Hermann attempts to save his vision by putting it on paper, but his faith is shaken when he finds he has committed a blunder through which the identity of the dead vagrant is made known; thereafter his "tale degenerates into a diary." With capture imminent, he reflects that "maybe it is all mock existence, an evil dream; and presently I shall wake up somewhere; on a patch of grass near Prague" (where the novel began). The novel concludes with Hermann's final attempt to impose a subjective, artistic illusion upon the world: he exhorts the crowd that has gathered to watch his arrest to stand aside; the whole business has been staged for the films, he announces, and the "getaway scene" is about to be recorded.

Both Hermann and Humbert Humbert, writes Nabokov in the Foreword, "are neurotic scoundrels, yet there is a green lane in Paradise where Humbert is permitted to wander at dusk once a year; but Hell shall never parole Hermann." If such is the case, it is not just a matter of Hermann's being more monstrous than Humbert, but, I think, a matter of Hermann's being more hopelessly entangled in his own mental nets. Yet even Hermann's mad solipsism is eclipsed by that of Charles Kinbote, the narrator of Pale Fire (1962),[7] whose artistic urges and imaginative capabilities are far more developed. Kinbote's story, revealed through his distorted annotations of a poem by "John Shade," is that of a deposed king from "Zembla," a "remote Northern land," who has taken refuge in an American university. As Clarence Brown argues in his comparison of the novel with the Onegin translation, Kinbote shows an artistic sensibility superior to that of his subject. Obsessed with the notion of having his experiences and his country immortalized, Kinbote forces himself upon Shade, the local poet, and imagines that he has inspired him to incorporate the exotic Zemblan material into a narrative poem. In the denouement, Shade is mistakenly killed by a man who apparently came from Zembla to assassinate Kinbote. As with The Eye, the reader is wholly at the mercy of the narrator (and of Nabokov

---

[7] Lancer Books, New York, 1963.

himself, who fills the work with puns, cryptograms, and cross-references). While one can deduce, by comparing the text of the poem with the annotation, that Kinbote is virtually insane, one has no way of judging precisely what is valid in his report, including the association with Zembla, if indeed there ever was such a place. (Miss Merivale has some interesting observations on the actual identity and motivation of Shade's killer.) One can be certain, however, that Kinbote did not write Shade's poem and that he is one of a long line of frustrated artists in Nabokov's fiction: "by mid-June I felt sure at last that he would recreate in a poem the dazzling Zembla burning in my brain. I mesmerized him with it, I saturated him with my vision, I pressed upon him, with a drunkard's wild generosity, all that I was helpless myself to put into verse." (p. 58)

Again, Kinbote's madness is the divine madness of the poet, and his judgment of Shade's poem, in a lucid moment, is not entirely inaccurate: "An autobiographical, eminently Appalachian, rather old-fashioned narrative in a neo-Popian prosodic style—beautifully written of course—Shade could not write otherwise than beautifully—but void of my magic, of that special rich streak of magical madness which I was sure would run through it and make it transcend its time." (p. 209) For the purposes of art, truth and reality are unimportant, and it is on this principle that Kinbote (whoever he is) is justified. Shade, unaware of Kinbote's "secret," asks him, "How can you know that all this intimate stuff about your rather appalling king is true?" And Kinbote answers, "Once transmuted by you into poetry, the stuff *will* be true, and the people *will* come alive." (p. 153) If this is the answer of a solipsist, it is an answer to which there is no reply.

It is characteristic of Nabokov that he should deny an interest in politics even when he is writing novels apparently concerned with totalitarian conditions. While in *Speak, Memory* he says that *Invitation to a Beheading* (1938),[8] for example, "deals with the incarceration of a rebel by the buffoons and bullies of a Communazist state" (p. 217), he writes in a foreword to the novel that the "question whether or not my seeing both [the Communist and Nazi regimes] in terms of one dull beastly farce had any effect on this book, should concern the good reader as little as it does me." He later calls the work "a violin in the void," and that, in a sense, is an adequate description of its narrator, Cincinnatus. Imprisoned for

---

[8] Capricorn Books, New York, 1965.

"gnostical turpitude," Cincinnatus sees the external world in much the same terms as Luzhin, with the exception that self-reflection in the face of an impending execution has replaced absorption with chess: "through the process of gradual divestment I reach the final, indivisible, firm, radiant point, and this point says: I am! like a pearl ring embedded in a shark's gory fat—O my eternal, my eternal . . . and this point is enough for me—actually nothing more is necessary." (p. 90) The central image for Cincinnatus' mind is the distorted mirror that accompanies a set of "nonnons," "absolutely absurd objects, shapeless, mottled, pock-marked, knobby things, like some kind of fossils." When these objects are reflected in the mirror, they acquire familiar shapes; "everything was restored, everything was fine." It is not simply the prison that dismays Cincinnatus but "the whole terrible, striped world" in which he sees himself as a misfit. This nonnon reality he has transfigured in his dreams; here "the world would come alive, becoming so captivatingly majestic, free and ethereal, that afterwards it would be oppressive to breathe the dust of this painted life." (p. 92) Waking life, on the other hand, is a reversal of the nonnon mirror, a "semi-sleep, an evil drowsiness into which penetrate in grotesque disguise the sounds and sights of the real [i.e., dream] world, flowing beyond the periphery of the mind—as when you hear during sleep a dreadful, insidious tale because a branch is scraping on the pane, or see yourself sinking into snow because your blanket is sliding off." (p. 92)

Again, what is real in Cincinnatus' world is problematic. Is the grotesque prison, with its banal or clownish antagonists, an actual world from which the narrator seeks to escape both literally and in dream, or is it the hallucination of a hypersensitive mind that can neither sustain an ideal dream vision nor live consistently in an antagonistic society? Perhaps the crime of gnostical turpitude is that of self-consciousness and the sense of existence (the opposite of "secure non-existence," for which, we are told, the average man is prepared from childhood). The true punishment for such a crime is not beheading, as we discover in the bizarre conclusion, but the endurance of a self-created hell of isolation and an abiding fear of death. Once "beheaded," Cincinnatus finds the demons of his mind, his prison tormentors, dwarfed before him, as the grotesque world splinters and he walks off "in that direction where, to judge by the voices, stood beings akin to him." (p. 223) The nightmare ends not in awakening, for awakening in this world has no meaning; it ends rather in a continuation of the dream, an ideal dream in which the

horrors of cerebration have been dispelled. Whether Cincinnatus has
entered heaven or simply an ultimate psychological refuge depends
upon how strictly one wishes to read the allegory.

Concerned with the intimidation of a university professor in an
East European country, who refuses to endorse the policies of the
dictator, a former school mate, *Bend Sinister* (1947) has a more
explicitly political context than *Invitation to a Beheading*. Still, one
is not surprised to find Nabokov saying, in the introduction to the
Time edition of the novel (1964), that the story "is not really about
life and death in a grotesque police state. My characters are not
'types,' not carriers of this or that 'idea.' . . . all of them are only
absurd mirages, illusions oppressive to Krug [the hero] during his
brief spell of being, but harmlessly fading away when I dismiss the
cast." (Nabokov is more evasive on this problem in the Interview.
L.L. Lee discusses both the political and psychological aspects of
the novel.) The statement about dismissing the cast actually adds
another dimension to the problem of solipsism: here the author
refuses to allow his characters to carry on a separate existence from
himself, and self-consciously emphasizes their attributes as mental
projections. Thus Nabokov speaks of "Krug's blessed madness when
he suddenly perceives the simple reality of things and knows but
cannot express in the words of his world that he and his son and his
wife and everybody else are merely my whims and megrims." ("It
was at that moment, just after Krug had fallen through the bottom
of a confused dream . . . just before his reality, his remembered
hideous misfortune could pounce upon him—it was then that I felt
a pang of pity . . . and slid towards him along an inclined beam of
pale light—causing instantaneous madness." [p. 210]) The novel
concludes with the author's looking up from his completed work as
the details of his own world begin to pervade his consciousness—a
final instance of the fusion of fiction with actuality.

A solipsistic relation between an author and his subject is treated
more explicitly in *The Real Life of Sebastian Knight* (1941),[9] ostensibly the story of an attempt by V., the narrator, to reconstruct
the "real" life of his half-brother, a generally neglected novelist, and
to determine the identity and influence upon him of his last mistress before his premature death. (Charles Nicol investigates the
similarities between Sebastian's fiction and V.'s own narrative.) In
trying to reconstruct the novelist, V. absorbs his identity: "Whatever
his secret was, I have learnt one secret, too, and namely: that the soul

---

9 New Directions, Norfolk, Connecticut, 1959.

is but a manner of being—not a constant state—that any soul may be yours, if you find and follow its undulations. The hereafter may be the full ability of consciously living in any chosen soul, in any number of souls, all of them unconscious of their interchangeable burden. Thus—I am Sebastian Knight. . . . or Sebastian is I, or perhaps we both are someone whom neither of us knows." (pp. 204–205) Needless to say, that "someone" is probably Vladimir Nabokov himself. (Nabokov has more to say on the theme of the dominant author in the Interview. Gleb Struve analyzes its appearance in the early novels, and Simon Karlinsky, in the plays.)

Although written in a realistic style and concerned with a broad range of characters, The Gift (1937),[10] a novel at least partly autobiographical, is Nabokov's most extensive treatment of the introspective literary mind. Its hero, Fyodor Godunov-Cherdyntsev, is a young émigré writer with a predilection for non-social artistic values and a capacity for inventing vivid and detailed imaginary experiences. The novel is an account of his growing self-awareness as a writer in an indifferent world, of his imaginative apprehension of the past, and of his love affair with a woman who responds to his values.

A consistent problem in the novel is Cherdyntsev's attempt to find the language adequate to his visions of the past, and the audience that will appreciate his work. Concerned with what he eventually calls "wordsmithy," he asks, early in the narration, "What, then, compels me to compose poems about my childhood if, in spite of everything, my words go wide of the mark, or else slay both the pard and the hart with the exploding bullet of an 'accurate' epithet?" (p. 28) His passion for finding right words and rhymes is akin to his father's passion, as a naturalist, for discovery and classification. Although the struggle for mastery of language often ends in failure (what should have been "the expression, the living connection" between divine and human worlds collapses into a "fatal gust of words"), Cherdyntsev refuses to make the conventional complaint that "words are incapable of expressing our thingummy-bob feelings," and he retains a belief in "inspired expressiveness."

His father's travels in Asia provide the material for one of Cherdyntsev's most vivid imaginative constructions. He recounts at length his adventures while accompanying the naturalist on far-flung expeditions, but the story is a fiction. For their author the actual excitement is in the telling of the tale, a "verbal adventure." But the fear of linguistic failure—of the inability to give the dream

---

[10] Popular Library, New York, 1963.

its proper expression—is apparent here as well. Cherdyntsev eventually abandons a projected biography of his father when he comes to accept the "impossibility of having the imagery of his travels germinate without contaminating them with a kind of secondary poetization, which keeps departing further and further from that real poetry with which the live experience of these receptive, knowledgeable and chaste naturalists endowed their research." (p. 159)

A kind of poetic solipsist himself, the elder Godunov-Cherdyntsev had been accused of "scientific aristocratism, of a haughty contempt for Man, of disregard for the reader's interests, of dangerous eccentricity—and of much more." (p. 131) This "humanitarian-liberal" attack represents for his son the insensitivity to "art" in general of a whole generation of Russian social critics, particularly of N. G. Chernyshevsky. Instead of doing a biography of his father, he chooses to write an unsympathetic one of Chernyshevsky, a work that is presented in full as a chapter of the novel. Just as was his father's treatise, the biography is attacked for its anti-humanitarianism. Cherdyntsev, still in need of an audience, chooses one of the few émigré literary figures he respects, Koncheyev, and constructs a long imaginary conversation with him in which the latter is critical but appreciative of his achievement. (Koncheyev accuses him of having "an excessive trust in words.")

The one figure who actually understands Cherdyntsev, intuitively if not intellectually, is Zina Mertz, who represents an ideal reader: "She was completely unconcerned whether or not the author clung assiduously to historical truth. . . . A deeper truth, on the other hand, for which he alone was responsible and which he alone could find, was for her so important that the least clumsiness or fogginess in his words seemed to be the germ of a falsehood, which had to be immediately exterminated. Gifted with a most flexible memory, which twined like ivy around what she perceived, Zina by repeating such word-combinations as she particularly liked ennobled them with her own secret convolution, and whenever Fyodor for any reason changed a turn of phrase which she had remembered, the ruins of the portico stood for a long time on the golden horizon, reluctant to disappear." (p. 231)

It is not surprising that Cherdyntsev, the "pure" artist, should propose to an imaginary Koncheyev a conception of time appropriate to artistic transcendence of the causal, material world. "Our mistaken feeling of time as a kind of growth is a consequence of our finiteness which, being always on the level of the present, implies its constant rise between the watery abyss of the past and the aerial abyss of the future. . . . The theory I find most tempting [is] that there is no time, that everything is the present situated like a radiance outside our blindness. . . ." (Nabokov discusses the problem of time in the Interview.) Such a theory, Cherdyntsev realizes, is "just as hopeless a finite hypothesis as all the others"; nonetheless, it is a theory that is at least congenial to the artistic need for escape from necessity. "And if one adds to this that nature was seeing double when she created us . . . that symmetry in the structure of live bodies is a consequence of the rotation of worlds . . . and that in our strain toward asymmetry, towards inequality, I can detect a howl for genuine freedom, an urge to break out of the circle. . . ." (pp. 384–385) Whatever the metaphysical coherence or incoherence of this statement, the theory reflects Cherdyntsev's reaction against the whole humanitarian tradition and what he takes to be the sentimental social values that it has imposed. It is precisely Cherdyntsev himself who is striving for "asymmetry," indeed for transcendence of the social, human condition—including his role as artist. Here is his account of an experience in the Grunewald prior to his "conversation" with Koncheyev (an experience out of D. H. Lawrence): "The sun licked me all over with its big, smooth tongue. I gradually felt that I was becoming moltenly transparent, that I was permeated with flame and existed only insofar as it did. As a book is translated into an exotic idiom, so was I translated into sun. . . . My personal I, the one that wrote books, the one that loved words, colors, mental fireworks, Russia, chocolate and Zina—had somehow disintegrated and dissolved; after being made transparent by the strength of the light, it was now assimilated to the shimmering of the summer forest. . . ." (p. 375) Perhaps it would be farfetched to suggest that this experience is one form of seeing into "the radiance outside our blindness" that represents non-chronological reality. Cherdyntsev's whole life, with its dedication to aesthetically reviving the past, is the most explicit representation of the attempt to overcome metaphysical blindness.

Like Nabokov's other novels, *The Gift* settles none of the problems it raises, but there is little doubt that for all his weaknesses (most of them self-acknowledged) Cherdyntsev is a sympathetic character. Nabokov clearly envisioned his life as the story of the émigré Russian writer seeking to recover his heritage. The heroine of the novel, he writes, "is not Zina, but Russian Literature. The plot of Chapter One centers in Fyodor's poems. Chapter Two is a surge toward Pushkin in Fyodor's literary progress and contains his attempt to describe his father's zoological explorations. Chapter Three shifts to Gogol, but its real hub is the love poem dedicated to Zina. Fyodor's book on Chernyshevsky, a spiral within a sonnet, takes care of Chapter Four. The last chapter combines all the preceding themes and adumbrates the book Fyodor dreams of writing some day: *The Gift*." That Nabokov himself wrote *The Gift* involves us in the same mirror-reality that appears in *Sebastian Knight* and *Bend Sinister*. In fact *The Gift* concludes with a declaration by its author, just as *Bend Sinister* does.

In *Speak, Memory* Nabokov wrote that Russian children of his generation passed through a period of genius when it came to hoarding up impressions "as if destiny were loyally trying [to do] what it could for them by giving them more than their share, in view of the cataclysm that was to remove completely the world they had known." (p. 7) The taste for imaginative invention and reconstruction of the past may well be considered the effects of exile, but, more broadly, they are no less comprehensible as conditions natural to the artist in an indifferent world. The story of Timofey Pavlovich Pnin, whose partly comic, partly pathetic vicissitudes as a Russian émigré in an American college town are recorded in the novel to which he lends his name (1957),[11] is a quiet variation on the theme of exile and the artistic sensibility. (In his interesting discussion Ambrose Gordon, Jr., distinguishes Pnin's personality as an exile from that as an alien.) Far from being a solipsist, however, Pnin, a gentle, sensitive, scholarly eccentric, seeks to adapt himself to his American environment, and when, "battered and stunned by thirty-five years of homelessness," he finally rents a house, he feels that his life in America as a college professor is essentially no different from what it would have been in Russia had there been no revolution. But Pnin's often-mimicked English is an indication that true naturalization is impossible, and he remains alienated from American society and the frequently insipid academic community in particular (only one of his colleagues, Laurence Clements, has any appreciation of his qualities).

Again, Pnin is not simply the Russian exile in America, but the isolated literary man in the modern world. His contacts with the Russian community, during a summer on an estate in New England, are more sentimental than profound and serve only to intensify his thoughts of the past. His marriage to a Russian poetess-psychoanalyst

---

[11] Atheneum, New York, 1965.

A. When I was young I liked Poe, and I still love Melville, whom I did not read as a boy. My feelings towards James are rather complicated. I really dislike him intensely but now and then the figure in the phrase, the turn of the epithet, the screw of an absurd adverb, cause me a kind of electric tingle, as if some current of his was also passing through my own blood. Hawthorne is a splendid writer. Emerson's poetry is delightful.

Q. You have often said that you "don't belong to any club or group," and I wonder if the historical examples of the ways Russian writers have allowed ideology to determine if not destroy their art, culminating in the Socialist Realism of our own time, have not gone a long way in shaping your own skepticism and aversion to didacticism of any kind. Which "historical examples" have you been most conscious of?

A. My aversion to groups is rather a matter of temperament than the fruit of information and thought. I was born that way and have despised ideological coercion instinctively all my life. Those "historical examples" by the way are not as clear-cut and obvious as you seem to imply. The mystical didacticism of Gogol or the utilitarian moralism of Tolstoy, or the reactionary journalism of Dostoevski, are of their own poor making and in the long run nobody really takes them seriously.

Q. Would you say something about the controversy surrounding the Chernyshevski biography in The Gift? You have commented on this briefly before, but since its suppression in the 'thirties expresses such a transcendent irony and seems to justify the need for just such a parody, I think your readers would be most interested, especially since so little is known about the émigré communities, their magazines, and the role of intellectuals in these communities. If you would like to describe something of the writer's relationship to this world, please do.

A. Everything that can be profitably said about Count Godunov-Cherdyntsev's biography of Chernyshevski has been said by Koncheyev in The Gift. I can only add that I devoted as much honest labor to the task of gathering the material for the Chernyshevski chapter as I did to the composing of Shade's poem for him. As to the suppression of that chapter by the editors of Sovremennye Zapiski, it was indeed an unprecedented occurrence, quite out of keeping with their exceptional broadmindedness for, generally speaking, in their acceptance or rejection of literary works they were guided exclusively by artistic standards. As to the latter part of your question, the revised chapter fourteen in *Speak, Memory* will provide additional information.

Q. Do you have any opinions about the Russian anti-utopian tradition (if it can be called this) from Odoevsky's "The Last Suicide" and "A City Without a Name" in *Russian Nights* to Briusov's *The Republic of the Southern Cross* and Zamiatin's *We* (to name only a few)?

A. I am indifferent to those works.

Q. Is it fair to say that *Invitation to a Beheading* and *Bend Sinister* are cast as mock anti-utopian novels, with their ideological centers removed—the totalitarian state becoming an extreme and fantastic metaphor for the imprisonment of the mind, thus making consciousness, rather than politics, the subject of these novels?

A. Yes, possibly.

Q. Speaking of ideology, you have often expressed your hostility to Freud, most noticeably in the forewords to your translated novels. Some readers have wondered which of Freud's works or theories you were most offended by and why. The parodies of Freud in *Lolita* and *Pale Fire* suggest a wider familiarity with the good doctor than you have ever publicly granted. Would you comment on this?

A. Oh, I am not up to discussing again that figure of fun. He is not worthy of more attention than I have granted him in my novels and in *Speak, Memory*. Let the credulous and the vulgar continue to believe that all mental woes can be cured by a daily application of old Greek myths to their private parts. I really do not care.

Q. Your contempt for Freud's "standardized symbols" extends to the assumptions of a good many other theorizers. Do you think literary criticism is at all purposeful, and if so, what kind of criticism would you point to? *Pale Fire* makes it clear what sort you find gratuitous (at best).

A. My advice to a budding literary critic would be as follows. Learn to distinguish banality. Remember that mediocrity thrives on "ideas."

Beware of the modish message. Ask yourself if the symbol you have detected is not your own footprint. Ignore allegories. By all means place the "how" above the "what" but do not let it be confused with the "so what." Rely on the sudden erection of your small dorsal hairs. Do not drag in Freud at this point. All the rest depends on personal talent.

Q. As a writer, have you ever found criticism instructive—not so much the reviews of your own books, but any general criticism? From your own experiences do you think that an academic and literary career nourish one another? Since many writers today know no other alternative than a life on campus I'd be very interested in your feelings about this. Do you think that your own work in America was at all shaped by your being part of an academic community?

A. I find criticism most instructive when an expert proves to me that my facts or my grammar are wrong. An academic career is especially helpful to writers in two ways: 1) easy access to magnificent libraries and 2) long vacations. There is of course the business of teaching but old professors have young instructors to correct examination papers for them, and young instructors, authors in their own right, are followed by admiring glances along the corridors of Vanity Hall. Otherwise, our greatest rewards, such as the reverberations of our minds in such minds as vibrate responsively in later years, force novelist-teachers to nurse lucidity and honesty of style in their lectures.

Q. What are the possibilities of literary biography?

A. They are great fun to write, generally less fun to read. Sometimes the thing becomes a kind of double paper chase: first, the biographer pursues his quarry through letters and diaries, and across the bogs of conjecture, and then a rival authority pursues the muddy biographer.

Q. Some critics may find the use of coincidence in a novel arch or contrived. I recall that you yourself at Cornell called Dostoevski's usage of coincidence crude.

A. But in "real" life they do happen. Last night you were telling us at dinner a very funny story about the use of the title "Doctor" in Germany, and the very next moment, as my loud laughter was subsiding, I heard a person at the next table saying to her neighbor in clear French tones coming through the tinkling and shuffling sounds of a restaurant —[turning to his wife] just as you can hear at this moment the trilling of that little grebe on the lake through the sounds of the traffic—"Of course, you never know with the Germans if 'Doctor' means a dentist or a lawyer." Very often you meet with some person or some event in "real" life that would sound pat in a story. It is not the coincidence in the story that bothers us so much as the coincidence of coincidences in several stories by different writers, as, for instance, the recurrent eavesdropping device in nineteenth-century Russian fiction.

Q. Could you tell us something about your work habits as a writer, and the way you compose your novels. Do you use an outline? Do you have a full sense of where a fiction is heading even while you are in the early stages of composition?

A. In my twenties and early thirties, I used to write, dipping pen in ink and using a new nib every other day, in exercise books, crossing out, inserting, striking out again, crumpling the page, rewriting every page three or four times, then copying out the novel in a different ink and a neater hand, then revising the whole thing once more, re-copying it with new corrections, and finally dictating it to my wife who has typed out all my stuff. Generally speaking, I am a slow writer, a snail carrying its house at the rate of two hundred pages of final copy per year (one spectacular exception was the Russian original of *Invitation to a Beheading*, the first draft of which I wrote in one fortnight of wonderful excitement and sustained inspiration). In those days and nights I generally followed the order of chapters when writing a novel but even so, from the very first, I relied heavily on mental composition, constructing whole paragraphs in my mind as I walked in the streets or sat in my bath, or lay in bed, although often deleting or rewriting them later. In the late 'thirties, beginning with *The Gift*, and perhaps under the influence of the many notes needed, I switched to another, physically more practical, method— that of writing with an eraser-capped pencil on index cards. Since I always have at the very start a curiously clear preview of the entire novel before me or above me, I find cards especially convenient when not following the logical sequence of chapters but preparing instead this or that passage at any point of the novel and filling in the gaps in no special order. I am afraid to get mixed up with Plato whom I do not care for, but I do think that in my case it is true that the entire book, before it is written, seems to be ready ideally in some other, now transparent, now dimming, dimension, and my job is to take down as much of it as I can make out and as precisely as I

am humanly able to. The greatest happiness I experience in composing is when I feel I cannot understand, or rather catch myself not
understanding (without the presupposition of an already existing
creation) how or why that image or structural move has just come
to me. It is sometimes rather amusing to find my readers trying to
elucidate in a matter-of-fact way these wild workings of my not very
efficient mind.

Q. One often hears from writers talk of how a character takes hold
of them and in a sense dictates the course of the action. Has this
ever been your experience?

A. I have never experienced this. What a preposterous experience!
Writers who have had it must be very minor or insane. No, the design
of my novel is fixed in my imagination and every character follows
the course I imagine for him. I am the perfect dictator in that private world insofar as I alone am responsible for its stability and truth.
Whether I reproduce it as fully and faithfully as I would wish, is
another question. Some of my old works reveal dismal blurrings
and blanks.

Q. Pale Fire appears to some readers to be in part a gloss on Plato's
myth of the cave, and the constant play of Shades and Shadows
throughout your work suggests a conscious Platonism. Would you
care to comment on this possibility?

A. As I have said I am not particularly fond of Plato, nor would
I survive very long under his Germanic regime of militarism and
music. I do not think that this cave business has anything to do with
my Shade and Shadows.

Q. Since we are mentioning philosophy per se, I wonder if we
might talk about the philosophy of language that seems to unfold
in your works, and whether or not you have consciously seen the
similarities, say, between the language of Zemblan and what Ludwig
Wittgenstein had to say about a "private language." Your poet's
sense of the limitations of language is startlingly similar to Wittgenstein's remarks on the referential basis of language. While you
were at Cambridge, did you have much contact with the philosophy
faculty?

A. No contact whatsoever. I am completely ignorant of Wittgenstein's works, and the first time I heard his name must have been in
the 'fifties. In Cambridge I played football and wrote Russian verse.

Q. When in Canto Two John Shade describes himself, "I stand before the window and I pare/My fingernails," you are echoing Stephen Dedalus in *A Portrait of the Artist as a Young Man*, on the artist who "remains within or behind or beyond or above his handiwork, invisible, refined out of existence, indifferent, paring his fingernails." In almost all of your novels, especially in *Invitation to a Beheading, Bend Sinister, Pale Fire*, and *Pnin*—but even in *Lolita*, in the person of the seventh hunter in Quilty's play, and in several other phosphorescent glimmers which are visible to the careful reader —the creator is indeed behind or above his handiwork, but he is not invisible and surely not indifferent. To what extent are you consciously "answering" Joyce in *Pale Fire*, and what are your feelings about his esthetic stance—or alleged stance, because perhaps you may think that Stephen's remark doesn't apply to *Ulysses*?

A. Neither Kinbote nor Shade, nor their maker, is answering Joyce in *Pale Fire*. Actually, I never liked *A Portrait of the Artist as a Young Man*. I find it a feeble and garrulous book. The phrase you quote is an unpleasant coincidence.

Q. You have granted that Pierre Delalande influenced you, and I would readily admit that influence-mongering can be reductive and deeply offensive if it tries to deny a writer's originality. But in the instance of yourself and Joyce, it seems to me that you've consciously profited from Joyce's example without imitating him—that you've realized the implications in *Ulysses* without having had recourse to obviously "Joycean" devices (stream-of-consciousness, the "collage" effects created out of the vast flotsam and jetsam of everyday life). Would you comment on what Joyce has meant to you as a writer, his importance in regard to his liberation and expansion of the novel form?

A. My first real contact with *Ulysses*, after a leering glimpse in the early 'twenties, was in the 'thirties at a time when I was definitely formed as a writer and immune to any literary influence. I studied *Ulysses* seriously only much later, in the 'fifties, when preparing my Cornell courses. That was the best part of the education I received at Cornell. *Ulysses* towers over the rest of Joyce's writings, and in comparison to its noble originality and unique lucidity of thought and style the unfortunate *Finnegans Wake* is nothing but a formless and dull mass of phony folklore, a cold pudding of a book, a persistent snore in the next room, most aggravating to the insomniac I am.

Moreover, I always detested regional literature full of quaint old-timers and imitated pronunciation. *Finnegans Wake's* façade disguises a very conventional and drab tenement house, and only the infrequent snatches of heavenly intonations redeem it from utter insipidity. I know I am going to be excommunicated for this pronouncement.

Q. Although I cannot recall your mentioning the involuted structure of *Ulysses* when you lectured on Joyce, I do remember your insisting that the hallucinations in Nighttown are the author's and not Stephen's or Bloom's, which is one step away from a discussion of the involution. This is an aspect of *Ulysses* almost totally ignored by the Joyce Industry, and an aspect of Joyce which would seem to be of great interest to you. If Joyce's somewhat inconsistent involutions tend to be obscured by the vastness of his structures, it might be said that the structuring of your novels depends on the strategy of involution. Could you comment on this, or compare your sense of Joyce's presence in and above his works with your own intention —that is, Joyce's covert appearances in *Ulysses*; the whole Shakespeare-paternity theme which ultimately spirals into the idea of the "parentage" of *Ulysses* itself; Shakespeare's direct address to Joyce in Nighttown ("How my Oldfellow chokit his Thursday-momum," that being Bloomsday); and Molly's plea to Joyce, "O Jamesy let me up out of this"—all this as against the way the authorial voice— or what you call the "anthropomorphic deity impersonated by me"— again and again appears in your novels, most strikingly at the end.

A. One of the reasons Bloom cannot be the active party in the Nighttown chapter (and if he is not, then the author is directly dreaming it up for him, and around him, with some real episodes inserted here and there) is that Bloom, a wilting male anyway, has been drained of his manhood earlier in the evening and thus would be quite unlikely to indulge in the violent sexual fancies of Nighttown. But I plan to publish my notes on *Ulysses*, and will not pursue the matter now.[1]

Q. Ideally, how should a reader experience or react to "the end" of one of your novels, that moment when the vectors are removed

---

[1] Nabokov is planning to publish in book-form both his Joyce and Kafka lectures.

and the fact of the fiction is underscored, the cast dismissed? What common assumptions about literature are you assaulting?

A. The question is so charmingly phrased that I would love to answer it with equal elegance and eloquence, but I cannot say very much. I think that what I would welcome at the close of a book of mine is a sensation of its world receding in the distance and stopping somewhere there suspended afar like a picture in a picture: *The Artist's Studio* by Van Bock.[2]

Q. It may well be a failure of perception, but I've always been unsure of the very last sentences of *Lolita*, perhaps because the shift in voice at the close of your other books is so clear, but is one supposed to "hear" a different voice when the masked narrator says "And do not pity C.Q. One had to choose between him and H.H., and one wanted H.H. . . . ." and so forth? The return to the first person in the next sentence makes me think that the mask has not been lifted, but readers trained on *Invitation to a Beheading*, among other books, are always looking for the imprint of that "master thumb," to quote Franklin Lane in *Pale Fire*, "that made the whole involuted, boggling thing one beautiful straight line."

A. No, I did not mean to introduce a different voice. I did want, however, to convey a constriction of the narrator's sick heart, a warning spasm causing him to abridge names and hasten to conclude his tale before it was too late. I am glad I managed to achieve this remoteness of tone at the end.

Q. Do Franklin Lane's *Letters* exist? I don't wish to appear like Mr. Goodman in *The Real Life of Sebastian Knight*, but I understand that Franklin Lane did exist.

A. Frank Lane, his published letters, and the passage cited by Kinbote, certainly exist. Kinbote was rather struck by Lane's handsome melancholy face. And of course "lane" is the last word of Shade's poem. The latter has no significance.

Q. In which of your early works do you think you first begin to

---

[2] Research has failed to confirm the existence of this alleged "Dutch Master," whose name is only an alphabetical step away from being a significant anagram, a poor relation of Quilty's anagrammatic mistress, "Vivian Darkbloom."

face the possibilities that are fully developed in *Invitation to a Beheading* and reach an apotheosis in the "involute abode" of *Pale Fire*?

A. Possibly in *The Eye*, but *Invitation to a Beheading* is on the whole a spontaneous generation.

Q. Are there other writers whose involuted effects you admire? Sterne? Pirandello's plays?

A. I never cared for Pirandello. I love Sterne but had not read him in my Russian period.

Q. The Afterword to *Lolita* is significant, obviously, for many reasons. Is it included in all the translations which, I understand, number about twenty-five?

A. Yes.

Q. You once told me after a class at Cornell that you'd been unable to read more than one hundred or so pages of *Finnegans Wake*. As it happens, on p. 104 there begins a section very close in spirit to *Pale Fire*, and I wonder if you've ever read this, or seen the similarity. It is the history of all the editions and interpretations of Anna Livia Plurabelle's Letter (or "Mamafesta," text included). Among the three pages listing the various titles of ALP's letter, Joyce includes *Try our Taal on a Taub* (which we are already doing), and I wondered if you would comment on Swift's contribution to the literature about the corruption of learning and literature. Is it only a coincidence that Kinbote's "Foreword" to *Pale Fire* is dated "Oct. 19," which is the date of Swift's death?

A. I finished *Finnegans Wake* eventually. It has no inner connection with *Pale Fire*. I think it is so nice that the day on which Kinbote committed suicide (and he certainly did after putting the last touches to his edition of the poem) happens to be both the anniversary of Pushkin's *Lyceum* and that of "poor old man Swift" 's death, which is news to me (but see variant in note to line 231). In common with Pushkin, I am fascinated by fatidic dates. Moreover, when dating some special event in my novels I often choose a more or less familiar one as a *point de repère*, which helps to check a possible misprint in the proofs, as for instance "April 1" in the diary of Hermann in *Despair*.

Q. Mention of Swift moves me to ask about the genre of *Pale Fire*; as a "monstrous semblance of a novel," do you see it in terms of some tradition or form?

A. The form of *Pale Fire* is specifically, if not generically, new. I would like to take this pleasant opportunity to correct the following misprints in the Putnam edition 1962, second impression: On p. 137, end of note to line 143, "rustic" should be "rusty." On p. 151, "Catskin Week" should be "Catkin Week." On p. 223, the line number in the reference at the end of the first note should not be "550" but "549." On p. 237, top, "For" should be "for." On p. 241, the word "lines" after "*disent-prise*" should be "rhymes." And on p. 294, the comma after "Arnold" should be replaced by an open parenthesis. Thank you.[3]

Q. Do you make a clear distinction between satire and parody? I ask this because you have so often said you do not wish to be taken as a "moral satirist," and yet parody is so central to your vision.

A. Satire is a lesson, parody is a game.

Q. Chapter ten in *The Real Life of Sebastian Knight* contains a wonderful description of how parody functions in your own novels. But your sense of what parody means seems to stretch the usual definition, as when Cincinnatus in *Invitation to a Beheading* tells his mother, "You're still only a parody . . . Just like this spider, just like those bars, just like the striking of that clock." All art, then, or at least all attempts at a "realistic" art, would seem to produce a distortion, a "parody." Would you expand on what you mean by parody and why, as Fyodor says in *The Gift*, "The spirit of parody always goes along with genuine poetry"?

A. When the poet Cincinnatus C., in my dreamiest and most poetical novel, accuses (not quite fairly) his mother of being a

---

[3] Since Mr. Nabokov has opened an Errata Department, the following misprints from the Lancer Books paperback edition of *Pale Fire*, 1963, should be noted: on p. 17, fifth line from bottom of middle paragraph, "sad" should be "saw." On p. 60, note to lines 47–48, line 21 should be "burst an appendix," not "and." On p. 111, fourth line of note to line 172, "inscription" is misspelled. On p. 158, last sentence of note to line 493, "filfth" should be "filth." Nabokov's other books are relatively free from misprints, except for the Popular Library paperback edition of *The Gift*, 1963, whose blemishes are too numerous to mention.

parody, he uses the word in its familiar sense of "grotesque imitation." When Fyodor, in *The Gift*, alludes to that "spirit of parody" which plays around the spray of genuine "serious" poetry, he is referring to parody in the sense of an essentially lighthearted, delicate, mocking-bird game, such as Pushkin's parody of Derzhavin in *Exegi Monumentum*.

Q. What is your opinion of Joyce's parodies? Do you see any difference in the artistic effect of scenes such as the maternity hospital and the beach interlude with Gerty Macdowell? Are you familiar with the work of younger American writers who have been influenced by both you and Joyce, such as Thomas Pynchon (a Cornellian, Class of '59, who surely was in Literature 312), and do you have any opinion on the current ascendancy of the so-called parody-novel (John Barth, for instance)?

A. The literary parodies in the Maternal Hospital chapter are on the whole jejunish. Joyce seems to have been hampered by the general sterilized tone he chose for that chapter, and this somehow dulled and monotonized the inlaid skits. On the other hand, the frilly novelette parodies in the Masturbation scene are highly successful; and the sudden bursting of its clichés into the fireworks and tender sky of real poetry is a feat of genius. I am not familiar with the works of the two other writers you mention.[4]

Q. Why, in *Pale Fire*, do you call parody the "last resort of wit"?

A. This is Kinbote speaking. There are people whom parody upsets.

Q. Are the composition of *Lolita* and *Speak, Memory*, two very different books about the spell exerted by the past, at all connected in the way that the translations of *The Song of Igor's Campaign* and *Eugene Onegin* are related to *Pale Fire*? Had you finished all the notes to *Onegin* before you began *Pale Fire*?

A. This is the kind of question that can be only answered by the interrogator himself. The task of pondering such juxtapositions and contrasts is above my capacities. Yes, I had finished all my notes to *Onegin* before I began *Pale Fire*. Flaubert speaks in one of his letters, in relation to a certain scene in *Madame Bovary*, about the

---

[4] Mrs. Nabokov, who graded her husband's examination papers, did remember Pynchon, but only for his "unusual" handwriting: half printing, half script.

difficulty of painting *couleur sur couleur*. This in a way is what I tried to do in retwisting my own experience when inventing Kinbote. *Speak, Memory* is strictly autobiographic. There is nothing autobiographic in *Lolita*.

Q. Although self-parody seems to be a vital part of your work, you are a writer who believes passionately in the primacy of the imagination. Yet your novels are filled with little details that seem to have been purposely pulled from your own life, as a reading of *Speak, Memory* makes clear, not to mention the overriding patterns, such as the lepidopteral motif, which extend through so many books. They seem to partake of something other than the involuted voice, to suggest some clearly held idea about the interrelationship between self-knowledge and artistic creation, self-parody and identity. Would you comment on this, and the significance of autobiographical hints in works of art that are literally *not* autobiographical?

A.   I would say that imagination is a form of memory. Down, Plato, down, good dog. An image depends on the power of association, and association is supplied and prompted by memory. When we speak of a vivid individual recollection we are paying a compliment not to our capacity of retention but to Mnemosyne's mysterious foresight in having stored up this or that element which creative imagination may use when combining it with later recollections and inventions. In this sense, both memory and imagination are a negation of time.

Q. C. P. Snow has complained about the gulf between the "two cultures," the literary and scientific communities. As someone who has bridged this gulf, do you see the sciences and humanities as necessarily opposed? Have your experiences as a scientist influenced your performance as an artist? Is it fanciful to use the vocabulary of physics in describing the structures of some of your novels?

A.   I would have compared myself to a Colossus of Rhodes bestriding the gulf between the thermodynamics of Snow and Laurentomania of Leavis, had that gulf not been a mere dimple of a ditch that a small frog could straddle. The terms "physics" and "egghead" as used nowadays evoke in me the dreary image of applied science, the knack of an electrician tinkering with bombs and other gadgets. One of those "Two Cultures" is really nothing but utilitarian technology; the other is B-grade novels, ideological fiction, popular art.

Who cares if there exists a gap between such "physics" and such "humanities." Those Eggheads are terrible philistines. A real good head is not oval but round.

My passion for lepidopterological research, in the field, in the laboratory, in the library, is even more pleasurable than the study and practice of literature, which is saying a good deal. Lepidopterists are obscure scientists. Not one is mentioned in Webster. But never mind. I have re-worked the classification of various groups of butterflies, have described and figured several species and sub-species. My names for the microscopic organs that I have been the first to see and portray have safely found their way into the biological dictionaries (which is poorly matched by the wretched entry under "nymphet" in Webster's latest edition). The tactile delights of precise delineation, the silent paradise of the camera lucida, and the precision of poetry in taxonomic description represent the artistic side of the thrill that accumulation of new knowledge, absolutely useless to the layman, gives its first begetter. Science means to me above all natural science. Not the ability to repair a radio set; quite stubby fingers can do that. Apart from this basic consideration, I certainly welcome the free interchange of terminology between any branch of science and any raceme of art. There is no science without fancy, and no art without facts. Aphoristicism is a symptom of arteriosclerosis.

Q. In *Pale Fire*, Kinbote complains that "The coming of summer represented a problem in optics." *The Eye* is well-titled, since you plumb these problems throughout your fiction; the apprehension of "reality" is a miracle of vision, and consciousness is virtually an optical instrument in your work. Have you studied the science of optics at all, and would you say something about your own visual sense, and how you feel it has served your fiction?

A. I am afraid you are quoting this out of context. Kinbote was simply annoyed by the spreading foliage of summer interfering with his Tom-peeping. Otherwise you are right in suggesting that I have good eyes. Doubting Tom should have worn spectacles. It is true, however, that even with the best of visions one must touch things to be quite sure of "reality."

Q. You have said that Alain Robbe-Grillet and Jorge Luis Borges are among your favorite contemporary writers. Do you find them to be at all similar? Do you think Robbe-Grillet's novels are as free of "psychology" as he claims?

A. Robbe-Grillet's claims are preposterous. Those manifestos die with the dadas. His fiction is magnificently poetical and original, and the shifts of levels, the interpenetration of successive impressions and so forth belong of course to psychology—psychology at its best. Borges is also a man of infinite talent, but his miniature labyrinths and the roomy ones of Robbe-Grillet are quite differently built, and the lighting is not the same.

Q. I recall your humorous remarks at Cornell about two writers experiencing "telepathy" (I believe you were comparing Dickens and Flaubert). You and Borges were both born in 1899 (but so was Ernest Hemingway!). Your *Bend Sinister* and Borges' story "The Circular Ruins" are conceptually similar, but you do not read Spanish and that story was first translated into English in 1949, two years after *Bend Sinister*'s birth, just as in Borges' "The Secret Miracle," Hladik has created a verse drama uncannily similar to your recently Englished play, *The Waltz Invention*, which precedes Borges' tale, but which he could not have read in Russian. When were you first aware of Borges' fictions, and have you and he had any kind of association or contact, other than telepathic?

A. I read a Borges story for the first time three or four years ago. Up till then I had not been aware of his existence, nor do I believe he knew, or indeed knows, anything about me. That is not very grand in the way of telepathy. There are affinities between *Invitation to a Beheading* and *The Castle*, but I had not yet read Kafka when I wrote my novel. As to Hemingway, I read him for the first time in the early 'forties, something about bells, balls and bulls, and loathed it. Later I read his admirable "The Killers" and the wonderful fish story which I was asked to translate into Russian but could not for some reason or other.

Q. As a matter of fact, Borges *does* know of your existence: he was supposed to contribute to the special issue of the French magazine *L'Arc* which was devoted to you, but, for some reason, he did not. Your first book was a translation of Lewis Carroll into Russian. Do you see any affinities between Carroll's idea of "nonsense" and your bogus or "mongrel" languages in *Bend Sinister* and *Pale Fire*?

A. In common with many other English children (I was an English child) I have been always very fond of Carroll. No, I do not think that his invented language shares any roots with mine. He has a pathetic affinity with H.H. but some odd scruple prevented me from alluding in *Lolita* to his wretched perversion and to those ambiguous photographs he took in dim rooms. He got away with it, as so many other Victorians got away with pederasty and nympholepsy. His were sad scrawny little nymphets, bedraggled and half-undressed, or rather semi-undraped, as if participating in some dusty and dreadful charade.

Q. I thought that you *did* allude to Carroll in *Lolita* through what might be called "the photography theme": Humbert cherishes his worn old photograph of Annabel, has in a sense been living with this "still," tries to make Lolita conform to it, and often laments his failure to capture her on film. Quilty's hobby is announced as "photography," and the unspeakable films he produced at the Duk Duk Ranch would seem to answer Carroll's wildest needs.

A. I did not consciously think of Carroll's hobby when I referred to the use of photography in *Lolita*.

Q. You have had wide experience as a translator and have made fictive use of translation. What basic problems of existence do you find implicit in the art and act of translation?

A. There is a certain small Malayan bird of the thrush family which is said to sing only when tormented in an unspeakable way by a specially trained child at the annual Feast of Flowers. There is Casanova making love to a harlot while looking from a window at the nameless tortures inflicted on Damiens. These are the visions that sicken me when I read the "poetical" translations from martyred Russian poets by some of my famous contemporaries. A tortured author and a deceived reader, this is the inevitable outcome of arty paraphrase. The only object and justification of translation is the conveying of the most exact information possible and this can be only achieved by a literal translation, with notes.

Q. Mention of translation brings me to one of the Kinbotian problems faced by critics who comment on your Russian novels in translation, but who themselves have no Russian. It has been said that translations such as *The Defense* and *Despair* must contain many stylistic revisions (certainly the puns), and moreover are in general much richer in language than *Laughter in the Dark*, written at about the same time but, unlike the others, translated in the 'thirties. Would you comment on this? If the style of *Laughter in the Dark* suggests it should have preceded *Despair*, perhaps it actually was written much earlier: in the BBC interview of four years ago,[5] you said that you wrote *Laughter in the Dark* when you were twenty-six, which would have been 1925, thus making it your first novel. Did you actually write it this early, or is the reference to age a slip in memory, no doubt caused by the distracting presence of the BBC machinery.

A. I touched up details here and there in those novels and reinstated a scene in *Despair*, as the Foreword explains. That "twenty-six" is certainly wrong. It is either a telescopation or I must have been thinking of *Mashenka*, my first novel written in 1925. The Russian original version (*Kamera Obskura*) of *Laughter in the Dark* was written in 1931, and an English translation by Winifred Roy, insufficiently revised by me, appeared in London in 1936. A year later, on the Riviera, I attempted—not quite successfully—to English the thing anew for Bobbs-Merrill, who published it in New York in 1938.

Q. There is a parenthetical remark in *Despair* about a "vulgar, mediocre Herzog." Is that a bit of added fun about a recent best seller?

A. Herzog means "Duke" in German and I was speaking of a conventional statue of a German Duke in a city square.

Q. Since the reissued edition of *Laughter in the Dark* is not graced by one of your informative forewords, would you tell us something about the book's inception and the circumstances under which you wrote it? Commentators are quick to suggest similarities between Margot and Lolita, but I'm much more interested in the kinship between Axel Rex and Quilty. Would you comment on this, and perhaps on the other perverters of the imagination one finds throughout your work, all of whom seem to share Rex's evil qualities.

A. Yes, some affinities between Rex and Quilty exist, as they do between Margot and Lo. Actually, of course, Margot was a common young whore, not an unfortunate little Lolita. Anyway I do not think that those recurrent sexual oddities and morbidities are of much

[5] Peter Duval-Smith, "Vladimir Nabokov on His Life and Work," *Listener*, LXVIII (Nov. 22, 1962), 856–58. Reprinted as "What Vladimir Nabokov Thinks of His Work," *Vogue*, CXLI (March 1, 1963), 152–55.

interest or importance. My Lolita has been compared to Emmie in *Invitation*, to Mariette in *Bend Sinister*, and even to Colette in *Speak, Memory*—the last is especially ludicrous. But I think it might have been simply English jollity and leg-pulling.[6]

Q. The *Doppelgänger* motif figures prominently throughout your fiction; in *Pale Fire* one is tempted to call it a Tripling (at least). Would you say that *Laughter in the Dark* is your earliest Double fiction?

A. I do not see any doubles in *Laughter in the Dark*. A lover can be viewed as the betrayed party's double but that is pointless.

Q. Would you care to comment on how the *Doppelgänger* motif has been both used and abused from Poe, Hoffman, Andersen, Dostoevski, Gogol, Stevenson, and Melville, down to Conrad and Mann? Which *Doppelgänger* fictions would you single out for praise?

A. The *Doppelgänger* subject is a frightful bore.

Q. What are your feelings about Dostoevski's celebrated *The Double*; after all, Hermann in *Despair* considers it as a possible title for his manuscript.

A. Dostoevski's *The Double* is his best work though an obvious and shameless imitation of Gogol's "Nose." Felix in *Despair* is really a *false* double.

Q. What are the criteria of identity which have made this theme so congenial to you? And what assumptions about identity have you reacted against in fashioning your own conception of the Double?

A. There are no "real" doubles in my novels.

Q. Speaking of Doubles brings me to *Pnin*, which in my experience has proved to be one of your most popular novels and at the same time one of your most elusive to those readers who fail to see the relationship of the narrator and the characters (or who fail to even notice the narrator until it's too late). Four of its seven chapters were published in the *New Yorker* over a considerable period (1953–57),

---

[6] A reference to Kingsley Amis' review of *Lolita*, "She Was a Child and I Was a Child," *Spectator*, CCIII (Nov. 6, 1959), 636. The "leg-pulling" persists in this issue; see "*Lolita*: The Springboard of Parody," p. 220.

but the all-important last chapter, in which the narrator takes control, is only in the book. I'd be most interested to know if the design of *Pnin* was complete while the separate sections were being published, or whether your full sense of its possibilities occurred later.

A. Yes, the design of *Pnin* was complete in my mind when I composed the first chapter which, I believe, in this case was actually the first of the seven I physically set down on paper. Alas, there was to be an additional chapter, between Four (in which, incidentally, both the boy at St. Mark's and Pnin dream of a passage from my drafts of *Pale Fire*, the revolution in Zembla and the escape of the king— that is telepathy for you!) and Five (where Pnin drives a car). In that still uninked chapter, which was beautifully clear in my mind down to the last curve, Pnin recovering in the hospital from a sprained back teaches himself to drive a car in bed by studying a 1935 manual of automobilism found in the hospital library and by manipulating the levers of his cot. Only one of his colleagues visits him there—Professor Blorenge. The chapter ended with Pnin's taking his driver's examination and pedantically arguing with the instructor who has to admit Pnin is right. A combination of chance circumstances in 1956 prevented me from actually writing that chapter, then other events intervened, and it is only a mummy now.

Q. In a television interview last year, you singled out Bely's *St. Petersburg*, along with works by Joyce, Kafka, and Proust, as one of the greatest achievements in twentieth-century prose (an endorsement, by the way, which has prompted Grove Press to reissue *St. Petersburg*, with your statement across the front cover). I greatly admire this novel but, unhappily enough, it is relatively unknown in America. What are its qualities which you most admire? Bely and Joyce are sometimes compared; is the comparison a just one?

A. *Petersburg* is a splendid fantasy, but this is a question I plan to answer in my essay on Joyce. There does exist some resemblance in manner between *Petersburg* and certain passages in *Ulysses*.

Q. Although I've never seen it discussed as such, the Ableukhov father-son relationship to me constitutes a doubling, making *Petersburg* one of the most interesting and fantastic permutations of the Doppelgänger theme. Since this kind of doubling (if you would agree it is one) is surely the kind you'd find more congenial, say, than the use Mann makes of the motif in *Death in Venice*, would you comment on its implications?

A. Those murky matters have no importance to me as a writer. Philosophically, I am an indivisible monist.

Q. Bely lived in Berlin in 1922–23. Did you know him there? You and Joyce lived in Paris at the same time; did you ever meet him?

A. Once, in 1921 or 1922, at a Berlin restaurant where I was dining with two girls. I happened to be sitting back to back with Andrey Bely who was dining with another writer, Aleksey Tolstoy, at the table behind me. Both writers were at the time frankly pro-Soviet (and on the point of returning to Russia), and a White Russian, which I still am in that particular sense, would certainly not wish to speak to a *bolshevizan* (fellow traveller). I was acquainted with Aleksey Tolstoy but of course ignored him. As to Joyce, I saw him a few times in Paris in the late 'thirties. Paul and Lucy Léon, close friends of his, were also old friends of mine. One night they brought him to a French lecture I had been asked to deliver on Pushkin under the auspices of Gabriel Marcel (it was later published in the *Nouvelle Revue Française*). I had happened to replace at the very last moment a Hungarian woman writer, very famous that winter, author of a bestselling novel, I remember its title, *La Rue du Chat qui Pêche*, but not the lady's name. A number of personal friends of mine, fearing that the sudden illness of the lady and a sudden discourse on Pushkin might result in a suddenly empty house, had done their best to round up the kind of audience they knew I would like to have. The house had, however, a pied aspect since some confusion had occurred among the lady's fans. The Hungarian consul mistook me for her husband and, as I entered, dashed towards me with the froth of condolence on his lips. Some people left as soon as I started to speak. A source of unforgettable consolation was the sight of Joyce sitting, arms folded and glasses glinting, in the midst of the Hungarian football team. Another time my wife and I had dinner with him at the Léons followed by a long friendly evening of talk. I do not recall one word of it but my wife remembers that Joyce asked about the exact ingredients of *myod*, the Russian "mead," and everybody gave him a different answer. In this connection, there is a marvelous howler in the standard English version of *The Brothers Karamazov*: a supper table at Zosima's abode is described with the translator hilariously misreading "Médoc" (in Russian transliteration in the original text), a French wine greatly appreciated in Russia, as *medok*, the diminutive of *myod* (mead). It would have been fun to recall that I spoke of this to Joyce but unfortunately I came across this incarnation of *The Karamazovs* some ten years later.

Q. You mentioned Aleksey Tolstoy a moment ago. Would you say something about him?

A. He was a writer of some talent and has two or three science fiction stories or novels which are memorable. But I wouldn't care to categorize writers, the only category being originality and talent. After all, if we start sticking group labels, we'll have to put "The Tempest" in the SF category, and of course thousands of other valuable works.

Q. Tolstoy was initially an anti-Bolshevik, and his early work precedes the Revolution. Are there any writers totally of the Soviet period whom you admire?

A. There were a few writers who discovered that if they chose certain plots and certain characters they could get away with it in the political sense, in other words, they wouldn't be told what to write and how to finish the novel. Ilf and Petrov, two wonderfully gifted writers, decided that if they had a rascal adventurer as protagonist, whatever they wrote about his adventures could not be criticized from a political point of view, since a perfect rascal or a madman or a delinquent or any person who was outside Soviet society—in other words, any picaresque character—could not be accused either of being a bad Communist or not being a good Communist. Thus Ilf and Petrov, Zoshchenko, and Olesha managed to publish some absolutely first-rate fiction under that standard of complete independence, since these characters, plots, and themes could not be treated as political ones. Until the early 'thirties they managed to get away with it. The poets had a parallel system. They thought, and they were right at first, that if they stuck to the garden —to pure poetry, to lyrical imitations, say, of gypsy songs, such as Ilya Selvinski's—that then they were safe. Zabolotski found a third method of writing, as if the "I" of the poem were a perfect imbecile, crooning in a dream, distorting words, playing with words as a half-insane person would. All these people were enormously gifted but the regime finally caught up with them and they disappeared, one by one, in nameless camps.

Q. By my loose approximation, there remain three novels, some fifty stories, and six plays still in Russian. Are there any plans to translate these? What of *The Exploit*, written during what seems to have been your most fecund period as a "Russian writer," would you tell us something, however briefly, about this book?

A. Not all of that stuff is as good as I thought it was thirty years ago but some of it will probably be published in English bye-and-bye. My son is now working on the translation of *The Exploit*. It is the story of a Russian expatriate, a romantic young man of my set and time, a lover of adventure for adventure's sake, proud flaunter of peril, climber of unnecessary mountains, who merely for the pure thrill of it decides one day to cross illegally into Soviet Russia, and then cross back to exile. Its main theme is the overcoming of fear, the glory and rapture of that victory.

Q. I understand that *The Real Life of Sebastian Knight* was written in English in 1938. It is very dramatic to think of you bidding farewell to one language and embarking on a new life in another in this way. Why did you decide to write in English at this time, since you obviously could not have known for certain you would emigrate two years later? How much more writing in Russian did you do between *Sebastian Knight* and your emigration to America in 1940, and once there, did you ever compose in Russian again?

A. Oh, I did know I would eventually land in America. I switched to English after convincing myself on the strength of my translation of *Despair* that I could use English as a wistful standby for Russian.[7] I still feel the pangs of that substitution, they have not been allayed by the Russian poems (my best) that I wrote in New York, or the 1954 Russian version of *Speak, Memory*, or even my recent two-years long work on the Russian translation of *Lolita* which will be published some time in 1967. I wrote *Sebastian Knight* in Paris, 1938. We had that year a charming flat on rue Saigon, between the Etoile and the Bois. It consisted of a huge handsome room (which served as parlor, bedroom and nursery) with a small kitchen on one side and a large sunny bathroom on the other. This apartment had been some bachelor's delight but was not meant to accommodate

---

[7] In 1936, while living in Berlin, Nabokov translated *Despair* for the English firm, John Long, who published it in 1937. The most recent and final edition of *Despair* (New York, 1966) is, as Nabokov explains in its Foreword, a revision of both the early translation and of *Otchayanie* itself.

a family of three. Evening guests had to be entertained in the kitchen so as not to interfere with my future translator's sleep. And the bathroom doubled as my study. Here is the *Doppelgänger* theme for you.

Q. Many people are surprised to learn that you have written seven plays, which is strange, since your novels are filled with "theatrical" effects that are patently unnovelistic. Is it just to say that your frequent allusions to Shakespeare are more than a matter of playful or respectful homage? What do you think of the drama as a form? What are the characteristics of Shakespeare's plays which you find most congenial to your own esthetic?

A. The verbal poetical texture of Shakespeare is the greatest the world has known, and is immensely superior to the structure of his plays as plays. With Shakespeare it is the metaphor that is the thing, not the play. My most ambitious venture in the domain of drama is a huge screenplay based on *Lolita*. I wrote it for Kubrick who used only bits and shadows of it for his otherwise excellent film.

Q. When I was your student, you never mentioned the Homeric parallels in discussing Joyce's *Ulysses*. But you did supply "special information" in introducing many of the masterpieces: a map of Dublin for *Ulysses*, the arrangement of streets and lodgings in *Dr. Jekyll and Mr. Hyde*, a diagram of the interior of a railway coach on the Moscow–St. Petersburg express in *Anna Karenina*, and a floor plan of the Samsa's apartment in *The Metamorphosis* and an entomological drawing of Gregor. Would you be able to suggest some equivalent for your own readers?

A. Joyce himself very soon realized with dismay that the harping on those essentially easy and vulgar "Homeric parallelisms" would only distract one's attention from the real beauty of his book. He soon dropped these pretentious chapter titles which already were "explaining" the book to non-readers. In my lectures I tried to give factual data only. A map of three country estates with a winding river and a figure of the butterfly *Parnassius mnemosyne* for a cartographic cherub will be the endpaper in my revised edition of *Speak, Memory*.

Q. Incidentally, one of my colleagues came into my office recently with the breathless news that Gregor is *not* a cockroach (he had read an article to that effect). I told him I've known that for twelve years, and took out my notes to show him my drawing from what was for one day only Entomology 312. What kind of beetle, by the way, was Gregor?

A. It was a domed beetle, a scarab beetle with wing-sheaths, and neither Gregor nor his maker realized that when the room was being made by the maid, and the window was open, he could have flown out and escaped and joined the other happy dung beetles rolling the dung balls on rural paths.

Q. How are you progressing in your novel, *The Texture of Time*? Since the *données* for some of your novels seem to be present, however fleetingly, in earlier novels, would it be fair to suggest that chapter fourteen of *Bend Sinister* contains the germ for your latest venture?

A. In a way, yes; but my *Texture of Time*, now almost half-ready, is only the central rose-web of a much ampler and richer novel, entitled *Ada*, about passionate, hopeless, rapturous sunset love, with swallows darting beyond the stained window and that radiant shiver...

Q. Speaking of *données*: At the end of *Pale Fire*, Kinbote says of Shade and his poem, "I even suggested to him a good title—the title of the book in me whose pages he was to cut: *Solus Rex*; instead of which I saw *Pale Fire*, which meant to me nothing." In 1940 *Sovremennye Zapiski* published a long section from your "unfinished" novel, *Solus Rex*, under that title. Does *Pale Fire* represent the "cutting" of its pages? What is the relationship between it, the other untranslated fragment from *Solus Rex* ("Ultima Thule," published in *Novyy Journal*, New York, 1942) and *Pale Fire*?

A. My *Solus Rex* might have disappointed Kinbote less than Shade's poem. The two countries, that of the Lone King and the Zembla land, belong to the same biological zone. Their subarctic bogs have much the same butterflies and berries. A sad and distant kingdom seems to have haunted my poetry and fiction since the 'twenties. It is not associated with my personal past. Unlike Northern Russia, both Zembla and Ultima Thule are mountainous, and their languages are of a phony Scandinavian type. If a cruel prankster kidnapped Kinbote and placed him, blindfolded, in the Ultima Thule countryside, Kinbote would not know—at least not immediately—by the sap smells and bird calls that he was not back in Zembla, but he would be tolerably sure that he was not on the banks of the Neva.

Q. This may be like asking a father to publicly declare which of his children is most loved, but do you have one novel towards which you feel the most affection, which you esteem over all others?

A. The most affection, *Lolita;* the greatest esteem, *Priglashenie na Kazn'*.[8]

Q. And as a closing question, sir, may I return to *Pale Fire*: where, please, are the crown jewels hidden?[9]

A. In the ruins, Sir, of some old barracks near Kobaltana (q.v.); but do not tell it to the Russians.

---

[8] *Invitation to a Beheading.*

[9] One hesitates to explain a joke, but readers unfamiliar with *Pale Fire* should be informed that the hiding place of the Zemblan crown jewels is never revealed in the text, and the Index entry under "crown jewels," to which the reader must now refer, is less than helpful. "Kobaltana" is also in the Index.

NOTES ON NABOKOV
AS A RUSSIAN WRITER

Gleb Struve

> The secret for which he strove was
> simplicity, harmonious simplicity,
> which can amaze one far more than
> the most intricate magic.
>
> V. Nabokov, *The Defense*

Vladimir Nabokov published (privately) his first book of juvenile poems at the age of sixteen; emigrated with his parents from Russia in 1919; wrote and published in Russian—at first prolifically, but, as time went on, more discriminately—in the 'twenties and 'thirties, and almost stopped writing in his native tongue after 1940. (There was no major fictional work after *Dar* [*The Gift*, 1938]. A few poems and stories appeared in the 'forties; the English autobiography was rewritten in Russian and published in 1954 under the title *Drugie berega* [*Other Shores*]; and now Nabokov has translated *Lolita* into Russian.) Nabokov appeared to his Russian readers under the pen name, "V. Sirin," which he adopted partly in order to avoid confusion with his father (whose name was also Vladimir), a well-known public man and journalist, and editor of the newspaper *Rul'* in which much of Nabokov-Sirin's early work was published. Most of the verse, the first two novels—even though they have been translated into German—most of the pieces in the first volume of stories, *Vozvrashchenie Chorba* (*The Return of Chorb*, 1930), the novel *Podvig* (*The Exploit*, 1932) remain unknown in the West.

The reception of Nabokov-Sirin by the Russian critics was mixed and recognition came slowly. It took one of the leading Russian émigré critics, George Adamovich, himself a poet and a talented essayist (in his autobiography Nabokov refers to him, without naming him, as the leader of the sect of "Adamites" among the young Russian writers in Paris), many years to admit the significance of Nabokov as a writer. For that matter, in the West, too, Nabokov achieved wide recognition only after the resounding success of *Lolita* (and his own opinion of it as his best work is certainly open to doubt): neither *The Real Life of Sebastian Knight* nor *Bend Sinister*, though they had a certain *succès d'estime*, won him the place he deserved in contemporary American literature. His Russian novels translated into other languages attracted little attention, even though they included *Zashchita Luzhina*, hailed by the critics upon its recent publication in English (under the title *The Defense*) as a masterpiece. One of the best of Nabokov's Russian novels, as well as one of his most typical, it was rendered into French (as *La Course du fou*) as early as 1934 by such an experienced and competent translator as Denis Roche who was known for his translations of Chekhov. Yet, when in the same year the present writer tried to find a British publisher for it, he failed completely. One of the best-known London publishers, himself a distinguished writer, said after reading the French translation that while he had found it "interesting," he did not think that it was a book for them. The same was true, with exceptions, of Nabokov's short stories for which I tried to find a place in British periodicals. It is even worth putting on record that in 1936 a highly reputable London literary magazine (let us be charitable and refrain from naming it) returned a story, because, as one of the editors put it, "Unfortunately, that he [Nabokov] is a Russian émigré precludes our using any of his work according to the recent policy of the directors of this paper"!

While Russian émigré critics (those inside Russia were to mention Nabokov first in connection with the reports about the filming of *Lolita*) disagreed about the merits of Nabokov's work, many of them did agree on one point: they kept referring to his "un-Russianness," to his lack of ties with Russian literature and its traditions. At the same time some of them made a point of establishing his dependence on contemporary European literature and spoke of the influence of such different writers as Proust, Kafka, Giraudoux, Céline, the German Expressionists, and so forth.[1] There were, it is true, exceptions: at one point some Russian critics began to speak of Nabokov's affinity with Gogol, to whom he was later to devote a

---

[1] In the "Foreword" to the American edition of *Despair* Nabokov mentions the critics who, in speaking of him, casually dragged in the influence of German Impressionists and adds: "I do not know German and have never read the Impressionists—whoever they are." This substitution of "Impressionists" for "Expressionists" is probably deliberate and rather typical of Nabokov's manner.

book in English, while the late Professor Peter Bitsilli, a well-known literary scholar and critic, in discussing Nabokov's *Invitation to a Beheading*, drew a curious parallel between Nabokov and the nine-teenth-century Russian social satirist Saltykov-Shchedrin, the author of *The Golovlyov Family*.

There was also one critic who after the publication of Nabokov's first novel, *Mashenka* (1926; the only translation of it is into Ger-man, under the title *Sie kommt—kommt sie?*, 1928; the author, regarding it as immature, will probably not want to see it translated now), predicted that Nabokov would develop into a writer of mores of the Russians in exile. This prediction was not borne out, for although Russian exiles appear in several of Nabokov's novels and in a number of early stories, only two of the novels—*Mashenka* and *Dar* (*The Gift*)—have the real émigré milieu for their setting. In *Zashchita Luzhina* (*The Defense*) and *Otchayanie* (*Despair*) the milieu is only partly Russian, while in some of the novels and in many stories there are no Russian characters at all. But even in the works in which the life of the Russians in exile is an important ele-ment of the story Nabokov is always more than a mere recorder of mores.

With all its immaturity, *Mashenka* reveals some of the essen-tials of Nabokov's literary technique. He is a "realist" (I know he himself detests the use of such labels in literature) in the sense that he nearly always uses material with which real life provides him, and in using it displays the astounding keenness of his vision and the uncanny power of his memory. But there is always in his work a blending of realism and artifice. Not content with recreating the natural flow of life, he artificially organizes his real life material. His artificiality is deliberate, a part of his artistic credo, which he has on more than one occasion formulated in the prefaces to his works in English. He had earlier put it into the mouths of his fictional char-acters. Thus the hero-narrator of *Despair*, who conceives his crime as a work of art ("There was in me, I felt, a poet, an author . . ."), coins the following aphorism: "The invention of art contains far more intrinsical truths than life's reality." It is he, too, who says that "every work of art is a deception." For Nabokov, real life and real people are the artist's "material," but he must never for a moment loosen his grip on them; he must not let their world, the world of his fiction, have an independent, "verisimilar" existence. He is the arbitrary master of that world, his characters must not give us an illusion of lifelikeness, of people whom we have met in real life, whom we sometimes seem to know better than real-life people (as has often been said, for instance, of Tolstoy's character creations). They are indeed puppets, products of the author's imagination and creative memory (of which we read again in *Despair*: "An artist's memory—what a curious thing! Beats all other kinds, I imagine"). Nabokov himself said in his autobiography that all conflicts in literature are clashes not between characters but between the author and the world. The reader must be constantly aware of the author's will, directing and shaping the destinies of his characters. He cannot allow them to get out of hand and follow the "natural" course of events. Contrivance is of the essence of art. Where other writers deal in probabilities, Nabokov prefers to choose bare possibilities. It is not accidental therefore that coincidences play such an important role in his novels and stories, or that he sometimes deliberately bares (as it were) the contrived nature of his fictional constructs and smashes them with the same delight with which a child smashes some of its elaborate constructions. Take, for instance, the ending of *Priglashenie na kazn'* (*Invitation to a Beheading*): it is reminiscent of the ending of *Alice in Wonderland* (a work which Nabokov is known to have admired very much—he translated it into Russian in the early 'twenties). Or the fact that in the last chapter of *Despair* the entry in the hero's account of what happened is dated "April 1st," that is, April Fools' Day. This date is found on the penultimate page of the novel (p. 221 of the American edition). How many readers will have noticed, however, that much earlier, on p. 34, the narrator says: "Tum-tee-tum. And once more—TUM! No, I have not gone mad. I am merely producing gleeful little sounds. The kind of glee one experiences upon making an April fool of someone. And a damned good fool I have made of someone. Who is he? Gentle reader, look at yourself in the mirror, as you seem to like mirrors so much." This is a kind of thing Nabokov takes a genuine delight in. And one can imagine his glee when his readers, including the critics, and especially those who like to talk gravely and ponderously about the symbolism of this or that situation or image, miss those little tricks of his, both verbal and compositional.[2]

---

[2] Unfortunately, I do not have at hand a copy of *Despair* in Russian (my own copy, with an inscription from the author, seems to have disappeared during the Second World War in London), and I do not know whether these particular passages are not afterthoughts to be found in the English version only.

Quite often Nabokov endows his characters with his own fondness for tricks and puns. Does not the same hero of *Despair* (who, after all, is an *artist*—an artist in crime) say: "I liked, as I like still, to make words look self-conscious and foolish, to bind them by the mock marriage of a pun, to turn them inside out, to come upon them unawares. What is this jest in majesty? This ass in passion? How do God and Devil combine to form a live dog?" These words could have been spoken by Nabokov of himself. His tendency to overindulge in this kind of verbal play is apt to irritate some and, in giving himself to it, Nabokov sometimes comes close to lapsing into bad taste. It is at the same time closely related to his great gift for parody and is something in which his linguistic genius finds expression.

Let us have another look at Nabokov's first novel, *Mashenka*. It is built around facts and situations of real life, well defined in time and place, and that life is described with masterful, satirically colored realism, the setting being the humdrum everyday life of an average Russian boarding-house in Berlin in the early 'twenties. In long flashbacks the author provides, through the memory of his hero, an equally "realistic" picture of life of a young, wealthy Russian before the Revolution, in which the reader of Nabokov's autobiography will easily recognize much of the author's own background. The hero relives the story of his love for Mashenka, the heroine of the novel, who turns out to be married to one of the hero's fellow boarders. She is expected to arrive from Russia and join him, but never appears in the flesh. The hero makes her husband drunk and goes to meet her in his place, but on the way to the station he changes his mind and goes off in a different direction. The novel ends on this note and the reader never comes to know Mashenka as she now is. Although the ending of *Mashenka* represents Nabokov's fondness for the unexpected, it is really a suspended denouement, the outcome of which is left to the reader's imagination. There is something similar in *Despair*, a much later and maturer novel, and this device enables Nabokov to engage in one of his favorite games with the reader; thus he writes in his preface to the American edition:

The "remote abode" to which mad Hermann finally scurries is economically located in the Roussillon where three years earlier I had begun writing my chess novel, *The Defense*. We leave Hermann at the ludicrous height of his discomfiture. I do not remember what happened to him eventually. After all, fifteen other books and twice as many years have intervened. I cannot even recall if that film he proposed to direct was ever made by him.

In the light of this whimsical "disavowal" and of the reference to April Fools' Day in the novel itself, the reader begins to wonder whether the elaborately conceived, executed, and described murder of Felix, Hermann's "double," is not a figment of Hermann's imagination. Are the author's references to Hermann's madness and to the film directed by him to be taken at their face value, and if so, which of them is the clue to his real intention? Or is the author deliberately leading the reader up the garden path?

Nabokov's second novel—*King Queen Knave*[3] (1928)—remains unknown to most of his English and American readers, for it has not been translated into English and I do not know whether there is any intention to do so. A German translation of it, under the title *König Dame Bube*, appeared soon after the publication of the original. Here the element of artifice, if not of sleight-of-hand, becomes almost too conspicuous, inasmuch as this motif is introduced into the story itself. While the title is an allusion to the cardboard nature of the novel's personages, it is also a hint at its subject—the trite eternal triangle. But this banal theme is handled by Nabokov in an original manner; the structure of the novel is simple and yet fascinating, and there is so much verbal freshness and felicity in it that the banality of the theme is easily forgotten by the reader. It is as though Nabokov had set out to prove that it is not "What" but "How" that matters in a work of art.

The scene is laid once more in Berlin, where Nabokov was living at the time after graduating from the University of Cambridge, but this time there are no Russians among the characters, and the satire is aimed at the philistinism of the German middle class. The three title characters are the only "real" people in the novel and the only ones who matter in the story. They are: Dreyer, a well-to-do German businessman; Martha, his pretty and flirtatious wife; and Franz, a poor relation of Dreyer's, a timid, awkward, myopic, provincial young man. Dreyer is a curious, elusive character: under a perfectly bourgeois, matter-of-fact, sober exterior he hides poetic imagination, a passion for far-off wanderings, an interest in things

---

[3] The commas were deliberately omitted by the author.

outlandish, and a subtly ironical and yet romantic attitude to life. Martha is, on the other hand, an embodiment of philistinism and vulgarity, as are some of the minor characters who appear as the couple's friends or Dreyer's business associates. A remote similarity may be seen here with the relationship between Hermann and Lydia in Despair, though Dreyer is no Hermann. And though his function in the novel is quite different, Ardalion may be seen as a distant reflection of Franz.

Fed up with Dreyer's apparent indifference, with his erratic moods, his mysterious preoccupations, Martha starts a love affair with Franz (her "seduction" of him is described with great comic gusto) and conceives the idea of doing away with Dreyer. The psychological interest of the novel lies in the presentation of the slow maturing of this plan in Martha's mind, of the way she "infects" Franz with her idea (he becomes her passive and involuntary accomplice). Perhaps one can see here also an anticipation of Despair, where the working out of the murder to be staged as a suicide is presented as a kind of creative process.[4] In the end, she works out a rather elaborate plan. Though the whole thing does not sound by any means natural and feasible, the reader expects it to succeed. But with Nabokov one never knows. Human destinies are ruled by blind hazard. Dreyer manages to thwart Martha's plan, she catches cold and dies of pneumonia, and Dreyer, who was seemingly so cold and aloof, suddenly realizes that he has always loved, and still loves, her.

Those who demand from literature "convincing," round characters and plausible situations will not find the novel to their taste. In keeping with his title Nabokov shows us, as I have said, flat, cardboard characters, and their mannequin-like behavior is emphasized by the introduction of some queer, almost fantastic, minor personages. One of them is the old inventor of robot mannequins with whom Dreyer has business dealings. Another is Franz's landlord, a funny old juggler who calls himself Mene-Tekel-Peres. In his person the author, who until then had kept aloof from the world created by him, seems to peep suddenly into the novel to remind us

---

[4] The well-known Russian poet Vladislav Khodasevich (1886–1939), in one of his perceptive articles about Nabokov, was the first to point out that the problem of creativity and of the creative process was quite obsessive with Nabokov. Indeed, not only is it all-important and central in The Gift and The Defense, but in one form or another it is to be found in nearly all his Russian novels, as well as in Sebastian Knight and Pale Fire. It is his primary artistic concern.

that he is the sole creator and arbiter of this fictional world of his and of the destinies of those who inhabit it.[5] Thus, towards the end of the novel (but not *at* the end of it) we read:

At eleven the old landlord passed soundlessly along the corridor. He listened, looked at Franz's door and then went back to his own room. He knew perfectly well that there was no Franz behind the door, that he had created Franz by a light stroke of imagination, but all the same he had to carry the joke through—and check whether his casual invention was asleep, whether it was not burning electricity at night. He was rather fed up with this lanky invention and its tortoiseshell glasses; it was high time to do away with it, to replace it by a new one. He did so by one beck of thought. Let this be the last night of the fictitious lodger. For this purpose he assumed that tomorrow would be the first of the month, and he himself thought that everything was quite natural: the lodger had decided to leave of his own, had paid up, everything was O.K. Thus, having invented the inevitable ending, Mene-Tekel-Peres added to it all that was, in the past, to lead to this ending. For he knew full well that the whole world was a trick of his own, and that all these people—Franz, Franz's girl friend, the noisy gentleman with the dog and even his own, Peres's, wife, a quiet old woman in a head-dress (and for the initiated, a man, his elderly companion, a mathematics teacher who had died seven years ago) —that all of them were but a play of his imagination, a suggestion, a sleight-of-hand. And he, too, could any moment turn into a centipede, a Turkish woman, a couch. . . . He was, after all, such an excellent conjuror, this Mene-Tekel-Peres.

In *King Queen Knave* the sleight-of-hand becomes an important motif of the novel, but it is also, in almost every work of Nabokov's, an essential element of his technique. In 1931, apropos of the publication of the short novel *Soglyadatay* (recently translated into English as *The Eye* and published in *Playboy* magazine), I wrote an anonymous article on Nabokov for a long since defunct Paris monthly, to which I gave the title "Les 'romans-escamotage' de Vladimir Sirine."[6] I concluded by saying that the author functions as a conjuror, similar to the old juggler in *King Queen Knave*, and that to the *roman-fleuve* of the nineteenth century and the impres-

---

[5] It can be said of Nabokov that, on the surface at least and in his earlier, Russian, period, he was one of the least subjective writers in Russian literature: there was no knowing his own views or feelings. Later, especially in his autobiography, Nabokov made many of his attitudes quite clear.

[6] See *Le Mois*, IV (avril-mai 1931), 145–152.

sionist novel of the twentieth century Nabokov was opposing the novel of artifice.

In *The Defense*, which seems to me to be one of Nabokov's best Russian works, we see the boy Luzhin fascinated by the art of conjuring before he discovers chess and succumbs to its ultimately fatal spell. But both conjuring and chess are shown to be preceded by his reading of two books, one by Jules Verne, the other by Conan Doyle, which Nabokov opposes to the boring writings of Korolenko and Goncharov (and on Luzhin's book shelf even Pushkin's large volume, with its "picture of a thick-lipped, curly-haired boy," was left unopened). Nabokov says, and there can be no doubt that he is speaking here also for himself, that it was not "a thirst for distant peregrinations that forced Luzhin to follow on the heels of Phileas Fogg, nor was it a boyish inclination for mysterious adventures that drew him to that house on Baker Street, where the lanky detective with the hawk profile, having given himself an injection of cocaine, would dreamily play the violin." But only much later did Luzhin

clarify in his own mind what it was that had thrilled him so about these two books; it was that exact and relentlessly unfolding pattern: Phileas, the dummy in the top hat, wending his complex elegant way with its justifiable sacrifices, now on an elephant bought for a million, now on a ship of which half has to be burned for fuel; and Sherlock endowing logic with the glamour of a daydream, Sherlock composing a monograph on the ash of all known sorts of cigars and with this ash as with a talisman progressing through a crystal labyrinth of possible deductions to the one radiant conclusion.

Even though Luzhin becomes a chess maniac who is driven to his doom, the whole of Nabokov's technique can be understood and interpreted only in the light of the pure delight in patterns and combinations which border on magic, on the art of the conjuror. To this Nabokov himself has since borne witness. When in his autobiography he writes about the delight he took in composing chess problems he is also writing about himself as a novelist:

Themes in chess . . . are such devices as forelaying, withdrawing, pinning, unpinning and so forth; but it is only when they are combined in a certain way that a problem is satisfying. Deceit, to the point of diabolism, and originality, grading into the grotesque, were my notions of strategy, and although in matters of construction I tried to conform, whenever possible, to classical rules, such as economy of force, unity, weeding out of

loose ends, I was always ready to sacrifice purity of form to the exigencies
of fantastic content, causing form to bulge and burst like a sponge-bag
containing a small furious devil.

It is one thing to conceive the main play of a composition and another to construct it. The strain on the mind is formidable; the element of
time drops out of one's consciousness altogether: the building hand gropes
for a pawn in the box, holds it, while the mind still ponders the need for
a foil or a stop-gap, and when the first opens, a whole hour, perhaps, has
gone by, has burned to ashes in the incandescent cerebration of the
schemer. The chessboard before him is a magnetic field, a system of
stresses and abysses, a starry firmament. The bishops move over it like
searchlights. This or that knight is a lever adjusted and tried, and readjusted
and tried again, till the problem is tuned up to the necessary level of
beauty and surprise. How often I have struggled to bind the terrible force
of White's queen so as to avoid a dual solution! [. . .] But whatever I can
say about this matter of problem composing, I do not seem to convey
sufficiently the ecstatic core of the process and its points of connection with
various other, more overt and fruitful, operations of the creative mind,
from the charting of dangerous seas to the writing of one of those incredible novels where the author, in a fit of lucid madness, has set himself
certain unique rules that he observes, certain nightmare obstacles that he
surmounts, with the zest of a deity building a live world from the most
unlikely ingredients—rocks, and carbon, and blind throbbings.[7]

Nabokov's conception of literature as an artifice, his interest in,
and concern with, the problems of composition, of pattern, his out-
spoken contempt for any kind of "message" in literature, be it social,
moral, or religious-philosophical, are all against the grain of the
Russian literary tradition, if not also of much of the European tradition of the nineteenth century. These attitudes lie behind Nabokov's
harsh criticism of so many established writers who are more or less
universally admired, particularly Dostoevsky, the "Dusty" of Hermann in Despair, but also such different writers as Racine, Goethe,
and Balzac. What makes Nabokov even more alien to the Russian
literary tradition is his lack of sympathy with, if not interest in,
human beings as such. Nikolay Berdyaev, the now famous Russian
philosopher, said that this love for one's fellow human beings was
the salient feature of Russian literature, that only one great Russian
writer lacked it, and this was Gogol (Gogol himself would have of
course denied this most hotly, and so would most of his nineteenth-

---

[7] Speak, Memory. A Memoir (New York, n.d.), pp. 219–220.

century Russian interpreters who saw "The Overcoat" as the acme of "compassion"). If Berdyaev is right, this is certainly a characteristic which Nabokov shares with Gogol, whatever differences their art may otherwise present. It is also something of which Nabokov himself is undoubtedly aware. I have written elsewhere that

. . . nearly all of Sirin's [i.e. Nabokov's] characters are 'negative.' He has an artist's predilection for the portrayal of morally and physically deformed creatures, but it would be no use to look in his portrayal of them, as one would in Dostoevsky, for love and pity for these monsters. Sirin is always artistically dispassionate and detached in his approach. Maybe this is another manifestation of that 'chastity' of which I spoke above. Yet, in The Luzhin Defense Sirin—perhaps against his own will—seems to escape from this circle of 'lack of love for man': in the fate of the mentally and spiritually defenseless monster and moral abortion there is something genuinely and pathetically human.[8]

I do not know what Nabokov thought of these words at the time, but now, more than thirty years later, he seems to have arrived at the same conclusion. In the Foreword to the American edition of The Defense, dated "Montreux Dec. 15, 1963," he says:

Of all my Russian books, The Defense contains and diffuses the greatest "warmth"—which may seem odd seeing how supremely abstract chess is supposed to be. In point of fact, Luzhin has been found lovable even by those who understand nothing about chess and/or detest all my other books. He is uncouth, unwashed, uncomely—but as my gentle lady (a dear girl in her own right) so quickly notices, there is something in him that transcends both the coarseness of his gray flesh and the sterility of his recondite genius.

It would be interesting to know why, in singling out The Defense, Nabokov deemed it necessary to speak of his Russian books only, for the same coldness, the same lack of human warmth, characterizes also his English novels. Or did he make here an exception for Pnin whose protagonist bears a certain family resemblance to Luzhin?

If chess and the art of conjuring are to be seen as the keys to

---

[8] See "Tvorchestvo Sirina," in Rossiya i Slavyanstvo (Paris, May 17, 1930). Earlier in the article I spoke of Nabokov-Sirin's "chastity" in the sense of his reluctance to lay his soul bare before his readers.

Nabokov's art as a writer, his interest—indeed, absorption—in lepi-
doptery provides another such key. Nabokov himself has written
enough about this subject and I need not expatiate on it here. Suffice
it to say that his keenness of vision, and the sharpness and colorful-
ness of the verbal garb in which that vision is clothed, seem to me
to be closely related to his lepidopteric pursuits and habits.

THE ARTIST AS FAILURE IN
NABOKOV'S EARLY PROSE

Andrew Field

The émigré poet Vladislav Khodasevich, who was Nabokov's best Russian critic, noted very early that in essence Nabokov writes only about artists and artistic problems, but that he does this under various allegorical guises.* The early works of Sirin-Nabokov do occasionally, however, confront the figure of the artist directly, and it is most curious that these direct statements concern artists who are failures either in their lives or their art.

The Eye, which was written in 1930, a year after *The Defense*, is a slighter work than *The Defense* in most respects including length. It is in fact really a short novella or a long short story which serves as the title story for a 1938 collection of Nabokov's short stories and was only promoted to the rank of a separate novel in its 1965 English translation—but in certain ways it is a more interesting work than *The Defense*.

As its very title shows, *The Eye*, like *Camera Obscura* (*Laughter in the Dark*), is concerned with problems of vision and appearance. *The Eye* also has a "break" in its narrative progression that is even sharper and more extraordinary than Kretschmar's sudden descent into blindness in *Camera Obscura*. Before *The Eye* has progressed past the one-quarter mark, its narrator-hero Smurov does the one thing that a narrator must never do until the last page—he shoots himself. Smurov's attempt on his own life doesn't succeed; after some time in a hospital he recovers from the shot, but the narrative proceeds as though he actually had killed himself. Its voice switches

---

* Reprinted from *Nabokov: His Life in Art*, copyright © 1967, by Andrew Field, with permission of Little, Brown and Company.

from first person to an impersonal third person "he." The trick of
this amazing transition is that Smurov does not identify himself by
name when he is speaking in the first person, and then a certain
Smurov enters the story "comparatively a newcomer, although he
hardly looks it." A long and winding sentence at the point of junc-
ture contains several clues that can be noticed by the careful reader,
and the excessively flattering description ("His manners were excellent. A quiet, somewhat melancholy smile lingered on his lips. He
spoke little, but everything he said was intelligent and appropriate . . .") is more than a little suspect. But there is really no trick
at all, since the "I" rambles on for fully three pages after he has shot
himself about how "after death human thought lives on by momentum. . . . I assumed that the posthumous momentum of my thought
would soon play itself out, but apparently, while I was still alive, my
imagination had been so fertile that enough of it remained to last
for a long time." And these comments, borrowed with certain elabo-
rations from Nabokov's 1923 verse drama, Death, should prepare
the reader for the practical application of the narrator's declaration:
"In respect to myself I was now an onlooker."

The change in the narrative is, whether one catches it early or
later, unusual, but it is fully justified both psychologically and
formally. I would compare it to one of the exceptional rules in chess
such as the convention that allows a pawn to be taken by an opposing pawn that lands beside it as a result of utilizing its first move
option to move ahead two squares instead of one—the pawn does
not actually "take" the other one by moving into its square, but
rather, it moves diagonally into its row and the pawn that had been
beside it is removed (the name of the move) en passant. In the
taking of a pawn en passant the question of timing is not left to the
discretion of the player, for the move may only be made at the proper
moment; that is, in the move immediately after the opposing pawn
has made its two-square move forward. All that happens in The Eye
is that two entirely distinct but actually closely connected occur-
rences, a suicide attempt and a change in the narrative, are made
in a single move. From a psychological point of view, the change to
the impersonal mode after the suicide attempt simply reflects the
complete dissociation of personality and lack of relatedness that led
to the suicide attempt in the first place.

The subject of suicide was a favorite theme among certain Paris-
ian émigré poets, and many prose works besides The Eye (to take
but one example, the excellent short story The Yid by the poet

Anatoly Shteiger) are concerned with this too frequent fact of émigré life. There are, of course, questions as to the degree that different cultures report suicides and especially the openness or lack thereof with which self-caused death is alluded to in newspaper obituaries, but the general assumption of a high suicide rate among Russian émigrés seems to be logically warranted on the basis of the enormous wrench in the lives of many émigrés, involving not only change of station in life and great material want but also separation from close members of one's family and lack of empathy with one's foster country.

Sergei Yablonovsky, a critic who wrote at some length about *The Eye*, reported that he had himself on two occasions heard exclamations of surprise expressed impersonally by people he knew who had tried unsuccessfully to shoot themselves. ("How can this be? I shot myself, and yet I still see, hear, and feel things?") And this alone, one realizes, disproves the generally accepted notion that suicide, like death in general, is a severely limited and terminal theme for a writer, one which may be vividly and convincingly presented (Luzhin hurling himself from a window at the end of *The Defense*) but not extended and examined from within. I cannot think of any more convincing description of the psychology of suicide than *The Eye*. It has been said that, because Smurov is such a "hospital type," *The Eye* is the Nabokov work which most clearly shows the influence of Dostoevsky. (In 1930 Nabokov had not yet expressed his opinion in print, apart from two short poems, on Dostoevsky, and because the two writers treat many similar psychological problems critics would quite often make the careless assumption that Sirin was under the influence of Dostoevsky.) In general terms there are certain broad similarities between Smurov and the underground man or Kirillov from *The Possessed*, but the philosophic uses to which Dostoevsky subjects his disturbed characters, and the meticulous and ingenious manner in which Nabokov presents his, make the similarity far more apparent than real. One might as well speak of Herman Melville as being a "disciple" of the author of *Two Years Before the Mast*.

Considering its brief length, one cannot help but note that *The Eye* contains more major characters—ten—than do some two or three of Nabokov's full length novels taken together. Like his first novel, *Mashenka*, *The Eye* is a group portrait of émigré life, but the characters in this novella are all reasonably well settled in terms of jobs and close personal ties. It is the narrator Smurov who stands apart from all of them. In his English Foreword to *The Eye* Nabokov writes: "The people in the book are the favorite characters of my literary youth," and he then proceeds to supply excellent thumbnail sketches of them with some further biographical speculation:

The expatriates in the Berlin of the book range from paupers to successful businessmen. Examples of the latter are Kashmarin, Matilda's cauchemaresque husband (who evidently escaped from Russia by the southern route, via Constantinople) and the father of Evgenia and Vania, an elderly gentleman (who judiciously directs the London branch of a German firm, and keeps a dancing girl). Kashmarin is probably what the English call "middleclass," but the two young ladies at 5, Peacock Street obviously belong to the Russian nobility, titled or untitled, which does not prevent them from having Philistine reading tastes. Evgenia's fat-faced husband, whose name [Khrushchov] sounds rather comic today, works in a Berlin bank. Colonel Mukhin, a nasty prig, fought in 1919 under Denikin, and in 1920 under Wrangel, speaks four languages, affects a cool, worldly air, and will probably do very well in the soft job into which his future father-in-law is steering him. Good Roman Bogdanovich is a Balt imbued with German, rather than Russian, culture. The eccentric Jew Weinstock, the pacifist woman doctor Marianna Nikolaevna, and the classless narrator himself are representatives of the many-faceted Russian intelligentsia.

All of these characters, except Matilda, who is Smurov's mistress while he is still speaking in the first person, are seen only insofar as they reflect a Smurov who, he says when he switches back to the first person at the conclusion, does not really exist: "There exist but the thousands of mirrors that reflect me." Smurov is seen in a half dozen quite contradictory ways, but the other characters who are merely Smurov's mirrors have only two images—the first incorrect one (Smurov is a very poor judge of mirrors) and the later images which come to us through the characters' own actions. The only character who, Smurov allows, is not a mirror is Vanya, whom he loves. But she is engaged to Mukhin, a character whom Smurov had scarcely taken note of. When Smurov blurts out to Vanya that she does not really know him and that he is always hidden behind a mask, she retorts: "Come, come . . . I know you very well indeed, and I see everything, and understand everything. You are a good, intelligent person." She is simply putting him off as nicely as she can. Smurov sets out to find "the real Smurov," and the reader's task is the same. It is, indeed, perhaps more difficult, but it may well be that the secondary mirror characters do indeed have a unified and reasonably accurate vision of Smurov that he, and consequently we the readers, are incapable of seeing. Or it may be that Smurov, the "secret artist," deliberately withholds the "true" image.

The most outstanding mirror image of himself—Smurov literally steals it—is a portion of a diary kept by Roman Bogdanovich "for posterity" and sent to a friend in Tallin. Smurov grabs the envelope saying he will mail it for him, but he keeps the letter to read himself. Previously he had searched Vanya's room while the family was out at the theater—he lives in the same apartment building as Vanya and her sister—to see if he could find any references to himself in letters. This intrusion into Vanya's room is quite different from the search Ganin made in Alferov's room in *Mashenka*—while reading the portion of Roman Bogdanovich's diary he has stolen, Smurov finds a description of himself as a kleptomaniac. And Roman Bogdanovich has an equally remarkable theory about Smurov's sexual nature:

Smurov belongs to the curious class of people I once called "sexual lefties." Smurov's entire appearance, his frailness, his decadence, his mincing gestures, his fondness for Eau de Cologne, and, in particular, those furtive, passionate glances that he constantly directs toward your humble servant —all this has long since confirmed this conjecture of mine. It is remarkable that these sexually unfortunate individuals, while yearning physically for some handsome specimen of mature virility, often choose for the object of their (perfectly platonic) admiration—a woman—a woman they know well, slightly, or not at all. And so Smurov, notwithstanding his perversion, has chosen Varvara as his ideal. This comely but rather stupid lass is engaged to a certain M. M. Mukhin, one of the youngest colonels in the White Army, so Smurov has full assurance that he will not be compelled to perform that which he is neither capable nor desirous of performing with any lady, even if she were Cleopatra herself.

Smurov is greatly concerned that he not be thought to be a thief, but he makes no comment at all on the remarks about his being a homosexual. In addition to plump Matilda, Smurov has had another mistress exactly like her in Russia, and he visits the Khrushchov's maid in her room. Weinstock, the owner of the bookstore where Smurov works, calls him a Don Juan and Casanova, but that may just be a reflection of Smurov's boasting and fabrication. He has been caught in a purposeless lie once by Mukhin. But if Smurov does indeed arrange, move, and control the other characters (and this is the one statement he makes that can be accepted without reservation), the corollary of that must be that Smurov himself, controlling the mirrors, also effectively controls the confusing picture of himself that emerges from them, and the most unflattering views then belong to him fully as much as do the naively flattering ones. We have, in other words, success by means of failure.

When psychological problems are seen as problems of composition, The Eye becomes a novel about the artistic process. The Smurov who speaks to us in the first person is the "easy" portrayal of the narrator-hero, and the many Smurovs which emerge when the narrative becomes impersonal are aspects of the whole that the artist must seek to fuse together. A casual remark by Evgenia Khrushchov towards the end of the narrative tells us that Smurov is a poet, or at least says that he is. Certain minute details seem to suggest compositional clues: when Smurov prowls through the Khrushchov's living quarters he sees a copy of a French novel, Ariane, Jeune Fille Russe, and we recall that at the very beginning of the novella Matilda had tried to persuade Smurov to read that work. It was on the pretext of giving him that book, in fact, that she first lured him into her apartment, while her husband was away, and seduced him. Smurov is beyond any doubt seen as a neurotic, but it is open to debate whether The Eye is a study of a writer who cannot separate himself from his creativity and so fails as an artist, or whether it is a diabolically cunning illusion performed by a first-rate artist: again, success in the guise of failure. Smurov's closing speech is an eloquent and somewhat pathetic panegyric justifying the artist's choice of solipsism:

What does it matter that I am a bit cheap, a bit foul, and that no one appreciates all the remarkable things about me—my fantasy, my erudition, my literary gift. . . . I am happy that I can gaze at myself, for any man is absorbing—yes, really absorbing! The world, try as it may, cannot insult me. I am invulnerable. And what do I care if she marries another? Every other night I dream of her dresses and things on an endless clothesline of bliss, in a ceaseless wind of possession, and her husband shall never learn what I do to the silks and fleece of the dancing witch. . . . Oh, to shout it so that all of you believe me at last, you cruel, smug people.

Nabokov has explained that, all signs and opinions of other characters to the contrary, Smurov is not actually a homosexual, but without the author's word, of course, the reader is free, indeed bound, to make as many mistakes as Weinstock, the Khrushchovs, and the others. Perhaps we are following a false path when we

search for the "real" Smurov in *The Eye*. The point of the novella
may be precisely the multiplicity and disparity of impressions and
images each of which becomes a "little Smurov" with an artistic life
of its own.

In the period immediately preceding the writing of *The Eye*,
Nabokov wrote two excellent short stories—"A Christmas Story"
(1928) and "Lips to Lips" (1929)—which concern unsuccessful
writers. "A Christmas Story" is about an older Soviet writer named
Novgorodtsev whose collected works have even been published in
a six-volume set but who is all the same little read or spoken of. A
literary critic of his acquaintance has brought a young writer named
Anton Goly (Anton the Naked) to Novgorodtsev to read a short
story he has written. Novgorodtsev had written the critic a short
time before to say that, although the twenty-fifth anniversary of his
writing career is approaching, he would prefer no celebration be
arranged "in view of the fact that my years of intensive work in
behalf of the Soviet Union still continue." The critic simply accedes
to his preference, and Novgorodtsev reflects that this Anton Goly
has probably been brought to him for his judgment in secret compensation for the celebration that he didn't receive.

As Novgorodtsev listens to Goly reading his story, he suddenly
realizes that he is listening to a continuation of the novella he had
published with great hope in the previous year but which had gone
unnoticed by the critics. Rather than say anything himself, Novgorodtsev waits to hear the critic remark on this—but the critic
evidently has not read Novgorodtsev's novella, for he says nothing. Novgorodtsev then begins to make gentle criticisms of the
story without saying anything about his own work: "And suddenly
Novgorodtsev became so sad—not offended, but simply sad—that
he stopped short and began to wipe off the lenses of his glasses
with his handkerchief, and he had very kind eyes." The critic and
Anton Goly get up to leave, and as they are going they talk briefly
about the sort of Christmas tale that used to be written when the
winter was as deep and beautiful as it is then. The critic talks about
a completely new sort of Christmas tale that could be written
"depicting the struggle of two worlds on the snow." After they have
gone, Novgorodtsev thinks bitterly that the critic undoubtedly considers that he has no more originality left in him.

Novgorodtsev sits down to write a Christmas tale and settles
on precisely the theme of "a struggle of two worlds" so that "later
he himself will remember it in print: I dropped in on him once

and in passing I happened to say, 'It would be a good idea, Dmitri Dmitrievich, if you were to depict the struggle of the old and the new against the background, so to say, of the Christmastime snow. That would complete the line you began so remarkably in *The Border*—remember the dream of Tumanov?' Well, that was the line. . . . And during that night there was born the work which. . . ."

After some hesitation—he can't imagine writing about the scrawny Soviet New Year's trees—the theme comes to him, at first in the form of a tale of émigrés weeping around their Christmas tree, but he can't see the émigrés whom he personally knew in Russia doing this. Then suddenly he enthusiastically begins to describe a beautiful and sumptuous tree in a store window in some European city with well-dressed and well-fed people passing by and a starving worker, the "victim of a lock-out," staring at it harshly and seriously. Novgorodtsev's theme is banal, not really his own, and, in spite of the starving worker, one knows (but Nabokov does not say) that he can never even print such a fantasy description of European affluence.

"Lips to Lips" is an even sadder tale, about an émigré widower named Ilya Borisovich who writes an unspeakably wretched novel (entitled *Lips to Lips*) and is maneuvered into underwriting the continuance of an almanac called *Arion* which promises to print it. Ilya Borisovich, whose previous literary production consists of two prose poems, a necrologue (pre-revolutionary and in a newspaper) and an étude called *Travelers by Land and Sea* (in a modest little émigré newspaper in Chicago). Ilya Borisovich's naiveté about literature is both hilarious and touching. *Travelers by Land and Sea* is the title of a novel by Mikhail Kuzmin, and the pseudonym he chooses for *Lips to Lips* is I. Annensky, the name of one of the foremost pre-revolutionary poets. When it is suggested that he use Ilya Annensky instead, he writes the editor (who has been recommended to him as "the Russian Joyce"): "You're completely right. I simply didn't know that there is a litterateur writing under this name." Annensky has been dead for twenty years. Ilya Borisovich knows Pushkin mainly by Chaikovsky's operas, and can recite by heart only two poems. He is familiar with some of the more popular decadent writers, and, though he feels they are corrupting youth, his own novel is strangely like their writing in all but its moral purity: "Take me, my chastity, my suffering . . . I am yours. Your loneliness is my loneliness, and no matter how long or short a time you love me I am ready for all, for around us Spring calls to humaneness and good, for the earth and the heavens glitter with divine beauty, for I love you . . ."

When *Arion* does appear, it first seems that they have not even printed *Lips to Lips*, but it turns out that they have printed about three pages under the title *Prologue to a Novel* and with the pseudonym A. Ilin. The editor of *Arion* visits Berlin, and he is to meet with Ilya Borisovich, but quite by chance the old man overhears a conversation in a theater lobby. A lady is telling a young man: "Pardon me, but I think that if you print him only because he gives you money. . . ." They are talking about him. His illusions of authorship shattered, he runs out of the theater when the editor is introduced to him. The old man's exclamations, and the editor's lame attempt to explain himself as they both struggle with Ilya Borisovich's coat, constitute a masterly scene that contrasts sharply with the opening scene in the story—Ilya Borisovich trying to get his ecstatic hero and heroine out of a theater into the spring night and worrying about how to deal with the awkward necessity to stop at the coatcheck room without breaking the romantic spell. The last paragraph is not at all funny, and it casts its shadow back on the story: "He thought about how old and alone he was, how few joys he had, and how old people must pay for their joys . . . He knew that it was necessary to forgive everything or else there would be no continuation."

It is not possible within the confines of an article to demonstrate adequately the many arguments supporting Khodasevich's casual observation that Nabokov really writes only about the artist and art. However it is not really true that Nabokov does this only by way of allegory. As a mature writer Nabokov would make a writer the protagonist of a major novel, *The Gift*, and, as we have seen, he touched directly upon the subject even as a young writer. The infrequency with which this is done in his writing may be related to the fact that the subject of art and the subject of the artist tend to work at cross purposes. *The Eye* is a superb demonstration of the tactical problems of art, but we have only a glimpse of Smurov as artist. When the artist is more important than his art, as in the two short stories I have discussed, that is tantamount to saying that he is a false or failed artist. Thus the artist can be best examined *as a person* by putting aside his occupation: in art the shortest distance between two points is sometimes not a straight line.

DESPAIR
AND THE LUST FOR
IMMORTALITY

Claire Rosenfield

Over the past eleven years readers of little magazines, whether in English or in Russian, or of scholarly books have become aware of Vladimir Nabokov's attitude toward translations. In the *Partisan Review* of 1955, while discussing his experience translating Pushkin's *Eugene Onegin*, he states that "The term 'literal translation' is tautological since anything but that is not truly a translation but an imitation, an adaptation or a parody."[1] The introduction of the completed work defines translation: the "attempts to render a poem in another language fall in three categories," the third of which is "Literal: rendering, as closely as the associative and syntactical capacities of another language allow, the exact contextual meaning of the original. Only this is true translation."[2] And, although Nabokov is speaking here of the translation of verse from one language into another, he would probably feel that prose, of which he is a master, deserves no less.

In translating his own novel *Otchayanie* into English, he does not apply the same rules: the author reserves the privilege—and rightly so—to correct, to amplify, to change extensively, as the Foreword of the recently published *Despair* makes clear. "For the present edition I have done more than revamp my thirty-year-old translation: I have revised *Otchayanie* itself."[3] Since the present English edition

---

[1] Vladimir Nabokov, "Problems of Translation: Onegin in English," *Partisan Review*, XXII (1955), 504.

[2] Vladimir Nabokov, "Foreword," *Eugene Onegin*, by Alexander Pushkin, trans. V. Nabokov (New York, 1964), I, viii.

[3] Vladimir Nabokov, "Foreword," *Despair* (New York, 1965–66), p. 8.

has itself a younger self, critics should be discouraged in seeing this present edition as simply an immature work, a paler *Pale Fire*, an *Ur-Faust*. What any critic or student fascinated by the mysteries of creativity would seize upon, however, is Nabokov's use of the Double at all stages of his career.

It is not enough to perceive that this is a novel about Doubles, a novel about a man who, believing that a free-spirited tramp resembles him exactly, allows that assumption about the existence of a "mirror image" to dictate the murder of his second self, ostensibly for profit. Events prove, however, that Hermann, the narrator, alone sees the similarity between himself and the derelict, Felix. What made Nabokov choose the theme of the Double as most congenial to the truths he wanted to dramatize is a far more interesting question. What, indeed, has dictated that choice in other Nabokovian novels? Most obviously Nabokov is the intellectual heir to a tradition in which the idea of the Double has been dramatized by one of its most troubled geniuses. Nor is Nabokov at all hesitant about exploiting our recognition of Dostoevsky's use of the motif. Hermann irreverently refers to "old Dusty's great book, *Crime and Slime*. Sorry: Schuld and Sühne (German edition),"[4] considers naming his own story "The Double." "But Russian literature possessed one already." At another point, the narrator, as a self-conscious author, makes an analogy: ". . . in spite of a grotesque resemblance to Rascalnikov"; but, with the assumed gesture of literary judgment, he follows it with "No, that's wrong. Canceled."

In analyzing Nabokov's authorial return to this conventional device, we might further have recourse to one of his dicta concerning the necessary tools of the translator: such a man must have a knowledge of the cultural context—both literary and social—of his subject. In another essay dealing with the problems of translating Pushkin, he insists that "The English translator of *Eugene Onegin* would seem to need not only a Russian's knowledge of Russian but also Pushkin's knowledge of French."[5] The original novel, *Otchayanie*, was written in a Germany where Thomas Mann was also working variations on the same theme. "Death in Venice," "The Blood of

---

[4] Vladimir Nabokov, *Despair* (New York, 1965–66), p. 187. All subsequent quotations of more than ten words are cited within the text immediately following the quotations.

[5] Vladimir Nabokov, "The Servile Path," *On Translation*, ed. by Rueben A. Brower (Cambridge, 1959), p. 97.

the Walsungs," *The Magic Mountain*—these, and more, were finally
to culminate in *Doctor Faustus*, Mann's most outrageous and most
traditional Double novel. So, perhaps, in spite of Nabokov's claim
in the Foreword of *Despair* that he knows "no German,"[6] one not
only needs to understand Nabokov's knowledge of the Russian cultural scene but also his knowledge of the German one. But, again,
the simultaneous existence of two creators in the same country, each
compelled to use the same theme, proves nothing. The uniqueness
of the result is what is important. Were it mainly a matter of chance
influence, Nabokov would never have returned obsessively to a pattern that was already a literary staple before Mann was born. Something about the possibilities inherent in the theme must have
exercised a fascination far in excess of the theme itself.

At least part of the truth may be gleaned from Otto Rank's
theoretical writings about the evolution of the Double.[7] Rank
assumes that man's persistent fear of oblivion caused the primitive,
"our remote ancestor," to create a body-soul which he might locate
in his shadow, in his reflection in a mirror, or in a lake, and which
survived the disintegration consequent upon the ever-present fact
of death. Dreams of the dead or the absent, the disappearance and
reappearance at dawn of one's shadow, gave assurance that somewhere a spiritual self existed and preserved that precious individuality, that identity, that totality that the ego of each man covets. But
modern, urban, sophisticated man makes the Double a symbol of
death rather than of eternal life. The Double may be a hallucination
defining a paranoid state, a literary representation of madness. While
Hermann, the narrator of *Despair*, does not create a second self who
has no bodily existence, an autoscopic image without any object, he
projects his own face upon the body of another man. Numerous,
indeed, are the hints of his extremely fragile grasp of reality long
before the denouement. He has headaches; he tells the reader of the

---

[6] Since Nabokov lived in Germany while writing *Despair* and since his
linguistic ability appears on every page, I am assuming that he simply means
that he does not have a command of German comparable to that of English
and French, that he has never had a love affair with the German language which
has produced a work of art. In other words, "no German" when applied to him
means the same as "small Latin" when applied to Shakespeare.

[7] For Rank's writings on the Double see *Psychology and the Soul*, trans.
by William D. Turner (New York, 1961) and *Beyond Psychology* (New York,
1958). The novelist's use of the Double motifs are analyzed in articles by Lawrence Kohlberg and me in *Daedalus* (Spring, 1963), pp. 326–362.

"clever Lett. . . . [who] said to me once that the clouds of brooding which occasionally and without any reason came over me were a sure sign of my ending in a madhouse." (p. 18) Immediately before meeting his Double in the historical time sequence but immediately after this event in narrative time, Hermann tells us that the pleasures of his intimate life with his wife are increased by a "certain aberration which, I understand, is not as uncommon as I thought at first among high-strung men in their middle thirties." (p. 37) By a curious dissociation he imagines himself during intercourse both the bed partner of his wife and the naked spectator of the sexual performance; and the presence of a mirror increases the images and, hence, the pleasure. But this "aberration" ceases when he chances upon Felix in Prague.

That he becomes a victim of this particular kind of delusion, that he assigns his own image to another man's living body, is also explainable in terms of the kind of man he is. He is, first of all, so vain about himself and the love his wife bears him that he cannot conceive of the possibility of her being unfaithful. Yet, as he admits, "I loved her because she loved me. To her I was the ideal man: brains, pluck. And there was none dressed better." (p. 35) What he loves is the image of himself he imagines is reflected in her face. His love is self-love. When he first encounters Felix and establishes the resemblance between them, he feels that "was not I, who knew and liked my own face in a better position than others to notice my double?" (p. 25)

But his enormous vanity is not sufficient reason for his madness to take the particular form it does. Part of his unconscious choice of his victim depends upon the kind of man Felix is, and Felix, is, after all, a dishevelled, dirty, unshaven, tasteless tramp, a pariah in the bourgeois world of the narrator, the antithesis of Hermann in social values as well as in dress. As a businessman, albeit an unsuccessful one, Hermann admits that he belongs to the "cream of the smug middle class." His nicety makes him take particular note of Felix's hands. "Blue-black, squat fingernails." A manufacturer of chocolate, he comes to Prague originally to convince a foreign firm "on the verge of bankruptcy to convert their manufacturing process to that of ours." (p. 15) Because his correspondent is away, he goes for a stroll to waste time and, by chance, happens upon a "second self." Felix, "the happy one," is that side of human nature that society has forced the businessman to submerge. He is uninhibited and unrestrained in his behavior, wandering unfettered by communal

ties, always wasting time. He is Bohemian and vaguely artistic in his
tastes, a lover of gardens, birds, and music. The "few faded violets"
he wears in his buttonhole indicate his closeness to the natural world.
Though he does not "believe in love," he longs for

"a friend who'd always be ready to share his slice of bread with me and
who'd bequeath to me a piece of land, a cottage. . . . I'd work for him as
a gardener, and then afterwards his garden would become mine, and I'd
always remember my dead comrade with grateful tears. We'd fiddle
together, or, say, he'd play the flute and I the mandolin." (p. 85)

Nor is he fond of confinement like jails that "sapped one's youth;
and . . . there was nothing like freedom and the singing of birds."
(p. 105) But unfortunately the anarchic, unrepressed self, because
it is beyond the conventions of social intercourse and responsibility,
is a bad self. Felix, in the pleasure he evinces at the possibility of
helping the narrator in an underhand action, in the "silver pencil"
he "forgets" to return, is by the standards of Berlin and Prague also
a criminal self.

That Hermann is saddled with a disintegrating business is
probably not the fault of his economic environment but of his own
temperamental inability to submit to the commercial life. The blue
Icarus he drives, a symbol of his status as a businessman, represents
the mechanization of his artist's soul. He is a "second-rate businessman with ideas." Everything he reveals about his past and present
shows the desire to become an artist. "As a child I composed verse
and elaborate stories,"—stories that become the lies of his adult
life. "There was in me, I felt, a poet, an author." He constantly
quotes from Pushkin or corrects the misquotations of others. After
the crime is committed, after he exchanges clothes with Felix, kills
him, and escapes—only to discover that no one else perceives the
physical similarity—after all these events, he decides to put his story
into the form of a novel. On the first page of Nabokov's book, beginning as it does at the end of the dramatic action, the narrator asserts
his abilities as an artist. "If I were not perfectly sure of my power
to write and of my marvelous ability to express ideas with the utmost
grace and vividness. . . ." (p. 13)

But art is as early as that same first page equated with the
illicit: "the breaker of the law . . . with a poet or a stage performer."
Part of the fascination his wife exercises over his person he attributes to her incompetence, her inability to remember anything, and
to the inordinate opportunity she gives him for free play of the

imagination. ". . . I took advantage of her confidence and during
the ten years we lived together told her such a heap of lies about
myself, my past, my adventures, that it would have been beyond
my powers to hold it all in my head, always ready for reference."
(p. 36) He is an "inspired" liar; he "lied as a nightingale sings,
ecstatically, self-obliviously." The perpetuation of his crime is part
of his deep-buried longing to be an artist, since it requires the
creation of plots as intricate as those of the writers of detective
stories whom he apostrophizes: "Conan Doyle, Dostoevsky, Leblanc,
Wallace—what are all the great novelists who wrote of nimble
criminals, what are all the great criminals who never read the nimble
novelists—what are they in comparison with me? Blundering fools!"
(p. 132) The nature of a crime is like that of "every art. If the deed
is planned and performed correctly, then the force of creative art is
such, that were the criminal to give himself up on the very next
morning, none would believe him, the invention of art containing
far more intrinsical truth than life's reality." (p. 132) Like the great
work of art rejected by the "mob," "the genius of a perfect crime
is not admitted by the people and does not make them dream and
wonder; instead, they do their best to pick out something that can
be pecked at and pulled to bits, something to prod the author with,
so as to hurt him as much as possible." And what are police but
"critics," and he, the murderer of another man and the celebrator
of the deed in a work of art, but "a poet misunderstood"?

Not simply the free self in Felix, not simply the criminal self,
but also the artist self, which Hermann equates with the criminal
and free, attracts the narrator. It is the "artistic perfection" of Felix's
sleeping face that he notices. The color of the few violets fading in
his buttonhole is the touch of natural beauty which in Hermann's
conventional sphere has to take the forms of civilization—a lilac
chocolate-wrapper, a lilac tie. He loves music and the singing of
birds, plays the fiddle, and is, according to his passport, dignified
to the profession of "musician."

Thus Felix, the dirty tramp, is chosen as a victim because he
represents all that Hermann can aspire to only in dreams; he is the
externalization of Hermann's buried instinctual life, a complementary self which Hermann admits that he "had been unconsciously
tracking." Once Hermann exchanges clothing with his victim and
kills him, once he "puts on Felix's external attributes," the repressed
emotions begin to assert their power completely. He speedily loses
his sense of identity, his Hermann-self. As he hides from the world

that recognizes only his criminality, he believes he becomes invisible
to himself merely by growing a beard: "I am disguised so perfectly,
as to be invisible to my own self." (p. 31) But this period of hiding
after the crime also coincides with his sudden hatred of mirrors,
manifestations of the resemblances that he earlier sought.

Now that is a word I loathe, the ghastly thing! I have had none of the
article ever since I stopped shaving. Anyway, the mere mention of it has
just given me a nasty shock, broken the flow of my story (please imagine
what should follow here—the history of mirrors; then, too, there are
crooked ones, monsters among mirrors: a neck bared, no matter how
slightly, draws out suddenly into a downward yawn of flesh, to meet which
there stretches up from below the belt another marchpane—pink nudity
and both merge into one; a crooked mirror strips its man or starts to squash
him, and lo! there is produced a man-bull, a man-toad, under pressure of
countless glass atmospheres; or else, one is pulled out like dough and then
torn in two. (p. 31)

He has, in fact, been torn in two—and the bourgeois self, the socially
functioning human being has been disposed of. Madness is the
psychic mark of that split; isolation, its social manifestation.

Although Hermann at once unconsciously seeks and is attracted
to Felix because, on the surface at least, the tramp personifies what
his middle-class preoccupations with sweetness and light scorn, yet
he does not want a complementary self: he wants an exact Double,
a "creature bodily identical" with himself, a mirror image which he
defines as a "soul." To Hermann, Felix's "trampness" is only a "sorry
disguise"; what counts is the resemblance that is "strikingly evident"
in "perfect repose." "Life only marred my Double." When he first
speaks to the newly awakened tramp, who, not being so surprised
to see Hermann as Hermann is to see him, gives the reader one of
the first hints of the truth, he tests the future victim. "Slowly I
raised my right arm, but his left did not rise, as I had almost expected
it to do. I closed my left eye, but both his eyes remained open. I
showed him my tongue." (p. 21) When the narrator returns to his
hotel, he confronts his own image in the mirror, but now he describes
the unreal reflection as if it were the real man—a Felix no longer
dirty or tarnished by life. "Pale-faced and solemn he drew near. He
was now well-shaven, his hair was smoothly brushed back. He wore
a dove-grey suit with a lilac tie. I took out my handkerchief; he took
out his handkerchief too. A truce, parleying." (p. 24) That his distorted vision does not see himself in the glass but a Felix made over

in his own image indicates his insane assumption about the living tramp he has made his Double: he has absorbed him into his being.

In Hoffman's "Story of a Lost Reflection" the hero who sells his reflection to the devil is, in the reality of this fantasy, selling his soul. So here, the narrator, by substituting Felix's name for his new reflection, assigns the tramp the role of soul-self. In his growing obsession with the man he considers his mirror image, he eventually extends the idea of the soul to the other's physical presence. At their first assignation he states that he "seldom . . . [has] occasion to take . . . [his] soul for an outing." (p. 95) As the two sit in the restaurant, the chocolate manufacturer contemplates the reaction of others to the sight of "the fortunate brother and the luckless brother." In the metaphor of kinship the longing of the self for communion with its soul is seen. Later, when he invents the story of a long-lost brother to engage Lydia in his plot ostensibly to get his insurance money, he entreats her to "believe" that he is really dead. "As things stand it won't be far from the truth, as my brother is a part of my soul." Again, Nabokov ironically employs the convention which uses the bird as a symbol of the soul. So Felix is a lover of birds. In assuming the name "Sparrow" to exploit his outlaw role, he adopts the qualities he assigns to that bird: he is the "beggar among birds."

Paradoxically, the narrator's longing for a bodily double, a "brother," is a modern perversion of the primitive's longing for immortality; it reveals the quality of his personal disintegration that he seeks his soul by destroying another's body. Once the deed is done, the claims of the "reflected image" make him aware that one cannot assure one's desire for immortality by usurping another's. Though he tries to imagine Felix's past, he discovers that the soul he "had inherited," he "had studied very cursorily, so that all . . . he knew of it were the bare outlines of his personality, two or three chance traits." (p. 186) "Having never been a tramp myself, I failed —and still fail—to rerun his life on my private screen." (p. 54) His soul has become a "vacant" one. He fears mirrors because, in being invisible to himself, he knows that he has lost his own soul.

But Hermann's impulse for immortality, an impulse possessed by all men, is intensified by the artistic longings within him. So all artists, according to Rank, have stronger yearnings after eternal life than ordinary men.[8] Hermann's union with his wife has produced

---

[8] Otto Rank, Art and Artist, trans. Charles Francis Atkinson, intro. Ludwig Lewisohn (New York, 1932).

no child, no extension of the self in a procreative Double. Rather, his Double is, unconsciously, his first creation—although Hermann, believing in the reality of Felix's resemblance, emphasizes the artistry of his crime. As he roams the countryside vaguely seeking something, he feels "secret inspiration." Nabokov hints at the fact that Felix's presence has for Hermann the unreality of the artifact by assigning May 9 as the day Hermann discovers what his interior being has been seeking—a second self; for, given the necessary differences between the Julian calendar (used by nineteenth-century Russians and not replaced until the Bolshevik revolution) and the Gregorian calendar of Western Europe, May 9 is the day Pushkin began writing *Eugene Onegin*. (And Hermann's love of Pushkin appears in his occasional quotations.) Only in retrospect can the reader, if he has been seduced by Hermann's cracked vision, understand why the waiter at the restaurant at Tarnitz does not note the resemblance between them as had been anticipated, why the maid can dismiss a stranger assumed to be Felix without marking the uncanny likeness, why Felix's passport picture does not resemble the narrator.

The imagery of their first planned meeting suggests that the Felix the narrator describes is really a creation of the narrator; it is the latter who has the power to complete or to leave half-finished; in his "genius" he is like a god—but a god gone mad.

I started working from his feet upward, as one sees on the screen when the cameraman is trying to be tantalizing. First came big, dusty shoes, thick socks sloppy about the ankles, then shiny blue trousers (the corduroy ones having presumably rotted) and a hand holding a crust of dry bread. Then a blue coat over a dark-grey sweater. Still higher the soft collar that I knew (though now comparatively clean). There I stopped. Should I leave him headless or go on building him? (pp. 83–84)

When he completes the reel, he momentarily sees the truth—that Felix is "as like . . . [him] as any man"—but the truth he regards as a "delusion, a hallucination." When he anticipates this meeting, he is convinced that were he not to appear, "Felix would defy the movement of time; he would still be loitering about the bronze duke, or resting on a neighboring bench, drawing with his stick from left to right and from right to left, the earthen rainbows drawn by every man with a stick and time to spare (our eternal subjection to the circle in which we are all imprisoned!)" (p. 73) As an artifact, Felix lives within the timelessness of the narrator's unconscious, but the circle which the madman's mind envisages is not the traditional symbol of eternity. Rather, it designates their bondage within time. Ironically, Hermann believes that the permanence he seeks in his second self can only be achieved in death. For Hermann, as for Gustave von Aschenbach, artistic perfection is tainted with the anarchy of death as well as the anarchy of crime. So the modern disintegrating personality sees in his Double not the promise of immortality but the imminence of death. Sleeping, the tramp presents "the flawlessly pure image of my corpse."

. . . we had identical features, and . . . , in a state of perfect repose, this resemblance was strikingly evident, and what is death, if not a face at peace—its artistic perfection? Life only marred my double; thus a breeze dims the bliss of Narcissus: thus, in the painter's absence, there comes his pupil and by the superfluous flush of unbidden tints disfigures the portrait painted by the master. (p. 25)

The moment of destruction is followed by his astonished recognition of the mystery of creativity; it can never "err."

Like an author reading his work over a thousand times, probing and testing every syllable, and finally unable to say of this brindle of words whether it is good or not, so it happened with me, so it happened—But there is the maker's secret certainly, which never can err. At that moment when all the required features were fixed and frozen, our likeness was such that really I could not say who had been killed, I or he. And while I looked, it grew dark in the vibrating wood, and with that face before me slowly dissolving, vibrating fainter and fainter, it seemed as if I were looking at my image in a stagnant pool. (pp. 181–182)

So the "frozen" face of the dead man appears to be the living face mirrored in a "stagnant pool." So the "maker's secret," his godlike knowledge, is equally changeless. But his art is the art of death rather than "a liberating process of life";[9] it is defined by such words as "stagnant" and "frozen."

Once the deed of murder is discovered, Hermann is shocked that the newspapers do not note the likeness between the two at all; that is, he assigns to a human face the permanence of the artifact because in his madness Felix is an artifact. The latter is created by his "genius" and so can only change if he changes him. "Now, one single night could not very well have decomposed him; on the con-

---

9 *Ibid.*, p. 398.

trary his countenace ought to have acquired a marble quality, making our likeness still more sharply chiseled. . . ." (p. 196) When he discovers that the world, as the world often does, denies him the immortality he wishes, he turns to a more conventional art form, a book, to explain his "masterpiece." "But enough, enough. All that disgusting mess is due to the inertia, pigheadedness, prejudice of humans, failing to recognize me in the corpse of my flawless double. . . . And so, in order to obtain recognition, to justify and save the offspring of my brain, to explain to the world all the depth of my masterpiece, did I devise the writing of the present tale." (p. 205) Not only is he the "maker" but he is also the "father"—the "brain child" being a parody of the biological Double, man's attempt at procreative immortality.[10]

But our truth about Felix is not Hermann's truth—though ours may be revealed in the same figures that Hermann's madness takes. Hermann's selective vision limits his perception, but the details he seizes upon to justify himself enable the reader to pierce the narrator's obtuseness. "Leftness" is not merely a complement to Hermann's "rightness," not merely a partner of Hermann's soul, not merely a sign of a free and/or criminal self; for us, it is a statement about his humanity. If his handwriting is awkward because "He wrote with his left hand," it is because he is like all mortals, imperfect. As a creature at once sinister and gauche, he is a part of nature, not an art object. While Hermann's fastidiousness notes that the violets Felix wears are faded, the former sees this imperfection as correctable in the eternity of art, in the ideal dead Felix, in the perpetuation of an artistic crime which is the extension of his soul. To Felix, they merely symbolize his love of the natural world, of gardens, birds, music, his desire for a plot of land. Felix sees friendship as a communal experience based on mutual need rather than as a corrupted passion for immortality that can end only in death. Hermann's choice of ground on which to kill Felix perverts the tramp's simple love of things wild. It is the isolated ground by the reflecting lake "owned—if one payment constitutes ownership" by Lydia's cousin and lover, Ardalion. The garden that Felix covets and maintains by the devotion of friendship becomes the disorder of the wooded, ownerless, pathless land which symbolizes the anarchy of the interior world.

The novel, Hermann's second attempt at eternalizing the self, is structured by the logic of insanity. In its temporal dislocation, its

----

10 *Ibid.*

playing of roles and direct address to the reader, it manages to convey a distorted image in the glass of the mind. He thinks that the world is only concerned with surfaces: when the waiter does not detect the resemblance between him and his "luckless brother," he attributes this failure to the presence of a new moustache. He thinks his wife Lydia believes his lies. Assuming that he kills Felix for financial reasons, the authorities cannot guess why he would dress a man in his clothing before shooting him. The form of the crime puzzles them because they do not understand its context. He resents the fact that the newspapers publish a passport picture of him that does not resemble him at all:

Another point that maddened me was that the papers printed my passport photo (in which I indeed look like a criminal, and not like myself at all, so maliciously did they touch it up) instead of some other one, that one, say, where I dip into a book—an expensive affair in tender milk-chocolate shades; and the same photographer took me in another pose, finger at the temple, grave eyes looking up at you from under bent brows; that is the way German novelists like to be taken. (p. 204)

He, unlike the crass world, sees the inner self, the artistic soul, the Felix within.

Moreover, the world that sees only surfaces is filled with poor artists and successful businessmen, with critics who do not recognize the maker's genius. Ardalion, who believes that the Sistine Chapel is in Dresden, who misquotes the poet Nekrasov, who does not like Dostoevsky, who sees the narrator's crime in the conventional mold —as an attempt to gain the money from his life insurance policies— exposes his inferiority in his belief that "every face is unique," that the artist perceives "primarily the *difference* between things." Ardalion begins a picture of Hermann, moves from the "honest slog of charcoal" to the "petty knavishness of pastel"; but in the finished product, according to Hermann, "none could see the ghost of a likeness!" While working, he leaves the eyes for last, an indication that he cannot grasp the inner self reflected through them. The eyes, which popular and literary convention has long regarded as the "windows of the soul," are also the organ by which the advocates of the devil, the possessors of the "evil eye," ensnare the unwary soul of the innocent and send it to eternal perdition.[11] That the narrator

---

[11] One need only reread the intricate figures of metaphysical poetry to see how often poets use the image of the eyes as both a mirror of the external self and a revelation of the soul of lover and beloved.

senses a vague uneasiness about the "meddlesome portrait painter" and regards him as "the only person of whom I ought to be aware" may stem from Hermann's recognition of his "dangerous eyes." Once when he feigns "nearsightedness" to deceive a child into mailing his letter to Felix, he associates this defect with Ardalion. As a bad artist Ardalion can never give to his work the stamp of immortality. To Hermann, in whose mad artistry the sleeping Felix presents "the flawlessly pure image of my corpse," the portrait by Ardalion that seeks to repeat his features is like a "death mask." The businessman Orlovius moves from contemplating it to another called "The Isle of the Dead."

Hermann's obtuseness is measured by his own failure to plumb the depths of other men's lives, by his concentration on surface reality. Although Lydia and Ardalion patently seek mutual satisfaction in a love affair, she has so long been "gay, empty, and not very bright," "rather formless," to her husband that he cannot assign her a role apart from his conception of her. The Lydia who briefly contemplates suicide when Ardalion supposedly departs for Italy, who herself possesses a hidden life, is a nonexistent Lydia to Hermann. Attracted to that which he sees in Felix's exterior, he, like Humbert Humbert who does not consider Lolita's independent longings in his efforts to stop time, denies the existence of his victim's inner being. When describing Felix, he notes the difference between their eyes, but discounts this fact. Instead, he emphasizes the similarity of the lids to dispel the discomfiture instilled by Felix's waking self.

Our eyes alone were not quite identical but what likeness did exist between them was a mere luxury; for his were closed as he lay in the ground before me, and though I have never really seen, only felt, my eyelids when shut, I know that they differed in nothing from his eye-eaves—a good word, that! (p. 39)

Nabokov's subtle intention—to inform the reader that Hermann cannot look beyond the eyes to the soul of another, beyond the image on the surface of the glass—becomes clear if the reader has a sense of the pattern involved. By exchanging clothes with the tramp, he symbolically assumes only an external disguise, a role with no substance. Because Hermann and Felix harbor no communal or fraternal feelings, he has no understanding of the other's being; he has inherited a "vacant soul." Psychologically, he loses his identity because the demands of his long-repressed unconscious have asserted themselves with a vengeance. "Not I sought a refuge in a foreign land, not

I grew a beard but Felix, my slayer." (p. 186) To grow a beard, to change his appearance, makes it possible for him "to hide . . . not so much from others as from my own self." (p. 187) Madness, moreover, also convinces him that by growing a beard he has become "invisible" to himself in the mirror, he has lost his reflection in the glass and, therefore, his immortal soul.

Nabokov's handling of the natural world through which Hermann walks indicates that the confrontation with Felix is an immersion within the self. The "heavy and barren country," the two humps of bald ground, the "vast stretch of land that at first glance seemed to me most rural and alluring" (p. 16) and that proves deceptive—all these uninhabited regions over which he wanders are but echoes of his "vast inward wilderness." Felix appears asleep under a thornbush. When he looks back at his second self, the tramp's "dark lank figure" lies among the bushes and the narrator feels "limp, dizzy, dead-tired, as after some long and disgusting orgy." (p. 24) The area he chooses as the site of the crime is equally wild—Ardalion's plot of land, imperfectly possessed, surrounded by ownerless plots, beyond the margins of the road. Before the crime, he obsessively returns to it "without ever meeting a soul in the forest." Finally, in the "heart" of the forest he consummates the crime as night is falling:

. . . although in my soul of souls I had no qualms about the perfection of my work, believing that in the black and white wood there lay a dead man perfectly resembling me, yet as a novice of genius, still unfamiliar with the flavor of fame, but filled with the pride that escorts self-stringency, I longed, to the point of pain, for that masterpiece of mine (finished and signed on the ninth of March in a gloomy wood) to be appreciated by men, or in other words, for the deception—and every work of art is a deception—to act successfully; as to the royalties, so to speak, paid by the insurance firm, that was in my mind a matter of secondary importance. (p. 188)

The crime does not prove to be the deception that is characteristic of "every work of art." Nor does it inspire the applause anticipated by the artist seeking immortality. Rather, the rewards of success elude him. It resembles the "drab landscape" which seemed to promise Hermann "a spot of wild and wonderful beauty." Death has not perfected the masterpiece "(finished and signed on the ninth of March in a gloomy wood)." Now the narrator abandons the attempt to achieve immortality in the mind-created second self, who belongs, after all, to the "book of nature" and whose ultimate existence as a spiritual self is as fragile as Hermann's reason. Now the authenticity of the interior life finds its mirror in a written book, an attempt at self-perpetuation through art. In insisting upon the creativity of his confused memory, he is denying that the events he records are the product of his "rational part." It is the "irrational memory of his senses," the "devious memory" that earlier felt compelled to seek repetitions, to return both to Felix's self and to the landscapes which were associated with him. So immersed is he in the psychotic belief in the "prejudice" of the public that he never admits that his "idea was radically wrong."

Mistakes—pseudo mistakes—have been imposed upon me retrospectively by my critics when they jumped to the groundless conclusion that my very idea was radically wrong, thereupon picking out those trifling discrepancies, which I myself am aware of and which have no importance whatever in the sum of an artist's success. I maintain that in the planning and execution of the whole thing the limit of skill was attained; that its perfect finish was, in a sense, inevitable; that all came together, regardless of my will, by means of creative intention. And so, in order to obtain recognition, to justify and save the offspring of my brain, to explain to the world the depth of my masterpiece, did I devise the writing of the present tale. (pp. 204–205)

The initial experience of writing is like his climbing of the mountain whose "splendor proved to be a deception"; it is a "tough uphill business." When he begins to read what he has written, he finds himself

. . . wondering whether I was reading written lines or seeing visions. Even more: my transfigured memory inhaled, as it were, a double dose of oxygen; my room was still lighter, because the panes had been washed; my past still more graphic, because twice irradiated by art. (p. 212)

The earlier recollections, dreams, and déjà vu experiences that permeate Nabokov's narrative become part of the texture of Hermann's story. The people he knows actually become his creations. "I went on reading, and one by one they appeared: my rosy wife, Ardalion, Orlovius; and they were all alive, but in a certain sense I held their lives in my hands." (p. 212) He assumes the role of magician, weaving his "spell" around Felix. "And again I wove my spell about him, and had him in my toils but he slipped away, and I feigned to give up my scheme, and with an unexpected potency the story blazed forth anew, demanding of its creator a continuation and

an ending. And once again on a March afternoon I was dreamily
driving along the highway, and there, in the ditch, near the post, he
was waiting for me." (p. 212) Rereading becomes reliving in his fascination with resemblances and repetition, becomes a ritual re-enact-
ment designed at once to make the past eternally present and to
make the personal experience part of the collective immortality of the
society. The images of magic, spell, and dream unite to suggest both
the unreality of life and the deception of art, a fusion which Hermann's mad actions make throughout.

In writing his book, the mad Hermann puts a new construction
upon the idea of religious immortality. Rank shows that the artist-
genius "embodies the same process and achievement, on earth and
individually, which in religious form we saw beginning with the
image of God. The idea of genius is, in its mythical origin, a *representation* of the immortal soul, that part of the personality which
can beget (gignere) what is immortal, be it a child or work."[12] But
Hermann reverses the process: "God was invented by a scamp who
had genius; it somehow reeks too much of humanity, that idea, to
make its azure origin plausible. . . ." (p. 111) Paradoxically, Hermann, assuming a godlike role as a creator, cannot believe in God
because he did not create Him: "the fairy tale about him is not
really mine, it belongs to strangers, to all men; it is soaked through
by the evil-smelling effluvia of millions of other souls that have spun
about a little under the sun and then burst. . . ." (pp. 111–112)
The necessity to share his immortality with another is as repugnant
to him as the need to share in the communal life of others, to understand Felix's desire for mutual friendship or Lydia's, for mutual love.

Ironically, Hermann's view of a religious eternity partakes of
those same deceptions that he attributes to art. "There is the rub,
there is the horror; the more so as the acting will go on and on, endlessly; never, never, never, never, never will your soul in the other
world be quite sure that the sweet gentle spirits crowding about it
are not friends in disguise, and forever, and forever shall your soul
remain in doubt, expecting every moment some awful change, some
diabolical sneer to disfigure the dear face bending over you." (pp.
112–113) Like the small white mock dog of his dreams, whose flesh
is the "fat of a white worm," a dog he equates with "everlasting life,"
it is subject to endless change. Unlike art and the creations of the
interior life, however, it lacks permanence. Indeed, all his dreams—

---

[12] Rank, *Art and Artist*, p. 12.

including the obsessive dream of the empty room in which, one night, appears a chair and its shadow—reveal Hermann's fear of change and death at the same time that they indicate the promise of death to the reader.

Rank defines the artist as the productive individual who is able to resolve the conflict between his two personalities: "the one which wishes to eternalize itself in artistic creation, the other which wants to spend itself in ordinary life—in a word, the mortal man and the immortal soul of man."[13] The artist creates to satisfy his need for individual immortality; yet he must surrender his "child," his artistic creature to society who wants to absorb this extension of his personality in that of the community in order to assure the collective immortality of the group. For it realizes that collective immortality is "no longer religious, but social."[14]

But Hermann is unable to reconcile life and art. He must abandon the self that shares society's values in order to exploit the free, timeless, artistic self, achieved only at the sacrifice of life. Or else he attempts to turn the life of natural creatures into art by denying human existence apart from his conception of it, by creating a Double whom he then robs of an independent reality. He sees little difference between the deceptions of life, lies used to achieve one's ends, and those of art.

When the world denies the artistry of his crime, he seeks immortality in the creation of a book. Ultimately, the book designed to prove the validity of his assumptions, cannot share in the ideology of his society; he cannot admit that "he is still dependent on the collective forces that he seeks to escape by autonomous creation."[15] As obtuse narrator who becomes a self-conscious writer, he constantly addresses his audience with disdain, or seeks to manipulate their responses. "How I long to convince you!" he cries. Or he speaks of the mystic bond by which the reader himself becomes a creator by means of the author's skill—and hence, shares in his immortality. "An author's fondest dream is to turn the reader into a spectator; is this ever attained? The pale organisms of literary heroes feeding under the author's supervision swell gradually with the reader's life-blood; so that the genius of a writer consists in giving them the faculty to adapt themselves to that—not very appetizing—food and

---

[13] *Ibid.*, p. 402.
[14] *Ibid.*, p. 410.
[15] *Ibid.*, p. 12.

thrive on it, sometimes for centuries." (p. 26) But the imperceptive public who fails to understand his first attempt at individual immortality, cannot, he feels, respond to his second. Gradually we become aware that he has elected a particular Russian writer, "a well-known author of psychological novels," to receive his manuscript. In his paranoia he imagines that his "reader-writer" will steal his property —and hence, his soul. "Theft is the best compliment one can possibly pay a thing." (p. 91) In his last notation on April 1st, after his book suddenly degenerates in a diary, he wavers between two impulses: the story may end by his waking from an "evil dream," a "mock existence," on "a patch of ground near Prague" or he may continue the story by attempting another lie, by creating a new role in order to escape—that of an actor playing an "arch-criminal" upon the stage of life. And who, indeed, is the victim of the April Fool joke—he who cannot reconcile life and art and who believes to the end that they are one, or the reader who is left with the ambiguities the novel presents?

Earlier the narrator claims that he has made a "damned good fool" of someone. "Who is he? Gentle reader, look at yourself in the mirror, as you seem to like mirrors so much." (p. 34) Of course, our experience as readers has proved that Hermann is not to be trusted. Nor do we know whether he is here addressing us or that particular Russian author whom he selects as his "first reader." And who is that "writer-reader"? Perhaps Nabokov.

No one will deny that the artist is fascinated by the problems of his craft. Equally valid is the assumption that the artist is fascinated by the possibilities for immortality that the work of art offers. Is it any wonder, then, that Nabokov, whose creative impulse has manifested itself in novels at once skillful, authentic, and successful, should work new aesthetic variations upon a motif conventionally assigned both to the belief in a spiritual self and to its modern perversion. If Rank is right, if there is a "change in the meaning of art-forms from similar changes in the idea of the soul,"[16] then Nabokov's complex and ambiguous themes—the relationship of life and art, the immortality of art, personal derangement and its consequent perversion of the desire for a spiritual self, the juxtaposition of the loss of mind and loss of soul—can best be explored by means of the images and forms assigned to the motif of the Double.

This is not to say that Nabokov, who as successful artist does

---

[16] *Ibid.*

not confuse life and art as his creations do, always shares Hermann's aesthetic or, if he does, that he is mad. Nabokov's skill in presenting the narrator always enables us to perceive the truth even when that truth is filtered through a distorted vision, a cracked mirror. And surely Hermann's ironic panegyric on the glories of Bolshevism and the possibilities inherent in "such faith in the impending sameness of us all" (p. 30) is not Nabokov's. But the author of *Despair* does strive to make his reader a "reader-writer," in a sense, a Double. All the devices employed to convince us of Hermann's madness—the juxtaposition of hysteric utterances, the temporal dislocation, the confusion between past and present, between outer and inner, the imperceptive narrator—all these tools are the same to which the author resorts when he wishes his reader to struggle, to immerse himself in the experience of art, to become a creator. "The pale organisms of literary heroes feeding under the author's supervision swell gradually with the reader's lifeblood; so that the genius of a writer consists in giving them the faculty to adapt themselves to that—not very appetizing—food and thrive on it, sometimes for centuries." (p. 26) The ambiguity of the conclusion enables the reader to finish the novel to his own taste. If Nabokov, whose manipulation of his audience is notorious, intends to make his reader the object of an April Fool's joke (as Melville does in *The Confidence Man*), then the mirror into which the reader must look is the novel itself. Like Hermann, whose fancy "runs riot" in describing his "elastic hopes for the future" to Felix, Nabokov knows "how sweet it . . . [is] to be able to make one's listener thoroughly uncomfortable." (p. 95) Finally, by publishing his book, he enables the audience to make his personal attempt at immortality part of its collective immortality; he allows us, whose collective immortality must depend upon biological procreation, to "steal" his property.

THE MIRRORS OF
SEBASTIAN KNIGHT

Charles Nicol

Vladimir Nabokov insists that a novel is not to be read, but to be studied: "You can only re-read a novel. Or re-re-read a novel."[1] This attitude makes heavy demands, for Nabokov's work, even more than that of James Joyce, requires an involvement with the author's private calculus. The idiosyncratic literalness of his translation of *Eugene Onegin* suggests that Nabokov regards literature as a collection of cabbalistic texts, an attitude also voiced by V., the narrator of *The Real Life of Sebastian Knight*:

I sometimes feel when I turn the pages of Sebastian's masterpiece that the "absolute solution" is there, somewhere, concealed in some passage I have read too hastily, or that it is intertwined with other words whose familiar guise deceived me. I don't know any other book that gives one this special sensation, and perhaps this was the author's special intention.[2]

Perhaps there is no religion but art. For Nabokov, as for Joyce, a work has submerged structures probably not grasped at first glance, designed to intensify the reading experience. It is all the more remarkable that these gnostic novels are couched in the most lucid prose; Nabokov's labyrinthine buildings have glass-and-steel, curtain-wall exteriors.

The beautiful and brief *Sebastian Knight* is more congenially designed for rereading than any novel I know. Tightly constructed, it does not employ the diffuse attitude toward its subject that

---

[1] John G. Hayman, "A Conversation with Vladimir Nabokov—with Digressions," *The Twentieth Century*, CLXVI (Dec., 1959), 449.

[2] Norfolk, Conn., 1959, p. 180. Hereafter, references in parentheses will refer to this edition.

weakens *The Gift* and *Bend Sinister*, novels that immediately precede and follow it in the Nabokov canon. Nabokov has stated that, like Joyce, he writes his novels not from beginning to end but at all points at the same time, slowly filling in the gaps. While rereading, one begins to acquire the same method as reader that Nabokov employs as writer: seeing the entire novel simultaneously, as numerous structures, interlocking syllogisms which may proceed in reverse as well as forward order. For example, Sebastian's experience visiting what he wrongly believes to be the house his mother died in becomes significant only after V. has a similar experience—one that leads to the triumphant, visionary announcement at the end of the novel —while visiting the wrong sickroom.

Should one venture beyond a first reading, the gate of the labyrinth, there is always the possibility that one might not be able to find one's way out, as Nabokov suggests in an interview: "Reality is an infinite succession of levels, levels of perception, of false bottoms, and hence unquenchable, unattainable."[3] Mary McCarthy, in a remarkable review of *Pale Fire*, seems to agree: "Each plane or level in its shadow box proves to be a false bottom; there is an infinite perspective regression, for the book is a book of mirrors."[4] Yet Miss McCarthy may have fallen for one of Nabokov's gambits, for a novel may have other rules than "reality," and mirrors may cast mutual or collective reflections without providing an infinite regression. Nabokov often compares his novels to chess problems, and "deception in chess, as in art, is only part of the game";[5] in his autobiography, he compares chess-problem composition to "one of those incredible novels where the author, in a fit of lucid madness, has set himself certain unique rules that he observes, certain nightmare obstacles that he surmounts."[6] Even the most deceptive chess problems have solutions, and Nabokov's novels promise to resolve themselves once the "false bottoms" have been opened. "I like composing riddles and I like finding elegant solutions to those riddles that I have composed myself."[7]

To describe a Nabokov novel as "a book of mirrors" is to employ an accurate metaphor, one that has been frequently used by

---

[3] Peter Duval Smith and Vladimir Nabokov, "Vladimir Nabokov on His Life and Work," *The Listener*, LXVIII (Nov. 22, 1962), 856.

[4] "Vladimir Nabokov's 'Pale Fire,'" *Encounter*, XIX (Oct., 1962), 72.

[5] Smith and Nabokov, *The Listener*, LXVIII, p. 856.

[6] *Speak, Memory: An Autobiography Revisited* (New York, 1966), pp. 290–291.

[7] Smith and Nabokov, *The Listener*, LXVIII, p. 857.

Nabokov himself. For instance, Nabokov describes a novella as "my rain-sparkling crystograms" and continues: "The theme of *The Eye* is the pursuit of an investigation which leads the protagonist through a hell of mirrors and ends in the merging of twin images."[8] (In this context we should remember that not only *The Eye* is concerned with dual identities, but so too are *Sebastian Knight, Despair, Pale Fire,* and even *Lolita*.[9]) Nabokov also calls his novels mirrors in other contexts, however. He tells us, for instance, that the title of *Bend Sinister* is "an attempt to suggest an outline broken by refraction, a distortion in the mirror of being, a wrong turn taken by life, a sinistral and sinister world."[10] The "unique rules" that "lucidly mad" Nabokov follows in *Sebastian Knight* require the construction of multiple mirrors, and the "elegant solution" of the novel is that these metaphorical mirrors are the novels written by Sebastian Knight.

The problem that Nabokov sets up and solves is outlined in V.'s discussion of Sebastian's first novel:

The Prismatic Bezel can be thoroughly enjoyed once it is understood that the heroes of the book are what can be loosely called "methods of composition." It is as if a painter said: Look, here I'm going to show you not the painting of a landscape, but the painting of different ways of painting a certain landscape, and I trust their harmonious fusion will disclose the landscape as I intend you to see it. (p. 95)

This idea can be applied to *Sebastian Knight* itself: the personality of Sebastian will be disclosed by different ways of writing about that personality (that is, different methods of biography). The resulting book will be a fusion of these different methods, a merging of the images reflected by these variously angled mirrors. It is as though one prism had broken a diffused light into its rainbow spectrum and a second prism had turned it back into one pure, concentrated ray.

One method of composition, of biography, that will *not* be used is the environmental method of correlating the author with the fluctuations of the society around him. For one thing, Sebastian is anything but a representative of his generation, or of any other. For another, this is the method so disastrously used by Mr. Goodman in

---

[8] *The Eye* (New York, 1965), Foreword.

[9] See Page Stegner, *Escape into Aesthetics: The Art of Vladimir Nabokov* (New York, 1966), pp. 34–35; 104–105, for an initial study of the doubles (Humbert, Quilty) in *Lolita*, a question that still needs study. Remarkably, each novel listed above treats duality in an unprecedented way.

[10] *Bend Sinister* (New York, 1964), p. xii.

The Tragedy of Sebastian Knight, the rival biography. V.'s deflation
of the fictitious Mr. Goodman is as vicious and satisfying as Dwight
MacDonald's best pricking of similarly bloated reputations. We must
remember, however, that it is Mr. Goodman's book, not Mr. Goodman, that is the farcical villain of *Sebastian Knight.* Its type of biography, showing the artist as a child of his age, is rejected as a method
of composition, for it provides a mirror of distortion rather than of
perspective. Goodman's world, in which society influences the artist
rather than the reverse, is a scaled-down version of the tyranny of
banality and conformity pictured in *Bend Sinister,* and is to Nabokov
equally absurd.

In spite of the apparently receding structure of *Sebastian Knight*
(the more V. talks about his half-brother the less we seem to know
about him) the novel leads convincingly to its last-page resolution:
"Thus—I am Sebastian Knight." All roads lead to this denouement.
I intend to reach it through Sebastian's five books, for V.'s increasingly vague focus on Sebastian's life corresponds to his increasingly
sharp interest in Sebastian's work.

Sebastian Knight's first novel, *The Prismatic Bezel,* is a detective story, or rather the parody of a detective story. Any biographer
worth his ink must be part detective, and *Prismatic Bezel* is a novel
of literary detection. V. tells us that Sebastian's first three books
employ the "research" theme, and the first part of a biographer's
quest, that of providing himself with a general background on his
subject's life, corresponds to the elementary, subliterary nature of
the detective genre. *Prismatic Bezel* shifts from hotel to country
house in its parody of contemporary novels, much as V.'s quest for
the mysterious woman in Sebastian's life (the killer?) shifts from a
resort hotel to a house in the country. Perhaps this is why, while
visiting Madame Lecerf, V. has the odd impression that there is a
corpse in the garden. (p. 169) Sebastian's novel is a murder mystery; the same, of course, can be said for *Sebastian Knight:* "One
corpse, one investigator, some obscure photographs and burned letters, a mysterious woman or two, faint clues dropped here and there,
and so on."[11] But the parallel is even more exact, for *Prismatic Bezel*
closes with the revelation that old Nosebag is G. Abeson, that the
murder victim is still alive, and *Sebastian Knight* ends with V.'s
defiant declaration that, in a sense, he is Sebastian.

Success is Sebastian's second novel: "Here he seems to have

---

[11] Stegner, *Escape into Aesthetics,* p. 69.

passed from one plane to another rising a step higher, for, if his first novel is based on methods of literary composition,—the second one deals mainly with the methods of human fate." (p. 95) Sebastian explores various avenues of chance leading to the accidental first meeting of a man and woman who become lovers, devoting *Success* to "one of the most complicated researches that has ever been attempted by a writer." (p. 96) The novel starts by pursuing several avenues that end in blind alleys, and we are reminded of V.'s unsuccessful but nevertheless duly reported inquiries, such as his interview with Mademoiselle; in *Speak, Memory* Nabokov calls these various frustrated pursuits "self-mates."[12] Finally, retracing the steps of the lovers, the novel not only establishes why they came to the right place at the right time, but discovers that they had almost met on several previous occasions where "every time, a minute mistake (the shadow of a flaw, the stopped hole of an unwatched possibility, a caprice of free will) [spoiled] the necessitarian's pleasure and the two lives [were] diverging again with increased rapidity." (p. 97) We are reminded of the obstacles placed in the way of V. as he tries to race death to Sebastian's bedside, or perhaps of the meeting of Clare and Sebastian that is narrowly averted when Sebastian spies the book he needs at a nearby stand. *Sebastian Knight* could have been written in the way described in *Success*; the method is only partially adopted, however, and this second potential version remains only a shadow, a mirror, or a dream move beyond the border of a chessboard. The first meeting of Sebastian and Madame de Rechnoy, however, does provide a concrete example of the method of *Success*. Not only is the situation identical (the first meeting of two lovers), but V. provides us with the reasons of both parties for going to Blauberg (Sebastian was tired and ill; Madame de Rechnoy was suffering from her restless hypochondria), just as Sebastian retraced the movements of his pair of lovers.

This concern with chance and fate also reminds us of the strokes of pure luck that Nabokov paints with a wide brush in *Sebastian Knight*. While interviewing Goodman, V. meets Helen Pratt, who can tell him about Sebastian's relationship with her close friend, Clare Bishop—this in spite of Nabokov's almost immediately preceding admonition, that this kind of accident does not happen in "real life." After an unsuccessful visit to Blauberg to find the mysterious woman who wrote letters to Sebastian in Russian, V. meets

---

[12] *Speak, Memory*, p. 257.

a curious traveler who is able to procure V.'s list of names. The first
of these leads, Helene Grinstein, provides, again by chance, an anecdote of Sebastian's Russian student days. The second provides the
background which will eventually allow V. to identify Madame
Lecerf as Madame de Rechnoy, Sebastian's lover, because Rechnoy's
cousin happens to be visiting. The third visit, to Helene von Graun,
yields Madame Lecerf instead, who happens to be staying at her
friend's house. It is no wonder V. speculates that Sebastian's shade
is hovering over him. (p. 101)

Sebastian's third book, *The Funny Mountain*, is not a novel but
a collection of three short stories. Of these stories we find out little
from V., but he does mention the last of the three, "The Back of
the Moon":

You remember that delightful character in it—the meek little man waiting
for a train who helped three miserable travellers in three different ways?
This Mr. Siller is perhaps the most alive of Sebastian's creatures and is
incidentally the final representative of the "research theme." . . . It is as
though a certain idea steadily growing through two books has now burst
into real physical existence, and so Mr. Siller makes his bow, with every
detail of habit and manner, palpable and unique. . . . (pp. 103–104)

It is Nabokov's (or V.'s?) little joke that this "real," "palpable"
character, Siller, demonstrates his reality by appearing in *Sebastian
Knight* as Silbermann, with every mannerism intact, and helpfully
mentions the title of the story he appeared in, in case the reader's
memory is poor. He helps V. on the train as he had earlier helped
three characters in Sebastian's story.

This surprising development leads us to some complex questions. Is V.'s meeting with Silbermann another of those instances
where V. finds the initial impulse which led to Sebastian's prose,
as he caught the original of "that stone melting into wing," also
from *Funny Mountain* (p. 74), in pigeons fluttering away from the
Arc de Triomphe? Or is it an example of art manifesting itself in
nature? There is no question, however, that Nabokov has provided
us with another method of writing Knight's biography, and an
example of that method.

Nabokov's third mirror (method of composition, level of biography) is the first one that is applicable only to a literary personality.
In this third potential biography, Nabokov is for the first time considering Sebastian primarily as an author. The biographer searches
his subject's books for clues to his personality, attempting to find

correspondences between his creations and his life. At the extreme, such as Aiken's *Ushant*, characters are merely disguises for actual faces; more commonly, characters are partially "drawn from life" and partly imaginary. V. has (perhaps without realizing it) achieved a literary triumph in finding the original of Sebastian's Siller. The *Funny Mountain* also reflects *Sebastian Knight* in that Nabokov's novel has one "real" character, Nabokov himself, who poses as Paul Rechnoy.[13] This double mirroring also occurs in Nabokov's use of Sebastian's last two novels.

Lost Property, Knight's fourth book, gives us another level of analysis. V. calls it Sebastian's "most autobiographical work" (p. 6), and this seems to be the position from which we should consider the novel. It is the only one of Sebastian's novels whose plot is not described, but it "appears as a kind of halt in his literary journey of discovery: a summing up, a counting of the things and souls lost on the way, a setting of bearings." (p. 111) One fertile mode of literary investigation has always been to trace remnants of an author's auto-biography in his fictional creations. V. uses this method occasionally in *Sebastian Knight*, almost always taking these autobiographical quotations from *Lost Property*; V. assumes that the "fiction" is very thin in *Lost Property*, that Sebastian is speaking throughout in his own voice.

Any reader acquainted with *Speak, Memory* soon discovers that all of Nabokov's novels teem with details from his own life, given to various characters almost haphazardly. In *Sebastian Knight* V.'s mother wears her dead husband's wedding ring tied to her own with black thread, an eccentricity which Nabokov also ascribes to his own mother, and there are countless similar details in any of his novels. Yet what V. says of Sebastian's works, that it is futile to trace their autobiographical aspects, applies equally to Nabokov's own:

He had a queer habit of endowing even his most grotesque characters with this or that idea, or impression, or desire which he himself might have toyed with. . . . I fail to name any other author who made use of his art in such a baffling manner—baffling to me who might desire to see the real man behind the author. (p. 114)

This method, then, although used successfully with *Lost Property*, has its hazards. Culling autobiography from an author's fiction is,

---

[13] As Stegner points out, *Escape into Aesthetics*, p. 73.

however, another useful method of composing a biography.

In a different way, the novel is indeed autobiographical, because Sebastian and V. seem to represent aspects of Nabokov's literary career. *Sebastian Knight* is the first of Nabokov's English novels, and marks the end of his composing in Russian. Sebastian wrote under the name Knight, his mother's maiden name, just as Nabokov had written his Russian novels under the name Sirin, his mother's maiden name. Nabokov has frequently stated that his Russian is far richer than his English, and thus V., his new self, is a worried, amateur author. In the last sentence of *Sebastian Knight*, V. speculates on his relationship not only to Sebastian but to Nabokov: "I am Sebastian, or Sebastian is I, or perhaps we both are someone whom neither of us knows."

Sebastian Knight's fifth and last book, *The Doubtful Asphodel*, provides a more obvious mirror for *Sebastian Knight* than any other of Knight's novels. V.'s summary of the novel could be considered a description of *Sebastian Knight* as well:

The theme of the book is simple: a man is dying: you feel him sinking throughout the book; his thought and his memories pervade the whole. . . . The man is the book; the book itself is heaving and dying, and drawing up a ghostly knee. (p. 175)

Not only does the protagonist of *Doubtful Asphodel* seem to be Sebastian, but the other characters also provide echoes of *Sebastian Knight*:

We follow the gentle old chess player Schwarz, who sits down on a chair in a room in a house, to teach an orphan boy the moves of the knight; we meet the fat Bohemian woman with that grey streak showing in the fast colour of her cheaply dyed hair; we listen to a pale wretch noisily denouncing the policy of oppression to an attentive plainclothes man in an ill-famed public-house. The lovely tall primadonna steps in her haste into a puddle, and her silver shoes are ruined. An old man sobs and is soothed by a soft-lipped girl in mourning. Professor Nussbaum, a Swiss scientist, shoots his young mistress and himself dead in a hotel-room at half past three in the morning. (p. 175)

Schwarz is "Uncle Black," Paul Rechnoy's cousin; the "fat Bohemian woman" is Lydia Bohemsky; the plainclothes man may be Silbermann again; the "lovely tall primadonna" seems to be Helene von Graun, who has a "fine contralto voice" and also steps into a puddle, although her silver shoes once belonged to Clare Bishop; the suicidal couple died in Blauberg, around the corner from Sebastian.

While each of Sebastian's novels provides a mirror for *Sebastian Knight*, each successive reflection has caught more of the finished book, and *Prismatic Bezel* provides the closest parallel to V.'s work. The burden of *Prismatic Bezel* is an expected revelation about the nature of life and death: "In a moment or two, at the end of this sentence, in the middle of the next, or perhaps a little further still, we shall learn something that will change all our concepts." (p. 178) Of course the revelation does not come, the man dies, and the eternal secret remains unrevealed. Nabokov coolly replays this situation twice again in the last pages of *Sebastian Knight*. First Sebastian appears to V. in a dream: "I knew he was calling me and saying something very important—and promising to tell me something more important still." (p. 189) Sebastian's letter, which prompted V.'s dream, had concluded with the ominous, "I don't much like those bare branches and twigs which I see from my window" (p. 186), echoing the last observation in *Doubtful Asphodel*, that "'the absolute solution' was written all over the world he had known" (p. 178), and V.'s subconscious has provided a nightmare continuation. Then V. receives word that Sebastian is dying, and this fantasy takes on substance; if V. can reach Sebastian in time the truth about life and death may yet be revealed. Again the answer is lost, for Sebastian has died and V. sits unknowingly at the wrong bedside.

Here is a final, astonishing level of biography, for V. has, through his affinity for, sympathy with, and rereading of *Doubtful Asphodel*, literally relived its central situation in his own life. Through his total immersion in the novel, he has become its author. "Sebastian's mask clings to my face, the likeness will not be washed off." (p. 205) What is still more astonishing is that V. reveals the secret that Sebastian did not, that "the soul is but a manner of being—not a constant state —that any soul may be yours, if you find and follow its undulations." (p. 204) V.'s revelation came as he sat by the wrong bed, listening to the "quick soft breathing" of an ill man asleep, and what he learned would have been the same had he been listening to Sebastian's breathing, that the physical part of a man is unimportant in a quest for his soul. Sebastian's life is almost irrelevant to his "real life."

It is, then, through his attention to Knight's novels, rather than to his autobiography, that V. *becomes* Sebastian Knight. Jorge Luis Borges, in his essay "A New Refutation of Time" (neither Sebastian nor Nabokov believes in time[14]), presents this idea in a condensed form:

We can postulate, in the mind of an individual (or of two individuals who do not know of each other but in whom the same process works) two identical moments. Once this identity is postulated, one may ask: Are not these identical moments the same? Is not one single repeated term sufficient to break down and confuse the series of time? Do not the fervent readers who surrender themselves to Shakespeare become, literally, Shakespeare?[15]

To Borges, whose writings Nabokov admires,[16] these fervent readers seem to be fairly numerous. Nabokov is more skeptical, for his reader begins with an "inner knowledge" of, and "some sort of common rhythm" with, Sebastian (pp. 33, 34); his success comes only after his intensive rereading of Sebastian's last novel and a literal reliving of its incidents. Still, Nabokov's argument is the same—in a sense, he goes even further than Borges, for in suddenly making the physical world irrelevant, V. is able not only to grasp Sebastian's soul but to make the visionary leap that "perhaps we both are someone else whom neither of us knows," a speculative discovery that drove the protagonist of another Nabokov novel mad.

"Two modes of his life question each other and the answer is his life itself, and that is the nearest one ever can approach a human truth." (p. 137) *Sebastian Knight* is not a biography but a presentation of methods by which to write that biography; each of the methods used is mirrored by one of Sebastian's novels; and each of these mirrors comes closer to providing a perfect reflection of the finished book. A final mirror is yet to come, for *Sebastian Knight* is the fictional biography which Sebastian was planning in the last year of his life. (pp. 40–41) This last mirror is a flawless and endless double reflection.

---

14 *Sebastian Knight*, pp. 65–66, and *Speak, Memory*, p. 139.
15 "A New Refutation of Time," *Labyrinths* (Norfolk, Conn., 1964), p. 224.
16 See "Playboy Interview: Vladimir Nabokov," *Playboy*, XI (Jan., 1964), 46. See also the present interview, pp. 33–34, above.—Ed.

BEND SINISTER:
NABOKOV'S
POLITICAL DREAM

L. L. Lee

Bend Sinister was Nabokov's second novel in English, written by a man who had experienced both Nazi and Communist regimes. And, although the novel is neither quite history nor an allegory of history, it is Nabokov's most explicitly political novel; that is, it deals most concretely with living political themes. In *Speak, Memory*, Nabokov states that *Invitation to a Beheading*, composed in Russian during the 'thirties, treats "the buffoons and bullies of a Communazist state."[1] He also says, in his foreword to the translated *Invitation*, that this novel and *Bend Sinister* are related stylistically, which means thematically. They are both visions of madness, political and personal—a madness that is the dream which, carried too far, begins to act in the world.

But there are other equally important themes in *Bend Sinister*. What one might call the positive message of the novel is contained in the words of Krug, the philosopher protagonist, when he says that he esteems his university colleagues "for two things: because they are able to find perfect felicity in specialized knowledge and because they are not apt to commit physical murder." (p. 54) In other words, there are human values which must be upheld against those mad abstractions which, as we shall see, would destroy the mind and the body, treating man at best as only a machine.

Yet, Nabokov announces, he neither writes nor reads "didactic

---

[1] Vladimir Nabokov, *Speak, Memory* (New York, 1951), p. 217. Hereafter references to *SM* will be given in the text by title letters and page numbers. Other works of Nabokov (indicated in the text by title letters and page numbers in parentheses—with the exception of *Bend Sinister*) used in this paper are: *Bend Sinister* (London, 1961) (indicated by page numbers only); *Nikolai Gogol* (New York, 1961) (*G*); *Invitation to a Beheading* (New York, 1959) (*I*); *Eugene Onegin* (New York, 1964) (*EO*); *Lolita* (New York, 1955) (*L*); *The Real Life of Sebastian Knight* (Norfolk, Conn., 1959) (*SK*); *Pnin* (New York, 1964) (*P*).

fiction." (*L*, p. 316) And "all great literary achievements . . . [are] a phenomenon of language and not one of ideas." (*G*, p. 150) One does not need to take this entirely seriously: Nabokov (along with Mallarmé) recognizes that in practice words do convey ideas. His own creature, the writer Sebastian Knight, puts this last statement in reverse order and makes it more accurate in asserting "that no real idea can be said to exist without the words made to measure." (*SK*, p. 84) *Bend Sinister* is an example of how words are made to measure; but it is also concerned with words and, therefore, with literature—which is the dream of the artist, a dream that makes nothing happen but just *is*.

The novel, however, is not these generalizations; it is a construction of words, no doubt, but is also a story about people in a world. And so, perhaps a summary of the story can help us see how these themes come alive in the novel. The action takes place in an unnamed but obviously modern European country, somewhere east of France; a revolution, led by Paduk, has just overthrown the Republic. As the novel begins, Krug, the hero, leaves the hospital where his wife has died. Crossing a bridge, he has a hallucinatory encounter with the soldiers of the insane dictator, Paduk; and this event is the emblem of those that follow. Krug talks himself past the soldiers on the north side of the bridge but is turned back at the south because his pass has not been signed at the other end. The soldiers on the north side, one of whom is Gurk ("Krug" spelled backwards), are illiterate. In brief, Krug does not exist as a person until he can get a signature from people who cannot write. "Doomed to walk back and forth on a bridge which has ceased to be one since neither bank is really attainable." (p. 17) Krug, as human being, is caught in time. Finally he and another man, also held up, sign one another's passes —a nice irony, for the two prisoners create one another as persons, through written words, and so escape.

Krug and Paduk had been schoolmates as children; the new State wants Krug's endorsement for propaganda reasons, although there is an overtone of homosexuality in Paduk's desire for Krug. It would not be an over-reading to interpret Paduk's implied homosexuality as a personal and political commentary: the dictator, the seeker for power (an essentially sterile personality), lusts after the life of the mind at the same moment that he needs to degrade it.

Since he wishes to retain his individuality, Krug refuses to endorse Paduk's regime: "I want to be left alone" (p. 82); and, too, "I am not interested in politics." (p. 9) There *is* a lesson here; he should be interested in politics. For, one by one his friends, people of no political importance, are dragged off to prison as a kind of blackmail. At last his son is taken. Krug collapses, willing to do and sign anything. "The nightmare may get out of control," he cries to a state functionary (p. 185). Unfortunately it does, and his son is killed in a brutal psychological "experiment." Krug, now insane, believes himself to be a school child again, attacks Paduk and is shot.

Paduk is the chief advocate of Ekwilism, "a violent and virulent political doctrine" that proposes "to enforce spiritual uniformity upon . . . [the] land through the medium of the most standardized section of the inhabitants, namely the Army, under the supervision of a bloated and dangerously divine State." (p. 69) Nabokov presents Ekwilism as a basically confused political idea with one clear aim: destruction of the individual. Communist and Nazi dogmas—racism, militarism, extreme nationalism—seem casually tossed in, although there is more Nazi, perhaps, than Communist doctrine in this list. Moreover, the emblem of the Ekwilist state bears "a remarkable resemblance to a crushed dislocated but still writhing spider . . . upon a red flaglet." (p. 34) This is obviously derived from the Nazi swastika and banner, although with an echo of the Red Flag. And Krug, certainly ironically (we must remember that Nabokov is quite as aware of the range of meanings of his words as Joyce), asks the unlettered soldiers to sign his pass with "a cross, or a telephone booth curlicue, or a gammadion, or something." (p. 17) The gammadion can be in the shape of a swastika and, possibly not too oddly, of an open-ended Greek cross. The swastika, in German, is a *hakenkreuz*, a hook-cross; but the Christian cross has also been used as a symbol by killers.

As I have written elsewhere,[2] however, Nabokov, pursuing the image of the circle that is so important to his art, sees the ends of the political circle joining, "a vicious circle as all circles are" (G, p. 149)—and the death of the heart, "spiritual uniformity," is the result, if not the purpose, of both Communism and Nazism. The *petit bourgeois* who does sign Krug's pass is, in his emptiness, as vicious as any revolutionist of Paduk's kind; *Bend Sinister* must not

---

[2] L. L. Lee, "Vladimir Nabokov's Great Spiral of Being," *The Western Humanities Review*, XVIII, 3 (Summer, 1964), 225–236; and L. L. Lee, "Duplexity in V. Nabokov's Short Stories," *Studies in Short Fiction*, II, 4 (Summer, 1965), 307–315.

be read as an apologia for capitalism. Nabokov gives it explicitly in
Speak, Memory:

> . . . a kind of family circle . . . [links] representatives of all nations, jolly
> Empire-builders . . . , the unmentionable German product, the good old
> church-going Russian or Polish *pogromshchik*, the lean American lyncher,
> the man with the bad teeth who squirts antiminority stories in the bar
> or the lavatory, and, at another point of the same *subhuman circle* [my
> italics], those ruthless, paste-faced automatons in singularly wide trousers
> and high-shouldered coats, those *Sitzriesen*, whom—or shall I say which?—
> the Soviet State has brought out on such a scale after thirty years of selec-
> tive breeding. (*SM*, p. 195)

This, then, is what the illogical truth of the dream tells us: it shows
us how apparently dissimilar political ideals are really, not just super-
ficially, identical.

Above all, Ekwilism is and must be opposed to the life of the
Mind. As an acquaintance of Krug's holds (repeating Krug's
thought): "Curiosity . . . is insubordination in its purest form."
(p. 42) Ekwilism would destroy curiosity (i.e., any search for truth),
although the lower kind of curiosity, the impulse to pry into other
people's business, is made a virtue. Ekwilism would certainly destroy
art, at least art as Nabokov understands it. "Popular commonsense
must spit out the caviar of moonshine and poetry, and the simple
word, *verbum sine ornatu*, intelligible to man and beast [!] alike,
and accompanied by fit action, must be restored to power." (p. 98)
These senselessly fumbled but frightening metaphors with their
accent on action, an action that can mean only violence, are the
language of the Ekwilist state—and the antithesis of art and artist.
(It is not too surprising to discover that this sentence and part of
the description of Fortinbras, which Nabokov gives to his Professor Hamm, are inspired variants of an actual sentence and certain
remarks of Franz Horn, a nineteenth-century German commentator
on *Hamlet*. I should add here that Nabokov levies on a number of
Shakespeare's commentators, many more than I have room to point
out.[3]) Under the Ekwilist regime, there will be no more magical
dance of words, so free and yet so ordered. It is the totalitarian,
utilitarian mind, not Nabokov's art, not Krug's thought, that Krug's
friend Maximov cries out against: "But the utterly nonsensical is a
natural and logical part of Paduk's rule." (p. 80)

---

[3] See Horn, *et al.*, in the Furness *Variorum Hamlet*.

The very form of Nabokov's novel is an actualization of this ironic strain between art and politics. Form here means style, structure, and imagery, those three elements of the literary work that Nabokov suggests, in the epilogue to Lolita (L, p. 315), as the truly important ones. It is almost impossible, however, to speak of the one without speaking of the other two in his fiction. One cannot, for instance, explain those digressions that really do not digress, those digressions that Nabokov thinks of, along with Sterne, as "the sunshine—. . . the life, the soul of reading" (EO, II, p. 195), without noting that they are imagistically interrelated with the other parts of the novel—and that the style changes but makes, too, its correspondences. Nevertheless, one must see how these things work, particularly in the Shakespearean conversation and the long dream that takes up Chapter 5, in order to understand that the novel does have order and meaning.

We can start with the novel's beginning and its ending. The first chapter is apparently set within the mind of Krug, but one cannot be certain. The time is a November: the observer sees a street, a peculiar, spatulate puddle, two leafless poplar trees, and two houses. The puddle will appear again when the police spy, Dr. Alexander, signs his acquiescence to the State philosophy and accidentally blots the paper. And, almost at the end of the novel, just as Krug rushes across the courtyard at Paduk who is crouched against a wall, "and just a fraction of an instant before another and better bullet hit him, he shouted again: You, you—and the wall vanished, like a rapidly withdrawn slide, and I stretched myself and got up from among the chaos of written and rewritten pages. . . ." (p. 210) This "I" is the author in another persona. It is now night. The "I" looks out upon two windows lighted; they are windows in one of the houses seen by "Krug" in the first scene. There is also a poplar and "a special puddle (the one Krug had somehow perceived through the layer of his own life). . . ." The season is different; it is warm and there are moths about, "a good night for mothing" for Nabokov the lepidopterist. Yet Krug and the author are certainly identified; and of that puddle, always "acquiring the same form," the "I" says that, "possibly, something of the kind may be said to occur in regard to the imprint we leave in the intimate texture of space." (p. 211) The puddle is Krug's, Alexander's, the "I's"; they share the same space. The author as God is god of a pantheistic word world; the dreamer is his own creation.

So, too, with structure: the beginning and the end of the novel contain one another as well as containing the novel. But one must still examine the actual line of the story. I have said that the digressions are not really digressions—there are admittedly times when Nabokov indulges himself, but the longest of the digressions, the Shakespearean one, is not only a functional, but an absolutely necessary, part of the novel—it is the assertion of the value of literature. And one element of literature is the sheer joy of using or seeing words used intelligently and sensitively.

The figure of Shakespeare enters the novel early: Ember is translating him; Krug and Ember entertain the absurd, marvelous fancy of "forging" his works. One must note that Shakespeare is important to Nabokov not only as the greatest poet of all time (G, p. 29), not only as the author of the "dream-plays Hamlet . . . [and] Lear" (G, p. 54), or because of the complexity and mystery of his plays, but also because he is a magnificent enigma in himself, a puzzling trickster who hides and reveals himself in his works. The point here is that Shakespeare's works are the type of literature: the poet, or, rather, his works are truly "not of an age, but for all time." They are outside of time, in fact, although if Shakespeare did not exist, we should have to invent him for our own time. Krug and Ember can invent him, make him meaningful for themselves as individuals. But we shall see that there is a wrong way of "inventing" him, one that is an assault on language and literature.

The digression, which takes most of Chapter 7, opens with a partial description of Ember's bedroom. Once again we cannot be sure who is doing the perceiving, Krug, Ember, or the author. Who, for instance, says, "Last chance of describing the bedroom"? (p. 96) The literary dream will not allow us aesthetic distance: the voice of the dreamer is at our ear, perhaps in our ear. On one wall there are three pictures, all of which have something to do with the Bacon-Shakespeare nonsense. Nabokov does not so inform us, but the first two pictures are derived from the title page of the Cryptomenytices, etc., published at Lunaeburg in 1624 as the work of a Gustavus Selenus. One of the English Baconians, Sir Edwin Durning-Lawrence, used Selenus' book to "prove" that Bacon wrote Shakespeare's plays (I have been unable to discover where the third picture comes from). Sir Edwin's own book, Bacon is Shake-speare, offers quite a bit more to Nabokov, including the statement that the Droeshout portrait from the 1623 folio "is cunningly composed of two left arms and a mask."[4] Nabokov gives this as: "Who is he? William X, cunningly

---

[4] Sir Edwin Durning-Lawrence, Bart., Bacon is Shake-speare (New York, 1910), p. 23.

composed of two left arms and a mask. Who else? The person who said (not for the first time) that the glory of God is to hide a thing, and the glory of man is to find it." (pp. 95–96) One could argue that Nabokov is simply pulling our legs; he says of Pushkin that he is "a deceiver as all artists are. . . ." (*EO*, I, p. 50) He does not, indeed, take the Bacon-as-Shakespeare faith seriously; Shakespeare is Shakespeare, the "Warwickshire fellow." (p. 96) All this is, I agree, a joke, but it is more than a joke and more than just an opportunity for Nabokov to make some obscure allusions.

On the immediate level, the Shakespeare discussion serves as a psychological relief for Krug and Ember: Olga, Krug's wife, has just died and the Maximovs have just been arrested. It is also "comic relief," or, better, a relaxation that heightens the horror of both the Maximovs' arrest in the preceding chapter and the following, weirdly farcical, arrest of Ember. But neither justifies the absurdity or the length of the digression, which is, in design, neither a wandering nor a psychological manipulation of the reader; rather, it is an enrichment, an attempt on the part of the author to reach out and gather in as much life (even if fantastic) as possible; it is also an attempt to use "language" as thoroughly as possible. One must also see that these seemingly irrelevant bits of knowledge, these puzzles, these creations of new worlds, are always in the main flow of the novel. They are, to use Pnin's words, "Rambling Comparisons" (*P*, p. 186), but just as the metaphor or the figure makes poetry, so these digressions make the novel. They are not just baroque ornaments; they connect and they comment.

Nabokov's borrowings, allusions, and images in the digressions (and elsewhere) work in the same way. Sir Edwin is used because he too has invented "Shakespeare"—but he has done it stupidly, without humor, and with a flawed language; his is the dream of literature and truth gone sour. He also offers an image with his insistence on Bacon's "left-handedly" putting out his "Shakespeare" plays. The left hand, or the idea of the left, appears repeatedly. The title of the novel refers to the band running from sinister chief to dexter base on the shield, a standard representation of bastardy in heraldry. Not that Bacon fathered Shakespeare's plays, but rather that the true work of art contains the world, the left as well as the right; it contains contraries that are dialectically related. And, too, like questions of parentage, the work of literature contains mysteries. We might add that Nabokov's digressions are a deliberately bizarre interweaving of the comic and the serious, an echo of the practice of Hamlet.

It is Hamlet and Ophelia that Krug and Ember talk about:

"Hamlet at Wittenberg, always late, missing G. Bruno's lectures. . . ." (p. 101) Bruno is the philosopher of the coincidence of contraries, who was, by the way, burned—if not by the State, at least by a system that could not allow variety (i.e., heretics). Bruno was also a man who gave his faith to argument in words; his faith and his fate thus correspond to Hamlet's and Krug's. Nabokov offers us Hamlet as the indecisive poet unwilling or unable to act so long as he lacks the necessary evidence or the proper moment, always on the horns of a dilemma; and Krug as the indecisive philosopher unwilling to act because, though he *knows* men are irrational, he cannot *believe* in their irrationality. At one moment, Ember "might have embraced his fat friend [Krug] in silence (a miserable defeat in the case of philosophers and poets accustomed to believe that words are superior to deeds). . . ." (p. 96) Words are superior—but only in value. Yet paradoxically Hamlet and Krug, and even Ember, are true individuals, that is, men of courage and strength.

The discussion of *Hamlet* is, then, an element in the satire on the *political* dream. The grotesque ideas of the stupid Professor Hamm in his "The Real Plot of *Hamlet*," which controls Ember's production of the play in the new State Theater, are a revelation of Ekwilism: spiritual leveling on the one hand, racism on the other, both intensely opposed to the individual. (Hamm and Durning-Lawrence, though opposed, are true brothers, since they both deny Shakespeare in the name of political and economic classes.) One must finally allow the other meanings of "sinister"; although all things in the universe may be related, Nabokov does not believe that all things are of equal value. Both Paduk and Durning-Lawrence are sinister.

In the same way, the linguistic game that Krug and Ember play with names, their indulgence in that human and civilized pleasure in words, is a spiritual activity which the Ekwilist mentality cannot tolerate nor comprehend (unless we grant that Paduk's silly anagrams on Adam Krug's name, Gumakrad, Gurdamak, Dramaguk, can be called a pleasure in language). Nevertheless, Paduk misses the real significance of Krug's name: Adam is "the Man," the first man, the archetype of the individual. And Krug is Russian for "circle," "the circle in Krug, one Krug in another one" (p. 37), and therefore the symbol of completeness as well as of contraries and complexity.

Ophelia also brings in things Russian, or at least Nabokov's joy in things Russian, as well as his joy in things sexual. But even the Russian, the sexual, and Ophelia are essentially elements in the serious game of words. Ember pursues the meaning and derivation of Ophelia's name. He, or rather Nabokov, again cribs enthusiastically from Shakespearean commentators: Ruskin and C. Elliot Browne. In his own text and by allusion Nabokov finds her name in Greek, Danish, Italian, and Latin—a name associated with serpents (with no Freudian meaning) and amorous shepherds. She is "lithe, lithping, thin-lipped Ophelia, Amleth's wet dream, a mermaid of Lethe, a rare water serpent, *Russalka letheana* of science (to match your long purples)." (p. 103) *Rusalka* is Russian for "mermaid," in particular a fresh-water mermaid with legs. (*EO*, II, p. 246) There is surely an allusion here to the mermaid of Pushkin's poem "Rusalka," a seductress who tempts a lonely hermit into a lake and thus to death, physical and spiritual. Thus, both the mermaid and Ophelia (the creations of Shakespeare and Pushkin, these two greatest of poets [*G*, p. 29]) are linked by allusion and description to the silly but destructive girl-child, Mariette, of Nabokov's novel. Mariette tempts Krug to a sexual death and hands him over to a physical death; and she is the youngest of the three sisters, Mariette, Linda Bachofen, and Doktor von Wytwyl, all of whom help to wreck Krug's life: a kind of diabolic Kore-Persephone-Hecate.

It is also in this chapter that Nabokov makes most striking and pleasurable use of such connective devices as parallelisms, alliterations, metaphor, and even rhyme. It is here he "quotes" Professor Hamm, whose style is a fog of clichés and blurred metaphors. Hamm is no Hamlet (let me laugh a little too, gentlemen): "Some dark deed of violence, . . . some masonic manoeuvre engendered by the Shylocks of high finance, has dispossessed" (p. 98) Fortinbras' family of its right to the Danish throne; or, "the poison poured into the sleeper's ear is a symbol of the subtle injection of lethal rumours. . . ." (p. 99) Once more we have, in Professor Hamm's language, the idiom of the bureaucratic propagandist (state or private), a truly dead language, but it is at least a delight in that it is a joke. Yet later, when Krug receives the various missives of the state, especially its newspapers, the gray pall is not funny; it is terrifying.

On the reverse side, though, a phrase as wild as "lusty old King Hamlet smiting with a poleaxe the Polacks skidding and sprawling on the ice" (p. 102), which is paraphrased Shakespeare-Krug and pure Nabokov, fits felicitously into its context, the sound evoking the image. And Ember's Hamlet says of Ophelia, "Quietly, with a kind of devilish daintiness she minced her dangerous course the way her father's ambition pointed" (p. 104), a line that elsewhere would be arch but which, in context, is both exact parody and significant statement.

One can add that the language of the country and the names of the characters are illustrations of this complex of associations. The language is a made-up tongue, just as is that of Zembla in *Pale Fire*. Its roots are Russian and Teutonic, although there are considerable patches of straight Russian, especially in the translations Ember is making. However, the intent of the game here is to connect Nabokov's "pasts," *his* linguistic worlds; and, more seriously, to suggest that it is man's language that creates, in major part, man's world. One may say, too, that language is man's way of stopping (or passing) time.

The names serve not only as linkages but as humor (puns, even if erudite, give pleasure *and* connect). Krug is, to repeat, "circle." Paduk is nicknamed the Toad; his surname is almost "paddock," a toad. The word "paddock" certainly hints at something more threatening than "toad" does; in Shakespeare it is almost always a symbol of evil. And the name of old Skotoma, the senile "philosopher" of Ekwilism, is a direct transliteration of the Modern Greek *skotoma*, that is, "murder" or "killing." The comic strip hero Etermon, who supplies a sartorial style and a manner of life for Paduk, is, Nabokov points out, Everyman; but there is a possible sarcasm here on *etymon*, the "true" or original meaning of a word, for Etermon is completely fake, both as individual and as symbol. Finally, we have the student Phokus, the nucleus of a resistance to Paduk, who appears in the novel only as a shape and a sound: Phokus is *fokus*, the Russian for "focus" as well as for "conjuring trick." Phokus is the novel's heart but he is hidden.

It is in Krug's dream in Chapter 5 that we see most clearly this combination of real and unreal, of fiction and actuality, in the absurdity that is the art dream. "It bristled with farcical anachronism. . . ." (p. 56) The dream is treated almost as a play, the play within the play. But "who is behind the timid producers?" And the dreamer, not Krug, answers, "A nameless, mysterious genius who took advantage of the dream to convey his own peculiar code message which has nothing," really, to do with "Krug's physical existence, but which links him up somehow with an unfathomable mode of being . . ., a kind of transcendental madness which lurks behind the corner of consciousness. . . ." (p. 57)

Yet the dream is also a flashback, a witty retelling of the story of old Skotoma. It also tells of Paduk senior and his padograph—a machine that reproduces handwriting and which "subsisted as an Ekwilist symbol, as a proof of the fact that a mechanical device can reproduce personality, and that Quality is merely the distributional aspect of Quantity." (pp. 62–63) And it tells of the founding of the Party of the Average Man by Paduk junior, the future dictator (all the schoolboy members are most unaverage; that is, each is deficient mentally or physically—Nabokov's ironies are sometimes neither subtle nor pleasant). This part of Krug's dream is not a true dream sequence; it is Nabokov once more entering, slyly, as guide, since

a closer inspection (made when the dream-self is dead for the ten thousandth time and the day-self inherits for the ten thousandth time those dusty trifles . . .) reveals the presence of someone in the know . . . and we start afresh now combining dim dreams with the scholarly precision of memory. (p. 58)

Here is, in summary, the process by which the artist works.

But for what purpose? We must agree, finally, that *Bend Sinister* makes the statement that there are kinds of lives and kinds of human activities—especially the activity that is art—which are of supreme value. And so we may conclude with two quotations from Krug and one from Yeats:

Lives that I envy: longevity, peaceful times, peaceful country, quiet fame, quiet satisfaction: Ivar Aasen, Norwegian philologist, 1813–1896, who invented a language. Down here we have too much of *homo civis* and too little of *sapiens*. (p. 139)

Sapiens. The man who invents languages, who invents Shakespeare (wittily), who invents art, art that is (although Krug is thinking directly of the individual human life) "consciousness, which is the only real thing in the world and the greatest mystery of all." (p. 163) And yet "in dreams begins responsibility."

LOLITA:
THE SPRINGBOARD
OF PARODY

Alfred Appel, Jr.

I

In the decade since its initial publication in 1955 by the Olympia Press, Vladimir Nabokov's *Lolita* has emerged as a virtual classic of contemporary literature. Although it has received much serious attention, the criticism which *Lolita* has elicited invariably treats Nabokov's twelfth novel as a special case quite apart from the rest of his fiction, and almost always forces a thesis which does not and in fact cannot accommodate the total design of the novel. Nabokov affords that rare and disarming spectacle of a man who seems to know exactly what he is about; the most incisive criticism of Nabokov is found in his own books and, fortified by these passages, this essay attempts a comprehensive view of *Lolita*. But before doing so, a few general remarks are in order.

A single trope describes the world of Nabokov's fiction and may serve to place *Lolita* in its rightful context. In "The Assistant Producer," a story published in 1943, Nabokov writes about the German film companies of the 'twenties who "found cheap labor in hiring those among the Russian émigrés whose only hope and profession was their past—that is, a set of totally unreal people—to represent 'real' audiences in pictures. The dovetailing of one phantasm into another produced upon a sensitive person the impression of living in a Hall of Mirrors, or rather a prison of mirrors, and not even knowing which was the glass and which was yourself."[1] The comic charade

---

[1] Vladimir Nabokov, *Nabokov's Dozen* (New York, 1958), p. 83. Wherever possible, page references to the following editions of Nabokov's books will

we call selfhood is played out in this roomy prison, and although the variously involuted designs of his novels make it clear that Nabokov himself has been able to see beyond its mirrored confines by writing these very novels, there is for his characters "no exit" from *their* prison of mirrors, and the phrase goes far towards telescoping the total impression of Nabokov's fiction,[2] and his vision of "reality" ("one of the few words that mean nothing without quotes," he says in the afterword to *Lolita* [p. 314]). " 'So that's the dead end' (the mirror you break your nose against)," the overwrought Humbert tells Lolita after catching her in a lie (p. 227), and on their first conjugal night at The Enchanted Hunters hotel, they enter a room which to Humbert is a bewildering little prison of mirrors, a metaphor for his solipsism and circumscribing obsession: "There was a double bed, a mirror, a double bed in the mirror, a closet door with mirror, a bathroom door ditto, a blue-dark window, a reflected bed there, the same in the closet mirror, two chairs, a glass-topped table, two bed-tables, a double bed." (p. 121) "In our earthly house, windows are replaced by mirrors," writes Nabokov in *The Gift*. (p. 322) His characters continually confront mirrors where they had hoped to find windows, and the attempt to transcend solipsism is one of Nabokov's major themes. Many readers overlook the deep moral resonance of his work, for characters hopelessly imprisoned within themselves must submit to Nabokov's irony, parody, or, most significantly, self-parody.

As a literal image and overriding metaphor, the mirror is central to the form and content of Nabokov's novels. If one perceives *Pale Fire* spatially, with John Shade's poem on the "left" and Charles Kinbote's Commentary on the "right," the poem is seen as an object to be perceived, and the Commentary becomes the world seen through the distorting prism of a mind, a monstrous concave mirror held up to an objective "reality." The narrator of *Despair* (1934)

---

be placed in parentheses in the text, and initials of a title will be used if necessary: *Despair* (New York, 1966) (*D*); *The Gift* (New York, 1963) (*G*); *Invitation to a Beheading* (New York, 1959) (*I*); *Laughter in the Dark* (New York, 1960) (*LD*); *Lolita* (New York, 1958) (*L*); *Pale Fire* (New York, 1962) (*PF*); *The Real Life of Sebastian Knight* (New York, 1941) (*SK*); *Speak, Memory* (New York, 1951) (*SM*);– edition of the latter under original title, *Conclusive Evidence*, has the same pagination. The new, revised *SM* does not.

[2] For an attempt at describing this "total impression," see my two-part essay, "Nabokov's Puppet Show," *New Republic*, CLVI (Jan. 14,1967), 27–30; (Jan. 21, 1967), 25–32.

loathes mirrors, avoids them, and comments on those "monsters of mirrors," the "crooked ones," in which a man is stripped, squashed, or "pulled out like dough and then torn in two." (p. 31) Nabokov has placed these crooked reflectors everywhere in his fiction: Doubles, parodies and self-parodies (literature trapped in a prison of amusement park mirrors), works within works, mirror-games of chess,[3] translations ("a crazy-mirror of terror and art"[4]), and language games. He manipulates the basic linguistic devices—auditory, morphological, and alphabetical, most conspicuously the latter. In *Pale Fire*, Zemblan is "the tongue of the mirror" (p. 242), and the fragmentation or total annihilation of the self reverberates in the verbal distortions in *Bend Sinister's* police state, "where everybody is merely an anagram of everybody else" (p. xv), and in the alphabetical and psychic inversions and reversals in *Pale Fire*, such as Botkin-Kinbote and the Index references to "Word Golf" and "*Sudarg of Bokay*, a mirror maker of genius," the anagrammatic reflection and poetic description of omnipresent death, represented in *Pale Fire* by the Zemblan assassin, J[y]acob Gradus, who throws his shadow across the entire novel.

There are many references to James Joyce in *Lolita*, and not surprisingly, for the pun is its principal mirror-language. Joyce rehabilitated the pun for modern literature and Nabokov has continued to dignify this much disparaged rhetorical resource. Like Joyce, Nabokov fashions his puns from literary sources, from any of the several languages available to him, from obsolete words, or the roots of arcane words. If the discordant associations are rich enough, Nabokov's puns succeed in projecting a theme central to the fiction, in summarizing or commenting on the action. In *The Defense* (1930), the name of chess grandmaster Luzhin is a portmanteau combination of losing-illusion, as well as the Russian word for *puddle* and the name of Raskolnikov's stolid brother-in-law in *Crime and Punishment*, the man Mrs. Luzhin would have her husband become. Even the most playful punning will turn out to be invested with this kind of significance, as evidenced by the verbal pratfalls staged in the name of Humbert's mysterious "shadow," ubiquitous Clare Quilty. Lolita gets a letter supposedly from her friend Mona, but written by Quilty, as certain hints suggest when the letter collapses into

---

[3] See Edmond Bernard, "La thématique échiquéene de Lolita," *L'Arc*, VII (Printemps 1964), 39–47.

[4] Nabokov, Introduction to *Time* Reading Program edition, *Bend Sinister* (New York, 1964), p. xvi. References are to this edition.

French: "*comme le lac est beau car il faut qu'il t'y mène.* [". . . it is necessary that he carry you there"] Lucky beau *Qu'il t'y*—What a tongue-twister!" (p. 225) The French strives for *Qui est-il*—and who *is* he? It is the question that sounds throughout modern literature, the question asked by countless characters engaged in the shadow game that is the search for themselves—to name but one of the shadow games which are in progress in Nabokov's fiction.

In both *The Gift* (1937) and the 1959 Foreword to the translation of *Invitation to a Beheading* (1935–36), Nabokov mentions *Discours sur les ombres,* by Pierre Delalande, "the only author whom I must gratefully recognize as an influence upon me at the time of writing this book . . . [and] whom I invented." (*I*, p. 6) Delalande's *Discours* provided the epigraph for *Invitation*—"Comme un fou se croit Dieu, nous nous croyons mortels"—and Nabokov's entire corpus might be described as a "Discourse on Shadows or Shades." John Shade is the author of the poem *Pale Fire,* and since Humbert Humbert was brought up on the French Riviera, he would pronounce his name with a French accent: *ombre, ombre,* a resonant pun which includes the popular seventeenth and eighteenth century card game of *ombre* and echoes the Spanish *hombre.* Lolita's given name, Dolores Haze, fittingly juxtaposes the Spanish *sorrow* with the German *rabbit,* and haze is an apt metaphor for her illusory and ephemeral charms. Humbert's narrative dramatizes a Shade's efforts to capture the essence of a Haze, and in *Pale Fire,* the poet's homely, suicidal daughter is named Hazel Shade. By "solipsizing" Lolita, Humbert condemns her to the solitary confinement of his obsessional shadowland. "She had entered my world, umber and black Humberland," says Humbert (p. 168), who, by choosing to chase the figurative shadows that play on the walls of his "cave," upends Plato's famous allegory.[5] Although Humbert has had the benefit of a journey in the sunny "upper world"—a Riviera boyhood, in fact, and a full-sized wife or two—he nevertheless pursues the illusion that he can recapture what is inexorably lost. As Humbert demonstrates, illusions are realities in their ability to destroy us. "I was the shadow of the waxwing slain/ By the false azure in the windowpane," writes John Shade in the opening lines of *Pale Fire,* while in Nabokov's poem "An Evening of Russian Poetry" (1945), the speaker says:

> My back is Argus-eyed. I live in danger.
> False shadows turn to track me as I pass

---

[5] For Nabokov *contre* Plato, see the Appel-Nabokov interview.

and, wearing beards, disguised as secret agents,
creep in to blot the freshly written page
and read the blotter in the looking-glass.
And in the dark, under my bedroom window,
until, with a chill whirr and shiver, day
presses its starter, warily they linger
or silently approach the door and ring
the bell of memory and run away.[6]

Seventeen years later in *Pale Fire* the "Shadows" are the Zemblan "regicidal organization" who dispatch Gradus, one of whose aliases is d'Argus, to assassinate the exiled King Charles (Kinbote). But the Shadows' secret agent accidentally kills Shade. Thus the delusive nature of identity and perception, the constricting burdens of memory, and a haunting sense of mutability are all capsuled in a reverberating pun.

Because Nabokov is not a vapid contriver, his most labyrinthine and involuted artifice is of the greatest significance. Nabokov is well known as a lepidopterist, and in his poem "A Discovery" (1943) and memoir *Speak, Memory* (1951), he writes evocatively of his entomological forays, of the fleeting moments of ecstasy experienced in catching an exquisite and rare butterfly. It is no accident, as Diana Butler points out, that the object of Humbert's passion, a nymph, should be, according to the dictionary, *a pupa or the young of an insect undergoing incomplete metamorphosis.* Responding to blatant clues planted by Nabokov himself in his essay, "On a Book Entitled *Lolita*," Miss Butler demonstrates that the substratum of *Lolita* contains an extensive literary game in which the author's passion for butterflies, including the congruent joy and horror of the discovery and the necessary kill, has been transferred into Humbert's passion for nymphets, with Lolita as the butterfly.[7]

That the seemingly inscrutable Nabokov would write this essay and reprint it in several places surely suggests the dismay he must have felt to see how many readers, including some old friends, had taken the book solely on an erotic level. It should be clear that the butterfly motif was crucial to Nabokov's realization of the book—a

---

[6] Vladimir Nabokov, *Poems* (Garden City, N. Y., 1959), p. 22.

[7] Diana Butler, "Lolita Lepidoptera," *New World Writing 16* (Philadelphia, 1960), p. 60. I will not rehearse Miss Butler's findings, which seem incontestable, but rather confine myself to general remarks on the significance of the butterfly motif. Miss Butler, however, makes many lepidopterological errors.

psychic necessity, reinforcing in his mind the sense that, insofar as it
has a definable subject, *Lolita* is not merely about sexual perversion
but rather about love and the search for ineffable beauty, and as such,
like Wordsworth's *Prelude* and Proust's *Remembrance of Things
Past*, it is ultimately "about" its own creation. As Humbert says,
rather than describe the details of the seduction, "Anybody can
imagine those elements of animality. A greater endeavor lures me
on: to fix once for all the perilous magic of nymphets." (p. 136)
Later in the book he is more explicit about this "magic": "Indeed,
it may well be that the very attraction immaturity has for me lies not
so much in the limpidity of pure young forbidden fairy child beauty
as in the security of a situation where infinite perfections fill the gap
between the little given and the great promised—the great rose-grey
never-to-be-had." (p. 266) Humbert's desires are finally closer to those
of the poet than of the pervert, and not surprisingly, since they reflect,
darkly, in a crooked enough mirror, the artistic desires of his creator.

Like Joyce's use of the *Odyssey* in *Ulysses* and the Viconian scaf-
folding of *Finnegans Wake*, the butterfly pattern in *Lolita* is intricate, ingenious, and elaborate. Careful readers should be able to
identify it, for many of the lepidopteral descriptions of Lolita are
explicit, and a familiarity with Nabokov's other books, especially
Speak, Memory, should alert one to this possibility. The butterfly
game serves as a controlling metaphor that enriches *Lolita* in a more
fundamental and organic manner than the *Odyssey*'s effect on *Ulysses*.
Just as the nymph undergoes a metamorphosis in becoming the butterfly, so everything in *Lolita* is constantly in the process of metamorphosis, including the novel itself—a set of "notes" being compiled
by an imprisoned man during a fifty-six day period for possible use
at his trial, emerging as a book after his death, and then only after it
has passed through yet another stage, the nominal "editorship" of
John Ray, Jr. As Lolita turns from a girl into a woman, so Humbert's
lust becomes love, his sense of a "safely solipsized" Lolita (p. 62)
now replaced by his awareness that she was his "own creation" with
"no will, no consciousness—indeed, no life of her own" (p. 64),
that he did not know her (p. 286), and that their sexual intimacy
only isolated him more completely from the helpless girl. These
"metamorphoses" enable Humbert to transform a "crime" into a
redeeming work of art, and the reader has watched the chrysalis come
to life. As if in anticipation of *Lolita*, the narrator of *The Real Life
of Sebastian Knight* (1941) mentions the readers who "felt baffled
by [*The Prismatic Bezel's*] habit of metamorphosis" (p. 95), and

when Nabokov in his lectures at Cornell discussed "The theme of transformation" in R. L. Stevenson's *Dr. Jekyll and Mr. Hyde,* Gogol's *The Overcoat,* and Kafka's *The Metamorphosis,* he said that Stevenson's tale is a "thriller and mystery only in respect to artistic creativity. It is a phenomenon of style, a transformation through the art of writing." He likened the Jekyll-Hyde transformation to the metamorphosis of the larva to the pupa to the butterfly, and imagined Jekyll's final emergence from the melting and blackened features of the evil Hyde as "the rush of panic" which must accompany "the feeling of hatching." Once again, as in his book on Gogol, Nabokov has described his own performance by defining the art of another. As a metaphor for the artistic process, the nymph's cycle is a transcendent design.

There always will be readers who disapprove of such involuted methods. One can answer them briefly by focusing on their charges that the puns and networks of coincidence in Nabokov are gratuitous fun when, in fact, they are basic and essential—"Not flimsy nonsense," writes John Shade, "but a web of sense." (l. 810) The occurrence of "those dazzling coincidences that logicians loathe and poets love" (p. 33), given the infinitesimal number of possible combinations, goes beyond frivolity and defines a firmly held notion about "reality" and the probability of the wildly improbable. The insidious Clare Quilty is staying at The Enchanted Hunters when Lolita and Humbert consummate their relationship. Quilty names his play *The Enchanted Hunters,* adopts an anagram, Ted Hunter, as one of his many pseudonyms, and the married Lolita ends up living in a house on Hunter Road. These coincidences serve a twofold purpose: they at once point to the authorial consciousness that has plotted them, and they can be imagined as coordinates situated in time and space, marking the labyrinth from which a character cannot escape. An irrevocable destiny—or McFate, to use Humbert's jocular designation—seems confirmed at every turn. The hunter is indeed enchanted. The past merges with the present, and the vocabulary of time is only a convenient abstraction.

The reverberating significance of a meaningful pun in Nabokov is akin to coincidence: words move into words and words into worlds, to paraphrase John Shade. But what about the shallow playfulness in *Lolita,* Humbert's "daymares" as opposed to the resonant puns on his and Quilty's names? Not only do the puns afford pleasure, which, hopefully, is still one of the intentions of literature, but they are also thematically appropriate. The puns underline a central problem in

Lolita, for some readers have been more put off by Humbert's use of language than by his abuse of Lolita. Any full sense of *Lolita* depends on our understanding the function of Humbert's verbal vaudeville, his unique voice and idiom. One should not forget that "Humbert Humbert" is a pseudonym; his name is first presented to us in "editor" John Ray's quotation marks. "Is 'mask' the keyword?" Humbert asks (p. 55), and his rhetoric is a mask: "Imagine me, reader . . . masking the frenzy of my grief with a trembling ingratiating smile." (p. 249) After stating that Humbert's "bizarre cognomen is his own invention," John Ray adds, "of course, this mask—through which two hypnotic eyes seem to glow—had to remain unlifted in accordance with its wearer's wish." (p. 5) As usual, Ray is wrong, for although Humbert never reveals his "real" name, he does lift the mask once. As his narrative approaches the first conjugal night with Lolita, Humbert is overcome by anguish, and in the bare six lines of chapter twenty-six, the shortest "chapter" in the book, he loses control, and for a moment the mask drops:

> This daily headache in the opaque air of this tombal jail is disturbing, but I must persevere. Have written more than a hundred pages and not got anywhere yet. My calendar is getting confused. That must have been around August 15, 1947. Don't think I can go on. Heart, head—everything. Lolita, Lolita, Lolita, Lolita, Lolita, Lolita, Lolita, Lolita, Lolita. Repeat till the page is full, printer. (p. 111)

Not until the very end of the passage does the voice sound like Hum the Hummer, when the desperation of "Heart, head—everything" suddenly gives way to the resiliently comic command to the printer. In that one instant Humbert's masking has taken place before the reader, who has just had a fleeting look into those "two hypnotic eyes," and has seen the pain in them. *Lolita* is so deeply moving a novel because of our precise awareness of the great tension sustained between Humbert's mute despair and his compensatory jollity. "Crime and Pun" is one of the titles the murderous narrator of *Despair* considers for his manuscript, and it would serve Humbert just as well.

Language is as much a defense to Humbert as chess is to grandmaster Luzhin. In order to control his tombal "confession," Humbert must create and maintain a totally self-conscious narrative mode. Hardly under way, he nevertheless wonders if the reader "can still stand my style." (p. 12) Only by projecting it in audacious if not brutal humor can Humbert hope to face the horror implicit in his memories, and the controlling humor makes possible an act of recollection that is anything but tranquil. Even Humbert's worst puns distract him from his anguish and guilt, and help stay the heart trouble and the incipient madness (not the most "reliable" narrator, Humbert has been in several institutions) which would make it impossible to write the narrative now at hand. Humbert's Conception Park, Insomnia Lodge, Lake Climax, and St. Algebra (the girls' school) are thus all admittedly limp jokes, but they are necessary: "let me laugh a little, too, gentlemen," Humbert says, following a harmless pun, as he struggles to create a humorous pattern and ultimately an artistic order out of the wild disorder of his life. Humbert is fully aware of the willful capriciousness of his baroque language, and the verbal absurdities of his Double, Clare Quilty, represent his liberating act of self-parody.

II

Although Humbert offers "mask," *parody* is the "keyword" in *Lolita*, and it provides a key to all of Nabokov. Like Joyce, Nabokov has shown how parody may inform a high literary art, and parody figures in the design of each of his novels. *The Eye* parodies the nineteenth-century Romantic tale, such as V. F. Odoevsky's "The Brigadier," which is narrated by a ghost who has awakened after death to view his old life with new clarity, while *Laughter in the Dark* is a mercilessly cold mocking of the convention of the love triangle; *Despair* is cast as the kind of "cheap mystery" story the narrator's banal wife reads, though it evolves into something quite different; and *The Gift* parodies the major nineteenth-century Russian writers. *Invitation to a Beheading* and *Bend Sinister* are cast as mock anti-utopian novels, after the fashion of Zamiatin, while *Pnin* masquerades as an "academic novel" and turns out to parody the possibility of a novel's having a "reliable" narrator. Pnin's departure at the end mimics Chichikov's orbital exit from *Dead Souls*, just as the last paragraph of *The Gift* conceals a parody of a Pushkin stanza. The texture of Nabokov's parody is unique because, in addition to being a master parodist of literary styles, he is able to make brief references to another writer's themes or devices which are so telling in effect that Nabokov need not burlesque that writer's style. He not only parodies narrative clichés and outworn subject matter, but genres and prototypes of the novel. Because chapter four of *The Gift* is a mock literary biography, it anticipates the themes of Nabokov's major achievements, for he is continuously parodying the search for a verifiable truth—the autobiography, the biography, the exegesis, the detective story—and these generic "quests" will coalesce in one work, especially when the entire novel is conceptually a parody, as in *Lolita* and *Pale Fire*, Nabokov's masterpieces.

In form, *Pale Fire* is a grotesque scholarly edition, while *Lolita* is a burlesque of the confessional mode, the literary diary, the Romantic novel that chronicles the effects of a debilitating love, the *Doppelgänger* tale, and, in parts, a Duncan Hines tour of America conducted by a guide with a black imagination, a parodic case study, and, as the narrator of *The Real Life of Sebastian Knight* says of his half-brother's first novel, *The Prismatic Bezel*, "It is also a wicked imitation of many other . . . literary habit [s]." Knight's procedures summarize Nabokov's:

As often was the way with Sebastian Knight he used parody as a kind of springboard for leaping into the highest region of serious emotion. J. L. Coleman has called it "a clown developing wings, an angel mimicking a tumbler pigeon," and the metaphor seems to me very apt. Based cunningly on a parody of certain tricks of the literary trade, *The Prismatic Bezel* soars skyward. With something akin to fanatical hate Sebastian Knight was ever hunting out the things which had once been fresh and bright but which were now worn to a thread, dead things among living ones; dead things shamming life, painted and repainted, continuing to be accepted by lazy minds serenely unaware of the fraud. (p. 91)

"But all this obscure fun is, I repeat, only the author's springboard" (p. 92), says the narrator, whose tone is justifiably insistent, for although Nabokov is a virtuoso of the minor art of literary burlesque, which is at best a kind of literary criticism, he knows that the novelist who uses parody is under an obligation to engage the reader emotionally in a way that Max Beerbohm's *A Christmas Garland* does not. The description of *The Prismatic Bezel* and the remainder of chapter ten in *The Real Life of Sebastian Knight* indicate that Nabokov is fully aware of this necessity, and, like Knight, he has succeeded in making parody a "springboard." There is thus an important paradox implicit in Nabokov's most audacious parodies: *Lolita* makes fun of Dostoevsky's *Notes from Underground*, but Humbert's pages are indeed notes from underground in their own right, and Clare Quilty is both a parody of the Double as a convention of modern fiction, and a Double who formulates the horror in Humbert's life, just as *Pale Fire* is at once a parody of mad and mindless scholarship—a *Tale of the Tub* for our time—and, to those who identify the distinctive "voices" in the Botkin-Kinbote-King Charles-authorial voice confluence, a haunting revelation of a tormented mind's efforts to order chaos, and a bracing vision of its success.

With the possible exception of Joyce, Nabokov is alone among modern writers in his ability to make parody and pathos converge and sometimes coincide. Joyce comes closest to this in *Ulysses*, not in the coldly brilliant "Oxen of the Sun" section, but in the "Cyclops" episode in Barney Kiernan's pub, which oscillates between parodic passages and a straightforward rendering of the dialogue and action; in the "Nausicäa" episode on the beach, which first projects Gerty MacDowell's point of view in a style parodying sentimental ladies' magazine fiction, and midway shifts to Bloom's non-parodic stream-of-consciousness; and in parts of the "Hades" Nighttown section, especially the closing apparition of Bloom's dead son, Rudy. Nabokov has built on Joyce in developing parody as a novelistic form, for in *Lolita* and *Pale Fire*, which are totally parodic in form, and may be the finest comic novels since *Ulysses*, the parody and pathos are always congruent, rather than adjacent to one another —as though the *entire* "Nausicäa" or "Cyclops" episodes were cast as parody, without in any way diminishing our sense of Bloom's suffering, or that Joyce had been able to express something of Bloom's humanity in the "Oxen of the Sun" *tour de force*. Nabokov has summarized in a phrase his triumph in *Lolita* and *Pale Fire*. Just before Humbert takes Lolita into their room at The Enchanted Hunters hotel in what is to be the most crucial event in his life, Humbert comments, "Parody of a hotel corridor. Parody of silence and death." (p. 121) To paraphrase Marianne Moore's well-known line that poetry is "imaginary gardens with real toads in them," Nabokov's is a parody of death with real suffering in it. With characteristic self-awareness, Nabokov defines in *The Gift* the essence of his own art: "The spirit of parody always goes along with genuine poetry."

This spirit in Nabokov represents not merely a set of techniques, but an attitude towards experience, a means of discovering the nature of that experience. *The Prismatic Bezel* is aptly titled; a "bezel" is the sloping edge on a cutting tool or the oblique side of a gem, and the luminous bezel of Nabokov's parody can cut in any direction, often turning in upon itself as self-parody. In *The Gift*, Fyodor, the young poet who is writing a mock biography of Cherneshevsky, says:

I want to keep everything as it were on the very brink of parody. You know those idiotic 'biographies romancées' where Byron is coolly slipped a dream extracted from one of his own poems? And there must be on the other hand an abyss of seriousness, and I must make my way along this narrow ridge between my own truth and a caricature of it. (p. 212)

This is an excellent description of the tightrope act Nabokov performs along the "narrow ridge" that extends through his fiction. He is constantly slipping into his books "dream[s] extracted," as it were, from one of his or his character's "own poems" in order to create self-parodies that often function in the manner which William Empson, in *Some Versions of Pastoral,* ascribes to the double plot in Shakespeare. According to Empson, the parodic double plot in Shakespearean drama releases the audience from the temptation or need to identify with one character. Having responded imaginatively in one way to a situation, the viewer or reader is then free to experience "the chief other response possible" and to focus on something other than the "psychology" of a character.

Parody is in *Lolita* the major means by which Nabokov breaks the circuit of reader-character identification one associates with the conventional novel. In his other novels this is accomplished by a complicated sequence of interacting devices which, by constantly reminding the reader of the novelist's presence in and above his book as a puppeteer in charge of everything, establishes the fiction as total artifice.[8] In this sense "mask" is the "keyword" in Nabokov, and one is continually aware of Nabokov's masked participation in his fiction, whether as chess player, actor, ventriloquist, conjurer, or as what Nabokov calls "an anthropomorphic deity impersonated by me"—the intruding authorial consciousness which eventually takes over the novel altogether, involuting it, denying it any reality except that of "book." There is intrusive direct address to the reader in *Lolita,* and it is important, but it is still in the narrator's voice rather than in the distinctively different voice of the "deity," as in *Invitation to a Beheading, Bend Sinister,* and *Pale Fire.* Even when Humbert momentarily loses control and lets the mask slip, one glimpses his despair, but not the "real" Humbert nor the manipulative author. As Nabokov says in chapter five of *Gogol* (1944), analogously discussing Akaky Akakyvich and the "holes" and "gaps" in the narrative texture of *The Overcoat:* "We did not expect that, amid the whirling masks, one mask would turn out to be a real face, *or at least the place where that face ought to be*" (italics mine).

---

[8] See Part II of my essay, "Nabokov's Puppet Show," *op. cit.,* 26–31.

Because *Lolita* is Nabokov's only uninterrupted narrative since *Despair* (1934) and Humbert his most "humanized" character since Luzhin (1930)—more so even than Pnin, who is the narrator's re-creation of other people's impersonations of Pnin—readers must consider the esthetic implications of parody, or they are liable to approach *Lolita* as though it were *The Turn of the Screw*. By definition, parody and self-parody suspend the possibility of a fully "realistic" fiction, since their referents are either other literary works or themselves, and not the world of objective reality which the "realist" or "impressionist" tries to reproduce. Only an authorial sensibility, outside the book, can be said to have ordered the texture of parody; the dizzying, multiform perspectives it achieves are beyond the capacities of any "point of view" within the book. In the terms of Henry James or Percy Lubbock, Humbert's is finally *not* a credible point of view. Aubrey McFate, who is following Humbert, turns up in the middle of the neatly alphabetized Ramsdale class list which Humbert incorporates in his narrative, thus undercutting the inviolable "reality" of much more than that list. (p. 54) The "coincidences," as has already been suggested, are not simply a matter of McFate's ominous work, since McFate only "exists" insofar as he has been invented.

Nabokov has laid into the parodic design of *Lolita* an elaborate system of involutions which, like the network of coincidences, helps to close the circuits by demonstrating that everything is being manipulated, all is a fiction, thus parodying the reader's desire for verisimilitude. Typical of these inlays is Clare Quilty's entry in *Who's Who in the Limelight* (a mother lode of involutions), where he is listed as the author of *The Lady Who Loved Lightning*. (p. 33) Almost two hundred pages later, during a thunderstorm, Lolita comments gratuitously, "I am not a lady and do not love lightning" (p. 222), an involuted cross-reference which reveals a capacity for organization and order that is completely beyond the possibilities of Humbert's alleged unrevised "first draft" manuscript, which has supposedly been composed furiously over a period of less than two months. While he recounts his first night with Lolita he tries not to lose control of the language, but at the same time manages to tell how he was served by Mr. Swine, the room clerk, who is assisted by Mr. Potts, who can't find any cots because Swine has dispatched them to the Swoons. (p. 120) Like the presence in the novel of Quilty's anagrammatic mistress, "Vivian Darkbloom" (Vladimir Nabokov), the verbal patterning points beyond his anguish to "Someone else [who] is in the know," to quote an intruding voice in *Bend Sinister*.

Since it is Nabokov and not Humbert who is the expert lepidopterist, the most significant authorial patterning in *Lolita* is the butterfly motif; it enables Nabokov to leave behind on Humbert's pages a trail of his own phosphorescent fingerprints. Nabokov himself casually underscored its considerable esthetic relevance when I visited him in Switzerland to interview him for this issue and in regard to my study of his work. As an example of the kind of humorous but telling detail whose significance critics often miss, I had singled out the moment in the Humbert-Quilty confrontation when Quilty notes that he is known as "the American Maeterlinck," but quickly adds, "Maeterlinck-Schmetterling, says I." (p. 303) Nabokov nodded and with complete seriousness said, "Yes. That's the most important phrase in the chapter." At first this may seem to be an extreme statement, but in the context of the involuted patterning it is perfectly just, for by mentioning the German word for *butterfly*, Quilty has superimposed the author's watermark on the scene, and it is the sole butterfly reference in the chapter.

Nabokov thus appears everywhere in the texture of *Lolita* but never in the text, although he "com[es] damn close to it" as he lures the reader on. As Humbert says of "Detective Trapp" (Quilty):

. . . he succeeded in thoroughly enmeshing me and my thrashing anguish in his demoniacal game. With infinite skill, he swayed and staggered, and regained an impossible balance, always leaving me with the sportive hope —if I may use such a term in speaking of betrayal, fury, desolation, horror and hate—that he might give himself away next time. He never did— though coming damn close to it. We all admire the spangled acrobat with classical grace meticulously walking his tight rope in the talcum light; but how much rarer art there is in the sagging rope expert wearing scare-crow clothes and impersonating a grotesque drunk. *I* should know. (p. 251)

"Trapp"'s balancing act lucidly describes the performance of both the narrator and his creator, whose novels, by virtue of their delusive, parodic form, are in themselves vast and grotesque "impersonations." To take them literally is possibly to suffer feelings of "betrayal, fury, [or] desolation," for the parody-novel fashions a self-contained world in a book; but the reader, in trying to make this kind of novel conform to his vision, is continually manipulated by the book, trapped by the parodies which reveal the speciousness or superficiality of his assumptions, the commonplace qualities of his expectations.[9] At the conclusion of his dramatic reunion with Lolita, Humbert says, "Then I pulled out my automatic—I mean, this is the kind of fool thing a reader might suppose I did. It never even occurred to me to do it." (p. 282) By creating a reality which is a fiction, but a fiction that is able to mock the reader, the author has demonstrated the fiction of "reality,"[10] and the reader who accepts these implications may even have experienced a change in consciousness.

The detachment created by parody and self-parody ultimately defines a way of viewing and judging the self. Characters (and their creators) can never objectively observe their own existence, but self-imitation is one way towards self-reflection and an expanded consciousness. Humbert describes this process and maintains an appropriately Nabokovian equilibrium between the "truth and a caricature of it" when he summarizes the essay he published in the *Cantrip Review*, "Mimir and Memory" (a "cantrip" is a charm, spell or trick, and describes Lolita's hold on him, while "Mimir" is a giant in Norse mythology who lived by the well at the root of Yggdrasill, the great tree symbolizing the universe. By drinking its water, he knew the past and future). The essay suggests a "theory of perceptual time based on the circulation of the blood and conceptually depending (to fill up this nutshell) on the mind's being conscious of its own self, thus creating a continuous spanning of two points (the storable future and the stored past)." (p. 262)

Although Nabokov has called attention to the elements of parody in his work, he has repeatedly denied the relevance of satire. One can understand why he says "I have neither the intent nor the temperament of a moral or social satirist," for he eschews the overtly moral stance of the satirist who offers "to mend the world." Nabokov might not argue, however, if *Pale Fire* were placed in the tradition of the Menippean satire as it is defined by Northrop Frye, and, Nabokov's denials notwithstanding, Humbert's observations of American morals and mores are satirical, the product of his maker's moral sensibility, although this "satire" is over-emphasized by readers who

---

[9] The reader-manipulation effected by the two "false endings" on the last page of the story "Signs and Symbols" (in *Nabokov's Dozen*) telescopes the methods of the Nabokovian trap-play and thus provides an excellent introduction to the monstrous trap that is *Lolita*.

[10] This involuted process is best described by Jorge Luis Borges in "Partial Magic in the *Quixote*," in *Labyrinths* (Norfolk, 1962).

fail to recognize the extent of the parody, or its full implications.

In the course of showing us our landscape in all its natural beauty and meretricious glory, Humbert satirizes American songs, ads, movies, magazines, products, tourist attractions, summer camps, Dude Ranches, hotels, and motels, as well as the Good Housekeeping Syndrome (*Your Home is You* is one of Charlotte Haze's essential volumes) and the cant of progressive educationists and child guidance pontificators. Nabokov offers us a grotesque parody of a "good relationship," for Humbert and Lo are "pals" with a vengeance; *Know Your Own Daughter* is one of the books which Humbert consults. Yet Humbert's terrible demands notwithstanding, she is as insensitive as children are to their actual parents; sexuality aside, she demands anxious parental placation in a too typically American way, and affords Nabokov an ideal opportunity to comment on the Teen and Sub-Teen Tyranny. It is poetic justice that Lolita should seduce Humbert at The Enchanted Hunters hotel; the irony is obvious, but telling. Nabokov underscores his point with a resonant pun, characteristic of both himself and Joyce. The seduction takes place in the town of Briceland (note the *i* rather than y). Anyone over thirty should recall the popular weekly radio program of the 'forties, "Baby Snooks," starring the late Fanny Brice. The show featured only Baby Snooks, a sappy but demanding little girl of indeterminate age, who spoke a patois of baby talk and teen jargon, and her helpless, ineffectual Daddums (twice Humbert calls himself this). Year after year the program celebrated the various ways the tyrannical Baby Snooks could victimize her poor Daddy. The town of Briceland is well named. Nabokov's book is Baby Snooks and Daddums in apotheosis; Lolita is a Baby Snooks who looms threateningly high above us all. No one would deny that ours is a child-centered culture in deep trouble. "Tristram in Movielove," remarks Humbert, and Nabokov has responded to those various travesties of behavior which too many Americans recognize as tenable examples of significant reality. A gloss on this aspect of *Lolita* is provided by "Ode to a Model," a poem which Nabokov published the same year as *Lolita* (1955).

Yet Nabokov's attitude towards both America and Lolita are similarly ambivalent; "there is a queer, tender charm about that mythical nymphet," he said in an interview, and Humbert's satires are effected with an almost loving care. But there is nothing ambivalent about Nabokov's parody of the "Viennese witch doctor." Proclaiming himself "King Sigmund the Second," Humbert mounts a frontal attack on many orthodox Freudian views, and the parodies are easily discerned. Nabokov burlesques the case study by purposely providing the childhood "trauma" which supposedly accounts for Humbert's nympholepsy: the incomplete coitus which the thirteen-year old Humbert experienced on the French Riviera with Annabel, who died four months later (p. 15). The incident seems to be a sly fictive transmutation of Nabokov's own considerably more innocent childhood infatuation with Colette (chapter six, *Speak, Memory*). When earnest readers, nurtured on the "standardized symbols of the psychoanalytic racket" (p. 287), leap to make the association between the two episodes—as several have done—and immediately deduce that *Lolita* is surely autobiographical, then the trap has been sprung: their wantonly reductive gesture justifies the need for just such a parody as Nabokov's. With a cold literary perversity, Nabokov has demonstrated the falseness of their "truth"; the implications are considerable. Even the exegetic act of searching for the "meaning" of *Lolita* by trying to unfold the butterfly pattern becomes a parody of the expectations of the most sophisticated reader, who finds he is chasing a mocking inversion of the "normal" Freudian direction of symbols which, once identified, may still remain mysterious, or explain very little.

The reader who has been unhappily deceived by the autobiographical trap or the butterfly motif may justifiably feel that he has been checkmated, for by reading *Lolita* carefully he is involved in a game, in the fullest and most serious sense. "Darling, this is only a game!" says Humbert at the outset (p. 22), and the pun on his name includes the game of *ombre*.[11] The readers who say they admire Nabokov in spite of his games are only demonstrating the failure of their responses. A hard distinction between play and seriousness would vitiate the effect of *Lolita*,[12] and the central importance of the game-element in Nabokov is expressed in *Speak, Memory* when the description of his composition of chess problems turns out to serve as well for his fiction: "Themes in chess, it may be explained, are such devices as forelaying, withdrawing, pinning, unpinning and so forth. . . . Deceit, to the point of diabolism, and originality, grad-

---

[11] *Ombre* is played in Canto III of *The Rape of the Lock*. For a summary of the "game" in *Lolita*, so uncannily accurate that Nabokov must have had them in mind, see lines 87–100.

[12] Apologies for the game-element in Nabokov should not have to be made. Those who find the play-concept antithetical to "seriousness" would do well to read J. Huizinga's *Homo Ludens*.

ing into the grotesque, were my notions of strategy." (p. 219) He explains that "competition in chess problems is not really between White and Black but between the composer and the hypothetical solver," just as in first-rate fiction "the real clash" is between the author and the reader, rather than between the characters. (p. 220) The "delusive opening moves, false scents, [and] specious lines of play" which characterize the chess problem are effected by parody in *Lolita*. The subject matter of *Lolita* is in itself a bravura and "delusive opening move"—a withdrawn promise of pornography. The first one hundred or so pages of *Lolita* are often erotic—Lolita on Humbert's lap, for instance—but starting with the seduction scene, Nabokov withholds explicit sexual descriptions, at which point Humbert, trying to draw the reader into the vortex of the parody, exhorts us to "Imagine me: I shall not exist if you do not imagine me." (p. 131) "I am not concerned with so-called 'sex' at all," Humbert says (p. 136); on the contrary, Nabokov is very much concerned with it, but with the reader's expectations rather than Humbert's machinations. "Anybody can imagine those elements of animality," he says, and yet a great many readers wished that he had done it for them, enough to have kept *Lolita* at the top of the bestseller list for a year, although librarians reported that many readers never finished the novel. The critics and readers who complain that the second half of *Lolita* is less interesting are not aware of the possible significance of their admission. Their desire for highbrow pornography is doubled in Clare Quilty, whose main hobby is making pornographic films. At the end of the novel, Lolita tells Humbert that Quilty forced her to star in one of his unspeakable "sexcapades," and more than one reader has unconsciously wished that Quilty had been the narrator, his unseen movie the novel. Two of Quilty's pseudonymous hotel guestbook registrations list his home as "Larousse, Ill." and "Hoaxton, Eng.," but the acute way in which Quilty parodies the reader's voyeurism suggests that the elements of ruse and hoax are deserved and entirely in earnest. Puns thus summarize the function of parody as game: "Lolita was playing a double game," says Humbert, referring to Lolita's tennis and to the *Doppelgänger* parody, and Humbert's search for his Double, Quilty, whom he at first believes to be "Detective Gustave Trapp," turns out to be the detective trap. The novel becomes a gameboard on which, through parody, Nabokov assaults the conventions and worst pretentions of his readers.

By naming Humbert's lost love "Annabel Lee," Nabokov fuses Freud with Poe. Humbert's extensive "search for a Kingdom by the

Sea, a Sublimated Riviera, or whatnot" (p. 169), is very funny, but
the parody finally reveals the painful consequences of any attempt
to relive the past. Poe is everywhere in Lolita,[13] and Humbert several
times rightly identifies himself with A. Gordon Pym, an earlier first-
person narrator whose tale resonates far beyond its initial conception
as burlesque and hoax. And "Edgar H. Humbert's" (as he once calls
himself) most bravura Poe parodies involve Clare Quilty, whose
mouldering mansion, Pavor [Latin for panic] Manor, burlesques Poe's
falling House of Usher. In modeling Quilty on the Doppelgänger of
the Gothic tale, Nabokov invokes R. L. Stevenson's Dr. Jekyll and
Mr. Hyde, a favorite of his, Hans Christian Andersen's "The Shadow,"
and Poe's "William Wilson." The course of Lolita and the Humbert-
Quilty relationship are telescoped in "William Wilson," which is a
first-person confession by a pseudonymous narrator who "fled in vain"
from the Double who pursued him from school to school, a rival in
scholarship rather than love. Wilson's "shadow" wears the same
clothes as he does (Humbert and Quilty share a purple bathrobe),
and when, after traveling to Paris, Rome, Vienna, Berlin, and Moscow,
Wilson cannot rid himself of his "brother," he kills him, just as
Humbert is "free to destroy my brother." "But all this obscure fun is,
I repeat, only the author's springboard." (SK, p. 91)

The Doppelgänger motif brings to mind Dostoevsky, who has
long been one of Nabokov's primary targets. In addition to his
"Dostoevskian grin" (p. 72), Humbert experiences several fits, and
like many of Nabokov's isolated or incarcerated characters, his gloomy
good looks are eventually enhanced by the requisite dark, Dostoevskian
beard. One of Dostoevsky's obsessive images, the spider, is parodied by
Humbert. In Crime and Punishment, Svidrigailov imagines eternity
as a roomful of spiders, while in Notes from Underground and The
Brothers Karamazov the spider personifies evil and lust, respectively.
Awaiting his "warm-colored prey," Humbert is like an "inflated pale
spider" in an old garden (p. 51). He is "Humbert the Wounded
Spider" (p. 56), down whose back crawl "cold spiders of panic."
(p. 142) These references are but part of a larger parodic scheme.
Most Dostoevskian of all is Nabokov's use of the confessional mode.

---

[13] Several of the Poe allusions have also been identified by Elizabeth Phillips, "The Hocus-Pocus of Lolita," Literature and Psychology, X, 97–101, and
Arthur F. DuBois, "Poe and Lolita," CEA Critic, XXVI, vi, 1, 7; neither has
made critical sense of them. Dr. Phillips' attempts are excessive, Mr. DuBois
throws up his hands in despair.

"Heart-to-heart talks, confessions in the Dostoevskian manner are also not in my line," he says (*SM*, p. 215), and Dostoevsky's "sensitive murderers . . . are not to be endured for one moment—by this reader anyway," he told an interviewer. But Humbert is the ultimate in sensitive murderers, and, as he says, "You can always count on a murderer for a fancy prose style," especially when he has an urge to confess. "I thought I would use these notes in toto at my trial, to save not my head, of course, but my soul," Humbert says at the end of *Lolita* (p. 310). The "of course" reveals the play-spirit, and underscores how, by casting Humbert's tale as a mock confession, Nabokov lets Dostoevsky plot the rules of the game and then beats "old Dusty" at his own game. Again, the process is best described when Nabokov compares the composition of a chess problem to "the writing of one of those incredible novels where the author, in a fit of lucid madness, has set himself certain unique rules that he observes, certain nightmare obstacles that he surmounts, with the zest of a deity building a live world from the most unlikely ingredients." (*SM*, p. 220)

Lolita's parodic design also includes another convention allied with the confession—the literary journal or diary. Nabokov regards with profound skepticism the possibilities of autobiographical revelation. When Fyodor shaves himself in *The Gift*, "A pale self-portrait looked out of the mirror with the serious eyes of all self-portraits" (p. 120); Nabokov does not abide such portraits. "Manifold self-awareness" (*SM*, p. 156) is not to be achieved through solemn introspection, certainly not through the diarist's compulsive egotism, candid but totally self-conscious self-analysis, carefully created "honesty," willful irony, and studied self-deprecation. Nabokov burlesqued the literary diary as far back as 1934. Near the end of *Despair*, Hermann's first-person narrative "degenerates into a diary"—"the lowest form of literature" (p. 218)—and this early parody is fully realized in *Lolita*, especially in chapter eleven, Part One, when Humbert incorporates into his narrative a diary "destroyed" five years before. His entire prison "journal" seems to be written before our eyes. "I notice the slip of my pen in the preceding paragraph, but please do not correct it, Clarence" [his lawyer and caretaker of the manuscript], Humbert remarks. (p. 34) Several other "mistakes" are left intact, thus creating the illusion that Humbert's manuscript is a first draft, unaltered, written in great haste but with passion, and the hapless literal-minded reader may embrace it as the most "sincere" form of self-portraiture possible. But of course all the worst propensities of the diarist are embodied in Humbert's rhetoric, parodying the First Person Singular's almost inevitable solipsism and most tendentious assumptions about Self, and the reader who is late in realizing this has had his own assumptions parodied.

Nabokov has rejected a romantic or transcendental notion of self; another of Humbert's jocose but significant appellations is Jean-Jacques Humbert. The unified, definitive self is a joke to Nabokov, for the infinite possibilities of its development are circumscribed by the warped mirror in which we perceive ourselves and the world. Unlike those modern writers who continually bemoan the loss of the self in the modern world, Nabokov accepts the fragmentation, and within the terrifying limitations he coolly acknowledges, Nabokov lets Humbert define himself however he must, and fulfill his human condition, albeit obsessional and aberrant. The reader who can follow the process of involution and calmly play the games effected by parody, and realize their implications, will not worry whether Nabokov "approves" or "disapproves" of his characters.

What is extraordinary about *Lolita* is not the presence or absence of the author's "moral position," but the way in which Nabokov enlists us, against our will, on Humbert's side. "Pity is the password," says John Shade, speaking for his creator. Nabokov purposely takes a shocking subject in *Lolita*, and when we are sympathetic to Humbert, Nabokov has successfully expanded our potential for compassion, and has demonstrated that the certainty of our moral feelings is far more tenuous than we ever care to admit. We know exactly what Nabokov means about the contest between the author and the reader when we almost find ourselves wishing Humbert well during his agonizing first night with Lolita at The Enchanted Hunters, or appreciating Humbert's situation when the drugged Lolita occupies an "unfair amount of pillow." (p. 131) "Mesmer Mesmer" is one of the pseudonyms Humbert considered but rejected. It would be a fitting cognomen, given the power and effect of his rhetoric, since Humbert has figuratively made the reader his accomplice in both statutory rape and murder. Needless to say, the rhetoric of morality can be just as manipulative, and what is worse, it may not connect meaningfully with emotion of any kind. Because Lolita seduces Humbert she might seem to be the agent of immorality, but the irony is another trap in the game: this is just the kind of easy release from culpability which we are too ready to accept; it does not mitigate the existence of their ensuing two years together, nor the fact that Humbert has denied Lolita her youth, whatever its qualities may be. It should be clear that when Nabokov says that there is "No moral in tow" in *Lolita,* he is not denying it any moral resonance, but simply asserting that his intentions are not didactic. (p. 316)

Lolita is a moral novel in the fullest sense. Humbert is both victimizer and victim, culprit and judge. Throughout the narrative he is literally and figuratively pursued by his Double, Clare Quilty, who is by turns ludicrous and absurd, sinister and grotesque. Prior to his full-dress appearance in chapter thirty-five, Part Two, when he is killed by Humbert, Quilty is seen or alluded to more than fifty times, not including the several references to Aubrey McFate (as Hum "dub[s] that devil of mine" [p. 58]). Although Quilty is usually not mentioned by name, direct clues are planted through allusions to his uncle, Dr. Ivor Quilty, who is the Hazes' neighbor and dentist, and in Humbert's mention of *Who's Who in the Limelight,* which includes an entry under "Quilty, Clare, American dramatist," where he is listed as the author of *Fatherly Love* and *The Little Nymph.* (p. 33)[14] For a while Humbert is certain that his "shadow" and nemesis is his Swiss cousin, Detective Trapp, and when Lolita agrees and says, "Perhaps he is Trapp," she is summarizing Quilty's role in the novel. (p. 221) So complete is the respective entrapment of both Humbert and the reader that hardly ten or fifteen pages can go by in the course of Part One without Quilty's fleeting presence, and in Part Two he becomes omnipresent, for even after killing him, Humbert still feels "all covered with Quilty." The creator of "private movies" of Sade's *Justine* is always in the wings, so to speak, because he formulates Humbert's sense of guilt and the reader's prurient curiosity, and his name lends itself to obvious but significant wordplay: Clare Quilty is clearly guilty.[15]

Humbert knows he is clearly guilty, though he goes about saying it in oblique and unexpected ways. As his narrative draws to a

---

[14] Since space limitations prevent any full explication of the labyrinth of Quilty references, I will provide page references and invite readers to embark on what Humbert calls "that cryptogrammic paper chase": pp. 6, 33, 34, 45, 65, 66, 71, 80, 91, 115, 123, 128–129, 140, 141; [Part Two] 158, 161, 165, 172, 188, 198, 202, 204, 205, 209–211, 213, 215, 217–225, 229, 230–231, 234, 237, 239–240, 243–245, 248–252, 264, 274–275, 277–278, 292–293, 295–307, 308, and 311. McFate appears on pp. 54, 58, 109, 118, 212–213, 253, and 258.

[15] The pun is also pointed out by Page Stegner in *Escape into Aesthetics: The Art of Vladimir Nabokov* (New York, 1966), p. 104. Since Mr. Stegner has been generous to me in his preface and in a footnote to his *Lolita* chapter, regarding my influence on his work both in and out of the classroom, let me say that he and I have happily shared some of our insights, which may be credited to spontaneous combustion as well as to formal "influences."

close, Humbert's stance becomes increasingly "moral," but readers must be wary of the most overtly confessional passages, such as Humbert's re-creation of the crucial scene in which, after a three-year search, he confronts a pregnant ex-nymphet and, in a long passage which should not be excised, realizes that as "clearly as I know I am to die, that I loved her more than anything I had ever seen or imagined on earth," in spite of her "ruined looks and her adult, rope-veined narrow hands and her goose-flesh white arms." (p. 279)[16] It would be an understatement to say that the tone of the entire passage is ambiguous: the baby's dream, the injunction to an imaginary judge and jury, the interpolations in French, the parodic echo of Billy Graham's exhortation ("Make those twenty-five steps. Now"), and the purposeful banality of Humbert's promise ("And we shall live happily ever after") almost annihilate Humbert's declaration of love, but not quite. Miraculously enough, one believes in his love, not because of any confession, but in spite of it. "I had always thought that wringing one's hands was a fictional gesture," Humbert says (p. 85), and the comic turns are a protection against such rhetorical gestures and serve to isolate, if only for a moment, the arresting image of a wan and helpless girl.

Humbert's fullest expressions of "grief" are qualified, if not undercut completely, and these passages represent a series of traps in which Nabokov again parodies the reader's expectations by having Humbert say what the reader wants to hear. "I was a pentapod monster, but I loved you. I was despicable and brutal, and turpid, and everything" (p. 286); it is easy to confess, but the moral vocabulary we employ so readily may go no deeper than Humbert's parody of it. Although Humbert "quote[s] an old poet," "The moral sense in mortals is the duty/ We have to pay on mortal sense of beauty," one may wonder if he does indeed pay any duty. (p. 285) The payment is in fact exacted throughout the narrative, and is in part expressed in the grotesque gyrations of Humbert's tone: "Ah, gentle drivers gliding through summer's black nights, what frolics, what twists of lust, you might see from your impeccable highways if Kumfy Kabins were suddenly drained of their pigments and became as transparent as boxes of glass." (p. 119) Gentle readers gliding through Humbert's prose are similarly subjected to jolting twists of tone—a rhetorical trapdoor that opens with absurd suddenness, an

---

[16] The complete passage on which I am commenting runs from the middle of p. 279 to the middle of p. 280.

unexpected downhill slide, a lyrical or humorous lift that momentarily relaxes the tension, then, without warning, another trapdoor.
Such passages are free of any transitional phrases that might allow a
logical and gradual shift in tone; the effect can be chilling. "She was
very tall," Humbert says of Jean Farlow, "wore either slacks with
sandals or billowing skirts with ballet slippers, drank any strong liquor
in any amount, had had two miscarriages, wrote stories about ani-
mals, painted, as the reader knows, landscapes, was already nursing
the cancer that was to kill her at thirty-three, and was hopelessly unattractive to me." (p. 106) The sudden oscillations between the hor-
rific and the humorous catch our laughter short, creating a tension
that Humbert's jollity can never quite release; what Nabokov has
called Humbert's "rhetorical venom"[17] is turned back upon the narrator, affording an implicit commentary on his own acts.

"We continued our grotesque journey," Humbert says at one
point, and the summary adjective is well-chosen, for the ultimate
morality of *Lolita* is expressed through the grotesque. Those who are
uneasy with Nabokov the *immoraliste* may find necessary solace in
the carefully manipulated changes on the grotesque which proliferate
in *Lolita*. Humbert's self-disgust and loathing and guilt are projected
into almost all the so-called human beings Humbert "sees" or, more
accurately, reports having seen: Quilty; Gaston Godin; Miss Opposite,
the crippled neighbor; random carhops, bellboys, and parking-lot
attendants; the room clerk, Mr. Swine; the old barber in Kasbeam
(p. 215); and Dick Schiller, Lolita's almost deaf husband, who is
assisted by a one-armed young man named Bill, of whom Humbert
comments, "It was then noticed that one of the few thumbs remaining to Bill was bleeding (not such a wonder-worker at all)." (p. 275)
The grotesque is meaningfully present in the most casual of encounters, as when Frank, a motel attendant, stands in the doorway, his
hand on its jamb:

At twenty paces Frank used to look a mountain of health; at five, as
now, he was a ruddy mosaic of scars—had been blown through a wall over-
seas; but despite nameless injuries he was able to man a tremendous truck,
fish, hunt, drink, and buoyantly dally with roadside ladies. That day,
either because it was such a great holiday, or simply because he wanted
to divert a sick man, he had taken off the glove he usually wore on his
left hand (the one pressing against the side of the door) and revealed to

---

[17] Foreword to *Despair*, p. 9.

the fascinated sufferer not only an entire lack of fourth and fifth fingers, but also a naked girl, with cinnabar nipples and indigo delta, charmingly tattooed on the back of his crippled hand, its index and middle digit making her legs while his wrist bore her flower-crowned head. Oh, delicious . . . reclining against the woodwork, like some sly fairy. (p. 247)

As Humbert quietly says to Lolita when they notice the fragmented and surreal limbs of a department store mannikin, "Look well. Is not that a good symbol of something or other?" (p. 228) But this potential booby trap is only a dud, for it *is* a good symbol, in a refreshingly direct way, and Humbert is only dissembling, though symbol-mongering critics may accept the warning. The entire physical world of *Lolita* seems to be maimed, and the animate and inanimate share each other's properties in startling and unsettling ways. The car which runs over Charlotte Haze has doors "open like wings," and the driver's old father lies on the lawn in a faint, "like a death-size wax figure," an "old man-doll," whom a nurse "watered on the green bank where he lay." (p. 100) Even Humbert's car limps. (p. 258) The hunchbacks, the tennis-playing "Boschian cripples" (p. 237), the broken nose of a man wiping down Hum's windshield, Humbert's terrifying dream of Lolita (p. 256), his self-styled animal characteristics of ape, spider, and octopus—the possible parodic allusions to Poe, Dostoevsky, and Stevenson notwithstanding—and the numerous other seemingly gratuitous grotesque details are all metaphoric for the horror implicit in Humbert's life, for his suffering, his sense of shame and guilt and self-hate. "And I have still other smothered memories," says Humbert towards the end of *Lolita*, "now unfolding themselves into limbless monsters of pain." (p. 286)

Thus Nabokov uses the grotesque to express the anguish behind Humbert's rhetoric, the pain at the center of his playfulness, the price he must pay for having loved the way he was fated to love; one should not forget that Humbert dies of a coronary shortly after finishing his "book." Because he knows that he has treated Lolita like a thing, Humbert's world seems to have been reduced to monstrous "thinghood," and his grotesque projections are by way of his "confession": " 'Did you happen to see—' [Lolita] I asked of a hunchback sweeping the floor . . . He had, the old lecherer." (p. 225) Although the mask has not been removed, it has been penetrated, for the "slipperyself" 's moral judgments on its "public" acts have been transposed to the scene—inscape as landscape—and Nabokov is sly enough to have Humbert say something almost to that effect: "I am afraid, Clarence . . . I did not keep any notes, and have at my disposal only an atrociously crippled tour book in three volumes, almost a symbol of my torn and tattered past." (p. 156) Nabokov has parodied all "literary" confessions that would offer a strident and rhetorical experession of egotism as a revelation of the soul, and at the same time has succeeded in suggesting the deepest reaches of that soul. In their own way, Humbert's "tragic notes" are indeed from underground, but only because they embody both the "truth and a caricature of it."

This hazardous equipoise is also sustained in the doubling of Quilty and Humbert, for Quilty is at once a projection of Humbert's guilt and a parody of the psychological Double. The Double motif figures prominently throughout Nabokov, from the early 'thirties in *Despair* and *Laughter in the Dark* (where the Albinus-Axel Rex pairing rehearses the Humbert-Quilty doubling), to *Sebastian Knight* and on through *Bend Sinister*, the story "Scenes from the Life of a Double Monster," *Lolita*, *Pnin*, and *Pale Fire*, which offers a monumental doubling (or, more properly, tripling). It is probably the most intricate and profound of all *Doppelgänger* novels, written at precisely the time when it seemed that the Double theme had been exhausted in modern literature, and this achievement was very likely made possible by Nabokov's elaborate parody of the theme in *Lolita*, which renewed his sense of the artistic efficacy of another literary "thing which had once been fresh and bright but which was now worn to a thread." (*SK*, p. 91)[18]

By making Quilty *too* clearly guilty, Nabokov is assaulting the convention of the good and evil "dual selves" found in the traditional Double tale. Humbert would let some of us believe that when he kills Quilty in chapter thirty-five, Part Two, the good poet has exorcised the bad monster, but the two are finally not to be clearly distinguished: when Humbert and Quilty wrestle, "I rolled over him. We rolled over me. They rolled over him. We rolled over us."

---

[18] The considerable amount of teasing ambiguity as to whether Humbert's pursuer is "real" or an autoscopic hallucination parodies Golyadkin Jr. and the central problem of Dostoevsky's *The Double* (the narrator of *Despair* considers "The Double" as a title for his book, "But Russian literature possessed one already," he says). When Humbert perceives Quilty and his Aztec Red Convertible (which also has a Double! [p. 229]) as a "red-beast," "red shadow," or "red fiend," Nabokov is parodying that archetypal Double, the Devil, and, more specifically, its predictable avatars in Thomas Mann's *Death in Venice* and *Doctor Faustus*, where the Doubles are inevitably devil-like and red-haired. The parody persists in *Pale Fire*.

Although the parody culminates in this "silent, soft, formless tussle on the part of two literati" (p. 301), it is sustained throughout the novel. In the traditional *Doppelgänger* fiction the Double representing the reprehensible self is often described as an ape. In *The Possessed*, Stavrogin tells Verkhovensky, "you're my ape"; in *Dr. Jekyll and Mr. Hyde*, Hyde plays "apelike tricks," attacks and kills with "apelike fury" and "apelike spite"; and in Poe's "The Murders in the Rue Morgue," the criminal self is literally an ape. But "good" Humbert undermines the doubling by often calling himself an ape, rather than Quilty, and when the two face one another, Quilty also calls Humbert an ape.[19] This transference is forcefully underscored when Humbert refers to himself as running along like "Mr. Hyde," his "talons still tingling." (p. 208) In Conrad's *Heart of Darkness*, Kurtz is Marlow's "shadow" and "shade." Although Humbert calls Quilty his "shadow," the pun on Humbert's name suggests that he is as much a shadow as Quilty, and like the shadow self in Andersen's tale, Humbert is dressed all in black. Quilty in fact first regards Humbert as possibly being "some familiar and innocuous hallucination" of his own (p. 296), and in the novel's closing moments the masked narrator addresses Lolita and completes this transferral: "And do not pity C.Q. One had to choose between him and H.H., and one wanted H.H. to exist at least a couple of months longer, so as to have him make you live in the minds of later generations." The book might have been told by "C.Q.," the doubling reversed; "H.H." is simply a better artist, more likely to possess the "secret of durable pigments." (p. 311)

If the Humbert-Quilty doubling is a conscious parody of "William Wilson," it is with good reason, for Poe's story is unusual among *Doppelgänger* tales in that it presents a reversal of the conventional situation: the weak and evil self is the main character, pursued by the moral self, whom he kills. Nabokov goes further and with one vertiginous sweep stands the convention on its head: in terms of the nineteenth-century Double tale, it should not even be necessary to kill Quilty and what he represents, for Humbert has already declared his love for Lolita *before* he goes to Quilty's Pavor Manor, and in asking the no longer nymphic Lolita to go away with him, he has

---

[19] Their confrontation also seems to parody the reunion of the professor and his shadow in Andersen's "The Shadow." Quilty's Pavor Manor is appropriately on "Grimm Rd." Nabokov's brilliant reading of this chapter is not to be missed. (Spoken Arts LP 902)

transcended his obsession. As a "symbolic" act, the killing is gratuitous; the parodic design is complete.

Quilty rightly balks at his symbolic role: "I'm not responsible for the rapes of others. Absurd!" he tells Humbert, and his words are well taken, for in this scene Humbert *is* trying to make him totally responsible, and the poem which he has Quilty read aloud reinforces his effort, and again demonstrates how a Nabokov parody moves beyond the "obscure fun" of stylistic imitation to connect with the most serious region of the book. It begins as a parody of Eliot's "Ash Wednesday" but ends by undercutting all the confessing in which "remorseful" Humbert has just been engaged: "because of all you did/because of all I did not/ you have to die." (p. 302) Since Quilty has been described as "the American Maeterlinck," it goes without saying that his ensuing death scene should be extravagantly "symbolic." Because one is not easily rid of an "evil" self, Quilty is almost impossible to kill, but the idea of exorcism is rendered absurd by his comically prolonged death throes, which, in the spirit of Canto V of *The Rape of the Lock*, burlesque the gore and rhetoric of literary death scenes ranging from the Elizabethan drama to the worst of detective novels. Quilty returns to the scene of the crime—a bed— and it is here that Humbert finally corners him. When Humbert fires his remaining bullets at close range, Quilty "lay back, and a big pink bubble with juvenile connotations formed on his lips, grew to the size of a toy balloon, and vanished." (p. 306) The last details emphasize the mock-symbolic association with Lolita; the monstrous self that has devoured Lolita, bubblegum, childhood and all, is "symbolically" dead, but as the bubble explodes, so does the Gothic *Doppelgänger* convention, with all its own "juvenile connotations" about identity, and we learn shortly that Humbert is still "all covered with Quilty." Guilt is not to be exorcised so readily—McFate is McFate, to coin a Humbertism—and the ambiguities of human experience and identity are not to be reduced to mere "dualities." Instead of the successful integration of a neatly divisible self, we are left with "Clare Obscure" and "quilted Quilty," the patchwork self (p. 308). Quilty refuses to die, just as the recaptured nose, in Gogol's extraordinary Double story of that name, would not at first stick to its owner's face. The reader who has expected the solemn moral-ethical absolutes of a Poe, Dostoevsky, Mann, or Conrad *Doppelgänger* fiction instead discovers himself adrift in a fantastic, comic cosmos more akin to Gogol's. Having hoped that Humbert would master his "secret sharer," we find rather that his quest for his "slippery

self" figuratively resembles Major Kovaliov's frantic chase after his
own nose through the spectral streets of St. Petersburg, and that
Humbert's "quest" has its mock "ending" in a final confrontation
that, like the end of *The Overcoat*, is not a confrontation at all.

The parodic references to R. L. Stevenson suggest that Nabokov
had in mind Henry Jekyll's painfully earnest discovery of the "truth"
that "man is not only one, but truly two. I say two, because the
state of my own knowledge does not pass beyond that point. Others
will follow, others will outstrip me on the same lines." The "serial
selves" of *Pale Fire* "outstrip" Stevenson and a good many other
writers, and rather than undermining Humbert's guilt, the Double
parody in *Lolita* locks Humbert within that prison of mirrors in
which the "real self" and its masks blend into one another, the
refracted outlines of good and evil becoming terrifyingly confused.

Humbert's search for the whereabouts and identity of Detective
Trapp (Quilty) invites the reader to wend his way through a labyrinth of clues in order to solve this mystery, a process which parodies
the Poe "tale of ratiocination." When Humbert finds Lolita and
presses her for her abductor's name,

> She said really it was useless, she would never tell, but on the other
> hand, after all—"Do you really want to know who it was? Well it was—"
> And softly, confidentially, arching her thin eyebrows and puckering
> her parched lips, she emitted, a little mockingly, somewhat fastidiously,
> not untenderly, in a kind of muted whistle, the name that the astute reader
> has guessed long ago.
> Waterproof. Why did a flash from Hourglass Lake cross my conscious-
> ness? I, too, had known it, without knowing it, all along. There was no
> shock, no surprise. Quietly the fusion took place, and everything fell into
> order, into the pattern of branches that I have worn throughout this
> memoir with the express purpose of having the ripe fruit fall at the right
> moment; yes, with the express and perverse purpose of rendering—she
> was talking but I sat melting in my golden peace—of rendering that golden
> and monstrous peace through the satisfaction of logical recognition, which
> my most inimical reader should experience now. (pp. 273–274)

Even here Humbert withholds Quilty's identity, though the "astute
reader" may recognize that "Waterproof" is a clue which leads back
to an early scene at the lake, in which Charlotte had said that Humbert's watch was waterproof and Jean Farlow had alluded to Quilty's
Uncle Ivor (by his first name only), and then had almost mentioned
Clare Quilty by name: Ivor "told me a completely indecent story

about his nephew. It appears—" but she is interrupted and the chapter ends. (p. 91) This teasing exercise in ratiocination—"peace" indeed!—is the detective trap—another parody of the reader's assumptions and expectations, as though even the most astute reader could ever fully discover the identity of Quilty, Humbert, or of himself.

Provided with Quilty's name, Humbert now makes his way to Pavor Manor, that latter-day House of Usher, where the extended and variegated parodies of Poe are laid to rest. All the novel's parodic themes are concluded in this chapter. Its importance is telescoped by Humbert's conclusion that "This, I said to myself, was the end of the ingenious play staged for me by Quilty." (p. 307) In form, of course, this bravura set piece is not a play, but as a summary parodic commentary on the main action, it does function in the manner of an Elizabethan play-within-the-play, and its "staging" underscores once more the game-element central to the book.

When indestructible Quilty dies, he fittingly subsides "in a purple heap," the color of his prose and of a good many of Humbert's quilted verbal patterns. Quilty's "genre, his type of humor," says Humbert, "had affinities with my own. He mimed and mocked me." (p. 251) Quilty's penchant for "logadaedaly and logomancy" double Humbert's own excesses, and Quilty's death scene rhetoric and trail of recondite, "insulting pseudonyms" (pp. 250–253), duly commented on by Humbert ("obvious"; "trite poke"; "in horrible taste"; "silly but funny"; "shoddy" [p. 252]) represent Humbert's act of self-criticism, and ultimately Nabokov's, too. "His main trait was his passion for tantalization. Goodness, what a tease the poor fellow was! He challenged my scholarship." (p. 252) Humbert's "cryptogrammic paper chase" after Quilty is Nabokov's self-parody of the involuted butterfly pattern running through the book's substratum and a compressed parody of the author-reader conflict sustained over the course of the trap-laden book (Quilty "succeeded in thoroughly enmeshing me . . . in his demoniacal game" [p. 251]; "*touché*, reader!" says Humbert, granting us a point in the game while mocking our delight in recognizing one of Quilty's most obvious literary jokes [p. 252]). Nabokov's own proclivities are reflected in Humbert's puns, which are in turn refracted in Quilty's worse puns. A double self-parody spirals in upon Quilty, who seals his own fate in the eyes of both the narrator and the author when he tells Humbert, "you know, as the Bard said, with that cold in his head, to borrow and to borrow and to borrow" (p. 303), and for that, Quilty deserves to die.

Nabokov has written thirteen books in Russian and ten in English (not including his translations). In the Afterword to *Lolita*, he corrects the critic who thought that *Lolita* was "the record of my love affair with the romantic novel," and suggests that "The substitution 'English language' for 'romantic novel' would make this elegant formula more correct." (p. 317) But *Lolita* doesn't chronicle the happiest "love affair," and "the second-rate brand of English" [sic] which Nabokov says he has adopted in place of his "untrammeled" and "rich" Russian idiom is belied by the eloquent and elegant English prose of *Speak, Memory*, the book previous to *Lolita*. This suggests that the language of *Lolita*—which might be termed colloquial baroque—is both a conscious parody of all efforts to acquire a "fine style" (including *Speak, Memory*) and a parodic record of the painful struggle to capture in any language the essence of what Albinus, in *Laughter in the Dark*, calls "a thing quite impossible to capture," whether it be the past, as in *Speak, Memory*, or the grace and beauty of a nymphet. "What a tale might be told," imagines Albinus, "the tale of an artist's vision, the happy journey of eye and brush" (p. 9), and Nabokov tells it in *Lolita*, but it is a journey through "black Humberland." By purposely making his narrator a decidedly second-rate man of letters—a "*manqué* talent"—Nabokov can not only show us the struggle more clearly, but may incorporate into Humbert's caprices a network of literary jokes and minor parodies which express concrete and consistent ideas concerning language, literature, and the limitations inherent in just such an effort as Humbert's.

Nabokov has said that poetry is the "mystery of the irrational perceived through rational words." Throughout his work he confronts the central problem of post-Romantic art and literature and, using parody and self-parody as "springboards," offers a critique of Romanticism. At its very best, Nabokov's verbal slapstick will thus suggest the inner tensions which threaten to break down a character and with him the language, especially when he is trying to communicate that "mystery," to re-create an abyss. Cincinnatus in *Invitation to a Beheading* tells Millie, his twelve-year old inamorata, "I'm exhausted—I didn't weep a slink last night," just as two decades later, in their "seduction" scene at The Enchanted Hunters, Humbert says to Lolita,

"What's the katter with misses?" I muttered (word-control gone) into her hair.
"If you must know," she said, "you do it the wrong way."
"Show, wight ray."

"All in good time," responded the spoonerette.

*Seva ascendes, pulsata, brulans, kitzelans, dementissima. Elevator clat-
terans, pausa, clatterans, populus in corridoro. Hanc nisi mors mihi adimet
nemo! Juncea puellula, jo pensavo fondissime, nobserva nihil quidquam . . .*
(p. 122)

The language of Horace and Catullus (both of whom are mentioned
in *Lolita*) is appropriate to this modern, if hysterical, elegiast—the
rush of "Latin" registering background noises and Humbert's panic
and garbled expression of undying love. At moments of extreme
crisis, Humbert croaks incomprehensibly, losing more than his expro-
priated English, for his attempts "to fix once for all the perilous
magic of nymphets" (p. 136) almost resist language altogether, carrying him close to the edge of non-language and a figurative silence.[20]
Thus Humbert significantly announces the scene as a "Parody of
silence" (p. 121), and far from being non-sensical, the ensuing nonsense Latin is a parodic stream-of-consciousness, affording a brief
critical comment on a technique which Nabokov finds unsatisfactory,
even in the novels of Joyce, whom he reveres. "We think not in words
but in shadows of words," Nabokov has said. "James Joyce's mistake
in those otherwise marvelous mental soliloquies of his consists in
that he gives too much verbal body to words." To Nabokov, the
unconnected impressions and associations that impinge on the mind
are irrational until they are consciously ordered; and to order them
in art is to fulfill a virtually moral obligation, for without rational
language, man has "grown a very/ landfish, languageless,/ a monster," as Thersites says of Ajax in Shakespeare's *Troilus and Cressida*.
Nabokov and his beleaguered first person narrators have looked into
the void, but they do not reproduce it; the "private language" of
Zemblan in *Pale Fire* is the nearest Nabokov has come, and its efficacy is totally rejected through parody. In contrast to the state of
"silence" towards which so much recent art variously evolves or
aspires—whether Samuel Beckett, William Burroughs, John Cage,
or Ad Reinhardt—Nabokov's deeply humanistic art reaffirms the
reality and majesty of language. Even the imprisoned and doomed
Cincinnatus is "already thinking of how to set up an alphabet"
which might humanize his dystopian world. (*I*, p. 139)

Humbert says of his artistic labors, "The beastly and beautiful

---

[20] G. D. Josipovici makes a similar point in "*Lolita*: Parody and the Pursuit of Beauty," *Critical Quarterly*, VI, 46.

merged at one point, and it is that borderline I would like to fix, and
I feel I fail to do so utterly. Why?" (p. 137) The rhetorical question
is coy enough because he answered it at the beginning of his narrative;
he hasn't failed, but neither can he ever be entirely successful, because
"Oh, my Lolita, I have only words to play with!" (p. 34)—an admission many post-Romantic writers would not make.[21] Nabokov's
remark about Joyce giving "too much verbal body to words" succinctly
defines the burden the Symbolists placed on the word, as though it
were an endlessly resonant object rather than one component in a
referential system of signs. As G. D. Josipovici observes, "To try
and use them as objects is . . . to repeat the mistake Humbert
made with Lolita: to try and possess carnally what can only be possessed imaginatively."[22] Nabokov's novels are filled with allusions to
other writers, but never more meaningfully than in *Lolita*, since
Humbert's acknowledgment of the limitations of language leaves so
many writers open to criticism, especially the Romantic poets. "Are
you troubled by Romantic Associations?" Charlotte inquires of her
new husband, and Keats, Byron, and Blake are humorously invoked.
Humbert calls Lolita a "fair daemon child" (p. 174), which makes
her a kind of Belle Dame Sans Merci in bobby sox. But the main
recipient of Nabokov's parody of Romanticism is Edgar Poe.

Like Poe's first-person narrators who incorporate poems into
their tales ("The Assignation," "Ligeia," "The Fall of the House of
Usher"), Humbert interpolates liberal amounts of his own verse, and
its comically blatant rhymes suggest an overly zealous application of
Poe's ideas on rhyme in "The Poetic Principle." Nabokov's choice
of both subject matter and narrator parody Poe's designation, in
"The Philosophy of Composition," of the "most poetical topic in
the world": "the death of a beautiful woman . . . and equally is it
beyond doubt that the lips best suited for such topic are those of a
bereaved lover." Both Annabel Lee and Lolita "die," the latter in
terms of her fading nymphic qualities and escape from Humbert,
who invokes yet another of Poe's lost ladies when he calls Lolita
"Lenore" (the subject of "Lenore" and "The Raven"), a reference
which also points to "The Philosophy of Composition," since that
essay concerns "The Raven."

---

[21] *Ibid.*, 45–48. I had developed this line of analysis before seeing Mr.
Josipovici's essay, but since his discussion of the relationship of language and
irrationality anticipates my remarks, I wish to acknowledge his contribution.
[22] *Ibid.*, 46.

The speaker in Poe's "Lenore" gropes for the right elegiac chord: "How shall the ritual, then, be read?—the requiem how be sung/ By you—by yours, the evil eye,—by yours, the slanderous tongue/ That did to death the innocence that died, and died so young?" How shall it be "sung" is also the main question in *Lolita*, and Nabokov found his answer in a parodic style that seems to parody *all* styles, including its own. This self-parodying tone is well-defined by a writer much admired by Nabokov. Jorge Luis Borges says that "the Baroque is that style which deliberately exhausts (or tries to exhaust) its possibilities and borders on its own caricature."[23] "You talk like a book, *Dad*," Lolita tells Humbert; and in order to protect his own efforts to capture her essence, he tries to exhaust the "fictional gestures," such as Edgar Poe's, which would reduce the nymphet's ineffable qualities to a convention of language or literature. "Only in the tritest of terms," says Humbert, "can I describe Lo's features: I might say her hair is auburn, and her lips are red as licked red candy, the lower one prettily plump—oh, that I were a lady writer who could have her pose naked in a naked light!" (p. 46) "Well-read Humbert" will imitate the locution of a famous writer, try it on for size—"We came to know—*nous connûmes*, to use a Flaubertian intonation" (p. 147)—toy with it— "*Nous connûmes* (this is a royal fun)" (p. 148)—and then abandon it for something else. More than fifty writers are treated in this spirit, ranging from Dante and Petrarch to Molnar and Maeterlinck, as though only through parody and caricature can Humbert prevent the possibility that his "memoir" might finally be nothing more than what the authorial voice in *Invitation to a Beheading* asks of its captive creation: "Or is this all but obsolete romantic rot, Cincinnatus?" (p. 139)

That *Lolita* is not in any way "obsolete" results from Nabokov's realization of the ultimate implications of Proust's injunction to writers "to indulge in the cleansing, exorcising pastime of parody."[24] Because Nabokov's use of parody is like Sebastian Knight's—"a clown developing wings, an angel mimicking a tumbler pigeon" (*SK*, p. 91)—he is able to have it both ways. Humbert's baroque

---

[23] Borges, *op. cit.*, p. xxii.

[24] Marcel Proust, "About Flaubert's Style," in *Pleasures and Days*, ed. F. W. Dupee (Garden City, 1957), p. 233. Proust was not suggesting that parodies should be incorporated into the novel, but rather that the practice of parody would release the novelist from the "spell" of a great writer and allow him to write his own novels.

language constitutes a virtuoso balancing or juggling act, for there are intervals when Humbert does capture Lolita's "essential grace," moments when, in the midst of the cascading puns and parodies, one has a glimpse of the "borderline [where] the beastly and beautiful merged," as in the scene where she plays tennis (pp. 233–236). It is a crucial necessity to recognize the tonal oscillations between his "beastly" and "beautiful" intonations, and to understand that one enables Humbert to realize the other. At the conclusion of Humbert's extended description of Lolita's tennis game, which occurs shortly before she is "kidnapped," the butterfly rises from its confines in the hermetic substructure of the novel, and in a single-line paragraph that it has to itself, flutters across the page: "An inquisitive butterfly passed, dipping, between us." (p. 236)[25]

Its appearance foreshadows the transcendent moment of felicity which has carried Humbert beyond the frightening solipsism of his lust and has enabled him to write his narrative. At the end of the novel, after crazily driving on the wrong, "mirror" side of the highway, Humbert turns off the road and rides up a grassy slope, coming to a "gentle, rocking stop." Immobile, suspended in felicity, he experiences "A kind of thoughtful Hegelian synthesis linking up two dead women" (p. 309), a realization of Quilty's play-within-the-novel, The Enchanted Hunters, which featured Lolita as a bewitching "farmer's daughter who imagines herself to be a woodland witch, or Diana" (p. 202), and seven hunters, six of them "red-capped, uniformly attired." A "last-minute kiss was to enforce the play's profound message, namely, that mirage and reality merge in love." (p. 203) When Humbert asks a pregnant and veiny-armed Lolita to go away with him, he demonstrates that the mirage of the past (the nymphic Lolita as his lost "Annabel") and the reality of the present (the Charlotte-like woman Lolita is becoming) have merged in love, a "synthesis linking up two dead women."

The play's "message" also describes the "aesthetic bliss" (p. 318) of artistic creation, and one involuted turn in the "plot" of The Enchanted Hunters almost reveals the hand of an enchanted hunter named Nabokov: "a seventh Hunter (in a green cap, the fool) was a Young Poet, and he insisted, much to Diana's annoyance, that she and the entertainment provided (dancing nymphs, and elves, and monsters) were his, the Poet's invention." (p. 203) Humbert is Nabokov's creation just as Lolita is Humbert's, and for a summary com-

---

[25] Miss Butler notes that this scene is the "most complete portrayal . . . of Lolita's butterfly nature," op. cit., pp. 77–79.

ment, one looks to the narrator of *The Real Life of Sebastian Knight*, who, in speaking of *The Prismatic Bezel*, has preempted Nabokov's critics by limpidly presaging the entire parodic design and progression of *Lolita*:

> I have tried my best to show the workings of the book, at least some of its workings. Its charm, humour and pathos can only be appreciated by direct reading. But for enlightenment of those who felt baffled by its habit of metamorphosis, or merely disgusted at finding something incompatible with the idea of a "nice book" in the discovery of a book's being an utterly new one, I should like to point out that *The Prismatic Bezel* can be thoroughly enjoyed once it is understood that the heroes of the book are what can be loosely called "methods of composition." It is as if a painter said: look, here I'm going to show you not the painting of a landscape, but the painting of different ways of painting a certain landscape, and I trust their harmonious fusion will disclose the landscape as I intend you to see it. (*SK*, p. 95)

III

The lepidopteral game is but one of several reminders that *Lolita* is to Nabokov a deeply personal book. Like many of his characters, Humbert is an émigré, and Nabokov has been an exile for his entire adult life. It is a fact which characterizes a state of mind and spirit. Since leaving Russia in 1919 he has never owned a house and even today resides in a hotel. But the theme of exile in Nabokov's work is not merely a matter of the special circumstances of his life, for the figure of the Exile embodies the human condition in our time, and no one has written more movingly about this figure than Nabokov. But the Exile has his past—like the movie extras in "The Assistant Producer," that may well be all that he does have—and in *Speak, Memory*, Nabokov re-creates the past, making it as vivid as the present. But the obsessive nostalgia that is so central to Nabokov's vision is ultimately no substitute for a viable life in the present, and among other things, *Lolita* is a devastating self-criticism of the reflexive attempt to move out of time, a self-parody of the psychological pastoral, and as such, it is Nabokov's own answer to his previous book, *Speak, Memory*. As Humbert says, near the end of the novel, "I was weeping again, drunk on the impossible past." (p. 284) Even Lolita tells him that "the past was the past," and his efforts to recapture it are made more than ludicrous by the congruent parody of Poe and psychiatry. If we envision Lolita and the brief time span of her nymphic years as a correlative for the past, we see how irrevocably self-destructive it is to live in that impossible past. "She had entered my world," says Humbert, "umber and black Humberland" (p. 168) —the shadowland of memory, a punning world where one shadow pursues another, and is destroyed in the process (see above).

As an exile, Nabokov of course had to write *Lolita* in English. "My private tragedy, which cannot, and indeed should not, be anybody's concern," he says, "is that I had to abandon my natural idiom." (p. 318) But his "private tragedy" *is* our concern, for in varying degrees it involves us all. Nabokov's search for the language adequate to *Lolita* is Humbert's search for the language that will reach Lolita, and it is a representative search, a heightened emblem of all of our attempts to communicate. "A penny for your thoughts, I said, and she stretched out her palm at once." (p. 210) It is the almost insuperable distance between those thoughts and that palm which Nabokov has measured so accurately and so movingly in *Lolita*: the distance between people, the distance separating love from lovemaking, mirage from reality—the desperate extent of all human need and desire. "I have only words to play with," says Humbert, and only words can bridge the gulf suggested by Lolita's palm. Humbert has failed once—"She would mail her vulnerability in trite brashness and boredom, whereas I use[d] for my desperately detached comments an artificial tone of voice that set my own teeth on edge" (p. 286)—but it is a necessary act of love to try, and perhaps Nabokov succeeds with the reader where Humbert failed with Lolita.

Nabokov's account of the book's origin is fitting. "The first little throb of *Lolita*," he writes,

went through me late in 1939 or early in 1940, in Paris, at a time when I was laid up with a severe attack of intercostal neuralgia. As far as I can recall, the initial shiver of inspiration was somehow prompted by a newspaper story about an ape in the Jardin des Plantes who, after months of coaxing by a scientist, produced the first drawing ever charcoaled by an animal: this sketch showed the bars of the poor creature's cage. (p. 313)

Humbert, the "aging ape" writing from prison, whose impossible love metaphorically connects him with that imprisoned animal, learns the language, in his fashion, and records his "imprisonment," and his book is the "picture" of the bars of the poor creature's cage.[26] Yet

---

[26] See Stegner, *op. cit.*, p. 103, who also reminds us that the Jardin des Plantes eventually housed the captured orangutan in Poe's "The Murders in the Rue Morgue."

from behind these bars, Humbert also exults. In *Gogol*, Nabokov notes how "one likes to recall that the difference between the comic side of things, and their cosmic side, depends upon one sibilant," a juxtaposition implicit in the early title, *Laughter in the Dark.* The title goes two ways: it records the laughter of the cosmic joker who has made a pawn of Albinus, blinding and tormenting him, but it also summarizes Nabokov's response to life, his course for survival. Towards the end of *Lolita,* the sick and despairing Humbert has finally tracked down Lolita, who is now the pregnant Mrs. Richard Schiller. He recalls how he rang the door bell, ready to kill Dick. The bell seems to vibrate through his whole exhausted system, but suddenly Humbert takes his automatic French response to the sound and playfully twists it into verbal nonsense: "*Personne. Je resonne. Repersonne.* From what depth this re-nonsense?" he wonders. (p. 271) It sounds from the depths of Vladimir Nabokov's profoundly humane comic vision; and the gusto of Humbert's narration, his punning language, his abundant delight in digressions, parodies, and games all attest to a comic vision that overrides the circumscribing sadness, absurdity, and terror of everyday life.

THE DOUBLE PNIN

Ambrose Gordon, Jr.

To the classic problems of freedom and necessity and the one and the many the present age seems to have added a certain bafflement about outsides and insides, the container and the thing contained. Like Peer Gynt peeling his onion in pursuit of its elusive core we have been brought to the tearful but absurd discovery that all is skin or all is core. In a non-Euclidean, post-Einsteinian world of "ever-changing viewpoints and interpenetration of inner and outer space" (Siegfried Giedeon) the intrinsic is not so much illusory or non-existent as somewhat problematic. As instance of the concern of one poet, consider these lines by Howard Nemerov:

> To fleece the Fleece from golden sheep,
> Or prey, or get—is it not lewd
> That we be eaten by our food
> And slept by sleepers in our sleep?[1]

Even advertising, in this period when we seem to be increasingly estranged from the substance and smells of our own bodies, has made its occasional contribution, as in the possibly apocryphal toothpaste slogan: "Your teeth are at your own throat always." While sometimes, as if for compensation, our remote and disincarnate bodies we project outward upon the universe, as in the following portion of dialogue from Vladimir Nabokov's *Pnin*. It is late. A party is breaking up:

> It was a fair fall night, velvet below, steel above.
> Joan asked:
> "You're sure you don't want us to give you a lift?"

---

[1] "The Scales of the Eyes," *New and Selected Poems* (Chicago, 1960), p. 61.

"It's a ten-minute walk. And a walk is a must on such a wonderful night."

The three of them stood for a moment gazing at the stars.

"And all of these are worlds," said Hagen.

"Or else," said Clements with a yawn, " a frightful mess. I suspect it is really a fluorescent corpse, and we are inside it."[2]

Such is the strange, funny, and sinister world of Nabokov's fiction, which remains determinedly non-Euclidean. What he has said of Gogol might be said of him: that his world "is somewhat related to such conceptions of modern physics as the 'Concertina Universe' or the 'ExplosionUniverse' " and that "there is a curvature in literary style as there is curvature in space."[3] The prose of Pushkin "is three-dimensional; that of Gogol is four-dimensional, at least. . . . If parallel lines do not meet it is not because meet they cannot, but because they have other things to do."

Nabokov's *Pnin*, published in 1957, was the fourth of his novels written in English to appear, and the second with an American setting (*Lolita* was the first). It is the shortest of these. In seven chapters covering five years we are given what has seemed to certain readers a charming but somewhat episodic portrait of a Russian refugee who finds himself a displaced person in the American academic scene. Even as discerning a critic as Howard Nemerov—certainly one of Nabokov's best—has expressed the view that "as a novel, this book looks somewhat accidental."[4] Agreement or disagreement may depend on how seriously we are meant to take the qualifying "somewhat." *Pnin*, indeed, probably does lack the complexity of the longer *Pale Fire* and *Lolita*—not to mention *The Real Life of Sebastian Knight*—but for this very reason, in its inner structure and outer occasion (or outer structure and inner occasion), it constitutes an admirable specimen for those interested in examining the dynamics of Nabokov's art.

We first encounter Professor Timofey Pnin aboard a train en route to the city of Cremona, where he has been scheduled to give a lecture before the local ladies' club. The year is 1950. It turns out to be the wrong train, and there is also some question as to whether he has

---

[2] *Pnin* (New York, 1957), pp. 165–166. Hereafter, references in parentheses will refer to this edition.

[3] *Nikolai Gogol* (Norfolk, Conn., 1944), pp. 144–145.

[4] *Poetry and Fiction* (New Brunswick, 1963), p. 261. Hereafter references in parentheses will refer to this edition.

the right lecture in his pocket. Nevertheless, Pnin finally arrives. His vicissitudes in Cremona occupy the book's opening chapter, near the end of which he suffers a cardiac seizure that causes to pass before his eyes, and ours, various figures and events out of his past. Born in Russia in 1898, the son of a prominent ophthalmologist, and escaping (like the author) from Red-invaded Crimea in 1919, Pnin completed his education at the University of Prague, and lived afterwards for nearly twenty years as an alien in Paris and then as a naturalized, if never quite acclimatized, citizen of the U.S. Since 1945 he has been Assistant Professor of Russian at Waindell College. Once married, Pnin is now divorced, and childless.

Subsquent chapters explore his homelessness: his distress in often noisy and drafty rented rooms ("It blows from the floor, and it blows from the walls—" [p. 36]), in one of which he has a pathetically brief reunion with his adored former wife, now married to a psychiatrist named Eric Wind, and in another room a far happier meeting with her (but not Pnin's) son. These meetings account for two of the novel's seven chapters; another is occupied with Pnin's summer visit to the country house of some old Russian acquaintances, where memories crowd upon him. In addition, we are permitted to see much of the ebb and flow of his relatively uneventful life. There is Pnin happily puttering in the stacks of the Waindell College library but also being miserably expelled, by a newly appointed professor, from the sanctuary of his office and by a landlord's returning daughter from his one thoroughly homelike, comfortable and quiet room. Finally we see him installed in a small, brick, two-story house of his own, only to learn, with Pnin, following a house-warming, that his contract is up and his stay at Waindell is at an end.

So much for the plot—what there is of it. As background to the shiftings of Pnin's uncomfortable evanescence there is the eternal return of the academic year, something that Nabokov sketches in with a few skilled satiric strokes: "Again the *Waindell Recorder* discussed the Parking Problem. Again in the margins of library books earnest freshmen inscribed such helpful glosses as 'Description of nature,' or 'Irony'; and in a pretty edition of Mallarmé's poems an especially able scholiast had already underlined in violet ink the difficult word *oiseaux* and scrawled above it 'birds.'" (p. 137) All this needs no comment, for it is part of what Mark Schorer refers to as the "hilarious comedy, which any academic person at least will recognize at once and delight in." But I think it is clear and generally recognized that satire of the academic world is no more this novel's chief concern than was satire of motels the chief concern of *Lolita*. What I am concerned with in these notes is Nabokov's brew of individual fancy. "How should we diagnose his sad case?" asks Nabokov at one point, and answers:

Pnin, it should be particularly stressed, was anything but the type of that good-natured German platitude of last century, der zerstreute Professor. On the contrary, he was perhaps too wary, too persistently on the lookout for diabolical pitfalls, too painfully on the alert lest his erratic surroundings (unpredictable America) inveigle him into some bit of preposterous oversight. It was the world that was absent-minded and it was Pnin whose business it was to set it straight. His life was a constant war with insensate objects that fell apart, or attacked him, or refused to function, or viciously got themselves lost as soon as they entered the sphere of his existence. (p. 13)

The worst of it is that Pnin's insides are no less extrinsic and no less erratic: his surroundings have got into him, are perhaps even of him. He is a man with "a shadow behind the heart." "My patient was one of those singular and unfortunate people," Nabokov writes,

who regard their heart ('a hollow, muscular organ,' according to the gruesome definition in Webster's New Collegiate Dictionary . . .) with a queasy dread, a nervous repulsion, a sick hate, as if it were some strong slimy untouchable monster that one had to be parasitized with, alas. Occasionally, when puzzled by his tumbling and tottering pulse, doctors examined him more thoroughly, the cardiograph outlined fabulous mountain ranges and indicated a dozen fatal diseases that excluded one another. (p. 20)

That weird cardiograph I take to be the signature of this particular novel. It suggests violation, penetration—a mountain range where no mountain range should be—and so on one occasion, by a metamorphosis of the image, becomes an even more rickety graph, the subjective correlative of intolerable noise from the outside: "Workmen," we are told, "came and started to drill holes in the street—Brainpan Street, Pningrad—and patch them up again, and this went on and on, in fits of shivering black zigzags and stunned pauses. . . ." (p. 63) These would appear to be nothing less than Pnin's outraged brain-waves, which dip and leap with each shiver of the pneumatic drill. There is also, and more strangely, the counter-movement outward. So, when sleep comes, if only in the blissful quiet of early morning, we are given as its correlative this image, the Pniniz-ing of the outer landscape. Pnin is asleep and all in the house are asleep. Consequently, it "was a pity nobody saw the display in the empty street, where the auroral breeze wrinkled a large luminous puddle, making of the telephone wires reflected in it illegible lines of black zigzags." (p. 110) Here, for once, the violated brain-waves, eased, have come to partial rest.

"I always think," writes Nabokov's celebrated fictional novelist, Sebastian Knight,

> that one of the purest emotions is that of the banished man pining after the land of his birth. I would have liked to show him straining his memory to the utmost in a continuous effort to keep alive and bright the vision of his past. . . . But because the theme has already been treated by my betters and also because I have an innate distrust of what I feel easy to express, no sentimental wanderer will ever be allowed to land on the rock of my unfriendly prose.[5]

Pnin could not imaginably have been written by the chilly Sebastian Knight, but it has been written—and expertly—by Nabokov.

The secret of Nabokov's success lies in his decomposition of the figure of the Banished Man into its dual components of the Exile and the Alien. These are then pitted against each other. The Exile (to consider him first) is a man separated from his world who yet *possesses it as a world* by the miracle of continually renewed synecdoche. He is stung by slivers of memory, heart's needles; but each vividly remembered part carries with it the whole. For example, the following recall by the novel's Russian narrator: "My first recollection of Timofey Pnin is connected with a speck of coal dust that entered my left eye on a spring Sunday in 1911." (p. 174) Remembrance of this painful incident now calls up for him the whole gusty morning by the waterfront of what, in those days, must have been Europe's most northern capital. "I had been trying out a beautiful new English bicycle given me for my twelfth birthday, and, as I rode home to our rosy-stone house in the Morskaya, over parquet-smooth wooden pavements, the consciousness of having gravely disobeyed my tutor was less bothersome than the granule of smarting pain in the far north of my eyeball." (pp. 174–175) When all home remedies proved of no avail, Dr. Pavel Pnin, the ophthalmologist, was at last consulted: "And what a divine relief it was when, with a tiny instrument resembling an elf's drumstick, the tender doctor removed from

---

[5] *The Real Life of Sebastian Knight* (Norfolk, Conn., 1959), pp. 26–27.

my eyeball the offending black atom!" (p. 176) Then follows this strange comment: "I wonder where that speck is now? The dull, mad fact is that it does exist somewhere." (p. 176) As for the black atom there is no telling, but "the granule of smarting pain" is where it always was, in the far north of memory's eyeball, enlarged, intensified, transfigured—but still called St. Petersburg.

The Alien, on the other hand, unlike the Exile, is never able to possess his world, although he too is penetrated by it. It remains a world in fragments, like the surface of the drilled street outside the window of Pnin's furnished room. The world for the Alien is always too close, yet always far away—an absurd predicament that is the source of continuous comedy. In this connection, Graham Greene was spokesman for more than one reviewer when he said of *Pnin*: "It is hilariously funny and of a sadness. . . ." That is true. He might have added that its protagonist and antagonist are less individual men than tonalities. Throughout, funny Pnin (the eternal Alien) and sad Pnin (the eternal Exile) struggle unknowingly for mastery, somewhat as when on a memorable occasion, summoned by the college library to return an overdue, and for Pnin indispensable, Russian tome—which he reluctantly does, out of consideration for another reader—Pnin discovers that the other reader is himself.

I could discourse at great length on Pnin the Alien, but I will not. Let me note in passing that it is not so much that the objects that float into his ken are utterly strange as that they are strangely distorted, drawn and elongated out of the perfect round. In a sporting-goods store he guilelessly orders a "football" and is given . . . a football: " 'No, no,' said Pnin, 'I do not wish an egg or, for example, a torpedo. I want a simple football ball. Round!' " (p. 99) And that is the way it goes, in an elliptic world. Ultimately, the trouble is, of course, less with objects than with words. While the Exile lives in his ocular organ (the eye of memory), the Alien remains trapped in his mouth—that unnaturalized mouth—where inner and outer, past and present, meet and overlap. Of Pnin we are told: "If his Russian was music, his English was murder. He had enormous difficulty ('dzeefeecooltsee' in Pninian English) with depalatization, never managing to remove the extra Russian moisture from t's and d's before the vowels he so quaintly softened." (p. 66)

Pnin seems to have known where the trouble lay and had once had a bold plan for making over his mouth, as the final stage, as it were, of his Americanization. He submitted to a fearful operation: he had his teeth out, *all* of them.

After that, during a few days he was in mourning for an intimate part of himself. . . . And when the plates were thrust in, it was like a poor fossil skull being fitted with the grinning jaws of a perfect stranger. . . . Ten days passed—and suddenly he began to enjoy the new gadget. It was a revelation, it was a sunrise, it was a firm mouthful of efficient, alabastrine, humane America. (p. 38)

With the advent of his new teeth, great new plans were made, a book, perhaps a marriage—but, alas, little comes of them and his English grows no surer. Until the end of the story (despite this dental bridge to a new world) it is as outcast aliens that Pnin and his poor mouth remain.

Pnin as Exile, on the other hand, is a far more subtle and complex matter. Unlike Pnin the Alien, Exile Pnin is not perceived by us as a "wonderful personality," and scarcely even as a separate identity. Like parallels reflected in shimmering water, his being and that of the narrator-author interpenetrate and merge. This is probably the strangest aspect of the novel. In addition to his pervasive presence (as the ghost of exile), the narrator, whose voice we have heard from the beginning, gradually emerges as a character, even a key character, in the story, and the more fully he emerges the more he takes on the familiar lineaments of Vladimir Nabokov. This author's ambiguous relation to his fictions recalls Marianne Moore's famous definition of poems ("imaginary gardens with real toads in them"); but perhaps real and imaginary is not quite the right opposition here: it is rather that the author is discovered to be both outside and inside the story he is telling.

Howard Nemerov has already remarked in *Poetry and Fiction* that Nabokov is "a practitioner whose relations with his narrators and theirs with their characters are so irregular as to make the sacred 'point of view' emit rabbits like a hat." (p. 261) As an illustration of this, there is a scene in the present novel where Pnin is lecturing to his small Russian class upon the death of Pushkin, and in particular upon Pushkin's morbid habit "of closely inspecting every passing day as he strove to find in its cryptogram a certain 'future anniversary'; the day and month that would appear, somewhere, sometime upon his tombstone." (p. 68) Once Pushkin wrote down with minute exactitude: "December 26, 1829, 3:03 P.M." " 'But,' exclaimed Pnin in triumph, 'he died on a quite, quite different day! He died—' The chair back against which Pnin was vigorously leaning emitted an ominous crack, and the class resolved a pardonable tension in loud young laughter." (p. 68) And then appears in the writing this parenthesis: "(Sometime, somewhere—Petersburg? Prague?—one of the two musical clowns pulled out the piano stool from under the other, who remained, however, playing on, in a seated, though seatless, position, with his rhapsody unimpaired. Where? Circus Busch, Berlin!)" (p. 68) Whose questions, we wonder, and whose memories are these? Pnin's? The narrator's? Or the author's? Apparently, when memory speaks of exile, it speaks for all three.

There is another queer aspect of Pnin's identity as Exile. If this identity on the left or sinister side merges with that of the author, on the right it partakes of myth. "His verbal vagaries add a new thrill to life. His mispronunciations are mythopeic. His slips of the tongue are oracular. He calls my wife John." (p. 165) —So Professor Clements on his friend, in what sounds like an epitaph. But there is more to it than that. Pnin's situation is mythopeic. It might be crystalized, somewhat as follows: A man of middle age and some resourcefulness, for twenty years banished to furnished rooms, seeks incessantly to find his way home, to what might have been. During his long travail he is brought, in a dark place, face to face with his own dead: "Murdered, forgotten, unrevenged, incorrupt, immortal, many old friends were scattered throughout the dim hall." (p. 27) At a later stage, he is recognized by the sympathetic youth whose "water father" we are told he is, and who reciprocally has long had a recurring fantasy of "The King, his father" who "alone—solus rex (as chess problem makers term royal solitude)—paced a beach." (p. 86) Once again he is embraced by his long-separated wife, to whose memory he has remained faithful. At last, he seems to be home: "And the tiny house was so spacious! With grateful surprise, Pnin thought that had there been no Russian Revolution, no exodus, no expatriation in France, no naturalization in America, everything—at the best, at the best, Timofey!—would have been much the same. . . ." (p. 144) But this domestic haven is not to be the end of his travels, and in a final glimpse we see him setting off with his faithful about him—one little white dog—into the unknown "where there was simply no saying what miracle might happen." (p. 191)

I trust that now to name Pnin's archetype would be nearly as superfluous as to name that of the hero of Sebastian Knight's first (unpublished) novel: "a fat young student . . . travels home to find his mother married to his uncle; this uncle, an ear-specialist, had murdered the student's father." To be sure, the events of Pnin's odyssey are recorded not continuously but in a manner somewhat scattered, and of course, like Leopold Bloom's it is essentially an odyssey manqué. Indeed, in reading Pnin, it is Joyce's Ulysses, rather than Homer's, that repeatedly comes to mind. I suppose there is no question here of influence—or if there is, it is not my intention to ask it—though Joyce is one of the few contemporary writers whom Nabokov mentions on various occasions, and apparently with respect. What I am concerned with establishing is, rather, an affinity. In cultivated Pnin we have no exact counterpart to Leopold Bloom, though Pnin's great interest in gadgets ("Plastics swept him off his feet. He had a deep admiration for the zipper" [p. 14]), his tendency to set others straight, and even an occasional turn of thought ("he sat down to the task of learning the language of Fenimore Cooper, Edgar Poe, Edison, and thirty-one Presidents" [p. 14])—all these have their Bloomian analogues. More to the point, however, are certain relationships, which may be set down proportionally as follows:

(1) Bloom : Molly (and her suitors) : : Pnin : Liza (and her suitors).

(2) Bloom : Stephen Dedalus : : Pnin : Victor Wind.

Of the former proportion little need be said. Both Molly Bloom and Liza Pnin are unfaithful Penelopes, and in relation to their wives' suitors both Bloom and Pnin are inadequate, or unsuccessful, versions of Odysseus. Both women are nevertheless like Penelope, not only as memorably statuesque mother-figures but in being passionately loved by their estranged husbands, who see embodied in them some lost homeland: for Bloom, a voluptuous but generally unspecified East; for Pnin, Russia. Both women feel toward their men a mingling of contempt and grudging respect, together with a belittling and rather patronizing affection.

Somewhat more complex and interesting is the second proportion. Different as their cultural levels may be, Leopold Bloom and Timofey Pnin are alike in being non-artists (yet with a bit of the artist about them) who are drawn into the mysterious bond of foster-fatherhood to a young, precocious, and gifted artist. As Stephen Dedalus is the portrait of an artist of a distinctly Joycean kind, so Victor Wind shares with Vladimir Nabokov more than a youthful insomnia and a penchant for clear but weirdly misleading sentences (example: "Bad reds should all be avoided; even if carefully manufactured, they are still bad"—quoted by Victor from an old book on the mixing of paints but "smacking of a political aphorism" [p. 98]). They share also an interest in the mingling of identities. We are told of Victor's bemused fascination with a brightly polished black car's relation to its visually interpenetrating environment, which is painted by him accordingly, so that the car is implied by the tilted planes of reflected sky, buildings, trees, but never distinctly beheld as a separate identity. An interesting idea.

In describing the meeting of Pnin with his foster son Nabokov shows great sensitivity. Reminiscent of the meeting of Bloom and Stephen, it is a meeting of persons but scarcely of minds. Never having seen the adolescent boy before, Timofey purchases a soccer ball and Jack London's *The Son of the Wolf* as offerings—only to learn that Victor is reading Dostoevsky and is not athletic. More happy is his choice of a suitable place for a ritual feast (it is the boy's first day of vacation): a diner, to be reached after a walk in the spring rain. After the meal Pnin quickly sets right his initial mistake, slipping upstairs to dispose of the ball through his bedroom window, but on his way down he loses his footing and falls heavily.

He lay supine for a moment, his eyes moving to and fro. He was helped to his feet. No bones were broken.

Pnin smiled and said: "It is like the splendid story of Tolstoy—you must read one day, Victor—about Ivan Ilyich Golovin who fell and got in consequence kidney of the cancer. Victor will now come upstairs with me." (p. 108)

Victor responds to the paternal affection; that night he suffers no insomnia. But Pnin, with an aching back from his recent accident, does. And then, when sleep finally comes, through the disguised stabs of pain, a very strange and moving thing happens: Pnin dreams his foster son's recurring fantasy (about which he knows nothing) of the royal exile by the shore:

He had fallen asleep at last, despite the discomfort in his back, and in the course of one of those dreams that still haunt Russian fugitives, even when a third of a century has elapsed since their escape from the Bolsheviks, Pnin saw himself fantastically cloaked, fleeing through great pools of ink under a cloud-barred moon from a chimerical palace, and then pacing a desolate strand with his dead friend Ilya Isidorovich Polyanski as they waited for some mysterious deliverance to arrive in a throbbing boat from beyond the hopeless sea. (pp. 109–110)

A word about the ending: "Harm is the norm," we are told: "Doom should not jam." (p. 25) Nor does it in the present instance, for Timofey's end is not happy. At the conclusion he is depicted as an aging Odysseus once again defeated by the suitors, the chief of whom is by now revealed to have been none other than the narrator, who had been Liza's lover before she married Pnin and who had not used her particularly well. Pnin knows and has not forgiven. When he is told who will replace him at Waindell, he is informed that he may stay on in a subordinate capacity—a proposal that he cannot accept with honor. He must leave.

The friendly and on the whole sympathetic narrator forces Pnin from the Waindell campus with a show of considerable reluctance. "I wrote to Timofey Pnin offering him in the most cordial terms I could muster to assist me. . . ." (p. 186) And so on. The real villain—if villain there be—is not the sympathetic narrator but his remorseless twin, the author. One recalls Nabokov's remark (in *Conclusive Evidence*) concerning his Russian-language avatar, V. Sirin: "His best works are those in which he condemns his people to the solitary confinement of their souls."[6] A certain remorselessness is no doubt characteristic of the short novel as a genre and of Nabokov as a practitioner. Moreover, there is added reason for his ruthlessness in *Pnin*, which occupies a very special place in the spectrum of works by this distinguished Russian-American novelist. "My private tragedy," Vladimir Nabokov once wrote, "which cannot, and indeed should not, be anybody's concern, is that I had to abandon my natural idiom, my untrammeled, rich, and infinitely docile Russian tongue for a second-rate brand of English. . . ."[7] Though we will demur—Nabokov's brand of English is *not* second-rate—we need not discount entirely what he is saying nor refrain from seeing Pnin as the scapegoat-hero of a "tragedy" whose fantastically interiorized scene is Pnin's own always-about-to-be-naturalized oral cavity: "this new amphitheater of translucid plastics [the hopefully acquired American teeth] implying, as it were, a stage and a performance." (p. 39) So viewed—and I trust it is not an impertinence to view it so—the novel *Pnin* is its author's ritual expunging of the alien in himself: an alien tongue.

But salvation of a kind is also Pnin's, and the book's ending, though sad, is not entirely hopeless. We first saw Timofey Pnin in motion on a train, the wrong train, bound for the wrong place; we last see him in a car bound for the unknown. Between the book's opening and close five years have passed and Pnin has got well nigh nowhere; yet these terminals, though similar, are not identical. Beginning and ending do not exactly coincide. The movement of Pnin's

[6] *Conclusive Evidence* (New York, 1951), p. 217. Hereafter, references in parentheses will refer to this edition. Nabokov's memoir has, of course, been revised and retitled *Speak, Memory*; see the Selected Bibliography.

[7] "On a Book Entitled *Lolita*," *The Anchor Review*, II (Garden City, 1957), 112.

journey has been spiral, for the spiral "is a spiritualized circle. In the spiral form, the circle, uncoiled, unwound, has ceased to be vicious; it has been set free." (p. 204) This hopeful view, taken from *Conclusive Evidence*, may also be matched from among the views of the painter Lake in *Pnin* (Victor's master):

Among the many exhilarating things Lake taught was that the order of the solar spectrum is not a closed circle but a spiral of tints from cadmium red and oranges through a strontian yellow and a pale paradisal green to cobalt blues and violets, at which point the sequence does not grade into red again but passes into another spiral, which starts with a kind of lavender gray and goes on to Cinderella shades transcending human perception. (p. 96)

Like Nabokov's other, sometimes even more remorseless books, *Pnin* as we read it is funny and pathetic simultaneously or by turns, but by the time we reach its last page it is neither: it is exhilarating. Earlier I suggested that within this novel the principal conflict was between Alien Pnin and Exile Pnin, a conflict of tonalities. It is resolved—to the extent that it *is* resolved—through the eventual elimination of both. This Nabokovian catharsis of Exile and Alien has been in two kinds. First, there is the freeing of the Exile, as with his prototype Odysseus, through the sheer force by which the Dead— Pnins' parents, his friends, childhood doctor, his first girl—are caused to rise, in active but spontaneous memory, bringing Russia with them. Such a violent process, happily, is not to be repeated forever. Secondly, there is the purgation of Alien Pnin through the exercise of an unremitting parody—by the deft author and by the something less than deft Chairman of the Waindell English Department, Jack Cockerell who, we are told, "acquired an unmistakable resemblance to the man he had now been mimicking for almost ten years." (p. 187) It is at this gentleman's house that the narrator stays on his first evening at Waindell, which is also the eve of Pnin's fifty-seventh birthday and his last day on campus.

The guest is regaled by a remarkable performance:

We got Pnin in the Stacks, and Pnin on the Campus Lake. We heard Pnin criticize the various rooms he had successively rented. We listened to Pnin's account of his learning to drive a car. . . . The performance, I repeat, was magnificent, but it was too long. By midnight the fun began to thin; the smile I was keeping afloat began to develop, I felt, symptoms of labial cramp. Finally the whole thing grew to be such a bore that I fell wondering if by some poetical vengeance this Pnin business had not become with Cockerell the kind of fatal obsession which substitutes its own victim for that of the initial ridicule. (pp. 187–189)

What remains after the dual sloughing off of Exile and Alien is the man, free and at home in his homelessness, like Ulysses in the last voyage, as celebrated by Dante and Tennyson. Our last—and perhaps our first—glimpse of the real Pnin is his setting out on that birthday morning. The narrator, taking a before-breakfast walk with his host's dog, sees Pnin suddenly:

Hardly had I taken a couple of steps when a great truck carrying beer rumbled up the street, immediately followed by a small pale blue sedan with the white head of a dog looking out, after which came another great truck exactly similar to the first. [Incidentally, are these trucks not the two stereotypes from which our intrepid hero is about to escape?] The humble sedan was crammed with bundles and suitcases; its driver was Pnin. I emitted a roar of greeting, but he did not see me, and my only hope was that I might walk uphill fast enough to catch him while the red light one block ahead kept him at bay.

I hurried past the rear truck, and had another glimpse of my old friend, in tense profile, wearing a cap with ear flaps and a storm coat; but next moment the light turned green, the little white dog leaning out yapped at Sobakevich, and everything surged forward—truck one, Pnin, truck two. From where I stood I watched them recede in the frame of the roadway, between the Moorish house and the Lombardy poplar. Then the little sedan boldly swung past the front truck and, free at last, spurted up the shining road. . . . (pp. 190–191)

But this is not quite our final glimpse of Pnin either. The saddened narrator returns "to a British breakfast of depressing kidney and fish" (p. 191)—and to Cockerell's further, probably quite fictitious, anecdotes. This strange excrescence remains like an aftertaste, a parody Pnin continuing his ghostly life.

PALE FIRE
AND THE
FINE ART OF ANNOTATION

John O. Lyons

Nabokov's *Pale Fire* is undoubtedly one of the wittiest (in the eighteenth-century sense of wit) novels since Joyce's *Ulysses*. What makes it so is largely its inheritance of a sly narrative pose from Pope, Sterne, and Byron. This is a scutcheon that on its dexter side has an impatience with cant and injustice expressed in a full range of satirical rhetoric. On its sinister side there is more than a little flippancy, innuendo, and playing of games with words and events that often make the work hated as a swallowed bait. This is in general terms the method. The purpose of this method is to convey the attitude (also inherited from the eighteenth century) that man is an animal both blessed and cursed with reason (or Reason), and equally despicable when he affirms or denies the existence of God at the end of his rational analysis of natural events. The works of Pope, Sterne, Byron, and Nabokov always return after the documentation of the ways of a blind Fate to the view that this very blindness must throw man back on a belief in an inscrutable Deity. Again and again the argument is that because this *is* such a perversely organized planet there must be a divine disorganizing principle; or, as Nabokov has put it, "There must be an original of the clumsy copy."[1]

It is this metaphor that leads Nabokov to his favorite narrative method, which is the examination of a text (or vision of aesthetic order) by some real or imagined artist who vies with God in disordering a universe. This explains his fervor in defense of his own

---

[1] Vladimir Nabokov, *Invitation to a Beheading*, tr. by Dimitri Nabokov in collaboration with the author (New York, 1959), p. 93.

literary Olympians: Shakespeare, Pope, Sterne, Byron, Pushkin,
Gogol, and Joyce, and why he expresses an unbounded contempt for
certain literary heretics like Dostoyevsky and Mann. For Nabokov
the true worshipper is the exegete of a profane text, but a text that
deceptively orders a world in praise and imitation of God's plan.
And, like most dissenting exegetes, Nabokov's (V. of *The Real Life
of Sebastian Knight*, Humbert Humbert of *Lolita*, Charles Kinbote
of *Pale Fire*) defend their Gods with whatever weapons they have:
pedantry, hauteur, slap-stick, acrimony, paranoia, ridicule, a sincere
wrath, and an insincere urbanity. This is precisely the range that
Pope uses in the notes to *The Dunciad* (1742–43), and that Nabokov often uses himself in his edition of *Eugene Onegin*. (1964)
These two works shed more light on the method and purpose of
Pale Fire than any other.

Robert Benchley once wrote a parody of the variorum style of
the British Vestry School of criticism called "Shakespeare Explained:
Carrying on the System of Footnotes to a Silly Extreme."[2] I think
that the modern reader's approach to both *Pale Fire* and the edition
of *Eugene Onegin* is colored by just such an easy parody as Benchley's so that the apparent lampoon of a scholarly method now fortu-
nately moribund tends to wear thin over such a long haul. But when
these works (and *Pale Fire* especially) are viewed in the light of
the Popean devices of *The Dunciad* Nabokov's intent is clearer.

The direct allusions to Pope in *Pale Fire* have often been noted,
but their purpose is a more complicated matter. The title is from
Shakespeare's *Timon of Athens* (but not from IV : 3, as Kinbote
says[3]) :

> I'll example you with thievery:
> The sun's a thief, and with his great attraction
> Robs the vast sea; the moon's an arrant thief,
> And her pale fire she snatches from the sun. . . . (IV: ii:441–444)

For the poet John Shade, and for Nabokov, this passage serves more
to explain the nature of art than the universality of theft. Art is the
thief which robs nature's pocket, and like the moon decks itself
in a borrowed glory. But the idea of the moon also suggests that art
is lunatic in its imitation of nature. By a process of infection the

---

[2] Robert Benchley, *Benchley Beside Himself* (New York, 1943), p. 87.

[3] Vladimir Nabokov, *Pale Fire* (New York, 1962), p. 79. Hereafter, this
edition is the one cited in the text.

artist himself is viewed as a madman, and his critic is also tainted. Then, in one of those Nabokovian paradoxes, sane and insane are inverted, and the work of art, because of its formal integrity, is sane, and the world, because of its inscrutability, is mad. Still, the exegete stands between, generously explaining and selfishly obscuring the mad-sane work to the sane-mad world.

Although Kinbote is a suspicious recluse in the same mold as Shakespeare's Timon, Nabokov uses the allusion for purposes very much his own. Pope is the more useful crutch. The story is that Swift rescued an early version of *The Dunciad* from the fire where Pope had thrown it during the summer of 1726 or 1727. Swift then went on as Martinus Scriblerus to write an introduction to *The Dunciad*, which was dedicated to him, and to contribute a number of facetious footnotes. So the rejected verses of "Pale Fire" are incinerated by Shade to the dismay of a voyeuristic Kinbote, but after the poet's death Kinbote is able to escape with the text and prefix a Foreword and add a Commentary and Index. John Shade is also a Popean. He has published a study of Pope called *Supremely Blest* (p. 195),[4] and conducts a seminar in Pope (p. 250). His own verse shows the influence of Pope, for "Pale Fire" is in pentameter couplets (although not heroic ones), and in four parts like *An Essay on Criticism*, the original *Rape of the Lock*, *An Essay on Man*, and *The Dunciad*. Two of Shade's rejected verses quote *An Essay on Man*: II: 267–268 (p. 202)—which send Kinbote into a finely restrained speculation since the lines mention a "lunatic a king"—and once there is a reference to Pope's Zembla (p. 272), also from *An Essay on Man*. (II: 224)

An Essay on Man is concerned with many of the issues meditated upon by John Shade, but when Nabokov adds the burden of Kinbote's material to the poem those meditations appear pompous. It is not a question of Shade's being a dunce, for he is one of the most respectable of Nabokov's creations. Yet a note in *The Dunciad* on "The high Priori Road" casts a Nabokovian doubt on the meanderings of Shade as well as those of the IPH ("Institute of Preparation for the Hereafter" [p. 52]):

Those who, from the effects of this Visible world, deduce the Eternal Power and Godhead of the First Cause, though they cannot attain to an adequate idea of the Deity, yet discover so much of him, as enables them

---

[4] The title is from *An Essay on Man*: II: 270.

to see the End of their Creation, and the Means of their Happiness: whereas they who take this high Priori Road (such as Hobbes, Spinoza, Des Cartes, and some better Reasoners) for one that goes right, ten lose themselves in Mists, or ramble after Visions, which deprive them of all sight of their End, and mislead them in the choice of wrong Means.[5]

Such a comment comes out of a long tradition of ridiculing idle and systematic theology, but this might be especially significant because it follows a reference to "Wilkins' wings," by which "one of the first Projectors of the Royal Society . . . entertained the extravagant hope of a possibility to fly to the Moon." (p. 350) There again is the moon, that mad-making symbol of the borrowed glory of art and a source for the figure of a "pale fire."

The exegete is caught between the work of art and life, and his mediation is awkward. He is afraid of murdering to dissect and yet out of reverence wishes to become the work of art. Its every detail and implication are paraded, and yet there is a suspicion of a more perfect work that is savored in private. The range of protective mock-pedantry is easily seen in The Dunciad. Puns and anagrams: "Alexander Pope hath sent abroad into the world as many Bulls as his namesake Pope Alexander.—Let us take the initial and final letters of his name, viz., A. P-E, and they give you an idea of an Ape" (this supposedly from John Dennis). (p. 282) Mock pedantry: as when Edmund Curl comments on his once being tossed in a blanket that "Here, Scriblerus! thou leeseth in what thou assertest concerning the blanket; it was not a blanket, but a rug." (p. 297) Worldly nonchalance: as in the comment on Leonard Welsted, "He writ other things which we cannot remember. You have him again in Book III." (p. 305) There is much more of the same, but the method is observed. The moral of the poem—and especially as it is reflected in the notes—is that

> Wit shoots in vain its momentary fires,
> The meteor drops, and in a flash expires.   (IV: 633–634)

Nabokov's translation of Eugene Onegin has more often been the object of criticism (famously by his old neighbor, Edmund Wilson) than his annotation. Little doubt has been cast on Nabokov's scholarship, but the tone is apt to raise eyebrows. Its ungraciousness

---

[5] Alexander Pope, The Best of Pope, ed. by George Sherburn (New York, 1929), p. 351. Hereafter, this edition is the one cited in the text.

toward Pushkin's translators and commentators has led several (most recently and vigorously D. J. Enright)[6] to see Nabokov as something of an inhuman monster. No doubt much of the spleen in Nabokov's work comes naturally to him and is a habit of years of literary infighting among disenfranchised émigré factions. Yet when Nabokov's aesthetic is seen as his theology, when that theology views certain writers as demigods, his acrimoniousness toward heretical corruptors of a sacred text makes more sense. This view is implicit in his flat and often awkward translation of *Eugene Onegin*. For Nabokov it is only the author's meaning that might be rendered in the vulgate of English, whereas his predecessors have (to his mind) attempted to vie with genius in their attempts to reproduce metrically Pushkin's intent. He mentions "four 'English' 'metrical' 'translations'" that are "unfortunately available to students. . . ." "Even worse than these is a new version, full of omissions and blunders, by Walter Arndt. . . ."[7]

Nabokov's attack upon what Pope called *Dullness* is arch and urbane more often than it is nasty, and he never uses Pope's scatological method (as Kinbote does with Gradus in *Pale Fire*), but this is the difference two centuries make. What is more remarkable is the way in which Nabokov's reverence toward the poem turns anything connected with it into a relique, so that he will lovingly linger over a printer's device (a butterfly), and snarl at his colleagues over the date of composition of a stanza. A psychoanalytic critic may be termed "silly" (II: 513), but his greatest contempt is reserved for the Soviet scholars:

> Every time a French novel crops up in the course of *EO*, Brodski dutifully (but always vaguely, as is the wont of Russian commentators) alludes to Russian translations of it. He forgets, however, that the Onegins and the Larins of 1820 read these books in French, whereas the grotesque, barbarous, monstrously stilted Russian versions were read only by the lower classes. (II: 65)

Or:

> The inimitable Brodski hints that the "bourgeois liberalism" of Jean

[6] D. J. Enright, "Nabokov's Way," *The New York Review of Books*, VII: vii (Nov. 3, 1966), 3–4.

[7] Aleksandr Pushkin, *Eugene Onegin*, tr. from the Russian, with a commentary by Vladimir Nabokov, 4 vols. (London, 1964), II, 3–4. Hereafter, this edition is the one cited in the text.

Baptiste Say's *Traité d' économie politique* (1803) and the "oracular babble" (teste Marx) of the learned jurist Jeremy Bentham (1748–1832) could not satisfy Onegin's subconscious Bolshevism. A delightful notion. (II: 164)

His attitude is summarized in a lament that he is "prevented . . . by a barbarous regime from traveling to Leningrad to examine old play-bills in its libraries" (II: 79), which must give him some sympathy for Kinbote who has no library in his hut in Cedarn where he edits "Pale Fire" and must quote his references from a very fallible memory. (p. 172)

All of this niggling pedantry is performed as an act of contrition before a great work, but Nabokov will also turn it into a mock ped-antry for use as a weapon against the dullards who pose as translators, critics, or poets. In glossing *pedant* in the poem he writes, "One variety of pedant is the person who likes to perorate, to air, if not to preach, his opinions, with great thoroughness and precision of detail," and then proceeds to perorate, to air, and preach, etc. (II: 46) This is the joke, for mock pedantry demands the writer alternate the guise of the fool with that of the cavalier. So he will also begin a note, "Everybody remembers the kindly lines (685–87) in James Thompson's *Summer* (1727) . . ." (II: 74), or he will speculate on verbal similarities between Pushkin and James Russell Lowell and call it a "charming coincidence" (II: 96), or he will indulge in a highly competitive personal image as when the mere word *rainbow* brings this:

My own fifty-year remembrance is not so much of prismatic colors cast upon snowdrifts by the two lateral lanterns of a brougham as of iridescent spicules around blurry street lights coming through its frost-foliated win-dows and breaking along the rim of the glass. (II:110)

Scholarly annotations are not supposed to indulge in prose poems, but in Nabokov's *Eugene Onegin* they do because the poem is a god-like rendering of life and his piety toward that may take an ecstatic as well as an exegetical form.

Most important to note in Nabokov's treatment of Pushkin is this sense that his poem is a heightened form of reality. He might acknowledge that the narrative voice called Pushkin in *Eugene One-gin* is not quite that of the historical Pushkin, yet he will often write as though Pushkin-narrator can be extracted from the letters of Pushkin-historical, and that both are real (not just fictional) contem-

poraries of Eugene Onegin. One note says that Pushkin's "and Onegin's youth may be gathered from a ribald letter Pushkin wrote to
another profligate . . ." (II: 76–77), or, "Onegin and Pushkin meet
on equal terms despite the difference in age; and if Onegin is Pushkin's master in Byronic gloom, Pushkin can teach him a number of
additional things about women, not found in Ovid." (II: 228)
Prose fiction always works in this grey area between life and art, but
few are as expert as Nabokov at charting its byways. He worked on
his edition of Eugene Onegin and Pale Fire simultaneously, and
no doubt the first was in large part the inspiration of the second. But
Pale Fire combines the method of the edition of Eugene Onegin
with that of The Dunciad, for Pope wrote the poem on which he
commented facetiously himself (with other helping hands), and in
Pale Fire Nabokov is not the worshipper, or leech, of Pushkin. With
full appreciation of the uses of anonymity he can play the roles of
both John Shade and Charles Kinbote.

In Nabokov's work the proof that a Creator exists is not that his
creation is orderly but that its order is eternally hidden from man. In
Pale Fire this Popean inversion of the traditional proof of God's
existence from the order of Nature is supported by other inversions.
The reader is first invited to think that the poem "Pale Fire," and
the life of New Wye, are real, whereas Kinbote's memory of Zembla
is entirely imaginary and fictitious. Normally the work of art (in this
case "Pale Fire") is the figment and the commentary on the work
is real. Then we gradually see that Nabokov intends—at first comically and then seriously—the commentary to be a shadow or reflection (to use the work's basic images) of the poem. In this way two
common assumptions are attacked; that life and art are separate and
distinct, and that reality or life adheres to the laws of natural causal-
ity. The Foreword ends with Kinbote asserting that

without my notes Shade's text simply has no human reality at all since
the human reality of such a poem as his (being too skittish and reticent
for an autobiographical work), with the omission of many pithy lines
carelessly rejected by him, has to depend entirely on the reality of its
author and his surroundings, attachments and so forth, a reality that only
my notes can provide. (pp. 28–29)

Such an attitude may appear to be stated in a slightly megalomaniac
way, but the general attitude is one that most readers accept. Then
those notes turn out to describe a "reality" that looks like a combination between an operetta by Franz Lehár and some early Marx

Brothers film. In the poem itself Shade, just after his reference to the Popean Zembla, writes, "Man's life as commentary to abstruse/ Unfinished poem. Note for further use." (p. 67) In spite of Shade's attack on the need for "sincerity" in art (p. 156), we might guess that he (and Nabokov) is here being most sincere, and that in spite of even Kinbote's doubts ("I have no desire to twist and batter an unambiguous *apparatus criticus* into the monstrous semblance of a novel" [p. 86]), for Shade (and, again, Nabokov) might well think Kinbote's Zembla relevant, for "life is a great surprise. I do not see why death should not be an even greater one." (p. 225)

NABOKOV'S
DIALECTICAL
STRUCTURE

Carol T. Williams

> Not only rainbows—every line is bent,
> and skulls and seeds and all good worlds are round.[1]

These lines contain the essence of Vladimir Nabokov's metaphysical division. The human eye, he implies, can see only half of the circle (the rainbow's arc); the other half must be taken on faith. This "twin-halved" mortal world is originally composed of opposites—"skulls and seeds"—in whose synthesis the contradiction between death and life is not eliminated, but honored as the basis of beauty—i.e., the human is a Hegelian synthesis in which the opposing thetic and antithetic *moments* (aspects) are *aufheben*—put aside and preserved.

Of his notion that "in the spiral form, the circle . . . has been set free," Nabokov writes,

I thought this up when I was a schoolboy, and I also discovered that Hegel's triadic series expressed merely the essential spirality of all things in their relation to time. Twirl follows twirl, and every synthesis is the thesis of the next series. If we consider the simplest spiral, three stages may be distinguished in it, corresponding to those of the triad: We can call "thetic" the small curve or arc that initiates the convolution centrally: "antithetic" the larger arc that faces the first in the process of continuing it; and "synthetic" the still ampler arc that continues the second while following the first along the outer side.[2]

An ideal chess problem, or novel, has a "fairly simple, 'thetic' solution," which the "unsophisticated" may "discover . . . without having

---

[1] Vladimir Nabokov, "An Evening of Russian Poetry," *Poems* (Garden City, 1959), p. 20.

[2] *Speak, Memory: A Memoir* (New York, 1960), p. 204. Subsequent references to *SM* are in the text.

passed through the pleasurable torments prepared for the sophisticated." The "latter" commits himself to the "pleasant experience of
the roundabout route," and "having passed through this 'antithetic'
inferno," an "ultra-sophisticated solver," he achieves "the simple key-
move [that] . . . provide[s] him with a synthesis of poignant artistic
delight." (SM, pp. 221–222)

Nabokov's "own life" is "Hegelian":

A colored spiral in a small ball of glass. . . . The twenty years I spent in
my native Russia (1899–1919) take care of my thetic arc. Twenty-one
years of voluntary exile in England, Germany and France (1919–1940)
supply the obvious antithesis. The decade I have already spent in my
adopted country (1940–1950) looks like the beginning of a synthetic en-
velopment. (SM, p. 205)

In The Gift Fyodor, the poet-hero, "tried to sort out the mish-
mash of philosophical ideas" of the 1860's and concluded that the
"burlesque consonance" of names "manifested a kind of sin against
thought, a mockery of it, . . . when some extravagantly praised Kant,
others Kont (Comte), others again Hegel or Schlegel."[3] Nabokov
seems to twit Hegel with a rhyme, but he does not in fact criticize
the idealist so much as those after him who implanted their own
notions in his philosophy. In Bend Sinister Ekwilism is a "metamorphosis" of the philosophy born in Fradrik Skotoma's "misty
senility," and it could be Hegel's philosophy of history; in fact,
Nabokov inserts quotation marks around " 'world consciousness,' " a
key term in Hegel's notion of history.[4] But he insists that "pathetic"
Skotoma (p. 73) is not to blame for the bestial totalitarianism that
took the name of his idealistic "idea of balance as a basis for universal
bliss." Like Hegel (though Nabokov does not say so), "while suggesting a remolding of human individuals in conformity with a well-
balanced pattern, . . . [Skotoma] prudently omitted to define . . .
the practical method to be pursued" (p. 75), and like Hegel, who
died before both Fascism and Communism claimed him as a foun-
tainhead, Skotoma, who "died soon after his treatise appeared . . .
was spared the discomfort of seeing his vague and benevolent Ekwil-

---

[3] The Gift, trans. Michael Scammell in collaboration with the author (New
York, 1963), p. 214. Subsequent references to G are in the text.

[4] Bend Sinister (New York, 1947), pp. 76, 74. Subsequent references to BS
are in the text.

ism transformed . . . into a violent and virulent political doctrine."
(p. 76) Thus, Nabokov's opinion of Hegel seems to be Fyodor's
judgment of those who "explained away . . . the smell of Gogol's
Petrushka . . . by the fact that everything existing was rational":

> the time for hearty Russian Hegelianism was now past. The molders of
> opinion were incapable of understanding Hegel's vital truth: a truth that
> was not stagnant, like shallow water, but flowed like blood, through the
> very process of cognition. (p. 256)

This "vital truth" is not, it seems, the misty philosophy of history,
but the Dialectic, the "very process of cognition" for Hegel and, it
seems, for Nabokov as well.

In itself, Hegel's Dialectic is complicated because it assumes a
dynamic condition or process, and because his definitions of it are
ambiguous and contradictory. Like an artist, Hegel ignores his own
theory. For example, he insists theoretically but not in his examples
that the stages in the Dialectical spiral are *necessarily* generated in
individual thought and action, as well as in social process, i.e., history. They are "produce[d]," Hegel says, by the thesis, i.e., by *Geist*
(Absolute Spirit), which is abstract in the thetic *moment*, but which,
because of its "indwelling tendency outwards," generates "the particular thought [or action] required."[5] In its third "side," that of
"positive reason," thought returns in "self-reference" to the thesis,
but enriched by its "Determination" and having unified its abstract
and concrete meanings in *aufheben*: "to discard" and "to preserve";
i.e., "the subjective and the objective are not merely identified but
also distinct."[6] Each synthesis is partial, and thus generates another
triad, until the final synthesis of the over-arching spiral, "the Abstract," "the Dialectical," and "positive reason."[7] Like Nabokov's
informal philosophy, Hegel's audacious psychology and history is
indebted to Plato's concept of "forms as synthesis of opposites."[8]
The root, however, of Hegel and Nabokov's similarity is that both
are artists—Hegel probably more than he knew, he who so valued
the antithetical *moment* that he termed it the "very soul" of "knowl-

---

[5] G. W. F. Hegel, *The Science of Logic*, trans. William Wallace, 2nd ed.
(Oxford, 1963), pp. 18, 34, 147–148.

[6] *Ibid.*, Chapter VI, pp. 143–155.

[7] *Ibid.*, pp. 135, 143. Hegel uses "Dialectic" to refer both to the cognitive
process as a whole and (as on p. 143) to only its second *moment*.

[8] G. R. C. Mure, *An Introduction to Hegel* (Oxford, 1940), pp. 117–119.

edge,"[9] and he who despite his own theory of necessity, chose his Dialectic's examples from the world's *freest* experiences: death, knowledge, and beauty.

Like Nabokov, Hegel conceives of art as a representation of the "good worlds" (although schematically he categorizes it as the thesis of a triad whose antithesis is religion and whose synthesis is—as one expects—philosophy). In his editor's Introduction to Scribner's *Hegel Selections*, Jacob Loewenberg presents Hegel as a "romantic iron-[ist]" who "impersonat[es]" with "apparent seriousness" a number of "heterogeneous moods," each of which is quickly discarded so that he may show himself its master through "parody and ridicule," and so that the ideas may be unmasked by their "internal contradictions" as "the partial masquerading as the complete."[10] But Loewenberg (who would have been a perceptive Nabokov critic) ignores Hegel's *real* "seriousness" and, above all, the critical fact that he did propose a final synthesis, the full consciousness of *Geist*, which he apparently believed was not doomed by the Dialectic's generative principle. To Loewenberg, Hegel's "happy ending" is either an artistic deceit or the delusion of a philosopher who does not understand his own system. But Hegel was no Beckett or Nabokov. The kind of artist he was is suggested by the similarity of his descriptions of the final synthesis and the end of an ideal tragedy. The tragic "spirit," Hegel says, "will, expanding into all particularity, step forth out of its repose, . . . and involve itself in the contradictions of the broken and confused medley of earthly existence," and "the true course of dramatic development consists in the annulment of contradictions viewed as such. . . . [Then] our emotional attitude is tranquillized . . . ; rudely shaken by the calamitous result to the heroes, but reconciled in the substantial facts."[11]

Thus, not only do the triadic movements of Nabokov's compositions resemble Hegel's Dialectic, in which opposing processes in time or the mind are interpeted as complements, but their conceptions of art and life are also similar. Both emphasize the nobility of the human striver as well as his destructiveness, and both reconcile the mortal conflict in an aesthetic synthesis in which two opposing

---

[9] Hegel, "Preface," *Phenomenology of Mind* [*Geist*], trans. J. B. Baillie, *Selections*, ed. Jacob Loewenberg (New York, 1957), p. 32; *The Logic*, p. 74.

[10] pp. xix–xxi, xxvii–xxxvii, xli.

[11] "Philosophy of Fine Art," I, trans. F. P. B. Osmaston, *Hegel on Tragedy*, ed. Anne and Henry Paolucci (Garden City, 1962), pp. 97, 71.

impulses are retained in stasis. It seems, then, that Nabokov's most Hegelian statement is one which does not refer to the philosopher directly; it is V.'s conclusion after he has searched for the "real life" of his half-brother, Sebastian Knight: "Two modes of his life question each other and the answer is his life itself, and that is the nearest one ever can approach a human truth."[12]

Nabokov's triple spiral of meaning is suggested by Cincinnatus C.'s definition of his "double": "the gangrel, that accompanies each of us—you, and me, and him over there—doing what we would like to do at that very moment, but cannot."[13] The double is the private self, masked, and hence in this world unreal. In Hegelian terms it is one's "Determination," as his thesis is himself as "Kind," i.e., Everyman. When Nabokov's "ultra-sophisticated" reader feels the synthesis "of poignant artistic delight," he is "reconciled in the substantial facts"—contradictions that are in stasis, yet stubbornly, splendidly discrete. Every Nabokov protagonist and work is this "triple dream."[14] In *Pale Fire* the man who is a poet, John Shade, and his mortal fate, Gradus, a man in his intestines, a machine in his mind, are synthesized in King Charles-Kinbote, a balance between the holy muse and the pitiful voyeur. The intense child and the chess-phobic adult Luzhin are synthesized in a brilliant but pitiful madness. Hermann, *Despair's* Utopian, and Hermann, the gross bourgeois reflected in his "double," Felix, generate the criminal. The artist Sebastian Knight and the would-be one, V., are synthesized in their omnipresent but enigmatic author, the "someone whom neither of us knows," as V. says in the novel's last words. In *The Gift*—as Nabokov says in the Foreword, a novel about art— lyricism and parody are typically suspended in the final paragraph ("Good-by, my book! . . ."), in which is hidden an "epilogic poem [that] mimics an *Onegin* stanza" (Foreword): lyricism creates emotional heightening, proper to the conclusion of a novel, until the rhyme's jangle obtrudes, suffusing lyricism with parody.

In many of the short stories, too, a *moment* of enlightenment —of which *Lolita's* Gray Star scene is the model—arranges each

---

[12] *The Real Life of Sebastian Knight* (Norfolk, Conn., 1959), p. 137. Subsequent references to *SK* are in the text.

[13] *Invitation to a Beheading*, trans. Dmitri Nabokov in collaboration with the author (New York, 1959), p. 25. Subsequent references to *I* are in the text.

[14] "Translator's Foreword," *A Hero of Our Time* by Mihail Lermontov, trans. Vladimir Nabokov in collaboration with Dmitri Nabokov (Garden City, 1958), p. vi.

work's discrete, contradictory moods into a complex "web of sense."
In "Signs and Symbols" (*Nabokov's Dozen*), for example, private
imaginativeness (the boy maddened by "'referential mania'") and
public dullness (his old parents' appearance and the world in which
they appear) are synthesized in the surprising revelation of the
woman's sensitive knowledge "of the incalculable amount of tenderness contained in the world" and its "simian . . . fate." An anagram is embedded in the conclusion of "The Vane Sisters," so that
for the reader who discovers the message Nabokov hides from the
narrator, a balance is made with the latter's conclusion that the dead
are "yellowly blurred, illusive, lost." The astronaut "Lance" (*Nabokov's Dozen*), who vanquished the "'Pass Perilous'" and "the
Bridge of the Sword leading to the Otherworld ('*dont nus estranges
ne retorne*'),'' and Lance, the outsider in a human world of "terrified" elders, are synthesized in the Hegelian way in the tale's last
paragraph, in which "the old Bokes," leaving their son to excited
reveries about his last and next trips in space, descend in the hospital
elevator with the human adventurer, "a girl with a baby," and the
human horror, "the gray-haired, bent, sullen elevator man, who
stands with his back to everybody."

In three of his novels, Nabokov's tri-arced structure is especially
clear: *Invitation to a Beheading*, in which the Hegelian pattern is
emphasized by Cincinnatus' decomposition into public aspects and
private "gangrel"; *Laughter in the Dark*, which, as Nabokov implies,
is a "Hegelian syllogism of humor";[15] and *Lolita*, in which Humbert
is decomposed, Humbert and Lolita's self-contradictory characteristics are exaggerated, and the synthetic spiral is initiated by a surprising revelation of character in the Gray Star scene.

Cincinnatus, the typical Nabokov protagonist, is an enigma. Is
he condemned by Nabokov for his certainty that he "knew what
it is impossible to know"? (*I*, p. 95) Or is he a sympathetic (and
sado-masochistic) self-portrait by an author certain "there is in the
world not a single human who can speak my language"? (*I*, p. 95)
Nabokov balances the two impressions, although, "relentlessly howl-
ing" (p. 93), Cincinnatus is less attractive than *Bend Sinister's* victim, Adam Krug. But Cincinnatus dreams of a better world and
quests for the words by which he might explain it, and he is as sensitive as Rodion, Marthe, Pierre, and his other "fate-mate[s]" (p. 16)

---

[15] *Laughter in the Dark* (New York, 1958), p. 78. Subsequent references
to *LD* are in the text.

are vulgar. In short, after decomposition into Rodion, Rodrig, etc.,
Nabokov's hero is still composed of two opposing aspects, which are
synthesized in one moment shortly before his death, in which Cincinnatus and a live creature "merge in love."[16]

In *Invitation*, as in all of Nabokov's works, "real life" is askew
from the beginning: "In accordance with the law the death sentence
was announced to Cincinnatus C. in a whisper. All rose, exchanging
smiles." (p. 11) Cincinnatus' name, like those of his keepers, Rodion
and Rodrig, and his lawyer, Roman, mitigates against one's recognizing his world in Cincinnatus', as do the facts that he is the "sole
prisoner (in such an enormous fortress)" (p. 13), and that Rodion
in his cell "offered to dance a waltz with him. Cincinnatus agreed.
They began to twirl." (p. 13) Only when Nabokov explicates Cincinnatus' crime of opaqueness does one recognize that what has
seemed the hero's dream is an allegory. In Chapter Two, Nabokov explains that Cincinnatus is "impervious to the rays of others,
. . . a lone dark obstacle in this world of souls transparent to one
another," whose "safe place," i.e., the "cell," is now so thoroughly
"penetrated" by "the solicitous sunshine of public concern" that
"there was not a single point that the observer on the other side of
the door could not pierce with his gaze." (pp. 24–25) Everyone in
Cincinnatus' world is "a reflection in a mirror." (p. 77)

In this "circus family" the spider in Cincinnatus' cell is "the
youngest member"; Pierre, the executioner, is the "star performer"
(pp. 115–116); Rodion is the clown ("bow-legged, in old faded
breeches, baggy in the seat" [p. 40]); and Rodrig is the "circus director" (p. 115), who wears "a perfect toupee, black as pitch," and who
moves his legs "evenly in his columnar trousers" (pp. 14–15): i.e.,
Rodrig is a tin soldier, a mechanical man like Gradus. All of the
entertainers are defective. Roman's "made-up face" has a "long hare-
lip" (p. 37) and "an edging of pinkish muslin at the back of his
head where the black wig ended" (p. 40): i.e., the doll's stuffing
obtrudes. Even Emmie, Lolita's "downy" twin and Cincinnatus'
romantic dream, is shin-scabbed (p. 149). But only at the end does
Nabokov unmask these puppets. On execution day, in contrast to
"attractively rouged M'sieur Pierre" (p. 207), Rodrig and Roman are
"haggard, . . . without any makeup, without padding and without
wigs." (p. 207) "They turned out to resemble each other, and their

---

[16] Nabokov, *Lolita* (New York, 1958), p. 203. Subsequent references to *L*
are in the text.

identical heads moved identically on their thin necks" (p. 207); so too Rodrig and Rodion are "perfectly identical" (p. 215), and after Cincinnatus leaves the platform on which he has been beheaded, he sees Roman, "many times smaller and . . . at the same time Rodrig." (p. 223) And, although it is he who frees Cincinnatus, the "fate-mate" Pierre is also diminished when Cincinnatus "dies." The buffoon in "honey-blond" wig (pp. 59, 159) who would woo Cincinnatus with acrobatics and card tricks, is a vulgar pederast (for is death not repulsive?); yet it is he who opens Cincinnatus' cell. Nabokov retains the paradox when he sentences the "operatic woodman." (p. 171) Pierre disintegrates, but into a "tiny" object "like a larva" (p. 223)—the embryo perhaps of a moth, the agent of *Invitation's* synthesis.

Shortly before Pierre comes for Cincinnatus, Rodion brings a moth, a succulent " 'treat' " for the cell's spider. The moth, "large as a man's hand," escapes, but after Cincinnatus returns to his journal of this "irreparabl[y] . . . crack[ed]" life, he sees it sleeping on the leg of his cot. This occurs just as Cincinnatus begins a new sheet of paper, on which he continues a sentence, " '. . . death,' " and then "crosse[s it] out" as not "precis[e]" enough. The moth has a blemish—"a bald spot . . . where the fuzz had rubbed off"—but it is this "little brown fuzz . . . stuck to the edge of the table" that creates Cincinnatus' experience, for it reminds him of the moth, and as he studies it "the perfect symmetry of all . . . [its] diverging lines" so "enchant" Cincinnatus that, "unable to restrain himself, [he] stroked with his fingertip the hoary ridge near the base of the right wing, then the ridge of the left one (what gentle firmness! what unyielding gentleness!)." (pp. 202–206) Because it is his only act of tenderness in the novel, this stroking is significant, and it seems to explain his remark to Pierre a moment later "that everything had . . . been written already" when he crossed out "death," and his novel "clarity . . . at first almost painful, so suddenly did it come, but then suffusing him with joy," as, on the execution block, he asks, "Why am I lying [note the double meaning] like this?" Cincinnatus gets up and makes "his way in that direction where, to judge by the voices, stood beings akin to him," because the platform, the "transparent" spectators, and the "reliefless" world are all "coming apart." (pp. 222–223) But Nabokov only "judge[s]" that Cincinnatus moves, and not to, but "in th[e] direction" of his dream of communication. Which of Cincinnatus' two worlds is "real"? Nabokov answers not with fact but with a dream, which is appropriately given in a Hegelian synthesis.

Invitation's world is that of allegory, fantastically real; *Laughter in the Dark* is a more realistic novel about people who live publicly in the world of make-believe. Albert Albinus is an art expert interested in movies. He contacts the cartoonist Axel Rex because he thinks paintings can be "brought to life" by animated drawings. Margot, Albinus and Rex's mistress, is an usherette in a cinema when Albinus discovers her and an inept starlet after she wins him from his wife and child. Even Elisabeth, the quiet matron, is the daughter of a theatrical manager. Only Paul, who represents *Laughter*'s thetic arc, is not connected by Nabokov with the arts. "A stout good-natured man," his solidity is imaged in the "two pencils and two pens" in his breastpocket (p. 7). These "secondary" artists enact a secondary pattern of the Hegelian syllogism, the "Hegelian syllogism of humor." *Laughter* is a triple construction of triads: its story, characters, and art are all composed of intertwining thetic, antithetic, and synthetic arcs.

In the story's thesis timid Albinus, for whom "romance had a trick of becoming flat" (p. 9), begins what he hopes will be a temporary liaison with "painfully beautiful" Margot (p. 13). But the ambitious teen-ager exposes their alliance, and Paul, who sees Margot as a "schoolgirl" (p. 40), comes to help Elisabeth leave Albinus wearing "black sticking plaster" on his "plump" cheek (p. 48): the scarred thetic arc disintegrates. The story's antithesis spirals when Elisabeth leaves and Albinus moves in with Margot. The flat he has rented for her is "dreadful" (p. 43), and Albinus "marveled how he, who prided himself on not being able to endure anything in bad taste, could tolerate this chamber of horrors. Everything, he mused, was beautified by his passion." (p. 52) Albinus, the reader is notified, is a different person, his "gangrel." He and Margot luxuriate on the Riviera, chauffeured by their good friend, Axel Rex: by Nabokovian coincidence Margot's first and only love. In an accident Albinus is blinded as literally as he has been figuratively, and he, Margot, and (secretly) Rex resume the *ménage à trois* in Switzerland, until Paul arrives to expose Rex's joke. At this point the synthetic arc dominates, as Albinus, who sought youth with a sixteen year-old and indirectly caused his own daughter's death, is placed in her nursery and cared for as a child by Elisabeth until, shot by Margot, he falls "like a big, soft doll." (p. 159)

As in *Lolita*, the thetic theme in *Laughter* is sounded lightly throughout the antithesis, whose grotesqueness is clear, for example, when Albinus re-enters his thesis for Irma's funeral and returns to his flat, unaware, says the narrator, that Rex, himself "well-contented," has just left Margot in it, "delirious[ly] content." (p. 97) And, again as in *Lolita*, each character has three aspects. Albinus is a seducer and a dupe, and eventually a child and a doll. Margot is sympathetic even as she destroys Albinus' marriage because of *his* selfishness, and even during the antithesis she receives some of the sympathy due an innocent egoist; she tries to be faithful to Albinus, the narrator says, but, however sensual, her love for Rex is real. On the Riviera, Rex plays his cruel-comic tricks on Albinus, and in Switzerland Margot is only his passive accomplice: Nabokov slowly turns his lens from her, so that one's permanent impression of Margot is mixed.

Even Rex, who in the final section becomes one of Nabokov's evilest villains, is not simply that. He is both "humorist" and "artist" (p. 79), and as an artist he has an aesthetic by which his author shapes the tale of which he is villain. Besides his own "triplicity," Rex, like *Lolita*'s Clare Quilty, also embodies Albinus' black "gangrel," the logical extension of "white's evil *moment*; and a passage in *The Gift* suggests that Rex is Nabokov's portrait of his own dark side. Rex composes this story: " 'A certain man . . . once lost a diamond cufflink in the wide blue sea, and twenty years later, on the exact day, a Friday apparently, he was eating a large fish—but there was no diamond inside. That's what I like about coincidence.' " (p. 74) To Rex, the world was a "roaring comedy," whose stage manager ". . . was an elusive, double, self-reflecting magic Proteus of a phantom, the shadow of many-colored glass balls flying in a curve. . . ." (pp. 100–101) This could be a Nabokov description of himself; yet Rex is eventually defeated by Paul. Romanov, a Berliner in *The Gift*, suggests that Rex is the artist Nabokov feared he might be. Romanov painted " 'Coincidence,' where, on an advertising post, among the vivid, remarkably harmonious colors of playbills, astral names of cinemas and other transparent motley, one could read a notice about a lost diamond necklace (with a reward to the finder), which necklace lay right there on the sidewalk, at the very foot of the post, its innocent fire sparkling." (G, p. 70) "I," says Fyodor (or is it Nabokov?), was "forestall[ed] and forewarn[ed]" by "Romanov's strange, beautiful, yet venomous art." Like Romanov (a "rex"), Axel Rex illuminates the "dangers of the [Romanov] way." (G, p. 71) Thus Nabokov adds to Rex's "Hegelian syllogism of humor": its venomous creator is also "made to look silly." (p. 78) Rex exemplifies his theory:

Uncle alone in the house with the children said he'd dress up to amuse them. After a long wait, as he did not appear, they went down and saw a masked man putting the table silver into a bag. "Oh, Uncle," they cried in delight. "Yes, isn't my make-up good?" said Uncle, taking his mask off. Thus goes the Hegelian syllogism of humor. Thesis: Uncle made himself up as a burglar (a laugh for the children); antithesis: it was a burglar (a laugh for the reader); synthesis: it still was Uncle (fooling the reader). (p. 78)

This "art of caricature" was, "as Rex understood it, . . . based (apart from its synthetic, fooled-again nature) on the contrast between cruelty on one side and credulity on the other." (pp. 78–79)

Laughter's art is another "Uncle" syllogism. The antithesis ("it was a burglar") is both ironic and false, as is Albinus' liaison with Margot, who shares "a laugh" with Rex and the reader. The synthesis (" it still was Uncle [Paul]") is perfectly Hegelian because "the reader is fooled" by Morality's disguise as a stolid clerk. Like the Uncle syllogism, Laughter's comic pattern moves from simple farce to an ironic antithesis and a grotesquely farcical synthesis in which the fundamental joke is on religious tragedy: a hero with a fatal flaw (blindness) destroys himself with the assistance of Coincidence—but vengeance is dealt by the Chorus (Paul), and at death Albinus has learned only of the "mess life has been." (p. 159)

As the title suggests, in Laughter story and characters both are subservient to comic art. Its jokes spiral from farce to grotesquery. The clearest "syllogism of humor" in the thesis is the joke begun by Margot and concluded by Chance. Visiting Albinus' flat without warning to frighten him, Margot (farcically) locks him into his own bedroom, from which he is released by Paul. While hunting the "burglars" with Paul, Albinus notices "just behind a revolving bookstand, the edge of a bright red frock" (p. 36), and all evening, among his family, he fears for Margot's exposure. But at last, and now "sinful[ly]" excited, " 'Margot, you mad little thing,' he whispered feverishly," creeping towards her, But "Margot" is "only a scarlet silk cushion which he himself had brought there a few days ago, to crouch on while consulting Nonnenmacher's History of Art—ten volumes, folio." (p. 38) The "laugh" on Albinus (the lock-up) returns to itself enriched because of his "credulity" and Fate's "cruelty" (pp. 78–79)—but "he himself" placed the pillow. This is crueler than the Uncle syllogism, and so is Rex's joke on Albinus.

But first, during the novel's antithesis, other comic themes are played: "burlesque" (in Rex's admiring opinion) when Albinus finds Margot and Rex on a couch, his coat button entangled in her lace

("Margot screamed [at Albinus], 'Don't you dare cut the lace; cut off the button!' 'Stop—it's my button!' yelled Rex" [pp. 90–91]); the Horner hoax (pp. 91–92); and a Bathroom Gag when the three lovers share two hotel rooms and a connecting bath. (pp. 111–113) After Albinus' blinding, Margot lovingly takes him to a Swiss "cottage . . . with a cup for holy water affixed to every door" (p. 137), where Rex, a delighted specter, sits at the table, eating "like a silent film diner, in perfect rhythm to Albinus' moving jaws." (p. 143) Synthesis, and Paul, arrive as Rex, "stark naked," deeply tanned, "with his hairy legs crossed and his chin cupped in his hand . . . in the pose of Rodin's 'Thinker,'" sits opposite Albinus in the "drawing room," tickling the blind man "gently" with a piece of grass, which Albinus, "bearded," wearing a "mouse-gray dressing-gown," and thinking the grass-stem a fly, wearily brushes away. (pp. 150–151) Then Rex sees Paul outside the window—a balance of Sherlock Holmes and The Tourist: "a stout gentleman in a checkered cap . . . looking on in amazement." Paul enters, saying simply, "'Of course, I know you. Your name is Rex,'" and the game is over. But not quite, for as Rex leaves the room—after a characteristically cool, "'Pity you've spoiled everything'"—Paul, "good-natured Paul who had never in his life hit a living creature," whacks Rex's head "mightily" with Albinus' stick—and the author unmasks: "Suddenly something very remarkable occurred: like Adam after the Fall, Rex, cowering by the white wall and grinning wanly, covered his nakedness with his hand." (pp. 151–152) Just so Morality, the fat-man comic, vanquishes Edmund, the "venomous" anarchist, and secures the peace of death for the tortured sinner—who is also the comic dupe: it is neither tragedy, nor parody of tragedy; it is Nabokovian tragic farce.

Lolita, too, is a "comic-horror" tale. Not only are Lolita and Humbert both triple characters, but Humbert is decomposed, and his antithetical "gangrel" appears as Clare Quilty.[17] Quilty is Humbert's guilt. (As Lolita's schoolmate Mona Dahl implies, in French, "Qu'il t'y" sounds almost "guilty" [p. 225].) After murdering his image, driving "on the wrong side of the road . . . [the] queer mirror side," Humbert, "with a graceful movement . . . turned off the road, and after two or three big bounces, rode up a grassy slope,

---

[17] Charles Mitchell ("Mythic Seriousness in Lolita," Texas Studies in Literature and Language, V [Autumn, 1963], 341) and G. D. Josipovici ("Lolita: Parody and The Pursuit of Beauty," Critical Quarterly, VI [Spring, 1964], 42) among others, have charted Quilty's role as "the parody of Humbert."

among surprised cows. . . . A kind of thoughtful Hegelian synthesis linking up two dead women" (pp. 308–309)—Dolly Schiller, dead if her tale is being read, and the nymphet Lolita, whom since Gray Star Humbert has known to be his own deadly creation, and whom he mercifully destroyed when he murdered Quilty.

But Quilty is only an enriching attendant on the spirals of Humbert and Lolita. In thetic Part I (until Humbert and Lolita become lovers), Humbert is pre-eminently Humbert the Horrible, but not entirely—never in Nabokov's or Hegel's dialectics entirely; for Hegel insists that the Dialectic is not a process in time, and Nabokov says that the "larger" antithesis "faces the first [arc] in the process of continuing it," and the "still ampler" synthesis "continues the second while following the first along the outer side." (*SM*, p. 204) Thetic Humbert is a sadistic impotent with a scholar's mine of information on the "girleen." What meliorates his repulsiveness is what prevents one remembering Lolita as merely her thesis, a twelve year-old American girl-child. Lolita, the *"gamine fatale"* antithetically, draws from perverted Humbert evidence of his antithesis: Humbert *cum* Dagwood Bumstead, the muddling American father. If he kissed her, he knew she would "even close her eyes as Hollywood teaches" and respond as to "a double vanilla with hot fudge." (p. 50) Thus does monstrous Lolita remain innocent even as monstrous Humbert secretly grasps her "little hot paw." (p. 53) As, after Charlotte Haze Humbert's death, one approaches Part II with Humbert, one hears from the (retrospective) narrator that "instead of basking in the beams of smiling Chance, I was obsessed by all sorts of purely ethical doubts and fears" (p. 107), and when Lolita, "her soft lips parted in a slightly foolish but wonderfully endearing smile," meets him at Camp Q., he considers a "sound education, a . . . clean home, nice girl-friends," but he concludes, "among whom . . . I might find . . . a pretty little *mägdlein* for Herr Doktor Humbert alone." (p. 113) Thetic Humbert is a baffling mixture of conscious (ironic) and natural repulsiveness.

As her antithesis spirals, Lolita, too, is both innocent and depraved; but her original character predominates. She makes them "technically lovers" (p. 134), but later, when he would park by the road, " 'Drive on,' my Lo cried shrilly," and "sweetly smiling," she claims he " 'raped' " her—Humbert wonders, "Was she just joking? An ominous hysterical note rang through her silly words." (p. 143) (Note that even from his retrospective, supposedly reformed perspective, they are "silly.") At the end of Part I, Lolita, "sobbing," real-

izes that she has "absolutely nowhere else to go" but to the bed of a
" 'dirty, dirty old man.' " (pp. 143–144) As the antithetic spiral
begins to dominate, one's impression is nearly balanced between
sympathy and distaste for each of the protagonists; and at the end of
Part II the reader will favor fatherly Humbert by about as much as
he does vulnerable Lolita at the end of Part I.

In "Kabins" across America and in Beardsley "Humbert le Bel"
becomes the bemused American Father: "I was not really quite prepared for her fits of disorganized boredom, intense and vehement
griping, her sprawling, droopy, dopey-eyed style, and what is called
goofing off." (p. 150) But psychotic Humbert and innocent Lolita
are still reported by "*Qu'il t'y*" Humbert: "a hazy blue view . . . and
the backs of a family enjoying it (with Lo, in a hot, happy, wild,
intense, hopeful, hopeless whisper—'Look, the McCrystals [from
Ramsdale], please, let's talk to them, please'—let's talk to them,
reader!—'please! I'll do anything you want.)" (p. 159); and he concludes his account of their first "circle" of America with "her sobs
in the night—every night, every night—the moment I feigned sleep."
(pp. 177–178) As Part II winds down, although (when Lolita is ill)
"I thought of poliomyelitis as any American parent would. Giving
up all hope of intercourse . . ." (p. 242), Humbert usually presents
himself as the vulnerable dupe who delivers Lolita to her "secret ter-
minus" and her next lover. For example, hearing a tapping on the
cabin door during their second (antithetical) American "tour," he
opened it and

noticed two things—that I was stark naked and that, white-glistening in
the rain-dripping darkness there stood a man holding before his face the
mask of Jutting Chin, a grotesque sleuth in the funnies. He emitted a
muffled guffaw and scurried away, and I . . . am not sure even to this day
that the visit was not a drug-provoked dream. . . . Did I see next morning
two urchins rummaging in a garbage can and trying on Jutting Chin?
(p. 219)

Humbert plays "Nabokov" instead of "the victim" in another passage: "all those identical detectives in prismatically changing cars
were figments of my persecution mania, recurrent images based on
coincidence and chance resemblance. *Soyons logiques.*" (p. 240)
But Quilty is following them—yet how real is Quilty?—and he will
take Lolita from Elphinstone Hospital while her worried step-
father prepares treats to make her tractable to *his* unnatural passion.
Again the balance is struck.

After Lolita leaves him, Humbert the madman uncoils, until, as normal as he can be, he answers Lolita's letter by driving to Gray Star, where, like him, she is suddenly no part of *art noir*. When Dolly Schiller opens the door of her "clapboard shack," he is a camera: "She was frankly and hugely pregnant. . . . Her pale-freckled cheeks were hollowed, and her bare shins and arms had lost all their tan, so that the little hairs showed." (p. 271) And, Humbert concludes, "I loved her." (p. 272) She is married to a "drab" deaf veteran who, when Humbert arrives, is helping repair the shack of his neighbor, another defective young man, one who has lost an arm in the war (because a simple man is only maimed physically). But even at Gray Star, even writing his journal in prison, Humbert perceives as an artist: "Curious: although actually her looks had faded, I definitely realized, so hopelessly late in the day, how much she looked—had always looked—like Botticelli's russet Venus." (p. 272)

Facing a new Dolores, Humbert remains a voyeur. "In her washed-out gray eyes, strangely spectacled, our poor romance was for a moment reflected, pondered upon, and dismissed like . . . a bit of dry mud caking her childhood. . . . I had been a good father, she guessed—granting me *that*." (p. 274) The pity Humbert gains by this irony is balanced by what neither he nor Lolita knows: that she will die in Christmas Day childbirth, and that in a mysterious way Humbert is her killer. Throughout the Gray Star scene this critical and often ignored fact of her approaching death depresses the reader's ascendant sympathy for "poor Humbert," and transforms Lolita's "accommodation" to Humbertian horror into tragedy. (*Time* found the "good life . . . emerg[ing] from a monstrous relationship," because Lolita is "pregnant and happy with a young goonlike husband. She has escaped." And the *New Republic* inquired editorially if a novel should be countenanced whose "moral is that a 12-year old . . . can be submerged in the kind of cesspool Mr. Nabokov describes . . . and come out of it."[18])

"Self-castigation" is only one Humbert *moment* that "faces" another to which it is synthesized in this concluding section of *Lolita*:

there she was . . . hopelessly worn at seventeen, with that baby, dreaming already of becoming a big shot and retiring around 2020 A.D.—and I . . . knew as clearly as I know I am to die, that I loved her more than anything

---

[18] "To the End of Night," *Time* (Sept. 1, 1958), 64; "*Lolita* and the Critics," *New Republic*, CXXXIX (Oct. 27, 1958), 3.

I had ever seen or imagined on earth, or hoped for anywhere else. She was only the faint violet whiff and dead leaf echo of the nymphet I had rolled myself upon . . . but thank God it was not that echo alone that I worshipped. (pp. 279–280)

It certainly is not "that echo alone," but it is that echo too, as his "violet" language reveals: ". . . my Lolita, *this* Lolita, pale and polluted, and big with another's child, but still gray-eyed, still sooty-lashed, still auburn and almond, still Carmencita, still mine. . . . No matter, even if . . . her nipples swell and crack, and her lovely young velvety delicate delta be tainted and torn—even then I would go mad with tenderness." (p. 280) Throughout the rest of the book, as Humbert plots his and Quilty's end, and Lolita, a "dear wan" (p. 280) gray ghost in the reader's consciousness, moves stately and innocent towards a Christmas death, this balance is struck between Humbert the tender and Humbert the "mad":

Unless it can be proven to me . . . that in the infinite run it does not matter a jot that a North American girl-child named Dolores Haze had been deprived of her childhood by a maniac, unless this can be proven (and if it can, then life is a joke), I see nothing for the treatment of my misery but the melancholy and very local palliative of articulate art. To quote an old poet:

> The moral sense in mortals is the duty
> We have to pay on mortal sense of beauty. (p. 285)

But, is "life" not "a joke" to "rex" Nabokov? And does not this "melancholy" couplet exactly convey *Lolita's* tragic contradictions? The artist envisions and immortalizes beauty that otherwise would not be, but he must destroy that mortal stuff to do so, for the two worlds are separate, and neither the artist nor the subject worthy of art may be in two at once. Does Humbert castigate himself as a man, or does he, a voyeur-artist in the mortal world, describe life as it appears to *his* author? The answer is not simple.[19]

---

[19] Except to (e.g.) Lionel Trilling (*Lolita* celebrates neo-Platonic passionlove" in a family-centered culture [The Last Lover: Vladimir Nabokov's 'Lolita,' " *Encounter*, XI (Oct., 1958), 19]), or Leslie Fiedler (*Lolita* is "the final blasphemy against the mythical innocence of the woman and the child" [*Love and Death in the American Novel* (New York, 1960), p. 328]). The best *Lolita* critique, Charles Mitchell's "Mythic Seriousness . . .," suggests it is Hegelian syllogism, but Mitchell seems not to fully understand the Dialectic. His analysis depends on time (e.g., on succeeding events of the plot), and he labels Lolita's

NABOKOV'S DIALECTICAL STRUCTURE 181

Certainly in the novel's final pages Lolita's thesis is revived, enriched now by her antithetical side, the dark lady of Romantic art. In his conclusion, however, Humbert describes only the child Lolita, debauched by himself, and his portrait is intensified by one's knowledge of her death. His emphasis is climaxed in the book's concluding image of the mining town whose "melody"—"of one nature," the "sounds . . . of children at play" (pp. 309–310)—teaches Humbert that "the hopelessly poignant thing was not Lolita's absence from my side, but the absence of her voice from that concord." (p. 310)

Can *Lolita* have a "moral in tow" (p. 316), and one so "conventional" (p. 289) as this panegyric to bourgeois mores? Again the answer is not simple, for as it is throughout Nabokov's "oeuvre," life—even the life of a gross tramp like Felix in *Despair*—is holy, and life—i.e., sex—is also an evil fate:

when . . . after fabulous, insane exertions that left me [Humbert] limp and azure-barred—I would gather her [Lolita] in my arms with, at last, a mute moan of human tenderness . . . —and the tenderness would deepen to shame and despair, and I would lull and rock my lone light Lolita in my marble arms, . . . and at the peak of this human agonized selfless tenderness (with my soul actually hanging around her naked body and ready to repent), all at once, ironically, horribly, lust would swell again—and "oh, no," Lolita would say with a sigh to heaven, and the next moment the tenderness and the azure—all would be shattered. (p. 287)

Humbert's arms are "marble"; Lolita "has individualized the writer's ancient lust" (p. 47); and he cries, "Imagine me; I shall not exist if you do not imagine me." (p. 131) To Humbert the "azure" world is, repeatedly, one of "tenderness," and in his essay, "On a Book Entitled *Lolita*," Nabokov synonymises "art" to "curiosity, tenderness, kindness, ecstasy." (*L*, p. 317) *Lolita*'s world is art, but also "mortal . . . beauty." The "peak of . . . selfless tenderness" is "human": i.e., were he Lolita's "real healthy sweetheart" (p. 286), Humbert's revived lust would not be monstrous; were she conscious

"thesis," "child or image," her antithesis, "woman," and her synthesis, nymphet, "image and flesh combined" (pp. 331, 342), although surely one's final impression of Lolita is not from the kingdom by the sea, but from Gray Star; it is not of a Carmencita but of a Dolores. Mitchell assumes, too, that contradictions are fully eliminated in a synthesis, e.g., Gray Star, "wherein Humbert unifies the real matronly Lolita and his former image of her" (pp. 342–343). But even at Gray Star, Humbert still creates Lolita; he sees in mortal fashion, through a crimson glass.

that, poised to serve a tennis ball, her "vital web of balance" effected a "powerful and graceful cosmos" (pp. 233–234), she would falter and become awkward. To her, tennis, and all of life, is "the very geometry of basic reality"; to Humbert it is "the art of make-believe." (p. 233) In the real world in which he finds Lolita at Gray Star, Humbert is tongue-tied: "Be true to your Dick. Do not let other fellows touch you. . . . I hope you will love your baby. I hope it will be a boy." (p. 311) (It was a "stillborn girl." [p. 6]) But without him, the artist, she would not endure: "the refuge of art . . . is the only immortality. . ., my Lolita." (p. 311) Nowhere more than in this concluding possessive does Humbert reveal that his final wisdom is less than Nabokov's, and, if all goes well, the reader's.

The Nabokov artist, the "eye" who never sleeps, knows "what it is impossible to know" (I, p. 95) of two worlds and the dark "dreams" that seem to be misty bridges, or "webs of sense," between them, but like Cincinnatus, he cannot "bring the words to bay" (p. 93); like Sebastian and V., he has only faith that "the word, the meaning" exists, and is "astonishing in its simplicity" (SK, p. 179), but like Humbert he is a mortal and hence blemished. He kills the beauty he mounts and names ("Lycaeides sublivens Nabokov," near the mining town in which the child Lolita belonged [L, p. 381]), because "nameless bliss no brain can bear."[20] He is balanced between two worlds themselves equipoised between union and separation, and, it seems, he is the "central intelligence" in the works that at their best, as in Lolita, are so precisely balanced between mortally conflicting meanings as to defy categorization and to attain the "superhigh level of art" which "appeals to that secret depth of the human soul where the shadows of other worlds pass like the shadows of nameless and soundless ships."[21] At this point precisely equidistant between the mortal and immortal "states of being" (L, p. 317)—an "unreal" point, created only by "the necessary ripple" stirred by the artist touching "real life" (NG, p. 145)—rests Nabokov's world of tragic farce, the shadow of both its real neighbors.

---

[20] Nabokov, "Restoration," Poems, p. 29.

[21] Nabokov, Nikolai Gogol (Norfolk, Conn., 1944), p. 149. Subsequent references to NG are in the text.

ILLUSION, REALITY,
AND PARODY IN
NABOKOV'S PLAYS

Simon Karlinsky

It was Vladislav Khodasevich who in 1937 characterized Nabokov as a writer obsessed with a single theme.[1] Nabokov's writings of the subsequent decades have confirmed the accuracy of this observation. Nabokov's central theme is, of course, the nature of the creative imagination and the solitary, freak-like role into which a man gifted with such imagination is inevitably cast in any society. Such a person may be shown pursuing his basic endeavor directly (e.g., Sebastian Knight or the hero of *The Gift*), but more often, as Khodasevich pointed out, Nabokov's artist-hero is disguised by means of some mask that may appear at first glance unrelated to artistic creation. Thus, the work of art that the hero strives to create, or at times actually achieves, may be presented in the guise of chess playing (*The Defense*), butterfly collecting ("The Aurelian"), a murder (*Despair*), seduction of a young girl (*Lolita*), preservation of one's own individuality in a nightmarish totalitarian world (*Invitation to a Beheading*), or of simply trying to reconstruct one's identity (*The Eye*). In all these cases, however, the hero uses his imagination to devise a reality of his own, which he seeks to impose on the surrounding reality. The question of which reality is *real*, that of the hero or that of his environment, is usually left open. What matters is which of the two realities is the more relevant one for the artistic conception of the particular novel or story.

With this constant and pervasive interest in the artificially produced illusion of reality and in the genuinely experienced reality of

---

[1] Vladislav Khodasevich, "O Sirine," in *Literaturnye stat'i i vospominaniia* (New York, 1954), pp. 245–254.

illusion, it would seem inevitable for Nabokov to become interested in drama as a literary form. Indeed, throughout his European period, when he wrote in Russian only, Nabokov repeatedly attempted the dramatic genre. His three brief verse plays, published in Berlin in 1923 and 1924 ("Death," "The Grandfather," and "The [North] Pole"), are not yet mature Nabokov. Reading these plays, one is struck by the testimony they offer to the autobiographical significance of those passages in The Gift that describe the hero's literary apprenticeship to Pushkin. The particular brand of iambic pentameter, the general diction, and occasionally even the sentence structure of Pushkin's "little tragedy," Mozart and Salieri, are effectively copied in Nabokov's three little plays, which could perhaps be more aptly characterized as narrative poems in dramatic form. Also evident is their stylistic relationship to the most neglected of Pushkin's verse narratives, Angelo (Pushkin's version of Shakespeare's Measure for Measure), which the hero of The Gift is also said to have studied. The most obviously Nabokovian of these early plays, "Death," uses a situation that was later to reappear in a pivotal passage in The Eye: an unsuccessful would-be suicide believes himself dead and takes his continuing life for a posthumous experience. Not much can be said of Nabokov's five-act play "The Man from the U.S.S.R." (1927), since only its first act has been published.[2] It is apparently a spy thriller with a film actress for a heroine and it seems to have been performed by an émigré company in Berlin soon after its writing.

The most interesting and significant work to date of Nabokov the playwright was all done in a single year. It consists of the two full-length plays, The Event (Sobytie) and The Waltz Invention (Izobretenie Val'sa), both written in 1938 and published the same year in the Paris émigré journal Russkie Zapiski. (The Waltz Invention is now also available in English, in a somewhat revised version.[3]) These two plays, written after such mature novels as The Exploit (Podvig), Despair, and The Gift, benefit from Nabokov's literary mastery at its most original and inventive. Both plays are firmly connected with Nabokov's central preoccupation with creative imagination. Like the novels, they are also "portraits of an artist as something

---

[2] For publication data on Nabokov's plays discussed in this article, the reader is referred to Dieter E. Zimmer's excellent bibliography, Vladimir Nabokov, Bibliographie des Gesamtwerks (Reinbek bei Hamburg, 1964), p. 29.

[3] Vladimir Nabokov, The Waltz Invention, trans. Dmitri Nabokov (New York, 1966).

else." The Event can be described as a portrait of an artist as a coward, and The Waltz Invention as a portrait of an artist as a madman-
politician. These descriptions are of course schematic, aimed at point-
ing out the basic similarity of the two plays to Nabokov's novels;
there are many additional aspects of these plays that such a scheme
could not even begin to indicate.

The principal character in The Event is an artist without disguise: he is a professional painter. Painting is an art form that, after
literature, interests Nabokov most, and discussions of it figure prominently in The Gift, The Real Life of Sebastian Knight, and Pnin.
In The Event, the passages about painting are central to the audience's understanding of the protagonist and the author's attitude
towards him. Nabokov seems to enjoy devising and describing imaginary paintings, which he then ascribes to his fictional painters, in
the same way Thomas Mann devised and described the musical compositions of his hero in Doctor Faustus. The personality and the
artistic development of the painter Vsevolod Romanov in The Gift
may contain a few remote references to the career of Nabokov's
fellow-émigré, Pavel Chelishchev (usually spelled Tchelitchew),
although Romanov's paintings, as described in the novel, evoke instead the work of René Magritte. On the other hand, the paintings
of Aleksei Troshcheikin, the hero of The Event, as they are outlined
in the stage directions and discussed in several of his speeches,
strongly recall the work of Chelishchev himself (and so, incidentally,
does the imaginary portrait of Sebastian Knight, with its reflecting
pool and aquatic spider). Troshcheikin's paintings in the play serve
as his credentials: they are the one wholly serious thing about this
weak and inept hero, whose genuine artistic gift cannot protect him
from triviality and humiliation in the other areas of his life.

Troshcheikin, his wife Liubov, his mother-in-law, and their
friends are apparently Russian exiles who live in a small provincial
town, possibly in one of the Baltic countries in the 'thirties. At the
beginning of the play, news is received that Liubov's former lover,
who had been serving a prison sentence for attempting to kill Troshcheikin, had been unexpectedly released and is probably intending
now to carry out his original plan. The rest of the play is primarily
a record of Troshcheikin's panicky reaction to this threat to his life.
Social amenities go on as usual: the mother-in-law celebrates her
birthday and receives guests; sympathy and concern for the hero's
predicament are ostensibly shown by those around him. Yet, as night
approaches, the hapless painter finds himself alone and unprotected

as logic and reality desert his world, leaving in their stead only danger and absurdity.

Reviewing the original Paris stage production of *The Event*, Khodasevich wrote that "Fear" would have been a more suitable title for this play. The "event," anticipated with mixed feelings throughout the play by Troshcheikin and the other characters, never does materialize. In the carefully contrived anticlimactic finale we learn that Troshcheikin's fears were groundless all along. By subjecting the artist-hero of this gay and sparkling comedy ("dramatic comedy in three acts" is the author's designation) to an intolerable ordeal by fear and betrayal, Nabokov not only restates his major theme of the artist's solitude, but illustrates, better than in any of his other works, Pushkin's oft-quoted statement that apart from his sacrifice to Apollo the artist may at times be the most insignificant of the insignificant, mindless children of this world.

When *The Event* was first published and then produced in Paris in 1938, émigré reviewers were quick to point out similarities between Nabokov's play and Gogol's *The Inspector General*. Russian reviewers and viewers, with their thorough knowledge of Russian classics, could not fail to spot the textual references and other allusions to Gogol's comedy. What can be termed the Gogolian reference series is set up early in the play, when a character named Revshin (a name formed from the first syllables of the Russian titles of *The Inspector General* and *The Overcoat*), who is the hero's best friend and the current secret lover of his wife, announces the impending danger in terms deliberately reminiscent of Bobchinsky and Dobchinsky's entrance in the first act of *The Inspector General*. The end of the first act finds Liubov hanging out of the window in a state of extreme curiosity and excitement, recapitulating the situation of the mayor's wife at the end of the first act of Gogol's play. The Gogolian references, all to *The Inspector General*, are repeated at various unexpected points in the other two acts of the play. Two ladies in the birthday party episode argue about who is to tell the story of Troshcheikin's predicament first, and thus evoke again Bobchinsky and Dobchinsky. The first name and patronymic of a minor but important character called Meshaev turn out to be Osip Mikheich, a name made up of Khlestakov's servant and the offstage Saint Petersburg janitor mentioned in the letter read at the end of the play. These textual references to Gogol are clear enough. What a closer examination of Nabokov's comedy reveals, however, is that its structure is in fact a kind of free variation on the main *peripeteia* of *The Inspector General*.

The action of Gogol's comedy hinges on three pivotal developments: the mayor's announcement that an inspector is on the way; the false news that Khlestakov is the inspector, which triggers off the main action; and the final revelation that the real inspector has arrived. (We can ignore for structural purposes the postmaster's discovery that Khlestakov was not the inspector, since the audience has known that all along.) Similarly, Nabokov has disposed the action of *The Event* around three announcements, made by characters whose function is analogous to heralds and messengers in classical drama. In the first act, Revshin, nicknamed "hairy tapeworm" by his business associates, reveals that the hero's enemy is at large; and for the rest of the play he keeps the hero and the audience informed of the enemy's movements, while consistently misconstruing his intentions and motives. In the second act, the second herald, Osip Mikheich Meshaev (while his first name and patronymic evoke the two Gogolian servants, the last name has connotations of meddlesomeness and ineptitude) causes some merriment at the afternoon birthday party for Troshcheikin's mother-in-law by rushing in with Revshin's original news, by now familiar to the entire cast. It is Meshaev's twin brother (played by the same actor, of course) who, arriving by mistake late in the evening after the party is finished, resolves the tension by his unexpected and casual revelation that the dreaded enemy has departed for good. This quasi-Gogolian structure gives the comedy a symmetry that is almost classical in its contrived elegance.

The obvious Gogolian references are solidly integrated within the framework of Nabokov's comedy. Less organic to the play and less apparent, but occurring more frequently, is the second major series of literary references. These references evoke the plays and stories of Anton Chekhov and his connections with the Moscow Art Theater. The Chekhovian references begin even before Revshin initiates the Gogolian ones, and they are associated mostly with Troshcheikin's wife, Liubov. Nabokov's heroine has a mother named Antonina Pavlovna, the feminine equivalent of Chekhov's first name and patronymic. Soon after her appearance on the stage, Liubov Troshcheikina launches into a lament for her long-dead little son, in a kind of serious parody on the similar first-act lament of her Chekhovian namesake, Liubov Ranevskaya, in *The Cherry Orchard*.

The scenes that involve Liubov are from then on quite regularly accompanied by some reference to Chekhov. There are citations of "A Dreary Story" and *The Three Sisters*; Liubov has friends named Stanislavsky and Vishnevsky (the latter being the name of a Moscow Art Theater actor who was a friend of Chekhov, who appeared in original productions of his plays, and whose name happens to suggest the Russian title of *The Cherry Orchard*); Liubov's husband, Troshcheikin, turns out to be named Aleksei Maksimovich (just like Gorky); and in the second act, Liubov ascribes to her former lover a carefully garbled version of Chekov's famous maxim about the use of firearms in dramatic structure of plays. Her current lover, Revshin, tells Liubov in a somewhat inept compliment that she was "conceived by Chekhov, executed by Rostand and played by Duse." Throughout the play there are deliberately twisted bits of dialogue from *Uncle Vanya*, *The Three Sisters*, and *The Cherry Orchard*. There is possibly even an echo of Chekhov's Mme Merchutkina (from *The Jubilee*) in the dialogue between the comical cook, Marfa, and Liubov at the beginning of the third act.

There are also more general ways in which one could connect Nabokov's play to the work of Anton Chekhov. The inability of Troshcheikin and his wife to achieve meaningful communication, to see the position in which the other spouse is placed, is of course a recurrent and typical Chekhovian situation, exemplified in such stories as "The Name-Day Party" or "The Calamity." The cowardly behavior of Chekhov's Laevsky in "The Duel" and his difficulties with his common-law wife Nadezhda likewise have similarities with the predicament and the marital troubles of Nabokov's hero. In both "The Duel" and *The Event*, the woman's infidelity is treated as a casual and insignificant factor so far as the hero is concerned, his inability to communicate with her being far more important. Finally, the play's title (*Sobytie*) happens to be identical with that of an early short story by Chekhov. This is one of Chekhov's stories about adult callousness to sensitive and impressionable children (the English version by Constance Garnett is called "An Incident"). The kittens of a house cat, which become for one day the very center of the universe for two small children, are devoured by a great Dane brought to the house by a visitor. The children are horrified and disconsolate, but the adults are indifferent and even mildly amused. The story is early Chekhov (1886), over-explicit and given to moralizing. At first glance, it seems to have nothing in common with Nabokov's play, except the coincidentally identical title, and, by further coincidence, a time structure that comprises a single day. And yet, a closer reading of Chekhov's story cannot fail to suggest a deeper parallel in the two works: the basic theme of both is the intrusion of danger and violence into an ordered existence, and the indifference with which this violence can be accepted by ordinary, decent people. The similarity of the theme and of the title may be purely accidental (*sobytie* is, after all, a common Russian word). Still, the conclusion of Chekhov's story, when read in the light of Nabokov's play, does seem to add a new dimension to the play's significance:

It seems to the children that all the people, every single one of them in the house, would become alarmed and pounce upon the villain Nero [the dog]. But the people sit calmly, each in his place, and only marvel at the huge dog's appetite. Papa and mamma laugh. . . . Nero walks around the table, wags his tail and smugly licks his chops. . . . The mother-cat alone is perturbed. Her tail stretched, she walks from one room to another, casts suspicious glances at the people and miaows piteously.
    —Children, it is after nine! Time to go to bed!—shouts mamma.
    Vanya and Nina go to bed, weep and keep thinking for a long time about the hurt cat and about the cruel, insolent and unpunished Nero.

The barrage of parodistic references in *The Event* to Russian classics becomes particularly dense with the appearance of the grotesquely incompetent detective Barboshin toward the end of the play. The entire role of this character is an excellent example of what later was to be called the theater of the absurd. In a play written in 1938, Barboshin's scenes offer an unmistakable foreshadowing of certain mannerisms of both Pinter and Ionesco; but much of the ostensible absurdity is simultaneously literary parody. The first entrance of Nabokov's comically Dostoevskian Sherlock Holmes is an outrageous parody on Zosima's bow to Mitya Karamazov. Before his major scene is over, the detective has run through several well-known quotations from Dostoevsky, made allusions to Turgenev's *Smoke* (apparently a favorite of Nabokov's, this novel is also alluded to in two of his novels), and engaged Troshcheikin in an argument based on a close similarity between his name and that of the offstage antagonist from whose violence he is supposedly protecting the hero. This argument is seemingly patterned after the equally senseless exchange between Chekhov's Doctor Chebutykin and Captain Soleny in *The Three Sisters* about *chekhartma* (a Georgian meat course) and *cheremsha* (a kind of scallion). The sound of the words that are the subject of the argument in Chekhov may furnish one possible clue as to why most of the male characters in *The Event* have such unusually raucous Russian names, with their clashes of r's and sibilants:

Troshcheikin, Revshin, Barbashin (the antagonist), Barboshin (the detective).

The parody of the Chekhovian argument is closely followed by the parodistic high point of the play, the detective's soliloquy, which is a truly vicious mockery of the more optimistic speeches of Chekhov's Colonel Vershinin from *The Three Sisters*, of his Sonya from *Uncle Vanya*, and of several of Dostoevsky's characters. For all its irreverence and seeming ridicule, the parodistic evocation of these idealistic literary characters has a definite function within the scheme of Nabokov's comedy. The climax of literary parody comes at the point when Troshcheikin's efforts to defend himself and to cope with his predicament take on a hopeless and ludicrous form. The much-vaunted "humanistic" traditions of his native literature (and, in this sense, it is irrelevant that the author of the play may love Chekhov and loathe Dostoevsky) are as powerless to help him as are his wife, his friends, and even his art.

The profusion of literary references in *The Event* recalls Nabokov's earlier novel *The Gift*, similarly saturated with allusions to Russian literature. In the novel, however, this material is used for serious literary and historical commentary, while in the play its function is parodistic and humorous. In their frequency of incidence, the literary quotations and allusions serve an additional purpose: they deliberately disrupt the carefully contrived realistic surface of the play. Several other devices are also used to sabotage the illusion of realism. These include the suggestions by Liubov's graphomane mother about how the dramatic situations onstage would have been handled had she been the author of the play in which she is one of the characters; the stage directions Liubov issues to the cook Marfa (or possibly to the actress playing this role) about how to achieve a more traditional characterization of a Russian peasant woman; and the remark of Meshaev II that both he and his twin brother are played by the same actor, though with varying degrees of success (ostensibly a metaphor but actually a description of an onstage fact). One of the lady guests at the birthday party keeps lapsing into verse. Nabokov's usual love of puns is given a free rein.[4] All this creates

---

[4] A particularly complex bit of verbal buffoonery is the pun on the second part of Hamlet's question, transcribed to convey a broad Russian accent ("Zad iz zyk veshchan") and thereby resulting in a vague Russian obscenity. The first half of the same Shakespearean quotation was later the subject of a trilingual pun in Nabokov's *Bend Sinister*, where "To be or not to be" is transformed in Russian into "ubit' il' ne ubit' " (instead of the traditional "byt' ili ne byt' "), which in turn results in French "L'égorgerai-je ou non."

a subtle and highly original tension between the ostensibly realistic comedy about believable people and the deliberate shattering of the realistic illusion through the author's sudden demonstrations of the literary and dramatic conventions he employs ("laying bare the device," as such practices were termed by the Russian Formalist critics).

In the most serious passage in the entire play (at the end of Act Two), the inner reality of the artist briefly asserts itself and results in a complete breakdown of external realism. While the birthday party guests become motionless "painted ghosts," and while real life thus becomes an immobile painting, Troshcheikin and his faithless wife achieve a moment of perfect communion as they converse in verbalized telepathy. The crude outer reality soon intrudes; the communion was inconclusive and it achieved nothing. Yet, taking place as it did while Troshcheikin and Liubov were lost in reverie during Antonina Pavlovna's reading of her new inept prose poem, the interlude underscores in a very Nabokovian way the difference between the genuine artistic insights of Troshcheikin and the amateurish pseudo-art of his mother-in-law.

The Event moves between the familiar reality of traditional Russian realistic fiction and drama and two other kinds of reality: the inner creative reality of the artist-hero, and the reality of literary references and conventions, which the author superimposes on the other two levels. The differentiation among the several levels of reality in Nabokov's other major play proceeds along different lines. The reality that surrounds the hero of The Waltz Invention is highly stylized in comparison with Troshcheikin's more realistic surroundings. The play is set in a generalized, hypothetical "never-never" land, situated equidistantly between science fiction and Viennese operetta. The inner reality of the creator-hero, Salvator Waltz, is that of his own megalomaniac imagination. This is the reality in which, as we learn only at the end, the entire action of the play takes place, with the exception of the introduction and the finale. The poor madman Salvator Waltz has imagined himself to be the possessor of a monstrously destructive invention which gives him unlimited power over other men—a power he seizes because he intends to use it for general welfare. But another kind of reality keeps breaking in periodically from the outside to thwart the hero's plans, despite the occasional boosts given to Waltz's flagging imagination by a strange, androgynous factotum named Dream (Son in the original Russian, Viola Trance in the new English translation). The selfless service to humanity, and

the abolition of suffering for which the dreamer strives, turn into
nightmare as he finds himself annihilating great masses of humanity
for their own good. His imagination does not possess the resources
necessary to conjure up the personal paradise of sensuality for which
he has secretly yearned; contrary to his intentions, the erotic visions
he has willed into existence turn ugly and absurd.

By the end of the second act, Waltz has gained absolute power
with the aid of Dream, but this power produces chaos in his dream
world once he tries to exercise it. When he perseveres, Dream deserts
him: the external reality fully invades his dream world, and Salvator
Waltz, like the peasant woman in Pushkin's "The Tale of the Fish-
erman and the Fish," is returned to the point where he began his
ascent to power. The entire action of the play has taken place within
the mind of a lunatic who was waiting to be received by the Minister
of War of a mythical country in regard to a non-existent invention.
And yet, the issues raised by Waltz's dream of power are real, his
dream world believable enough in its own terms, and the tragedy and
suffering of the hero important.

The Waltz Invention takes up two major themes often encountered in Nabokov's fiction. The interpenetration of two contiguous
worlds, of which one or the other is imaginary, was treated by Nabokov in *The Defense* and in *Invitation to a Beheading*. In the short
story "Terra Incognita" and in *The Gift* (the hero's imaginary conversations with the poet Koncheev), Nabokov had developed a set
of subtle devices for indicating that the action or dialogue described
is taking place within a character's reverie. Similar techniques are
widely used in *The Waltz Invention*. While Waltz is achieving his
fantastic triumphs, irritating little incidents—holes or slits in the
fabric of his imaginary reality—keep inflicting themselves on his
dream. A toy automobile that belongs to his other existence reappears
periodically under unlikely circumstances, upsetting Waltz's confidence and equilibrium. One character recites a poem that Waltz
himself had composed (the character attributes the poem to Tour-
valski, i.e., *un tour de valse*); and, before the hero's imagination
forces him to re-assume the role assigned to him in the dream world,
another character almost turns into a psychiatrist from the mental
institution where Waltz is being treated. The entire role of Dream-
Trance is also a device constantly used to cast doubts on the reality
of Waltz's triumphs and disappointments.

The other basic Nabokovian theme that this play treats is the
nature of absolute tyranny—both its horror and its unreal, illusory

character. This theme had been treated by Nabokov in *Invitation to a Beheading* and in the short story "Extermination of Tyrants" ("Istreblenie tiranov"), as well as in the novel, written in English, for which this short story seems to have been a preliminary sketch, *Bend Sinister*. The tyrants in the short story and in *Bend Sinister* were crude scoundrels who used idealistic verbiage to cover up their vulgar lust for power. The madman Waltz is a genuine idealist who believes his own humanitarian speeches; but, since he also resorts to brutal and autocratic methods to achieve his high-minded goals, he ends up being no better than any other tyrant, and even the corrupt but human and flexible government he has replaced seems preferable by comparison. The point Nabokov makes here about the uses of power is not too distant from Camus' point on the same subject in *La Peste*.

While *The Event* is steeped in Russian literary traditions (a fact which poses grave problems for the translator), the native Russian birthmarks of *The Waltz Invention* are few. There is a faint flavor of Pushkin's *Mozart and Salieri* in the iambic pentameter of Waltz's blank verse speeches (which are not broken into verse lines in the original Russian). The alliterative names of the lesser dream-officials, with their permutations of the same three consonants (Grib, Grab, Grob, Berg, Breg, etc.), have a possible double Russian literary parentage. The alliterative series of names itself originates in Vladimir Mayakovsky's onomatopoetic evocation of the clacking horse's hooves in his well-known poem "Kindly Treatment of Horses" ("Khoroshee otnoshenie k loshadiam"), in which the hooves apparently say: "Grib. Grab . Grob. Grub. " i.e., "Fungus. Rob. Coffin. Crude." But, while the sound pattern comes from Mayakovsky, the uses to which these names are put suggest the satirically treated and similarly alliterative group of government officials in Alexander Sukhovo-Kobylin's nineteenth-century play *The Affair* (*Delo*)—Messrs. Hertz, Schertz, Schmertz, Ibisov and Chibisov. No other Russian literary precedents suggest themselves with any degree of immediacy.

For all that, the English translation of *The Waltz Invention* did present definite difficulties, which Nabokov discusses in his introduction to the new English edition. To overcome some of those difficulties, the translator at times resorts to explicating the text rather than merely translating it. The result is that the English *The Waltz Invention*, while on the whole a reasonable equivalent of the original, loses some of its subtlety. For one thing, the puns have become broader and more obvious. Furthermore, much that was colorful and expressive in the original Russian becomes oddly neutral in English; but then, as Nabokov's preface explains, this was the effect he wanted. His attitude toward the reader of the English versions of his earlier work is mellower and more forbearing than the one he had toward the reader of the Russian originals. The literary allusions, puns, and false leads in the original version of *The Gift* have largely been elucidated and deciphered in the translation. Similarly, the reader of *The Waltz Invention* in English has a somewhat simplified text and is thus deprived of the creative collaboration with the author in which the reader of the original Russian text was privileged to participate. At the end of his English preface, the author obligingly tells the reader just where the action of the play is taking place; he further tips his hand by referring to Salvator Waltz as "a fellow author" in the newly provided list of *dramatis personae*, which the original lacked. This list also labels and compartmentalizes all the episodic Bumps and Thumps (the Mayakovskian horse's hooves in the original) which tumbled about in unlabeled confusion in the Russian version. These additions would probably make a stage production easier, but in the reading version of the play the removed obstacles also take away some of the pleasure.

Vladimir Nabokov has not returned to the drama since his two important plays of 1938. The contrast between these two works is all too evident, yet both clearly fit within the rest of his work and contribute to our understanding of Nabokov's depth and scope. A parallel from another art would be offered by Maurice Ravel's two masterpieces in piano concerto form, both written within the same year (1929–1930). The Piano Concerto in G is witty and sparkling; the Concerto in D for the Left Hand Alone is brooding and introspective. Vastly different from each other in conception, execution, and mood, the two concerti are major and typical works of Ravel. *The Event* and *The Waltz Invention* are also major and typical Nabokov in their exploration of his basic themes and in their relevance to his fundamental concepts of life and art.

NABOKOV'S PUSHKIN AND
NABOKOV'S NABOKOV

Clarence Brown

> Man's life as commentary to abstruse
> Unfinished poem. Note for further use.
>
> John Shade, Pale Fire, ll. 939–40

Vladimir Nabokov, the author of Lolita, as his publishers tirelessly remind us, and of many other novels in Russian and English, undertook in 1950 to prepare an English version of and a commentary on one of the greatest works of his native Russian literature: Alexander Pushkin's verse-novel Eugene Onegin, written between 1823 and 1831.* Fourteen years later his work was published in four beautiful sky-blue volumes which contain, among other matter too recondite for quick description: a long introduction of nearly a hundred pages, an almost unbearably literal translation of everything in and near the poem, including rejected variants and extensions, with long stretches of white unprinted paper to indicate omitted or never-composed stanzas (the non-existent lines of these non-existent stanzas are numbered for easy reference), an immensely personal, entertaining, and erudite commentary, two long appendices, one a sort of genealogical novelette dealing with Pushkin's African ancestor, and the other a comparative study of English and Russian prosody (both have appeared separately), and finally, an index and a facsimile of the last Russian text of the poem to have appeared while Pushkin was alive.

When this work appeared it was followed by a short silence, apparently prompted by disbelief. There was a preliminary article in the New York Times Book Review which, in the manner of that journal, apprised us at some length that a book had been published. Then the barrage began. In the New York Review of Books, the

---

* This essay is the written version of a lecture originally delivered at the University of California, Berkeley, in December 1965. The fifth paragraph of the essay has been added to the lecture version to update matters.

New Republic, Poetry and elsewhere there was a collective commotion probably best described in a phrase by Wodehouse: the raised eyebrow, the sharp intake of breath. To the virtual exclusion of everything else, the attention of the reviewers has been mesmerized by one thing: that incredible translation. It was preposterous, gauche beyond words, intentionally ugly, a travesty of a great work of art, sickeningly cute, incomprehensible. There was, to be sure, some other matter, but it was dreadfully boring stuff and would doubtless prove to be insupportable even to readers who were not, like the reviewers, limp from their exertions with the translation.

Nabokov replied. Mr. Edmund Wilson replied to the reply. The letters column in the NYRB bristled with the opinions of those eager to take public positions in the matter. Mr. David Magarshack wrote to say that he warmly agreed with "the views of Nabokov's incompetence as a translator." Mr. Magarshack, who rechristened Dostoevsky's Raskolnikov "Roddy," closed with a lofty moral insight into Nabokov's trouble: "It is yet one more sad example of how a man can be blind to his own shortcomings."

And finally, with a lightning change of venue, Nabokov resorted to the pages of Encounter (February 1966), whence he replied to all his massed assailants at once in the verbal equivalent of falling upon them like a tower. No one, to my knowledge, has yet replied to the reply, though the arrière garde has fired a few short rounds. Edmund Wilson did write a letter (April) in which he represents himself as doubled up on the floor "exsufflicate with cachinnation" over Nabokov's use of the word byre. Poor Quilty—also doubled up on the floor, as it chances—sought to counter vengeful Humbert Humbert's revolver with better jokes but with the same result. In the May Encounter Robert Lowell wrote to say, rather obscurely, that "whatever the devious dictionary meanings of English and Russian words" he still has a feeling, prompted by "commonsense and intuition," that Wilson is right and Nabokov wrong. To this Nabokov replied rather gently that Lowell's opinion, since he knows no Russian, is of no interest—but would he, in the meantime, stop mutilating Mandelstam? In September Professor Maurice Friedberg of Indiana University, a more or less innocent and justly outraged bystander, wrote to complain that Nabokov had misspelt his name. That must surely be the end of it; and now that the affair has petered out, we can perhaps survey it as a whole.

Let us begin with certain observations which are for me axiomatic. Nabokov is a consummate master of style. He is capable of more exquisite modulation, nuance, beauty, and power than is any person who has written of his work. His mastery of English is not quite the incredible anomaly that it has often been made out to be. Comparisons with Conrad are unfair to the latter, since he learned English comparatively much later in his life. Nabokov grew up in a thorougly Anglophile family and knew how to write English before he knew how to write Russian. Still, it is remarkable for a writer of such foreign origin and temperament to serve as a model in many matters of style for indigenous authors—e.g., John Updike—and to have produced in *Lolita*, I believe, a more entrancingly verisimilar version of teenage talk than our own poet-laureate of the soiled white cotton sock, J. D. Salinger.

The second axiomatic observation is that such masters of style as Nabokov simply do not begin all at once to commit unwitting lapses of style. Tolstoy and Gogol, in the latter part of their lives, denied themselves many kinds of excellence, but they did not become helpless in the matter of putting together Russian sentences of great cogency ånd beauty. They may have committed a crime, but they did not and could not commit that which, Talleyrand is supposed to have said, is worse than a crime: a blunder.

These two simple and certainly unoriginal axioms seem to have been completely ignored in the discussion of Nabokov's Pushkin, and it is they that force me to a quite different and I hope much less sterile approach. I emphasize approach, for these axioms are happily only heuristic and commit one to no prepackaged conclusion. They allow one to admit as accurate many of the strictures against Nabokov's translation, but they force one to seek an explanation. One is perfectly free, that is, to like or dislike his version, but it seems to me that one ought first to be much surer (1) what it is that one is judging, and (2) on what grounds one is judging it.

Mr. Wimsatt and others have now schooled us away from asking Goethe's first question—What was the writer attempting to do?—and we earnestly avoid the intentional fallacy. But I think it worth asking whether it is quite proper to substitute for the author's intention the reader's intention. Nabokov has been so much attacked for not doing what the reviewers expected him to do that it is perhaps only fair to listen to what he himself expected to do.

He begins by defining three kinds of translation. At one end of the scale is free translation, which he calls paraphrase; at the other end is word for word mechanical transposition, which he calls lexical; and in the middle of these is his choice, the literal translation, which

is for him the only true translation. He defines the latter in words
that have now become rather famous: "rendering, as closely as the
associative and syntactical capacities of another language allow, the
exact contextual meaning of the original." The aim of the literalist,
he says, is "to achieve some semblance of English construction and
retain some vestige of Russian rhythm." This is how his literal
version begins:

> My uncle has most honest principles:
> when he was taken gravely ill,
> he forced one to respect him
> and nothing better could invent. . . .

"And," Nabokov concludes, "if he is still not satisfied with his version, the [literal] translator can at least hope to amplify it in a detailed
note."

Nabokov's insupportable haughtiness has been so often reproved
that I think we should credit him with the modesty of this extremely
important passage. "As closely as the capacities allow . . . some semblance . . . some vestige . . . hope to amplify it in a detailed note."
Like all reasonable men, Nabokov is perfectly aware that true translation is impossible, or, like synonymy and parthenogenesis, very rare
to say the least. As his definition of translation is a compromise
between two extremes, so his translation itself is a compromise between two languages. It is frankly unsatisfactory—neither one thing
nor the other—but it is the best that under the circumstances and
under the sway of Nabokov's inexorable principles is possible. The
best that is possible means for him the best that is true, a thought
to which I shall return.

Let me now bluntly put to you a thesis which I hope to defend.
The translation of *Eugene Onegin* is relatively unimportant among
the contents of this work. It occupies only about two-thirds of the
slenderest of these four volumes, and it would have occupied even
less had Nabokov not allotted all that white, enumerated space to
all those non-existent stanzas. I believe that those who devote themselves to very easily made observations about the ways in which this
translation differs from ordinary translations are throwing themselves
with great energy at a door which Nabokov himself is obligingly
holding open. But lest one think that this hint of deviousness is another complaint about his character, let me say at once that I believe
him to be, like Onegin's uncle, a man of "most honest principles."

I shall later suggest other and perhaps less conscious reasons for the quality of this translation, but let me now point out that I think Nabokov hates "readability" not because it is readable but because it is false. The reader is allowed too cheaply, with too little exertion, to imagine that he has mastered the difficult, intricate, multiplex original. In *Speak, Memory*, his overt autobiography, Nabokov tells of the special sort of chess problem which he likes best to compose: the sort which even moderately skillful players can solve by taking certain obvious moves. Only the ideal solver will see that the obvious move—though it *does* lead to a solution—is a trap to lure the unworthy away from the real beauty of the problem. Nabokov has an extraordinary capacity for simultaneously dispersed and concentrated attention. He knows the supreme intricacy of Pushkin's achievement and he knows all the comfortable delusions by which that intricacy can seem to have been mastered. He knows the great novel-poem syllable by syllable, holds all the lines simultaneously in his memory, ever mindful when reading one line of all the others in this work and in the possible but unwritten poem which *Onegin* might have been with all the gaps filled, all the variants recognized, all the rejections restored. To put *this* Onegin, which no one except Nabokov has ever apprehended, into a readable translation is to cheapen a transcendent miracle of art, to betray it to those who will complacently congratulate themselves on having "read *Onegin*." It would be, in short, to lie about it, and Nabokov has a very Tolstoyan passion for the truth. The translation is the easy solution to the mystery of *Onegin*, the obvious route which, once taken, traps the brash traveller and holds him forever distant from the sanctum of Pushkin's art.

I realize that these ideas will probably seem fanciful and even rather too Nabokovian. Surely it is going a bit far to say that so much distinguished energy has been spent in the reviews of Nabokov's Pushkin in attacking what is only a sort of decoy, the translation, and that this translation is in fact of only secondary, not to say minor, importance. In order to substantiate my position I shall have to leave the first part of my title—"Nabokov's Pushkin"—and go to the second—"Nabokov's Nabokov."

It seems to me that the most cogent support for my interpretation is to be found in his other work. In passing, let me credit Edmund Wilson with one sentence of which I entirely approve. He writes, "This *Onegin*, it is important to mention, has, aside from its intrinsic merits, a special interest as a part of Nabokov's whole 'oeuvre.'" Unfortunately, he immediately diminishes the value of this insight by showing, in the sentence following next, that he has no comprehension whatsoever of what that "oeuvre" is: "The principal theme of his work . . . is the situation, comic and pathetic, full of embarrassment and misunderstanding, of the exile who cannot return, and one aspect of this is the case of the man who, like Nabokov, is torn between the culture he has left behind and that to which he is trying to adapt himself." It is little wonder, I think, that Nabokov, having read this statement of his "principal theme," publicly thanked Wilson for never having reviewed any of his novels.

If we examine this other work, what we find is, I think, a little surprising. This writer—one of the most Protean and entertaining masters of modern prose—is extremely repetitious. For well over a quarter of a century now he has been writing in book after book about the same thing. And I maintain that when he switches in his study of Pushkin to what is apparently a new subject and even a different genre he is in fact presenting us with the culmination of that unique thing which he has been doing all along, with remarkable consistency, in fact with almost monomaniacal persistence, in *The Real Life of Sebastian Knight, The Gift, The Eye, Pale Fire, The Defense*, and so on. More than anything else, it is this absolute unity in Nabokov's writing which gives me great confidence that my view of his work on Pushkin is the right one.

The essence of repetition is, of course, the unvarying unity of its object. Unity itself, oneness, the subtle linkages in the observer's mind that impart identity to all experience: this, I think, is one of the principal ideas in the formation of Nabokov's style as well as the larger forms of his art. I believe that this is something new, that the old circularity of art for art's sake is wholly inadequate to describe the phenomenon of Nabokov. Here, to begin with, is a quotation from one of the imagined novels (*Lost Property*) of an imagined writer named Sebastian Knight whose memory is being tracked down by a half-brother: "All things belong to the same order of things, for such is the oneness of human perception, the oneness of individuality, the oneness of matter, whatever matter may be. The only real number is one, the rest are mere repetition." (*SK*, p. 105)

And if it seems irrelevant to go back to Nabokov's first English novel for the sake of elucidating the most recent of his works, let me go back even further, to a novel written in Russian in 1935–37, *The Gift*, where we find in one paragraph (p. 198), the entire plot of *Lolita* and then, a few pages later (p. 206) the following remark by Fyodor Godunov-Cherdyntsev, the writer-hero: "It's queer, I seem to remember my future works." Of course Nabokov was here as always, in spite of all his denials in all of his interviews, writing about himself.

As no line in *Onegin* exists by itself, so no word in the English language exists without the company of other words, of all similar words, of all the conceivable transformations of itself, and finally, bursting through the thin linguistic partitions in Nabokov's mind, of all its translations, homophones and cognates in other languages. He can neither think nor see without etymologizing the universe. This is the most hypnotic and infectious element of his style, and to the limit of one's lesser abilities one begins to do it almost automatically, putting Nabokov's novel down on the green park bench to observe how the grey squirrel trembles and flicks toward the proffered peanut while keeping an eye out for the fluffy shadow of his pursuing tail as though it were one of the Greek monsters, Skía and Ourá, in his nomenclatorial history. The forte of Nabokov's style is the utter concentration of attention, masquerading as the utter dispersion of attention.

One of the commonest words in the Nabokovian lexicon is fate. It is fate who wills the unity of all things, who prompts the little unity of alliteration and the other poetic devices of sound repetition so common in the prose of Nabokov, who seeks out for words of one language unsuspected cousins in another language, who provides that abundance of Pasternakian and Lermontovian coincidence which informs the novels. In his translation of Lermontov's novel *A Hero of Our Time* Nabokov refers to all these lucky encounters and overheard conversations as "the barely noticeable routine of fate." Nabokov's account of his own life in *Speak, Memory* is a kind of diary of the workings of fate. Fate is really one of the guises of the muse of Nabokov.

If we turn to one of the larger elements of Nabokov's art, the structure of the character relationships, we find fate busily at work, inevitably with the same result, since fate has only one passion—the passion for unity. In these character relationships we begin, typically, with an apparent duality, which is then reduced to unity—two men who in the course of the novel strangely coalesce. "The only real number is one, the rest are mere repetition." The central position in the novel is usually occupied by the charismatic figure of some poet or novelist of genius. The other figure is the person in the foreground, usually the narrator, whose entire function consists in surrounding the genius at the middle. He researches this genius, seeks him out, comments upon him and in fact draws his existence from him. We know the character at the center only through the efforts of our narrator and guide, who is himself a sympathetic but a less interesting, less gifted, and somehow flawed, incomplete figure.

Take for instance *The Real Life of Sebastian Knight.* Here the narrator, the peripheral figure, is the half-brother of a distinguished novelist named Sebastian Knight, the genius at the center. Nabokov is apt to grow rather abusive if one ever mentions this sort of thing, but it is interesting to note that Knight was born in 1899, as was Nabokov; he grew up in an Anglophile Russian family, as did Nabokov; he went to Cambridge, Nabokov's university, and began to write novels in English. Even his pronunciation is described in such a way as to make it, for anyone who has heard Nabokov speak, unmistakably that of Nabokov.

Sebastian Knight is already dead when the novel opens, so we never meet him except in the retrospective vision of his half-brother. This half-brother is seeking for the sources of Knight's many novels. He is searching not so much for his brother's memory as for that part of his life which occasionally emerged as art. It is not, therefore, a family quest or a search prompted by some emotional need to know, by love's desire to possess a memory: it is a literary investigation, a kind of research into the abstruse question, how does reality become art? I need hardly say that he finds truth and fiction to be strangely identical. The question itself is misleading, for it is central to Nabokov's art that one thing does not *become* another; one thing *already is* the other.

The relationship of the characters in *The Gift* does not have the paradigmatic clarity of that in *Sebastian Knight,* but it is nevertheless there and it is the same. Nabokov tells us in the foreword to the English translation of this, the last of his Russian novels, that the real heroine is Russian literature. The central character is an émigré poet named Fyodor Godunov-Cherdyntsev. Like most of the characters in the foreground of Nabokov's works, he is not especially admirable; he is only moderately good as a poet, but he is improving and shows great promise. There is, however, a really good poet in the émigré colony in Berlin—Koncheyev—and he serves, along with the heroine defined in the foreword, as the center for Fyodor's centripetal movements. Of course the real conversations that Fyodor occasionally manages to have with this admired poet are utterly banal, but the imagined conversations (like the imagined idyll of Sebastian Knight's half-brother with his hero) are miraculously urbane and wise. One of them amounts to a little survey of Russian literature, in the course of which Nabokov manages to make one more payment on his old account with Dostoevsky: "Bedlam turned back into Bethlehem— that's Dostoevski for you." (*Gift*, p. 84) In another imagined conversation Fyodor listens to Koncheyev pronounce the most devastating judgments upon his, Fyodor's, works. These judgments, citing faults which the wise Koncheyev thinks Fyodor will overcome, are delivered in tones of glacial balance and objectivity, which makes it all the more remarkable, I think, that they are incidentally the most insightful and damaging things ever said about the work of Nabokov himself. (It is tempting to recall at this point Mr. Magarshack's remark about Nabokov as one more sad example of a man blind to his own shortcomings.) We see, then, in the relationship between Fyodor and Koncheyev essentially the same relationship that obtained between the rather moderately gifted narrator of *Sebastian Knight* and the hero of that novel.

The novel which bears the most striking resemblance to Nabokov's work on Pushkin and which, I think, actually developed out of that enterprise is, of course, *Pale Fire*. It appeared in 1962, that is to say, near the end of Nabokov's long occupation with *Eugene Onegin*. In *Pale Fire* not only the relationship of the characters but the very structure of the book itself partakes of the nature of a paradigm.

To begin with the characters, we meet in the foreground as our narrator (and in this case commentator) a person whose name, if we start from more or less objective reality, is Botkin. He is not only a Russian émigré teaching in an American university but also completely mad—a situation not without its near parallels in Nabokov, or for that matter in life. Throughout the novel Botkin occurs as the mirror image of his name, Kinbote, and he is of course the flawed peripheral character with whom we are by now familiar. Who is the central genius of talent and grace? He is the great American poet, John Francis Shade. Kinbote the madman worships Shade the poet. He literally spies on him through uncurtained windows, invites himself to the Shade house, and imagines himself to be Shade's good friend and confidant—that is to say, he is in every essential way the same character as Sebastian Knight's worshipful half-brother and all the others.

Pale Fire provides a natural and fluent transition to the next larger element in Nabokov's Nabokov that bears on the four-volume Pushkin, and that is the question of the structure of his novels. The

work consists of an introduction by Kinbote, a narrative and ruminative poem entitled "Pale Fire" by John Shade, a much longer, very
detailed, even more ruminative, certainly more narrative, and I think
more poetic commentary by Kinbote, and, finally, a hilarious index
to the whole book.

The poem itself deals with the central tragedy of John Shade's
life, the suicide of his plump, unattractive teenage daughter and then
of Shade's musing on reality and art (the same thing), on life and
death (the same thing). It is 999 lines long, the last, unwritten, one-
thousandth line being in Kinbote's imagination identical with the
first line, which is to say that the beginning and the ending are the
same. Since Kinbote is mad and imagines himself to be the deposed
and exiled King Charles the Beloved of a mythical kingdom to the
north of Russia, the commentary bears no relationship whatsoever
to the real poem. Kinbote sees it all as a deftly disguised account of
his own saga, with which he has been boring the great poet to death.

It is irresistible to recall at this point the identical situation in
the novelette, *The Eye*, recently translated into English. There the
hero, Smurov, shoots himself early in the story and like certain other
Nabokovian characters survives the vividly imagined experience of
death (he missed the vital organ) in order to return as a kind of spy
on his own subsequent life. The Russian title of *The Eye* is "Soglja-
dataj" (Spy). Smurov makes his way surreptitiously into the apartment of friends seeking overt evidence of his own existence. In a
letter lying open on a table, which he greedily reads, there is no mention of him; a snapshot of a group of people has had his image (if
it was ever there) trimmed off; a conversation that he overhears is
depressingly banal, without the least mention of him. In exactly this
way, poor mad Kinbote in *Pale Fire* inches toward the agonizing conclusion that the great poem of John Shade in fact contains nothing of
his royal tragedy. Smurov, Kinbote, Sebastian Knight's half-brother,
Fyodor Godunov-Cherdyntsev can all be seen as astonishingly late
and literal embodiments of one of the most exploited character types
in nineteenth-century Russian literature: the Superfluous Man.

Pale Fire, then, consists of a poem and a commentary, the
length and worth of the commentary being out of all proportion to
these qualities in the poem, and this is precisely the structure and
the nature of the work on Pushkin. It is also the form of Nabokov's
translation of and commentary on a late twelfth-century Russian epic
known as *The Igor Tale*. It is also the form of Nabokov's translation
of and commentary on Lermontov's novel *A Hero of Our Time*

(where Nabokov collaborates with Lermontov almost as exasperatingly as Kinbote collaborates with Shade).

These resemblances are easily seen, but I think it is not so often noticed that the poem-and-commentary form is the essential structure of the novels *The Real Life of Sebastian Knight*, *The Gift*, and even *The Defense*. I believe that I have already said enough about *Sebastian Knight*, in which the *included poem*, if I may now make a sort of shorthand use of this phrase, consists of the lengthy plot summaries and other features of the novels of Sebastian Knight. Perhaps a few more words about *The Gift* would be in order.

In this novel there are two included poems. The first is a book of poetry, Fyodor Godunov-Cherdyntsev's first book, made up of "about fifty twelve-line poems all devoted to a single theme: childhood." (p. 21) We are not given the texts of all these poems, but we are given a great many of them and there is a long and detailed commentary on them. The second included poem, occupying all of the nearly one hundred pages in chapter four, is another work by Godunov-Cherdyntsev, *The Life of Chernyshevski*. Like Pushkin, Nikolai Gavrilovich Chernyshevsky (1828–1889) was a real person, though here his resemblance to Pushkin ends. He was a sympathetic but essentially ungifted writer and critic whose views on the social function of art, much admired today in the U.S.S.R., could not more neatly oppose every view held by Nabokov on the same subject. Following this long included work come the reviews of it, and they constitute in effect a kind of commentary upon it. This commentary is supposed to come from various émigré critics, some of whom are densely incapable of understanding it, with the result that their responses are in fact a parody of a commentary.

My point is that Nabokov's Pushkin, his four-volume translation of and commentary on the great novel-poem *Eugene Onegin*, is only in detail different from what this extremely repetitious and extremely varied writer has been doing throughout all of his mature career. It is to be noted that in every case the *included poem*, the base or source work, in this peculiarly Nabokovian structure is inferior to the commentary. The poem of John Shade in *Pale Fire* is only occasionally of some interest. It is really not terribly good. Nabokov, let us admit it, is, both in Russian and in English, only moderately gifted as a maker of verses. Shade's poem is valuable chiefly in characterizing its author through the apparently tough-minded but actually rather sentimental account of the suicide of his unfortunate daughter. It gives to Shade a sharper and more vivid existence than he might otherwise have had if we had been obliged to see him only through the mad eyes of Kinbote. But no one could claim that it approaches the artistic level of the commentary that surrounds it. I do not think that a man could write a very good poem if it was meant to be only a pretext—or pre-text—for a comment upon it.

In the novel *The Gift*, the included poetry of Godunov-Cher-dyntsev is again not very good. It is in fact quite flat and prosaic. When we come to the monograph on the life of Chernyshevsky, which occupies a long chapter in the middle of the novel, we are, I think, uncomfortably aware that it is perhaps just a shade too inferior. There are several pages that would never be missed. But the moment we come to the reviews, that is to say, to the commentary on the novel, then we are back in the novel proper, and it is absorbing.

I think that the relationship between Nabokov's translation of *Eugene Onegin* and his commentary on *Eugene Onegin* is exactly the same as the relationship that we have seen in these other cases. The translation itself does not seem—and I think really that it was not particularly meant to seem—sufficient cause for the commentary. I am not speaking now, of course, of Pushkin's original masterpiece, which is superior to all conceivable commentaries upon it, including Nabokov's. But Nabokov's translation of it is not, and in this respect also his work on Pushkin is exactly like the preceding works of which we have just spoken.

And finally we come to what is for me the most fascinating aspect of all—the character relationships. We recall that Pushkin's *Onegin* contains, as one of the characters of the poem, an acquaintance of Onegin, the poet Alexander Pushkin. It contains its creator. There is much of Pushkin in his hero Onegin, to be sure, but there is also Pushkin himself *in propria persona*. He leans on the stone parapet on the bank of the Neva in St. Petersburg and chats with his character. He receives the letter that Tat'yana, his heroine, writes to Onegin and translates it for us out of French into Russian, and so on.[1] He is always there. He occasionally takes us aside to comment upon this and that event in the real world, to relate some anecdote concerning a friend of his. He is a peripheral character. But this is also the situation that we have in the major novels of Nabokov and in Nabokov's Pushkin, because Nabokov himself bears the same relation to his hero Pushkin that he has pictured in novel after novel. It

---

[1] In his commentary Nabokov puts it back into French.

is the relation which I think he learned in the first instance from this poem.

I said that fate was the muse of Nabokov. I might with equal justice have said that Pushkin is and has always been the muse of Nabokov. Nabokov is very much a Russian writer, and whenever Russian literature of the modern period has risen above the humdrum and everyday it has risen on the wings borrowed from Alexander Pushkin. Fate and Pushkin are identical. Pushkin is Nabokov's fate. Nabokov was long ago remembering his future work, remembering the great translation of and commentary on Pushkin's masterpiece.

It has been often remarked that Nabokov has a phenomenal visual acuity and an equally phenomenal ability to render the objects of that visual acuity in words. No one currently practicing the art of the English novel can see as well as he can. We speak rather glibly sometimes of the "heightened reality" of this or that work. Since the phrase is so worn we ought perhaps to modify it slightly when applying it to Nabokov: a "sharpened reality"? a "focussed reality"? a "clarified reality"? Whatever we choose, the meaning is that he makes us more acutely aware of what had always struck us as familiar things; and in doing so he makes them both real and new. Reading Nabokov is using, for a time, his central nervous system. We cease to be ourselves and become the person whom he supplies. And that is the point of his art. He has said that what he seeks in writing is best described as "aesthetic bliss." He means by this "ecstasy," with its etymological sense of being taken outside of oneself. The chief value of his work on Pushkin's great poem is that he makes it pass through his intelligence to us. We become Nabokov reading Pushkin. It is literally a kind of aesthetic ecstasy, but like all ecstasy it is temporary. We must become ourselves again, but we will not be or see exactly what we were and saw before. To read Pushkin not with Nabokov but as Nabokov is an experience that leaves us pleased, instructed, and altered.

Much has been made of Nabokov's discourtesy, and his supposed discourtesy has been adduced as justification of the discourtesy, not to say impudence, offered him in return. I dare say it is not easy to regain one's sense of equilibrium after having just received a full, mortifying dose of Nabokov's opprobrium. But I should nevertheless like to suggest that hurt feelings and petulant complaints about deportment are rather beside the point. Nabokov is not, after all, indifferent to or only mildly concerned with the fate of Pushkin's heritage. Nor, as I have tried to show, does he have any wish or indeed ability to distance himself from it. Pushkin's fate is a part of his fate, and their fate as artists is a part of the only fate with which Nabokov has ever been in the least concerned: the fate of art itself.

THE FLAUNTING OF ARTIFICE
IN VLADIMIR NABOKOV
AND JORGE LUIS BORGES

Patricia Merivale

Vladimir Nabokov never lets his readers forget that he is the conjuror, the illusionist, the stage-manager, to whom his characters owe their existence; this flaunting of artifice, not merely as technique but also as theme, can perhaps be elucidated by a closer examination of one type of Nabokovian device, the book that, in whole or in part, explicitly imitates another book: a "discovered manuscript," a fictitious confession, a book about imaginary books, or a book that parodies such an already conventionalized structure as the detective story, the scholarly commentary, or the literary biography. Of the large number of contemporary writers employing such devices, Jorge Luis Borges, the Argentine poet, essayist, and author of disturbingly effective philosophical-fantastic tales, offers the closest and most illuminating parallels with Nabokov. Yet the similarity of their forms and structures brings into focus a fundamental difference in their premises about the relationship of art and reality.

Both Borges and Nabokov could be called "modern mannerists";[1] Borges, who said that "la irrealidad es condición del arte"[2]

---

[1] For Borges and "Manierismus," see Gustav Hocke, *Manierismus in der Literatur* (Hamburg, 1959), pp. 22–23, and Marianne Kesting, *Vermessung des Labyrinths* (Frankfurt am Main, 1965), pp. 50–56. See also John Updike's excellent article on Borges, "The Author as Librarian," *The New Yorker* (October 30, 1965), pp. 223–246.

[2] Borges, "El milagro secreto" ["The Secret Miracle"], *Ficciones*, in *Obras Completas* (Buenos Aires, 1956), V, 162. Further references to tales in this edition will be given in the text, using the abbreviation *F*. Where English translations are readily available, either in *Ficciones*, ed. Anthony Kerrigan (New York, 1962), or in *Labyrinths: Selected Stories and Other Writings*, ed. Donald

("unreality is the necessary condition of art"), has often been called "baroque" as well, a term that reminds us that *Don Quixote* is the father of the book-conscious-of-its-bookness. Both Borges and Nabokov exploit, for their own thematic purposes, all the narrative tricks and devices of the Gothic fantasy writers of the last two centuries, and they blend mannerism and Gothicism together in their single most important parodic pattern, the metaphysical detective story.

Borges' tales, rational and horrid, in the manner of Poe, yet paradoxical and philosophically teasing, in the manner of G. K. Chesterton, blend paradox, wonder and fear in a way that has often been compared with the nightmare logic of Kafka; the comparison is both obvious and justified. Both men see the world as a labyrinth of passages, a series of unopened doors, a thwarted or negated quest, a pointless wait separating the hero from a doubtfully existent Law, from a somehow menacing Judgment. Both authors are masters of the short poetic parable with much paradox and riddling in it, a form hovering somewhere between "fiction" and philosophic or even mythic tale-telling. But Borges, motivated by a passionate, highly intellectual curiosity, seeks to know what, if anything, is true; Kafka, motivated by a deep anxiety, seeks to know where, if anywhere, he belongs; the distortions of "laconicas pesadillas"[3] seem more relevant to his quest than do the distortions of self-conscious and explicit artifice that charm both Borges and Nabokov. Even Nabokov's *Invitation to a Beheading*, so Kafkaesque in structure and effect, if not in intention,[4] seems rather to lead back towards a world of the sane and normal, where something could perhaps be both real and beautiful at once.

The logical extrapolation of Borges' brief tales into novel form would be not *Das Schloss* or *Der Prozess*, but a real metaphysical detective story like Alain Robbe-Grillet's *Les Gommes* (1953), where the detective hero himself becomes, by "accident" or by "destiny," the murderer he has been seeking. Wallas, Robbe-Grillet's stoical

---

A. Yates and James E. Irby (New York, 1962), the English titles will be given in the text in square brackets. English translations have been supplied, in parentheses, for all quotations, and for the titles of stories not found in these editions.

[3] (Laconic nightmares.) See Borges' introduction to his translation of nine Kafka stories, *La metamorfosis* (Buenos Aires, 1938), p. 7.

[4] See Nabokov's Foreword to *Invitation to a Beheading* (New York, 1965), p. 6, where he firmly denies the possibility of a "Kafkaesque" strain, as he had read no Kafka at the time he wrote the book.

hero, lives out not only the rigid, deliberately conventional fiction of a *roman policier*, following the web of clues to a "surprise" ending, but also, through a labyrinthine city, he re-enacts the search of his literary predecessor, the detective Oedipus, who likewise pitted an ironic ignorance and the power of reason against the riddling clues to his own guilt and walked into the trap of his own accord. Wallas' victim, like Oedipus', is his "father," rather than, as in the Borgesian pattern, his own self or his anti-self; otherwise for both authors the "solution"—truth and identity—is found in violence and annihilation at the center of the labyrinth. The fatal gunshots that climax or conclude five of Nabokov's major fictions and the sudden deaths that end two others serve a less readily definable purpose; at times it appears that, in a very serious and complex Nabokovian sense, "Death often is the point of life's joke."[5]

While Nabokov seems, in actuality, to have preferred the patterns of Mayne Reid's Wild Westerns[6] to detective stories per se, Borges has always admired and enjoyed detective stories, and indeed translated, anthologized and parodied them.[7] In his own volume of detective stories, pointedly entitled *Seis problemas para don Isidro Parodi* (*Six Problems for Isidro Parodi*, 1942), the detective's purity of ratiocination, of armchair detection, is guaranteed by his being in jail the whole time. But the Chestertonian tricks of Parodi, presented without deep thematic purpose, fall flat in comparison with those in, for instance, "Abenjacán el Bojarí, muerto en su laberinto" ("Abenjacán el Bojarí, Dead in his Labyrinth"). This tale retains the device of the uninvolved detective, reasoning out, from the evidence presented in the apparent story, the real story, or "solution," an elaborately Chestertonian paradox: the labyrinth was not the refuge where the king was hiding, but instead the trap where the slave was waiting, to rob the king of life and, thematically more important, of identity as well.

Justly the most famous of the detective stories is "La muerte y la brújula" ["Death and the Compass"], where Borges' detective-reasoner is, like Robbe-Grillet's, also the active follower of clues. The detective, Lönnrot, using clues from the Jewish cabbalistic tra-

---

[5] *Laughter in the Dark* (New York, 1938), p. 182.

[6] *Conclusive Evidence: A Memoir* (New York, 1951), p. 137.

[7] Wilkie Collins, Chesterton, Agatha Christie and Ellery Queen are among the many authors represented in his anthology *Los mejores cuentos policiales*, 2d series (Buenos Aires, 1951). See also his *Antología de la literatura fantástica* (Buenos Aires, 1940).

dition of the four letters of the mystic name of God, works out with map and compass where a fourth murder will take place, extrapolating from the locations of the first three. At the point where the structure is logically completed, a solitary, labyrinthine building, he discovers, again like Robbe-Grillet's Wallas, that he is not a mere investigator but a chief participant—in fact, the victim. The villain now plays the detective's role of explaining the true story. The clues were planted, so that Lönnrot could build from them his own four-sided labyrinth, or trap, and then walk into it. The real labyrinth was, paradoxically, merely a simple straight line from starting-point to doom. After the explanation, the fourth murder occurs.[8]

Not only the opportunities but also the limitations of the detective story form suit Borges' purposes. It has been said that he builds "a world of shadows" in his fiction;[9] perhaps a better term would be "abstractions." Though the more intellectual emotions of curiosity and awe at the marvellous are abundant, the less intellectual ones of sexuality, love, and the entanglements of human relationships are replaced by a little hate and fear and, a quality not unlike that of a Conrad hero, the strange, free honor of the solitary man.

While none of Nabokov's heroes are, strictly speaking, detectives, many of them follow out clues to self-discovery according to the structure of the metaphysical detective story. Indeed, the author Sebastian Knight has written just such a story, *The Prismatic Bezel*, where, as in Borges or Robbe-Grillet, the alleged victim turns up alive—in this case, by the simple, farcical device of removing his false beard.[10] More important, Knight's brother has embarked on the detective-like quest of the literary biographer, to find out what his brother's "Real Life" was, and perhaps what his own life is. The hero of *The Eye* is a voyeur rather than a detective, but Nabokov describes his quest in these terms:

The texture of the tale mimics that of detective fiction . . . the pursuit of an investigation which leads the protagonist through a hell of mirrors

---

[8] In numerous other stories ("El Sur" ["The South"], or "Hombre de la esquina rosada," for instance), where the hero follows a devious route to his doom, Borges leaves to the reader the detective's function of reasoning from clues, of supplying the missing scene or the true explanation. Detective-story structure is still there; "story" still equals "puzzle," but some of its paraphernalia has dropped away.

[9] Ana María Barrenechea, *Borges the Labyrinth Maker*, ed. and tr. Robert Lima (New York, 1965), p. 22.

[10] *The Real Life of Sebastian Knight* (Norfolk, 1959), pp. 91–95.

and ends in the merging of twin images. . . . The stress is not on the mystery but on the pattern.[11]

But the quest of Smurov, a "superfluous man," to discover, from the mere reflections of himself in other people, whether he really exists or not, is but a pale prefiguration of the detective quests that pattern three of Nabokov's major novels: *Despair*, *Pale Fire* and *Lolita*.

Despair is the clearest and the least interesting. The narrator (Hermann), impassioned by creativity as well as greed, murders his own double, and, failing both as criminal and as artist, is caught at once when no one perceives any resemblance between them. Hermann is the weakest of the three heroes, as his fancies do not rise as far above the flat and hackneyed as he supposes; he merely wishes to turn his life into a good detective story, by slaying some necessary but imagined externalization of himself. The last third of *Lolita* is a sequence of stalkings and pursuits, including a "cryptogrammic paper chase" (Chapter 23) of puns and allusions, which ends with Humbert's slaughter, in a rather Gothic house, of Quilty, the man who resembles him in quasi-artistic perversity and who shares the guilt of Lolita's corruption. In effect, Humbert is, like Hermann, killing "himself," his sin externalized in the form of Quilty, and will shortly die for doing so.[12] *Pale Fire*, an amazingly complex book, again includes the slow approach of an assassin through a maze of words and inventions to slay the narrator's "double," the poet whose name is "Shade." But, as in *Despair*, a very ordinary, squalid murder is made into a metaphysical detective story by the imagination of the narrator. An escaped lunatic, a criminal who has come to kill his judge and executioner (compare the vengeance of Borges' gangster upon the detective Lönnrot), is turned into an invented "agent" journeying through the labyrinths of the poem's lines, of geography, and of the clues the narrator plants in his way. Gradus kills a "dou-

---

[11] *The Eye* (New York, 1965), pp. 9–10.

[12] This idea is interestingly corroborated in Martin Green's valuable article, "The Morality of Lolita," *Kenyon Review*, XXVIII:3 (June 1966), 357. The Quilty-Humbert-Lolita triangle is foreshadowed in many ways by the Rex-Albinus-Margot triangle in *Laughter in the Dark* (New York, 1938), with Rex a phonier, more corrupt Albinus ("Rex was Albinus' shadow," p. 208), and Albinus a feebler, but equally possessive and unwanted Humbert, seeking a blind man's revenge upon his fickle mistress by stalking her, horribly, in the "dark."

ble," to be sure—among Nabokov's well-hidden clues is one indicating the close physical resemblance of John Shade, the poet, to his absent neighbor, the Judge—but not the narrator's double, for that, by refusing to write Kinbote's poem of Zembla,[13] John Shade has steadfastly refused to be. Ironically the mad Kinbote is right in thinking that Shade is his true friend, for only Shade, of all those who know him to be mad, has pity and some understanding for him: "One should not apply [the word "mad"] to a person who deliberately peels off a drab and unhappy past and replaces it with a brilliant invention. That's merely turning a new leaf with the left hand." (p. 238)

Nabokov's novelistic method of characterization stresses the individual personality, whose separateness will be marked by whims, quirks, eccentricity, perversion, and insanity, and whose complete fictional existence will be filled out by the fictional dimensions of memory, nostalgic nuance, and the pieced-together events of a whole life, thus implicitly denying the very possibility of the "doubles" whose supposed existence means so much to his narrators. Shade, Hermann's vagrant, and Quilty are all reluctant doubles, refusing to acknowledge the alleged resemblance.[14]

In Nabokov's work true doubles only occur as unreal grotesques, like the director and the lawyer in *Invitation to a Beheading* (p. 207) or the doubled spies of *Bend Sinister*, who might even be "Rosenstern and Guildenkranz, those gentle interchangeable twins." (p. 100) But again and again characters give an effect of double-ness by looking at themselves from the outside, vividly imagining the actions of, for instance, "the other Cincinnatus"; Hermann makes a fetish of self-voyeurism (pp. 37–39); *The Eye* depends upon the division the hero imagines in himself to render the complexity of his personality.

On the other hand, Borges, the *conteur philosophique*, is concerned not with personality, but only with identity, which is a defi-

---

[13] New York, 1962. See Kinbote's Foreword, p. 26, and Commentary on lines 47–48, p. 83. For Gradus' labyrinth, see especially p. 78 (Commentary on lines 17 and 29). Shade's Zembla is merely his own unshaven face in the mirror (ll. 937–8). But cf. Swift, scattering innuendoes for Rosicrucian commentators (as Nabokov plants clues for his Freudian interpreters), and the elaborate artifices of *The Battle of the Books*: "a malignant Deity, call'd *Criticism* . . . dwelt on the Top of a snowy Mountain in *Nova Zembla*."

[14] Even Pnin, in the novel which has perhaps less "flaunting of artifice" than any of the others, insists that his colleague, Wynn, has a "double," a "T. Wynn."

nition of self, archetypal, abstract, inexplicable, to be sure, and yet in a way very simple. By a binary moral arithmetic, Borges strips down his characters to victim and executioner, slave and monarch, coward and hero, and distinguishes between the polar opposites in terms of a single moment of unequivocal symbolic action. In the story called "La otra muerte," for example, the question is whether the protagonist has run away or has fought and died bravely; a writer of realistic war fiction would insist that it is not so easy to say. The writer of philosophic parable can simply describe "la noche en que por fin vio su propia cara, la noche en que por fin escuchó su nombre" ("the night when he finally saw his own face, the night in which he finally heard his name"), asserting that "cualquier destino, por largo y complicado que sea, consta en realidad de un solo momento: el momento en que el hombre sabe para siempre quién es"[15] ("any destiny, however long and complicated, consists, in reality, of a single moment: the moment when a man knows once and for all who he is"). The protagonist then knows himself to be hero or coward, or both together, or discovers himself to be identical with someone else in past or future or dream, or perhaps with all men at once, or perhaps with no one at all. Nabokov is never more Borgesian than in the concluding lines of *The Real Life of Sebastian Knight*: "Sebastian's mask clings to my face, the likeness will not be washed off. I am Sebastian, or Sebastian is I, or perhaps we both are someone whom neither of us knows."

Borges' "La forma de la espada" ["The Shape of the Sword"] is a well-made story in which, like the pistols in a "well-made play," the crescent-shaped scimitar on the wall at the beginning will be used by the end. But, oddly, though John Vincent Moon bears the scimitar-shaped scar of guilt, the Mark of Cain, his brother's slayer, and is at the same time Judas, the informer, we see that he has in a way achieved what, in "Abenjacán el Bojarí," the lackey only attempted: pretending to the identity of the brave man as he tells his own story, Moon has attained that identity, along with the strength and purpose of his victim—exchanged it for his former self,

---

[15] "Biografía de Tadeo Isidoro Cruz (1829–1874)," *El Aleph* (Buenos Aires, 1962), p. 66. See also "El espejo de tinta," in *Historia universal de la infamia* (Buenos Aires, 1935), for a good example of the paradoxical identity of victim and executioner. The theme of mirrors runs through the whole work of both authors, and along with their other images of artifice—chess and card games, maps, juggling and conjuring, masks and disguises, invented languages, and so on—it deserves to be discussed at length.

the trembling, cowardly fugitive. Hero and betrayer have become the same. Likewise, in "Los teólogos" ["The Theologians"], driven by the subtler violence of an obsessive life-long hatred, the two theologians battle to death at the stake, only to discover that in the eye of God there is no difference between the two abstrusely intellectual heresies that had made them enemies, or indeed between the two men themselves. They are now indistinguishable, "una sola persona," doubles of each other after all.

There are numerous possibilities in this Borgesian concept of identity, yet all the permutations of character are virtually reducible to a formula of "fire" and "algebra" in a way in which Nabokov's Humbert Humbert, or Kinbote, or even the rather stiffly contrived Hermann are not. Nabokov's characters are "real," even while following out the apparently patterned destiny, shaped by artifice, which they have created or imagined for themselves.

The stylized, patterned, cliché properties of the detective story, its very nature as a labyrinthine exercise of ingenuity, make it, or its parody, an especially valuable form for a book conscious of its book-ness, whether it is used alone or is gracefully combined with some other artifices of book-ness which have had a long literary history. There is, for instance, that manuscript, not to be published until after its author's death, edited by a fictitious editor, the confession of that arraigned criminal, Humbert Humbert. It is, in effect, a Manuscript Found in a Bottle, a Gothic device, like such notable works as the story found in the trunk in the Inn in *Don Quixote*, or the papers in the ebony cabinet in *Northanger Abbey*, or the dusty, charred and, unfortunately, torn and fragmentary manuscripts found in, say, *Melmoth the Wanderer*, which always break off at the point of greatest suspense. From Charles Maturin to Arthur Machen and beyond, any author of fantastic fiction is likely to employ the device: we think of Ambrose Bierce, H. G. Wells, M. P. Shiel, and of course Poe, author of the story called "MS Found in a Bottle." Less perfunctory and more integral to the theme, the device is a staple of narrative technique in such more characteristically modern authors as François Mauriac, Hermann Hesse, Junichiro Tanizaki, Max Frisch, John Barth, Lawrence Durrell and Abram Tertz. It is a device of pseudo-realism, "giving an air of verisimilitude to an otherwise bald and unconvincing narrative," distancing, relieving the alleged author or editor of responsibility for what is said. It is especially useful in making possible the first-hand story of an Arthur Gordon Pym, a man distant or dead. The Manuscript Found in a Bottle comes to shore, like an inky Ishmael: "And I only am escaped alone to tell thee. . . ."

The device, originated for fantastic fictions, became available for fictionalized philosophies, whence the elaborate interplay of pseudonym, persona and editor in Kierkegaard's *Either/Or* and in Carlyle's *Sartor Resartus*, from both of which Borges has learned that the line between fiction and philosophy may be a blurred one. If "la metafísica es una rama de la literatura fantástica" ("metaphysics is a branch of fantastic literature," "Tlön, Uqbar, Orbis Tertius," *F*, p. 23), then Gothic devices can be parodied for the purposes of metaphysics. At least half of Borges' tales are what he calls "notas sobre libros imaginarios" ("notes on imaginary books," Prologue to *F*, p. 12), having inner books as a major structural element: for instance, the imaginary Herbert Quain's imaginary detective story, *The God of the Labyrinth*, and the other Quain story from which Borges claims to have derived an actual story of his own (see "Examen de la obra de Herbert Quain" ["An Examination of the Work of Herbert Quain"]). The manuscript of the story of Marcus Flaminius Rufus, the Immortal, is found in a copy of Pope's *Homer*, and part of the imaginary encyclopedia of Tlön, describing the imaginary literature of that realm, is found in (among other places) a set of the *Anglo-American Cyclopedia*, a good instance of the "imagined" taking up residence in the world of the "actual."

Nabokov's *Pale Fire* contains, of course, the most notable of his many invented manuscripts, John Shade's own poem called "Pale Fire"; Nabokov's novel consists of Shade's poem plus Kinbote's lengthy scholarly commentary upon it.[16] Kinbote, the editor, "finds" the manuscript, or rather snatches it away from the dying poet. But when, in the scholarly prose of the commentary, he tries to turn the domestic New England realism of John Shade's verse into the romantic fantasy of his own exile from his kingdom of Zembla, he inevitably fails. The externally verified artifact, the Manuscript Found, maintains a stubborn life of its own, and it is the Commentary that becomes Kinbote's subjective, solipsist confession (like Humbert's and Hermann's), where deliberate self-justification and unconscious self-revelation throw into the sea an encoded message that may never be unraveled. The reader will find himself frustrated indeed when

---

[16] Life imitates art; see Edward J. Brown, "Nabokov and Pushkin," *Slavic Review* (December, 1965), 688 ff., for a discussion of Nabokov's real scholarly commentary on a real poem as an extension of the techniques of *Pale Fire*.

he tries to find the Zemblan Crown Jewels concealed somewhere in Kinbote's Index to his Commentary.

Borges' Hladik, in "El milagro secreto" ["The Secret Miracle"], lives and is condemned to death in a simpler, a more nearly solipsist world than Kinbote's. His miraculous reprieve of a year's imaginary life in the instant between the aiming and the firing of the guns suffices for him to complete his masterpiece, the work which justifies his life; it is a play about an action taking place outside of time. The last word needed to complete the play comes to him just before the bullets hit. Just as Sebastian Knight and his brother come closest to being "doubles" in the Borgesian sense, so Sebastian's own book, *The Doubtful Asphodel*, comes closest to being a true inner parallel in the Borgesian manner. Sebastian writes about a man dying while he himself is dying. His brother says of the work:

The man is the book; the book itself is heaving and dying. . . . We feel that we are on the brink of some absolute truth. . . . And the word, the meaning which appears is astounding in its simplicity. (pp. 175, 178–179)

But of course the inner hero dies before this word can be uttered; of course Sebastian dies before his brother can thread the infuriating labyrinth that separates him from Sebastian's death-bed, and before he can receive from Sebastian's own lips the answer to the puzzle of both their lives.[17]

In Nabokov's *Bend Sinister* the most important inner artifact (among so many) is a distorted reflection, the "bend sinister," of Shakespeare's *Hamlet*. The central parodies, of cinematic, pedantic, and especially of totalitarian interpretations of the play are evident enough, as are the numerous specific allusions throughout the book,

---

[17] Again there is a false double; Sebastian is already dead, and the brother sits all night by the side of the wrong man. Nabokov's numerous books-within-books more often provide a mocking contrast to the outer book, as in the false life of Sebastian which his brother must explicitly refute by writing "the real life" (a Cervantean touch), and as in *Pale Fire* itself. But cf. Cincinnatus' Journal, Krug's writings on philosophy, the literary biography within *The Gift* and especially the elaborate concept (*Bend Sinister*, p. 73) of inventing the works of Shakespeare as a hoax, and making all the interpolations in subsequent books that are needed to certify to the existence of the plays. This hoax is remarkably like the composition of the Encyclopedia of Tlön, which got away from its makers and became real, or like Pierre Menard's re-writing *Don Quixote* word for word. Cf. "La escritura del Dios," for the phrase that solves everything, the phrase of magic power.

for instance, to a Protean Shakespeare "composed of two left arms and a mask" (p. 94); the forthcoming production would have constituted a play within the "play." But simmering below the distorted surface, where the tyrant Paduk (nicknamed "the Toad") sees himself as the redeemer Fortinbras, is a shadowy *Hamlet* structure extending through the book (like the Oedipus structure of *Les Gommes*), in which Krug and the reader know Paduk to be Claudius: "A toad . . . on the late king's favourite garden seat." (p. 99) The bereaved and grieving hero, an image of integrity, stands aloof and disdainful in the first "court" scene where the academics rally around the new regime; he rejects the bribes and wooings of his old school enemy, Paduk, so anxious for his support; he escapes into philosophy and meditates upon death when he should be escaping to another country; and in a "court" that reeks of a coy sexual corruption, he is constantly spied upon by, among others, an "Ophelia" sent to discover his secrets by seducing him. "Osric and Fortinbras have acquired a tremendous ascendancy over the rest of the cast" (p. 95); the first of death's summoners is grotesquely foppish. In the final "court" scene, the themes of madness and revenge coalesce at last, but Nabokov, the stage-manager, breaks off our heightened involvement in the "tragedy" of the logical ending:

Death is but a question of style, a mere literary device, a musical resolution. . . . And Krug ran towards him, and just a fraction of an instant before another and better bullet hit him, he shouted again: You, you—and the wall vanished, like a rapidly withdrawn slide, and I stretched myself and got up from among the chaos of written and rewritten pages. . . . (pp. xvii, 216)

We have had some hints throughout that Nabokov is staging a play in which Krug dreams of a world even less real than he is himself, from which Nabokov must rescue him first by "blessed madness," and then by dismissing him, along with the rest of the cast, his other inventions, his "whims and megrims."[18]

Invitation to a Beheading, and that much slighter work, *The Waltz Invention,* being comic versions of the nightmare-reality situation, require only an act of heroic will by one of the characters to break the illusion; Nabokov's direct intervention is not needed. In *The Waltz Invention,* the mad inventor's dream of holding the

---

[18] *Bend Sinister* (New York, 1964). See especially Nabokov's introduction (1963), pp. xii, xiv, xviii, the whole of chapter 7 and p. 116.

whole world up to ransom becomes the world's nightmare, until at a touch of defiance from the actual, the nightmare villain collapses back into seedy nothingness. In *Invitation to a Beheading*, we are given, from beginning to end, clues that Cincinnatus is "realer" (more "opaque") than the grotesques around him, whom he himself is dreaming into existence, and that his prison is an artifice, a stage-set. At the end, with the prison collapsing like a house of cards, he realizes that he need not wait for the nightmare axe to fall; he simply gets up and walks towards "where, to judge by the voices, stood beings akin to him." (p. 223)

Both Borges and Nabokov like to make an appearance from time to time as characters within their own stories. Borges is the stage-manager of "La busca de Averroes" ["Averroes' Search"], whose hero disappears the moment Borges ceases to believe in him. "Borges" as a character appears in "Tlön, Uqbar, Orbis Tertius," "La forma de la espada" ["The Shape of the Sword"], and elsewhere, much as Nabokov appears in the guise of the Russian émigré author to whom Hermann will send his manuscript, or of the Russian émigré lecturer who is coming to take over Pnin's job, or the Russian writer in exile of whom Kinbote thinks at the very end of *Pale Fire*, or the "I" who cannot possibly be any of the characters, yet who often helps to narrate a third-person novel. But Borges goes further and contemplates a world in which this "I" too is dreamed, a book in which he too is written. The Rabbi of Prague created a Golem, a stupid, clumsy creature who mimicked the Rabbi's pious gestures in a somehow frightening way; but "¿Quién nos dirá las cosas que sentía/Dios al mirar a su rabino en Praga?"[19] ("Who can tell us the things God felt while looking at His rabbi in Prague?") In "Las ruinas circulares" ["The Circular Ruins"], the hero, with great suffering and effort, dreams into existence a man who can live independently of his creator. But the creator discovers that, in turn, someone has been dreaming *him* into existence. Again and again it seems as characteristic for Borges to use the devices of artifice to trap us and him-

---

[19] "El Golem," *Poemas 1923–1958* (O.C. II), p. 173. See also the conclusion of "Magias parciales del *Quijote*" ["Partial Enchantments of the *Quixote*"] for the key image of infinite regression, the perfect map which must contain a map of itself within it, which must in turn contain . . . and for the proposition that the metaphysical significance of plays within plays is simply that it reminds us that "if the characters in a story can be readers or spectators, then we, their readers or spectators, can be ficticious [also]." *Other Inquisitions*, tr. Ruth L.C. Simms (Austin, 1964), p. 46.

self in infinite regression—in an exitless labyrinth, a hall of mirrors, a dream within a dream—as it does for Nabokov to prick the richly iridescent bubble of artifice with a tiny touch from a world more actual.

Nabokov, writing fiction, asserts the primacy of "reality" over insane fantasy: Hermann, Humbert, and Kinbote are defeated as they attempt to impose their imagined structures—the perfect crime, the romantic kingdom, or the quintessence of ideal passion—on an unwilling world.[20] The walking-stick is left at the scene of the crime, when Hermann should have known that, by the rules of the literary genre, the "perfect criminal" always overlooks something. The real nature and needs of the person, Lolita, will not be denied. John Shade refuses to play "double" to Kinbote. In each case reality disrupts fantasy as a mode of action. The heroes are left only with the books they have written, their self-created artifices, for only a lunatic would behave as if the world were his own work of art, would try to make the world book-shaped.

But for Borges the world *is* book-shaped. Consider the complex series of "Chinese boxes," of story within story, in his tale "El jardín de senderos que se bifurcan" ["The Garden of Forking Paths"]. The tale is a fragmentary manuscript—we are told that the first two pages are missing—found and anonymously edited. It tells a story which must be placed in the context of historical events as given in a real book, Captain Liddell Hart's history of the First World War. It is the deposition or confession of an arraigned criminal, and its main action is that of a metaphysical detective story: a complex double pursuit—detective-assassin-victim—through a labyrinth to truth and violent death. And within these frames is an invented book, called, of course, *El jardín de senderos que se bifurcan*, written by an ancestor of the assassin. It is a novel structured upon a labyrinth, forking in time, showing the endlessly bifurcating possibilities of choice; it is very like the actual labyrinth-Garden, forking in space, which seemed to the assassin as he wound his way through it to be as large as the world. The victim, in effect supplying a commentary upon this invented book, explains that it is "una imagen, incompleta, pero no falsa" ("an image, incomplete, but not false," *F*, p. 109) of its author's universe, where every future possibility, including those

---

[20] As, in a different way, Luzhin (*The Defense*) turns life into the pattern of a chess-game and the world into a giant chess-board: a dangerous trifling with the actual from which only death can release him.

of this very encounter, may be actualized.[21] Two of these possibilities
are diametrically opposed: the two men will understand each other
and be friends, or one will come as an enemy to kill the other. Both,
of course, are true. But, as in "La muerte y la brújula," actuality
draws a straight line through the labyrinths of possibility; all this
occurs within a frame where the spy must kill the victim and in turn
be captured, in order that a message, in the world of history, may be
delivered. But "reality," if the spy story is any realer than the metaphysical novel it contains or than what the spy has imagined about
the novel, does not negate fantasy for Borges; "reality" is simply
another frame of the structure of artifice. The world can be seen as
a labyrinth, and transcribed as a detective story which can be sub-
sumed into an absolute Book, like Mallarmé's,[22] which perhaps can
explain the world.

In the parable of the "La biblioteca de Babel" ["The Library
of Babel"], where man is "el imperfecto bibliotecario" ("the imperfect librarian," F, p. 87), we have an ironic variant of the familiar
topos of the World as God's second sacred book.[23] "La biblioteca
total," the universe, is

la vasta Biblioteca contradictoria, cuyos desiertos verticales de libros corren
el incesante albur de cambiarse en otros y que todo lo afirman, lo niegan y
lo confunden como una divinidad que delira.[24]

---

[21] See not only Olaf Stapledon's *Starmaker* (1939) for a source of these
ideas, but also the selection from *Starmaker* that Borges translated and included
in his *Antología de la literatura fantástica*. (p. 182)

[22] See Jacques Scherer's commentary, Le *"Livre"* de Mallarmé (Paris,
1957). Cf. Shade's lines 939–40: "Man's life as commentary to abstruse/Unfin-
ished poem. Note for further use," and Kinbote's paraphrase of them. (p. 272)

[23] Ernst Curtius, *European Literature and the Latin Middle Ages* (New
York, 1963), gives some interesting early examples of "The Book as Symbol,"
pp. 302–347. See also Borges' "Del culto de los libros" ["On the Cult of
Books"], *Otros Inquisiciones*, where he gives a brief yet detailed history of the
topos of the Absolute Book, with references to Carlyle, Léon Bloy, Sir Thomas
Browne, Sir Francis Bacon, and the *Koran*, among others. Marianne Kestner
summarizes Borges' relation to the Baroque world-theatre or world-book as follows: "aber immerhin noch Gott die Fäden in den Händen halten liess,
während hinter Borges Metaphern sich das unendliche Nichts verbirgt." (*Vermessung*, p. 54)

[24] "La biblioteca total," *Sur* LIX: 59 (August 1939), p. 16. A case of a
pure essay giving literary antecedents and historical facts, later to be turned into
the "fiction," or philosophical parable, of "La biblioteca de Babel," where this
quotation, slightly altered, is used again, along with a similar list of hypothetical books.

(the vast contradictory library whose vertical deserts of books run the never ending risk of changing themselves into others, and which affirm all, deny all, and confuse all like a divinity in the midst of delirium.)

The library contains every conceivable combination of twenty-five symbols, and will thus yield, eventually, the unwritten chapters of *Edwin Drood*, the song the Sirens sang, the autobiographies of the archangels, the true catalog of the Library, thousands of false catalogs, and even Borges' own story; but mainly, stretching out perhaps to the size of the Universe itself, perhaps to infinity, there will be shelf after shelf of nonsense. If the parable is serious, we are compelled either to search hopelessly for the true book through the endless nightmare of the Library, or else to mimic the Absolute book by means of dream, or magic, or art, to make a human sub-creation, obedient to human rules rather than to the non- or in-human rules of the Library. And of course Borges, though not in this despairing parable, has chosen the latter: art, with its imperfect, merely provisory reality, which may well be futile. Poetry can dream into existence only tigers stuffed or flimsy like the Golem; yet Borges must continue "esta aventura indefinida/Insensata y antigua"[25] ("this indefinite, senseless and ancient adventure") the search for the real tiger who escapes art, since Artifice, the realest thing we can know, is the only thing that can make reality endurable. With this Nabokov would agree. Thus Borges, "desde los laberintos de cartón pintado del truco" ("from the painted pasteboard labyrinths of the card-trick") from the artifices and devices of his literary tradition, feels that "nos hemos acercado a la metafísica: unica justificación y finalidad de todos los temas"[26] ("we have approached metaphysics: the sole justification and end of all themes"). With this, perhaps, Nabokov would not agree: insofar as he is asking at all the question "what is true?" he is giving a commonsense, empirical answer, to counterpoint against what is beautifully or horribly imagined. Borges, the stoic artificer, tries to make his book mirror the world, however feebly, and yet "poco antes de morir, descubre que ese paciente laberinto de líneas traza la imagen de su cara"[27] ("just before dying, he discovers that the patient labyrinth of lines traces [only] the image of

---

[25] "El otro tigre" ["The Other Tiger"], and also the prose poem "Dream-tigers," both in *El Hacedor* (Buenos Aires, 1960), pp. 76, 12. Translated in *Dreamtigers* (Austin, 1964).

[26] "El truco," *El idioma de los argentinos* (Buenos Aires, 1928), p. 34.

[27] "Epílogo" ["Epilogue"], and "Una rosa amarilla" ["A Yellow Rose"], *El hacedor*, p. 109, pp. 31–32.

his [own] face"). He has only written his own Confession; he has only added one object or artifact more to the world. For Nabokov, the comic artificer, however, "the lunatic, the lover and the poet" (and Nabokov's heroes are generally all three at once)[28] will go on projecting fantasies simply because they must, and Nabokov will go on writing about them for the aesthetic conjuror's fun of it. And, as for identity, about which Borges has to be metaphysically solemn, if richly ironic and paradoxical, perhaps Kinbote of *Pale Fire*, handsome, bearded, Zemblan, wretched, crazy and incurably pederastic, will turn up "on another campus" (in another book?) as an "old, happy, healthy, hetero-sexual Russian, a writer in exile . . . sans anything but his art." (p. 301)

These Prosperos, the poet-conjurors of our own day, flaunt the complex artifices of their revels with equal skill; but while Nabokov usually dismisses his actors "into thin air" and returns us to the real world, Borges takes the argument to its conclusion, and perpetually reminds us that both author and reader "are such stuff/As dreams are made on."

---

[28] Humbert, for instance, calls himself "an artist and a madman, a creature of infinite melancholy," and then identifiies himself with "poets and lovers," *Lolita* (New York, 1959), p. 19 and p. 50.

VLADIMIR NABOKOV'S
CRITICAL REPUTATION IN ENGLISH:
A NOTE AND A CHECKLIST

Jackson R. Bryer

Assessments of an author's literary reputation and checklists of criticism are at best tentative for they are often obsolete or incomplete within a few months of publication. In the case of Vladimir Nabokov this circumstance is even more pertinent than usual; for there could hardly be a more inappropriate moment at which to attempt a summary and estimate of the reception of Nabokov's work in English than the present. Nabokov criticism appears to have reached a significant point of transition and the future promises to be of far more interest than the past. Among the important events one can contemplate are the appearance of the first book-length critical studies of Nabokov by Andrew Field and Page Stegner, a revised edition of *Speak, Memory*, published by Putnam's in late 1966, a new collection of short stories, future English translations of the Russian-language novels, a new novel, the idea for which is supposedly "germinating" in the author's mind, and British editions of the titles recently published in the United States.

The books by Field and Stegner undoubtedly will not only contain new insights but should also provoke reviews which themselves will, in some cases, constitute important contributions to Nabokov criticism. The publication of additional fiction in English by Nabokov will similarly elicit review-essays as well as, hopefully, much-needed independent critical articles in scholarly journals.

It is the latter kind of material which is most conspicuously absent from Nabokov criticism to date. Within the last two years, however, there have been indications of a change in this situation. One of the few general appraisals of Nabokov's major works is the recent and significant essay by R. H. W. Dillard in the June 1966 issue of the *Hollins Critic*. Ostensibly a review of *Despair*, Dillard's piece is actually a study and comparison of Nabokov's seven major novels. It makes a convincing and unique attempt to see connections between the protagonists of several of these works and to trace a pattern of development in Nabokov's fiction. On a somewhat less ambitious scale, Henry Grosshans' essay in the Winter 1966 issue of *Texas Studies in Literature and Language* similarly takes a wider view, as Alan Pryce-Jones (*Harper's*, April 1963) and F. W. Dupee (*NY Review of Books*, December 12, 1963) have done in earlier articles.

But these are exceptions to a trend in Nabokov criticism which has tended to focus intensively on individual novels, most generally in lengthy reviews but occasionally in critical articles. Thus, W. R. Johnson (*Carleton Miscellany*, Fall 1963) and Page Stegner (*Southern Review*, April 1966) have written essays on *The Real Life of Sebastian Knight*; while Carol T. Williams (*Critique*, Winter 1963), Jack Handley (*Northwest Review*, Spring 1963), and Richard Kostelanetz in his edition of *On Contemporary Literature* have coped with the complexities of *Pale Fire*.

More often, however, serious critical analyses of the individual novels can be found in reviews. *Bend Sinister*, perhaps the least widely-recognized of Nabokov's full-length fictional works, has been the subject of an extremely perceptive review-essay by Frank Kermode (*Encounter*, June 1960). Richard G. Stern (*Prairie Schooner*, Summer 1957) has assessed *Pnin* at considerable length; British novelist John Wain has done the same with *Invitation to a Beheading* (*New Republic*, December 21, 1959); Stanley Edgar Hyman (*New Leader*, October 14, 1963) and Donald Malcolm (*New Yorker*, April 25, 1964) have studied *The Gift*; *The Defense* has been subjected to similarly detailed scrutiny by Robert M. Adams (*NY Review of Books*, January 14, 1965), Andrew Field (*New Leader*, October 26, 1964), and John Updike (*New Republic*, September 26, 1964); and, most recently, excellent essays on *Despair* by Brigid Brophy (*Book Week*, May 15, 1966), Andrew Field (*NY Times Book Review*, May 15, 1966), and Quentin Anderson (*New Republic*, June 4, 1966) have appeared. *Pale Fire* aroused a heated exchange of views among several critics, most notably Mary McCarthy (*New Republic*, June 4, 1962), Dwight Macdonald (*Partisan Review*, Summer 1962), Frank Kermode (*New Statesman*, November 9, 1962), and Gilbert Highet (*Horizon*, July 1962).

But by far the single most notable—and deplorable—characteristic of Nabokov criticism is the disproportionate amount of attention devoted to *Lolita* and the resultant lack of serious comment on the other fiction, poetry, and translations. Vladimir Nabokov is the author in English of eleven novels, two collections of short stories, a volume of poetry, a play, and two translations, one of which, a four-volume edition of *Eugene Onegin*, he has called "the great work of my life." Yet, aside from book reviews, well over two-thirds of the criticism prompted by his work deals with *Lolita*, which very few serious critics consider his most significant book. Further, a good deal of this comment on *Lolita* can at best be described as quasi-literary, dealing as it does with the question of whether the novel is pornographic or not.

To be sure, important essays and reviews on *Lolita* are in print. F. W. Dupee's famous "Preface" to the first appearance of the work in a 1957 issue of the *Anchor Review* and Lionel Trilling's "The Last Lover" (*Griffin*, August 1958) certainly rank with the best of Nabokov criticism to date; while reviews by John Hollander (*Partisan Review*, Fall 1956), Kingsley Amis (*The Spectator*, November 6, 1959), Howard Nemerov (*Kenyon Review*, Spring 1957), Richard Schickel (*The Reporter*, November 28, 1957 and *The Progressive*, November 1958), and Rebecca West (London *Sunday Times*, November 8, 1959) are of much greater value than all but a very few of the critical essays published.

This last situation, as suggested earlier, is one of the several peculiar aspects of Nabokov criticism: most of the serious and inci-sive commentary has appeared in the form of book reviews. Given this fact, it is not surprising that Richard Kostelanetz, when faced with the task of selecting three pieces on Nabokov for his 1964 an-thology *On Contemporary Literature*, chose to reprint two reviews and to do a short essay himself rather than choose any of the articles then available to him. As Kostelanetz must have discovered very quickly, there is a great dearth of worthwhile critical essays on Nabo-kov. When one adds to this the lack of attention paid to him in books on contemporary literature and the impressive number of reviews which his novels have received, more of the paradoxes and ironies of his present literary reputation are apparent. Nabokov simply has not yet been "discovered" by the critical quarterlies, many of which have devoted entire numbers to the writings of contemporaries whose pub-lished work does not amount to half of his in quantity, let alone quality. The needs are clear: more general studies of the relationships between his works and their major characters; an increased amount of attention to novels other than *Lolita*; and perhaps even some attempts at analyzing the famous and puzzling Nabokov style.

Considering the length of the checklist which follows this note and the number of leading critics whose names appear therein, it is striking what little critical ground has actually been covered by the literally hundreds of reviewers and scholars who have grappled with the intricacies of Nabokov's work. Samuel Beckett is a writer whose career resembles Nabokov's in several respects: they have approximately the same amount of work available to readers in English; they both have challengingly complex styles; they both are multilingual; they both have achieved critical recognition within the last twenty years; and, at the risk of arousing controversy, it can be said that general critical opinion of the merits of their work is roughly about the same. Yet there are now just about a dozen full-length books available on Beckett, the great majority of them in English; and the number of consequential critical articles on Beckett in English is perhaps ten times the number of similar pieces on Nabokov. Surely this is one of the great oddities of modern literary criticism. The complaint cannot be raised with Nabokov, as it can with Salinger, Ellison, Cheever, Updike, and others of the post-Second World War generation, that they have not got a sufficient body of work in print to permit worthwhile assessments. The corpus is there; the burden now rests with those critics who are willing and able to take up the challenges of its complexities.

A CHECKLIST OF NABOKOV CRITICISM IN ENGLISH

Jackson R. Bryer and Thomas J. Bergin, Jr.

The form and arrangement of this checklist are, to a great extent, consequences of the situation in Nabokov criticism outlined in the preceding note. Because most of the important work is in the form of book reviews, a good deal of effort has been made to include as many of these notices as possible. Any success attained in this endeavor could not have been achieved without the cooperation of the Publicity Departments of G. P. Putnam's (especially Miss Donna

Onasch), George Weidenfeld & Nicolson (particularly Miss Bud McLennan), Trident Press, New Directions, and Doubleday, and the generous assistance of many reference librarians and newspaper editors who helped verify references unavailable to us. Again, because many reviews constitute significant contributions to Nabokov criticism, we have used an asterisk before those which we felt were in this category of review-article.

Comment on Nabokov in books is very scanty and we have included a section of this material just for this reason and also because often such material consists of reprinted reviews or essays which are probably more readily available to the reader in book form than in the original newspaper or periodical. Annotations after book references of this sort indicate where the item originally appeared.

In the Articles section, because there is, again, relatively little periodical criticism of Nabokov, we have made no effort to be selective but rather have tried to include virtually everything about him we could find. Thus, news items about *Lolita* censorship are here, along with interviews, brief mentions in general articles, and entire essays dealing with him. Frequently, a brief annotation indicates into which of these several categories the particular item falls.

In general, the form of the checklist follows the recommendations of the MLA Style Sheet. No extensive use of abbreviations has been made, except in the case of New York (both city and state) which has been shortened in all cases to NY. When only part of a review or essay deals with Nabokov, this has been indicated by first listing the page numbers of the entire piece and then, in brackets, the pages on Nabokov. No attempt has been made to list works by Nabokov. This job has already been done extremely fully and ably in a 1964 issue of the French journal *L'Arc*. The publication information given after the titles of Nabokov's writings in the Book Reviews section of this checklist is not intended to be exhaustive but merely to represent the major printings and those to which the reviews listed refer. Nabokov's works are listed in order of their first publication in English.

Finally, no work of this kind can be completed without the help and encouragement of a large number of persons, only two of whom can be acknowledged here. Mrs. Vladimir Nabokov has made several useful suggestions and Andrew Field has given generously of his time and his considerable knowledge of Nabokov studies.

I. BOOKS

Dupee, F.W., "The Coming of Nabokov." In his *The King of the Cats" and Other Remarks on Writers and Writing*. NY: Farrar, Straus and Giroux, 1965. Pp. 117–141 [Reprinted essay on *Lolita* from *Anchor Review* and reprinted review of *The Gift* from *NY Review of Books*].

Fiedler, Leslie A., *Love and Death in the American Novel*, rev. ed. NY: Stein and Day, 1966. Pp. 335–336, 416 [*Lolita*].

————, *No! In Thunder*. Boston: Beacon Press, 1960. Pp. 3, 4, 260, 289–290 [Emphasis on *Lolita*].

Field, Andrew, "The Defenseless Luzhin." In Richard Kostelanetz, ed. *On Contemporary Literature*. NY: Avon Books, 1964. Pp. 473–476 [Reprinted review of *The Defense*].

Green, Martin, "American Rococo: Salinger and Nabokov." In his *Re-Appraisals: Some Commonsense Readings in American Literature*. NY: W.W. Norton, 1965. Pp. 211–229.

Hollander, John, "The Perilous Magic of Nymphets." In Richard Kostelanetz, ed. *On Contemporary Literature*. NY: Avon Books, 1964. Pp. 477–480 [Reprinted review of *Lolita*].

Kostelanetz, Richard, "Nabokov's Obtuse Fool." In his ed. *On Contemporary Literature*. NY: Avon Books, 1964. Pp. 481–485 [*Pale Fire*].

Nemerov, Howard, "The Morality of Art" and "The Ills From Missing Dates." In his *Poetry and Fiction: Essays*. New Brunswick, N.J.: Rutgers University Press, 1963. Pp. 260–269 [Reprinted reviews of *Pnin*, *Lolita*, and *Nabokov's Dozen*].

Pryce-Jones, Alan, "The Fabulist's Worlds: Vladimir Nabokov." In Nona Balakian and Charles Simmons, eds. *The Creative Present—Notes on Contemporary American Fiction*. Garden City, NY: Doubleday, 1963. Pp. 65–78 [Reprinted essay from April 1963 *Harper's*].

Rougemont, Denis de, "*Lolita*, or Scandal." In his *Love Declared—Essays on the Myths of Love*, tr. Richard Howard. NY: Pantheon Books, 1963. Pp. 48–54. See also pp. 55–57.

Stegner, Page, *Escape Into Aesthetics: The Art of Vladimir Nabokov*. NY: Dial Press, 1966 [Focus primarily on the five novels written in English: *Sebastian Knight*, *Bend Sinister*, *Pnin*, *Lolita*, and *Pale Fire*].

West, Paul, *The Modern Novel*. London: Hutchinson, 1963. Pp. 277–280, 303, 306, 313, 417.

Witham, W. Tasker, *The Adolescent in the American Novel—1920–1960*. NY: Frederick Ungar, 1964. Pp. 22, 43, 61, 95, 241 [*Lolita*].

II. ESSAYS IN PERIODICALS

Allsop, Kenneth, "*Lolita,*" *New Statesman,* LVII (January 24, 1959), 108–109 [Letter to the Editor].

Aldridge, A. Owen, "*Lolita* and *Les Liaisons Dangereuses,*" *Wisconsin Studies in Contemporary Literature,* II (Fall 1961), 20–26.

Alvarez, A., "London Letter—Exile's Return," *Partisan Review,* XXVI (Spring 1959), 284–289 [288–289: *Lolita* in England].

"American Fiction—The Postwar Years, 1945–65," *Book Week* (Washington *Post,* NY *Herald Tribune,* San Francisco *Examiner*), September 26, 1965 [See esp. pp. 2, 5, 6, 18, 20, 22, 24].

Baker, George, "*Lolita:* Literature or Pornography?" *Saturday Review,* XL (June 22, 1957), 18.

Balakian, Nona, "The Prophetic Vogue of the Anti-heroine," *Southwest Review,* XLVII (Spring 1962), 134–141 [140–141: *Lolita*].

"Ban on 'Lolita' Lifted," London *Times,* September 21, 1959, p. 9 [News item].

Beaver, Harold, "A Figure in the Carpet: Irony and the American Novel," *Essays and Studies,* XV (1962), 101–114 [113–114: *Lolita*].

Breit, Harvey, "Talk With Mr. Nabokov," *NY Times Book Review,* July 1, 1951, p. 17 [Interview].

Brenner, Conrad, "Nabokov: The Art of the Perverse," *New Republic,* CXXXVIII (June 23, 1958), 18–21.

Brick, Allan, "The Madman in His Cell: Joyce, Beckett, Nabokov and the Stereotypes," *Massachusetts Review,* I (Fall 1959), 40–55 [52–55: *Lolita*].

B[urns], M[ildred] B[lair], "Books By Vladimir Nabokov," *Hollins Critic,* III (June 1966), 6–7 [Checklist].

Butler, Diana, "Lolita Lepidoptera," *New World Writing,* No. 16 (1960), 58–84.

C.,T., "Vladimir Nabokov," *Hollins Critic,* III (June 1966), 5 [Biographical sketch].

Coleman, John, "Nabokov," *The Spectator,* No. 6854 (November 6, 1959), 619 [Interview].

Cranston, Maurice, "Obscenity in the Eye of Only Some Beholders— Contradictions in the Case of 'Lolita,'" *Manchester Guardian,* May 14, 1957, p. 5.

Dalwood, Hubert, "*Lolita*—A Postscript," *Geste* (University of Leeds), IV (March 12, 1959), 13–14.

Davis, C.K., "Lolita," Books and Bookmen, IV (April 1959), 3 [Letter to the Editor].

Davis, Douglas M., "On the Banks of Lake Leman—Mr. Nabokov Reflects on 'Lolita' and 'Onegin,'" National Observer, June 29, 1964, p. 17 [Interview].

Drew, Philip, "British Ex-C.-in-C. Flays Ike's Battle Strategy," Cleveland Plain Dealer, November 15, 1958, p. 10-F [Includes brief comment on Lolita in England].

DuBois, Arthur E., "Poe and Lolita," CEA Critic, XXVI (No. 6, 1963), 1, 7.

Dupee, F.W., "Lolita in America," Encounter, XII (February 1959), 30–35. See also Columbia University Forum, II (Winter 1959), 35–39.

————, "Nabokov: The Prose and Poetry of It All," NY Review of Books, December 12, 1963, pp. 10–12. Reprinted in his "The King of the Cats" and Other Remarks on Writers and Writing. NY: Farrar, Straus and Giroux, 1965.

————, "A Preface to Lolita," Anchor Review, No. 2 (1957), 1–13. Reprinted in his "The King of the Cats" and Other Remarks. . . .

"Exclusive on 'Nymphet'?" Publishers' Weekly, CLXXVIII (August 8, 1960), 28.

Fiedler, Leslie A., "The Profanation of the Child," New Leader, XLI (June 23, 1958), 26–29.

Flint, R.W., "Lolita: The Moral Issues," New Republic, CXXXIX (November 3, 1958), 3, 23 [Letter to the Editor].

"French Ban 'Lolita' In English," London Times, December 18, 1959, p. 8 [News story].

"The Fuss About 'Lolita,'" The Spectator, No. 6812 (January 16, 1959), 80–81 [Letters to the Editor from A.E. Moore, Herbert Van Thal, and "Chelsea Artist"].

Gardiner, Harold C., "Clichés Are Dangerous," America, XCIX (August 30, 1958), 552–553.

Girodias, Maurice, "'Lolita,'" The Spectator, No. 6855 (November 13, 1959), 672 [Letter to the Editor from official of Olympia Press, French publishers of first edition of Lolita].

————, "Lolita, Nabokov, and I," Evergreen Review, IX (September 1965), 44–47, 89–91 [Account of first publication of Lolita].

Gold, Joseph, "The Morality of 'Lolita,'" British Association for American Studies Bulletin, n.s. No. 1 (September 1960), 50–54 [Comparison suggested between Lolita and Crime and Punishment].

Grosshans, Henry, "Vladimir Nabokov and the Dream of Old Russia," Texas Studies in Literature and Language, VII (Winter 1966), 401–409.

Hale, Nancy, "Hemingway and the Courage to Be," Virginia Quarterly Review, XXXVIII (Autumn 1962), 620–639 [621–623: Lolita].

Handley, Jack, "To Die in English," Northwest Review, VI (Spring 1963), 23–40 [Emphasis on Pale Fire].

Harris, Harold J., "Lolita and the Sly Foreword," Mad River Review (Dayton), I (Spring-Summer 1965), 29–38 [Comparison made between N's Foreword to Lolita and Defoe's Foreword to Moll Flanders].

Hayman, John G., "After 'Lolita'—A Conversation With Vladimir Nabokov—with Digressions," *Twentieth Century*, CLXVI (December 1959), 444–450.

"He Wrote *Lolita*," *Books and Bookmen*, IV (March 1959), 9 [Biography].

Hickey, Neil, "The Author of 'Lolita,' " *American Weekly*, October 4, 1959, pp. 16–17 [Interview-essay].

Hicks, Granville, "American Fiction in 1958," *Saturday Review*, XLI (December 27, 1958), 11–12 [11: *Lolita*].

———, "A Man of Many Words," *Saturday Review*, L (January 28, 1967), 31–32 [N's vocabulary].

"The Hidden Dissuaders: *Lolita* and the Libraries," *Quill and Quire* (Toronto), XXV (January-March 1959), 23–24, 29 [*Lolita's* reception in Canada].

High, Roger, "*Pnin*—A Preposterous Little Explosion," *Geste* (University of Leeds), IV (March 12, 1959), 16–18.

Hinchliffe, Arnold P., "Belinda in America," *Studi Americani*, VI (1960), 339–347.

Hogan, William, "Controversial 'Lolita' To Appear Next Month," San Francisco *Chronicle*, July 10, 1958, p. 29.

———, "Two Russians Set Off the Year's Literary Bombs," San Francisco Sunday *Chronicle*, December 28, 1958, *This World* Magazine, pp. 12–13 [13: *Lolita*].

"Holier Than Thou," *Books and Bookmen*, IV (February 1959), 3 [Editorial comment on *Lolita* as pornography].

Hughes, D.J., "Character in Contemporary Fiction," *Massachusetts Review*, III (Summer 1962), 788–795 [792–793: *Lolita*].

———, "Reality and the Hero: *Lolita* and *Henderson the Rain King*," *Modern Fiction Studies*, VI (Winter 1960–61), 345–364.

Hutchens, John K., "The National Book Awards," NY *Herald Tribune*, March 5, 1959, p. 15.

"Ithaca and 'Lolita,' " *Newsweek*, LII (November 24, 1958), 114–115 [Interview and reactions to *Lolita* on Cornell campus].

Ivask, George, "The World of Vladimir Nabokov," *Russian Review*, XX (April 1961), 134–142.

Johnson, W.R., "The Real Life of Sebastian Knight," *Carleton Miscellany*, IV (Fall 1963), 111–114.

Josipovici, G.D., "*Lolita*: Parody and the Pursuit of Beauty," *Critical Quarterly*, VI (Spring 1964), 35–48.

Karlinsky, Simon, "Vladimir Nabokov's Novel *Dar* as a Work of Literary Criticism: A Structural Analysis," *The Slavic and East European Journal*, VII (Fall 1963), 284–290.

King, Adele, "*La Meprise*," *Geste* (University of Leeds), IV (March 12, 1959), 18, 19–20 [On *Despair*].

King, Bruce, "*Lolita*—Sense and Sensibility at Mid-century," *Geste* (University of Leeds), IV (March 12, 1959), 3–9.

Kinser, Samuel, "*Speak Memory!*" *Geste* (University of Leeds), IV (March 12, 1959), 15–16.

Kostelanetz, Richard, "The New American Fiction," *Ramparts*, III (January-February 1965), 57–60, 62 [60, 62: *Pale Fire*].

Lauter, Paul, " '. . . elementary errors,' " *New Republic*, CXXXIX (November 3, 1958), 23–24 [Letter to the Editor about *Lolita*].

Lawrenson, Helen, "The Man Who Scandalized the World," *Esquire*, LIV (August 1960), 70–74.

Lee, L.L., "Duplexity in V. Nabokov's Short Stories," *Studies in Short Fiction*, II (Summer 1965), 307–315.

————, "Vladimir Nabokov's Great Spiral of Being," *Western Humanities Review*, XVIII (Summer 1964), 225–236.

"Letters to the Editor—'Lolita,' " *NY Times Book Review*, September 14, 1958, p. 33 [Letters from Frances Winwar, Catherine Deininger, and Bernard Sobel].

Levin, Alan, "Nabokov Says 'Lolita' Is More Art Than Life," *NY Post*, September 18, 1963, p. 8.

Levin, Bernard, "Why All the Fuss?" *The Spectator*, No. 6811 (January 9, 1959), 32–33 [Publication history of *Lolita*].

" 'Lolita,' " *London Times*, January 23, 1959, p. 11 [Letter to the Editor protesting possible English ban of novel, signed by Walter Allen, Isaiah Berlin, Storm Jameson, Frank Kermode, Compton Mackenzie, Iris Murdoch, Peter Quennell, Herbert Read, Stephen Spender, Angus Wilson, and others].

" 'Lolita,' " *The Spectator*, No. 6815 (February 6, 1959), 192 [Letters to the Editor from Douglas Woodruff and Derek Parker].

" 'Lolita,' " *The Spectator*, No. 6816 (February 13, 1959), 231 [Letters to the Editor from Douglas Woodruff, Brian Osborne, and Herbert R. Barton].

"*Lolita*," *The Spectator*, No. 6854 (November 6, 1959), 616 [Editorial comment].

"*Lolita* and the Critics," *New Republic*, CXXXIX (October 27, 1958), 3 [Editorial criticism].

"The *Lolita* Case," *Time*, LXXII (November 17, 1958), 102.

" 'Lolita' in London," *Encounter*, XII (February 1959), 34 [Brief excerpts from English critics' reviews and views of *Lolita*].

"*Lolita* in Tunbridge Wells," *Time*, LXXIII (March 2, 1959), 72 [British debate over *Lolita*].

" 'Lolita' Obscene? Not to Its Author," *NY Post*, August 6, 1958, p. 10 [N's comments recorded at Harvard Club cocktail party].

"Lolita's Creator—Author Nabokov, a 'Cosmic Joker,' " *Newsweek*, LIX (June 25, 1962), 51–54.

"*Lolita*—Technically Pornographic," *Books and Bookmen*, IV (March 1959), 3 [Letters to the Editor from J.C.M. Barnes and Anthony Gower].

" 'Lolita' Test Case Sought By Publisher," *London Observer*, February 1, 1959, p. 1 [N's English publisher interviewed on efforts to get *Lolita* published in Britain].

Lund, Mary Graham, "Don Quixote Rides Again or Some Co-ordinates Are Outside," *Whetstone*, III (Fall 1959), 172–178 [*Lolita*].

MacGregor, Martha, "The Author of 'Lolita'—An Unhurried View," *NY Post*, August 17, 1958, p. M10 [Interview].

————, "*Lolita*: Comment From the Critics," *NY Post*, August 31, 1958, p. M11 [Excerpts from reviews].

Maslin, Marsh, "A Letter About *Lolita*," San Francisco *Call Bulletin*,

September 13, 1958, p. 16.

————, "Something About *Lolita*," San Francisco *Call-Bulletin*, December 27, 1958, p. 9.

————, "What To Say About Book French Banned?" San Francisco *Call-Bulletin*, August 23, 1958, p. 12 [*Lolita*].

"Minister Tells Why *Lolita* Was Banned," Wellington (New Zealand) *Dominion*, November 19, 1959.

Mitchell, Charles, "Mythic Seriousness in *Lolita*," *Texas Studies in Literature and Language*, V (Autumn 1963), 329–343.

Mosley, Nicholas, "The Contemporary Novel," *Theology* (London), LXVI (July 1963), 266–271 [269: *Pale Fire*].

Moynahan, Julian, "Speaking of Books: Vladimir Nabokov," *NY Times Book Review*, April 3, 1966, pp. 2, 14.

Nabokov, Vladimir, "On a Book Entitled *Lolita*," *Anchor Review*, No. 2 (1957), 105–112. See also *Encounter*, XII (April 1959), 73–76.

Nichols, Lewis, "In and Out of Books—Mr. Nabokov," *NY Times Book Review*, August 17, 1958, p. 8.

————, "In and Out of Books—Nymphet Abroad," *NY Times Book Review*, November 22, 1959, p. 8 [Reception of *Lolita* by English reviewers].

————, "Speaking of Books—'*Lolita*,'" *NY Times Book Review*, March 22, 1959, p. 8 [Concerns forthcoming English edition].

Oliphant, Robert, "Public Voices and Wise Guys," *Virginia Quarterly Review*, XXXVII (Autumn 1961), 522–537 [530–535: *Lolita*].

"People," *Time*, LXXVI (July 18, 1960), 31 [Brief note on censorship of *Lolita* in New Zealand].

Pharos, "A Spectator's Notebook," *The Spectator*, No. 6814 (January 30, 1959), 138–139 [*Lolita*].

————, "A Spectator's Notebook," *The Spectator*, No. 6815 (February 6, 1959), 179–180 [*Lolita*].

————, "A Spectator's Notebook," *The Spectator*, No. 6816 (February 13, 1959), 216 [*Lolita*].

————, "A Spectator's Notebook," *The Spectator*, No. 6818 (February 27, 1959), 283, 285 [285: *Lolita* compared to Isherwood's *Seascape With Figures*].

Phillips, Elizabeth, "The Hocus-Pocus of *Lolita*," *Literature and Psychology*, X (Summer 1960), 97–101.

Pitman, Robert, "*Lolita*," *New Statesman*, LVII (January 17, 1959), 71 [Letter to the Editor].

————, "*Lolita*," *New Statesman*, LVII (February 7, 1959), 190 [Letter to the Editor].

"*Playboy* Interview: Vladimir Nabokov," *Playboy*, XI (January 1964), 35–41, 44–45.

Pritchett, V.S., "*Lolita*," *New Statesman*, LVII (January 10, 1959), 38.

Probyn, Hugh, "*Lolita*—Nabokov By Poe Out of Rabelais," *Geste* (University of Leeds), IV (March 12, 1959), 10–12.

Pryce-Jones, Alan, "The Art of Nabokov," *Harper's*, CCXXVI (April 1963), 97–101. Reprinted, revised and expanded, in Nona Balakian and Charles Simmons, eds. *The Creative Present—Notes on Contemporary American Fiction*. Garden City, NY: Doubleday, 1963. Pp. 65–78.

————, "On 'Lolita,' " *Book Week* (Washington *Post*, NY *Herald Tribune*, San Francisco *Examiner*), September 26, 1965, pp. 4, 12, 14.

"Publishers' Hopes of Lolita Test Case," London *Times*, February 18, 1959, p. 13 [News story].

"Publishers of 'Lolita' Fight Ban on Novel," NY *Post*, September 22, 1958, p. 34.

Rubin, Louis D., Jr., "The Self Recaptured," *Kenyon Review*, XXV (Summer 1963), 393–415 [403: *Lolita*].

Russell, Leonard, "The Years With *Lolita*," London *Sunday Times*, November 1, 1959, p. 17 [*Lolita* in England].

Saroyan, Amie R., "*Lolita*," *New Republic*, CXXXIX (November 10, 1958), 23 [Letter to the Editor].

Scott, W.J., "The *Lolita* Case," *Landfall*, XV (June 1961), 134–138 [Concerns *Lolita* in New Zealand].

Segal, Lee, "Under Cover," Louisville *Courier-Journal*, January 25, 1959, Sec. 4, p. 7 [Report of interview with N].

"Sisters Under the Skin?" *Time*, LXXII (December 29, 1958), 40 [Concerns possible connections between current comic-strip characters and Lolita].

Slonim, Marc, " 'Doctor Zhivago' and 'Lolita,' " *International Literary Annual*, No. 2 (1959), 213–225 [221–225].

Smith, Peter Duval, "Vladimir Nabokov on His Life and Work," *The Listener*, LXVIII (November 22, 1962), 856–858 [Text of BBC television interview]. See also *Vogue*, CXLI (March 1, 1963), 152–155.

Speakman, P.T., "*Lolita*—What Are Humbert's Motives?" *Geste* (University of Leeds), IV (March 12, 1959), 12–13.

Stegner, S. Page, "The Immortality of Art—Vladimir Nabokov's *The Real Life of Sebastian Knight*," *Southern Review*, n.s. II (April 1966), 286–296. Reprinted in his *Escape Into Aesthetics: The Art of Vladimir Nabokov*, pp. 63–75.

Strainchamps, Ethel, "Nabokov's Handling of English Syntax," *American Speech*, XXXVI (October 1961), 234–235 [*Lolita*].

Struve, Gleb, "The Double Life of Russian Literature," *Books Abroad*, XXXVIII (Autumn 1954), 389–406 [399, 403–404, 405, 406].

Teirlinch, Herman, "Notes on Nabokov's *Lolita*," *Literary Review*, VII (Spring 1964), 439–442.

Theall, D. Bernard, O.S.B., "*Lolita*," *Commonweal*, LXIX (November 28, 1958), 234–235 [Letter to the Editor].

Trilling, Lionel, "The Last Lover—Vladimir Nabokov's 'Lolita,' " *Griffin*, VII (August 1958), 4–21. See also *Encounter*, XI (October 1958), 9–19.

Wain, John, "Small World of Vladimir Nabokov," London *Observer*, November 1, 1959, p. 21 [Criticism-biography-interview].

Williams, Carol T., " 'Web of Sense': *Pale Fire* in the Nabokov Canon," *Critique*, VI (Winter 1963), 29–45.

Woodruff, Douglas, " 'Lolita,' " London *Times*, January 28, 1959, p. 9 [Letter to the Editor].

Zall, Paul M., "*Lolita* and *Gulliver*," *Satire Newsletter*, III (Fall 1965), 33–37.

III. BOOK REVIEWS

CAMERA OBSCURA (LAUGHTER IN THE DARK). London: John Long, 1936, 1938; Toronto: McClelland & Stewart, 1938; NY: Bobbs-Merrill, 1938; NY: New Directions, 1960; London: George Weidenfeld & Nicolson, 1961.

Atlanta *Journal and Constitution*, December 25, 1960, p. 2-C.

Bauer, Malcolm, Portland *Sunday Oregonian*, December 4, 1960, p. 49.

Blake, Nicholas, "Waif on the Make," London *Sunday Telegraph*, April 2, 1961, p. 7.

Bryden, Ronald, "So Wild," *The Spectator*, No. 6925 (March 17, 1961), 375.

Bunting, Harold, "Winks and Nods of Deceit," Sheffield *Morning Telegraph*, April 1, 1961, Weekend Magazine, p. 2.

Burgess, Anthony, "A Rich Quarry For the Novelist," *Yorkshire Post* (Leeds), March 23, 1961, p. 4.

Butler, G. Paul, NY *Mirror*, January 1, 1961, p. 22.

Carrew, Rivers, "Love and Thunder," *Irish Times* (Dublin), March 31, & April 1, 1961, p. 6.

Cleveland *Plain Dealer*, November 20, 1960, p. 7-H.

Dietrich, Henry, San Francisco *Sunday Chronicle*, November 6, 1960, *This World* Magazine, p. 35.

Fletcher, Raymond, London *Tribune*, March 24, 1961, p. 10.

George, Daniel, "Recent Fiction—The Maharajah Comes Home," London *Daily Telegraph and Morning Post*, March 17, 1961, p. 19.

Gilbert, T.R., "Something to Read," *Dark Horse* (London), XLII (April 1961), 257.

Gillon, Diana, and Meir Gillon, "Lessons Taught By Love," London *Sunday Times*, March 19, 1961, p. 30.

Grauel, George E., *Best Sellers*, XX (January 1, 1961), 388–389.

Hall, James B., "Early Work of Nabokov Spotlighted," Los Angeles *Times*, November 27, 1960, p. C-7.

Hay, Sara H., "Predecessor to 'Lolita' Deeply Compassionate," Pittsburgh *Press*, November 20, 1960, Sec. 7, p. 2.

K., A., *Books Abroad*, XII (Autumn 1938), 523.

Merton, Thomas, "Realism and Adventure," *NY Herald Tribune Books*, May 15, 1938, p. 10.

"New Novels: Humour From a Carved Box," *The Scotsman* (Edinburgh), March 18, 1961, Week-end Magazine, p. 2.

"New Sidelights on a Lepidopterist," *Times Literary Supplement*, April 7, 1961, p. 218.

Nottingham Guardian Journal, March 30, 1961, p. 4.

Ort, Dan, "Nabokov Returns to Young Girl, Old Man Theme," Fort Wayne *News-Sentinel*, November 12, 1960, p. 4.

"Pachyderm in a Panic," *Time*, LXXVI (November 21, 1960), 112.

Pagones, Dorrie, Washington *Post*, January 1, 1961, p. E7.

Phelps, Robert, "Nabokov: Pre-*Lolita*," *NY Herald Tribune Book Review*, December 25, 1960, p. 33.

Psychiatric Quarterly, XXXIV (Supplement—Part 2, 1960), 353.

Sandford, Antonia, "Out of Apathy," *John O'London's*, IV (March 30, 1961), 354.

Sandrof, Nancy, "Man Who Played the Pipes and Paid the Piper," Worcester *Sunday Telegram*, November 13, 1960, p. E7.

Schott, Webster, "Nabokov's Special Talent Again," Kansas City *Star*, December 10, 1960, p. 6.

Schultz, Howard, "A Lack of Preachment," Richmond *Times-Dispatch*, November 20, 1960, p. 12.

Seymour-Smith, Martin, "Novels," *Encounter*, XVII (August 1961), 81–84 [81–82].

Shapiro, Charles, "Forerunner of 'Lolita,'" Louisville *Courier-Journal*, December 4, 1960, Sec. 4, p. 7.

Sherman, Thomas B., "Reading and Writing," St. Louis *Sunday Post-Dispatch*, December 25, 1960, p. 4C.

Shrapnel, Norman, "Crossing the Colour Bar," Manchester *Guardian*, March 17, 1961, p. 10.

"The Silent Lover," *Reynolds News and Sunday Citizen* (London), March 19, 1961, p. 10.

Simon, John, "Before *Lolita*, What?" *The Mid-Century*, XIX (November 1960), 8–13.

Spread Eagle (London), April 1961, p. 115.

S[tevens], L[eslie], *Midbank Chronicle*, April 1961.

W[edgewood], M[aurice], "The Nabokov Collection," *Northern Echo* (Darlington), April 14, 1961.

Willy, Margaret, "Debut at 'A' Level," Birmingham *Post*, March 28, 1961, p. 4.

Wilson, Andree, "Bookshelf," *What's On In London*, September 1, 1961, p. 73.

"Working Backwards From Fame," Birmingham *Mail*, March 22, 1961, p. 12.

DESPAIR. London: John Long, 1937, 1939; NY: G.P. Putnam's, 1966 (rev. ed.).

*Anderson, Quentin, "Nabokov in Time," *New Republic*, CLIV (June 4, 1966), 23–28.

Benke, Dick, "New-Old-Novel By Vladimir Nabokov," *Pasadena Independent Star-News*, May 22, 1966, Scene Section, p. 5.

Bleck, Tim, "Masterfully-Told Story," *Dayton Journal Herald*, May 21, 1966, p. 30.

"Book Beat," Portland (Me.) *Sunday Telegram*, May 22, 1966, p. 4D.

Bowerman, Wendell J., "Nabokov's Broken Mirror," *Boston Sunday Herald*, May 15, 1966, Show Guide Section, p. 20.

B[rady], C[harles] A., "Murder Tale, Circa 1932, Translated From Russian," *Buffalo Evening News*, May 21, 1966, p. B-12.

*Brophy, Brigid, " 'Lolita' and Other Games," *Book Week* (Washington *Post*, San Francisco *Examiner*), May 15, 1966, pp. 2, 10.

C[aldwell], S[tephen] F., "Why Bother?" Hackensack (N.J.) *Record*, May 31, 1966, Magazine Section, p. 16.

Clark, Rose Marie, "Author of 'Lolita' Turns to Despair," *Memphis Commercial Appeal*, May 22, 1966, Sec. 5, p. 8.

Colbert, Haines, "Despair, Indeed," *Miami News*, May 22, 1966, MIAMI Magazine, p. 19.

The Critic, XXV (August-September 1966), 62.

Darack, Arthur, "Trouble With Doubles," *Saturday Review*, XLIX (May 21, 1966), 32–33.

Davenport, Guy, "Dazzlers and Astounders," *National Review*, XVIII (June 28, 1966), 636–638 [636–637].

D[avis], D[ouglas] M., "Perils Are Apparent in Reissuing Early Nabokov, Vonnegut Works," *National Observer*, May 23, 1966, p. 23.

*Dillard, R.H.W., "Not Text, But Texture: The Novels of Vladimir Nabokov," *Hollins Critic*, III (June 1966), 1–12 .

"Face Value," *Time*, LXXXVII (May 20, 1966), 124, 126.

*Field, Andrew, "Hermann and Felix," *NY Times Book Review*, May 15, 1966, pp. 5, 36–37.

Fremont-Smith, Eliot, "Books of The Times—Mirror Magic," *NY Times*, May 10, 1966, p. 47.

Gibbs, Wayne E., "Flexing Literary Muscles," Camden (N.J.) *Courier-Post*, May 14, 1966, p. 4.

Hayes, E. Nelson, "By the Author of 'Lolita,' " *Worcester Sunday Telegram*, May 15, 1966, Sec. E, p. 12.

Hill, Virginia, "Another Neurotic By Lolita's Author," Burlingame (Cal.) *Advance-Star & Green Sheet*, May 29, 1966, Peninsula Living Section, p. 36.

Hill, William B., S.J., *Best Sellers*, XXVI (June 1, 1966), 90–91.

Hobby, Diana, "2 Nabokovs," *Houston Post*, June 5, 1966, Spotlight Section, p. 13.

Hofmann, Frank, "Perfect Crime Stirs Nabokov to Artful Prose," *Dayton*

Daily News, May 1, 1966, *Dayton Leisure* Section, p. 19.

Howe, Marjorie, "Russian Writer's 'Despair' Is Brilliant, Entertaining," Burlington (Vt.) *Free Press*, June 3, 1966, p. 4.

Hubler, Richard G., "More Tongue in Cheek By Nabokov," Los Angeles *Times*, May 15, 1966, *Calendar* Section, p. 26.

Hyman, Stanley Edgar, "Nabokov's Distorting Mirrors," *New Leader*, XLIX (May 9, 1966), 11–12.

Idema, James, "Nabokov Novel Tricky Mixture," Denver *Post*, May 29, 1966, *Roundup* Section, p. 28.

Jackson, Paul R., "Artistic Perfection of a Crime," *Chicago Tribune Books Today*, May 29, 1966, p. 3.

Johnson, Lucy, "Macabre Wit," *The Progressive*, XXX (June 1966), 49–51.

Journal (Screen Producers Guild, Beverly Hills, Cal.), June 1966, p. 43.

Knickmeyer, Naomi, "Nabokov's In Great Form Again," Ada (Okla.) *Evening News*, May 22, 1966, p. 9.

"The Last European," *Newsweek*, LXVII (May 16, 1966), 121–122.

Morse, J. Mitchell, "Fiction Chronicle," *Hudson Review*, XIX (Autumn 1966), 507–514 [513–514].

Murray, James G., "3 Novels With a Touch of Old World," *Long Island Catholic*, May 26, 1966, p. 9.

Newquist, Roy, Chicago *American*, May 15, 1966, Sec. 4, p. 8.

Oates, Joyce Carol, "Mr. Nabokov's Too-Thin Book," Detroit *Free Press*, May 15, 1966, p. 5-B.

O'Donnell, John B., "Story of a Nabokov Story," Baltimore *Sunday Sun*, May 15, 1966, Sec. D, p. 5.

O'Neill, John, "Your Flesh Creeps . . . At a Petty Pace," Atlanta *Journal and Constitution*, May 29, 1966, p. 2-B.

Pasley, Virginia, "Nabokov's New-Old Double-Dealing Novel," *Newsday* (Garden City, NY), May 14, 1966, p. 15W.

Peterson, Virgilia, "Understudy for Humbert," *The Reporter*, XXXIV (June 2, 1966), 42–44.

Pickrel, Paul, "Sad, Sinister, and Sane: Some New Novels," *Harper's*, CCXXXII (June 1966), 98–100 [99].

Prescott, Peter S., "A Streak of Madness," Chicago *Daily News*, May 14, 1966, *Panorama* Section, p. 8.

Q., G., " 'Lolita' Fans Can Rejoice With 'Despair,' " Waco *Tribune-Herald*, June 5, 1966, p. 14-D.

Ravitz, Abe C., "Nabokov's Travesty on Human Values," Cleveland *Plain Dealer*, May 22, 1966, p. 9-H.

Rogers, W.G., "Disclaims Any Message—Nabokov Spins a Tale With Tongue in Cheek," Grand Rapids *Press*, May 15, 1966, p. 37.

Root, Bertram, "Within the Spacious Circle," *North American Review*, n.s. III (May 1966), 36.

[Smith, Miles A.], "New 'Heel' Is Created By Nabokov," Anniston (Ala.) *Star*, May 15, 1966, p. 11C. See also Allentown (Pa.) *Sunday Call-Chronicle*, May 15, 1966, p. E-7; Gary *Post-Tribune*, May 15, 1966; Fort Lauderdale *News-Sun-Sentinel*, May 22, 1966; Appleton (Wis.) *Post Crescent*, June 5, 1966.

Stern, Jerome, "If Nabokov Despairs, It's Always With Wit," Charlotte *Observer*, May 29, 1966, p. 5F.

Strong, Barbara, "Another Neurotic Scoundrel," Houston *Chronicle*, May 22, 1966, *Zest* Magazine, p. 14.

Thrope, Day, "Books: New Nabokov Novel Employs 'Double' Plot," Washington (D.C.) *Sunday Star*, May 15, 1966, p. E-2.

Wilkie, Curtis, " 'Hell Shall Never Parole' Narrator of 'Despair,' " Clarksdale (Miss.) *Press Register*, May 14, 1966, p. 2.

Wolff, Geoffrey A., "Don't 'Despair', Viva la Difference," Washington *Post*, May 28, 1966, p. A14.

THE REAL LIFE OF SEBASTIAN KNIGHT. NY: New Directions, 1941, 1959; London: Nicholson & Watson, 1945; London: George Weidenfeld & Nicolson, 1961.

Aldiss, Brian W., "In the Back Alleys of Human Nature," Oxford *Mail*, September 15, 1960, p. 4.

Allen, Walter, "Fiction," *The Spectator*, No. 6149 (May 3, 1946), 462, 464.

Ashton, Eddie, "New Books," Glasgow *Evening Times*, October 7, 1960, p. 10.

Barry, Iris, "Novels of the Opening Season," *NY Herald Tribune Books*, January 25, 1942, p. 12.

B[ecker], D[on], *The Argus* (Seattle, Wash.), LXVI (September 4, 1959), 4.

Betts, Doris, "Nabokov's Reality," Houston *Post*, October 4, 1959, *Houston Now* Section, p. 13.

Boyle, Kay, *New Republic*, CVI (January 26, 1942), 124.

Bryden, Ronald, "Quest for Sebastian," *The Spectator*, No. 6900 (September 23, 1960), 453–454.

Buchanan, Leigh M., "Early Nabokov Novel Describes Dim-Lit World of Artists' Soul," *Cornell Daily Sun* (Ithaca, NY), January 20, 1960, p. 9.

Burlington (Vt.) *Free Press*, November 9, 1959, p. 8.

Churchill, R.C., Birmingham *Post*, October 4, 1960, p. 4.

C[lepper], P[atrick] M., "Nabokov's First Novel Reissued," St. Paul *Dispatch*, October 17, 1959, p. 4.

Cole, Connolly, "Love's Labour's Lost," *Irish Times* (Dublin), September 24, 1960, p. 6.

Coogler, Edith Hills, "Real Sebastian Knight Theme of Skillful Book,"

Atlanta *Journal and Constitution*, September 13, 1959, p. 2-E.

"Curious Quest," *Times Literary Supplement*, September 30, 1960, p. 625.

Davenport, Dorrie, " 'Lolita' Really Came From the Steppes," Washington *Post*, November 1, 1959, p. E7.

Dill, Marshall, Jr., "Two Earlier Novels By *Lolita's* Author," Oakland *Tribune*, December 6, 1959, p. C-9.

Doherty, R.B., "Words Run in Delightful Packs," Birmingham *News*, August 23, 1959, p. E-7.

"Early Nabokov," *Time*, LXXIV (September 28, 1959), 94.

East Anglian Daily Times (Ipswich), October 1, 1960, p. 10.

E[vans], E[ric], "Nabokov," Oxford *Times*, October 7, 1960, p. 26.

Fleishmann, Wolfgang Bernard, *Books Abroad*, XXXIV (Spring 1960), 180.

Fulford, Robert, "A Big Season for Nabokov," Toronto *Star*, August 31, 1959, p. 23.

Gilbert, T.R., "Something to Read," *Dark Horse* (London), XLI (October 1960), 623.

Gillon, Diana, and Meir Gillon, "Tearing Off Strips," London *Sunday Times*, September 18, 1960, p. 27.

Gobi, Nunzio, "The Magician's Rope," *Brunonia Book Review* (Brown University, Providence, R.I.), Winter 1960, pp. 24–26.

Hutchens, John K., " 'The Real Life' . . .," *NY Herald Tribune*, August 27, 1959, p. 13.

J., P.M., "Novelist's Life," *NY Times Book Review*, January 11, 1942, pp. 7, 14.

Jones, Bess, "Nabokov . . . ," *Saturday Review*, XXV (January 17, 1942), 6.

London *Evening Standard*, September 20, 1960, p. 13.

Millstein, Gilbert, "Books of The Times," *NY Times*, August 27, 1959, p. 25.

Morse, Samuel F., "Sample of Each," Hartford *Courant*, September 6, 1959, Magazine Section, p. 13.

"Nabokov's Art Fully Revealed in Early Novel," St. Louis *Globe-Democrat*, August 30, 1959, p. 4F.

N[esbitt], W.J., "Quest For a Brother," *Northern Echo* (Darlington), October 7, 1960.

"New Fiction," London *Times*, September 22, 1960, p. 15.

"New Novels: Pursuit in the Jungle," *The Scotsman* (Edinburgh), October 15, 1960, Week-end Magazine, p. 3.

New Yorker, XVII (December 27, 1941), 60.

Norris, Hoke, "Nabokov Spins Profound Magic in Two Works," Chicago *Sun-Times*, September 6, 1959, Section Three, p. 4.

Peterson, Virgilia, "Search For a Lost Soul," *NY Times Book Review*, August 30, 1959, p. 5.

Phelps, Robert, "The Unique Vision of Vladimir Nabokov," *NY Herald Tribune Book Review*, November 22, 1959, p. 10.

Pickrel, Paul, "Vintage Nabokov," *Harper's*, CCXIX (November 1959), 104, 106.

Prina, L. Edgar, "Nabokov Literary Gem Comes Back to Light," Washington (D.C.) *Sunday Star*, September 13, 1959, p. C-5.

Reed, Henry, "New Novels," *New Statesman and Nation*, XXXI (May 4, 1946), 323–324 [324].

Schickel, Richard, "Hurrah for Our Side," *The Progressive*, XXIII (December 1959), 57–58 [58].

Schott, Webster, Kansas City *Star*, September 5, 1959, p. 18.

Segal, Lee, "Under Cover," Louisville *Courier-Journal*, September 20, 1959, Sec. 4, p. 7.

Shackleton, Edith, "New Books," *Lady* (London), CLII (November 3, 1960), 579.

Shapiro, Charles, "Nabokov's First Novel," Louisville *Courier-Journal*, October 4, 1959, Sec. 4, p. 7.

Sherman, John K., "Nabokov Novel Shows Mastery of the Oblique," Minneapolis *Sunday Tribune*, October 11, 1959, p. E6.

Sherman, Thomas B., "Reading and Writing—More Superb Writing By Author of 'Lolita,'" St. Louis *Sunday Post-Dispatch*, September 13, 1959, p. 4C.

Shrapnel, Norman, "Living in a Nightmare," Manchester *Guardian*, September 30, 1960, p. 8. See also Manchester *Guardian Weekly*, LXXXIII (October 6, 1960), 11.

Singer, Burns, "Utopia and Reality," *Encounter*, XIV (January 1961), 77–79 [78].

Smith, Winifred, "Clever Acrobatics in Literary Technique," *Books Abroad*, XVI (October 1942), 444.

Tanzy, C.E., *English Journal*, XLIX (February 1960), 141–142.

Toronto *Star*, January 31, 1959, p. 28.

Vogler, Lewis, "'Lolita' Produced a Haul of Nabokov," San Francisco *Sunday Chronicle*, December 13, 1959, *This World* Magazine, p. 36.

White, Donald B., "Predecessor of *Lolita*," Worcester *Sunday Telegram*, September 6, 1959, p. E7.

NIKOLAI GOGOL. NY: New Directions, 1944, 1959; London: Editions Poetry London, 1947.

Deutsch, Babette, "Creator of Dead Souls," NY *Herald Tribune Weekly Book Review*, December 24, 1944, p. 8.

Farber, Marjorie, "Nikolai Gogol the Man—and His Nightmare," NY *Times Book Review*, November 5, 1944, p. 29.

"Gogol," *Commonweal*, XL (September 1, 1944), 471–472.

Guerney, Bernard Guilbert, "Great Grotesque," New Republic, CXI (September 25, 1944), 376, 378.
Ivask, Astrid, "What Nabokov Has Done For Gogol. . . .," Books Abroad, XXXV (Autumn 1961), 391.
Posin, J.A., Books Abroad, XX (Spring 1946), 204–205.
Rahv, Philip, "Strictly One-Sided," The Nation, CLIX (November 25, 1944), 658.
Saturday Review, XLII (September 12, 1959), 27.
W., J.T., NY Herald Tribune Book Review, August 9, 1959, p. 10.
Walter, Raymond, Jr., NY Times Book Review, July 12, 1959, p. 12.
Wilson, Edmund, "Nikolai Gogol—Greek Paideia," New Yorker, XX (September 9, 1944), 72–74 [72–73].

NINE STORIES. NY: New Directions, 1947.

"Cosmopolitan Collection," The Cresset (Valparaiso, Ind.), XI (March 1948), 60–61.
Garoffolo, Vincent, New Mexico Quarterly Review, XVIII (Summer 1948), 248.
Newark (N.J.) Evening News, April 5, 1948, p. 8.
New Yorker, XXII (December 20, 1947), 85.
*Weiss, Neil, "Nabokov: 'Cluster Around an Image,'" New Leader, XXXI (April 10, 1948), 11.
Woolsey, F.W., "9 Short Stories Tinged By Irony," Nashville Tennessean, January 18, 1948, p. 29-A.

BEND SINISTER. NY: Henry Holt, 1947; Toronto: Oxford University Press, 1947; London: George Weidenfeld & Nicolson, 1960; NY: McClelland, 1960; NY: Time Reading Program, 1965.

"As For Book," *Jewish Chronicle* (London), March 25, 1960, p. 26.
Basso, Hamilton, "Hands Across the Sea," *New Yorker*, XXIII (June 14, 1947), 86–87.
Bernt, H.H.A., *Library Journal*, LXXII (June 1, 1947), 888.
Borland, Hal, "Strategy of Terror," *NY Times Magazine*, June 15, 1947, p. 10.
Bradbury, Malcolm, *Punch*, CCXXXVII (April 20, 1960), 562.
Coleman, John, "Style and The Man," *The Spectator*, No. 6874 (March 25, 1960), 444–445 [444].
Forbes, Anthony, "New Translation Shows Russian Author at Best," *Nashville Banner*, January 15, 1965, p. 21.
Furbank, P.N., "New Novels," *The Listener*, LXIII (April 14, 1960), 678.
George, Daniel, "Recent Fiction—Mr. Nabokov's New Horror-Comic," London *Daily Telegraph and Morning Post*, March 18, 1960, p. 16.
Harvey, E[lizabeth], "Stinging Satire," Birmingham *Post*, November 22, 1960, Christmas Books Supplement, p. 10.
James, Edith, San Francisco *Chronicle*, June 29, 1947, *This World* Magazine, p. 10.
*Kermode, Frank, "Aesthetic Bliss," *Encounter*, XIV (June 1960), 81–86.
Kippax, H. G., "Novel By Vladimir Nabokov—Ugly Story of Tyranny and Sadism," Sydney *Morning Herald*, June 11, 1960, p. 15.
London *Evening Standard*, March 15, 1960, p. 17.
London *Tribune*, May 6, 1960, p. 10.
Metcalf, John, "Denunciation & Diversion," London *Sunday Times*, March 20, 1960, p. 17.
Millard, John, "New Novels," London *Evening News*, March 24, 1960.
Miller, Karl, "Monsieur Butterfly," London *Observer*, March 27, 1960, p. 21.
"Nabokov and The Toad," London *Daily Express*, March 17, 1960, p. 6.
Naipaul, V.S., "New Novels," *New Statesman*, LIX (March 26, 1960), 461–462.
"New Fiction," London *Times*, March 24, 1960, p. 15.
"New Novel—Round the Sinister Bend?" Glasgow *Herald*, March 19, 1960, p. 9.
"New Novels: Elegantly Patterned Horror," *The Scotsman* (Edinburgh), March 26, 1960, p. 6.
Oldroyd, D.B., *Oxford Mail*, March 17, 1960, p. 6.
Potts, J.C., *Yorkshire Evening Press*, March 31, 1960, p. 6.
Rothman, Nathan L., "Puppet Under Tyrant," *Saturday Review*, XXX (August 2, 1947), 33.
S., B.W., *Shell Magazine* (London), XL (May 1960), 165.
Schossberger, Emily, "The Individual and the State," *Chicago Sun Book Week*, June 22, 1947, p. 4.

Share, Bernard, "No Place For Little Girls," *Irish Times* (Dublin), March 19, 1960, p. 8.
"Superior Amusement," *Time*, XLIX (June 16, 1947), 104.
Trilling, Diana, *The Nation*, CLXIV (June 14, 1947), 722.
Van Sommers, Tess, "New Novels," Sydney *Sun*, July 6, 1960, p. 37.
"Varieties of Behaviour," *Times Literary Supplement*, May 6, 1960, p. 293.
W., R.L., *Canadian Forum*, XXVII (September 1947), 143.
Watts, Richard, Jr., "Comic-Strip Dictator," *New Republic*, CXVII (July 7, 1947), 26.
Webb, W.L., "Shot in Glorious Nabokolor," *Manchester Guardian*, March 18, 1960, p. 9. See also *Manchester Guardian Weekly*, LXXXII (March 24, 1960), 11.
Young, Phyllis, "A Choice of Novels," *Yorkshire Post* (Leeds), March 24, 1960, p. 12.

CONCLUSIVE EVIDENCE: A MEMOIR (SPEAK MEMORY: A MEMOIR; SPEAK MEMORY: A MEMOIR REVISITED). NY: Harper & Bros., 1951; Toronto: Mussen Book Co., 1951; London: Victor Gollancz, 1951; NY: Grosset & Dunlap, 1960; NY: G. P. Putnam's, 1966 (rev. ed.).

*Appel, Alfred, Jr., "Nabokov's Puppet Show—II," *New Republic*, CLVI (January 21, 1967), 25–28, 32.
Arnold, G.L., "Two Russians," *Manchester Guardian*, December 4, 1951, p. 4.
Bookmark (NY State Library, Albany), X (March 1951), 132.
Clark, John, "Nabokov Goes Into His Past," *Chicago Sun-Times*, July 3, 1960, Section Three, p. 5. See also *Toledo Blade*, May 15, 1960, Sec. 2, p. 7.
Crane, Milton, "An Ornament to a Language By Adoption," *Chicago Sunday Tribune Magazine of Books*, March 11, 1951, p. 9.
Cranston, Maurice, "Last Enchantments," *The Spectator*, No. 6443 (December 21, 1951), 859.
Hicks, Granville, "All About Nabokov," *Saturday Review*, L (January 7, 1967), 27–28 [27].
Hindus, Maurice, "Gentle Russian Yesterdays," *Saturday Review*, XXXIV (April 14, 1951), 29.
*Hingley, Ronald, "An Aggressively Private Person," *NY Times Book Review*, January 15, 1967, pp. 1, 14, 16.

Jackson, Paul R., "A Fragile World Made On a Sunday," *Chicago Tribune Books Today*, January 8, 1967, p. 1.

Jones, Frank N., *Library Journal*, XCI (December 15, 1966), 6076.

Kirsch, Robert R., *Los Angeles Times*, July 15, 1960, Part III, p. 5.

Lane, Margaret, "Paradise Lost," *New Statesman and Nation*, XLII (December 1, 1951), 634, 636.

Laut, Stephen J., S.J., *Best Sellers*, XXVI (January 15, 1967), 380.

The Nation, CLXXII (June 16, 1951), 572.

NY Herald Tribune Book Review, August 28, 1960, p. 10.

Paulding, Gouverneur, "Enchanting Recollections of Childhood In Old Russia," *NY Herald Tribune Book Review*, February 25, 1951, p. 7.

Providence Sunday Journal, July 24, 1960, p. W-16.

Pryce-Jones, Alan, "Refining Old Gold," *Book Week* (NY *World Journal Tribune*, Washington *Post*, Chicago *Sun-Times*), January 29, 1967, p. 8.

Raeff, Marc, *Books Abroad*, XXIX (Summer 1955), 307.

"The Reality of The Past," *Time*, LXXXIX (January 20, 1967), 84.

Sherman, Thomas B., "Author of 'Lolita' Tells of His Childhood and Youth," St. Louis *Post-Dispatch*, June 5, 1960, p. 4C.

Slonim, Mark, "Glimpses Into a Vanished World," *NY Times Book Review*, February 18, 1951, p. 7.

Snell, George, "A Man From St. Petersburg in the Western World," San Francisco *Chronicle*, March 18, 1951, *This World* Magazine, p. 21.

Updike, John, "Nabokov's Look Back: A National Loss," *Life*, LXII (January 13, 1967), 11, 15.

Weeks, Edward, *Atlantic*, CCXIX (January 1967), 115–116.

Wolff, Geoffrey A., "Capital Reading—Nabokov Recounts His Past Brilliantly," Washington *Post*, January 14, 1967, p. A14.

LOLITA. Paris: Olympia Press, 1955; NY: G.P. Putnam's, 1958; Toronto: Longman's Green, 1959; London: George Weidenfeld & Nicolson, 1959; NY: Crest, 1959.

Allen, Walter, "Simply Lolita," *New Statesman*, LVIII (November 7, 1959), 631–632.

*Amis, Kingsley, "She Was a Child and I Was a Child," *The Spectator*, No. 6854 (November 6, 1959), 635–636.

Avery, David, "Funny as Crutches," *Mainstream*, XI (December 1958), 51–52.

Baro, Gene, "Wry Comedy of One Man's Sad Obsession," NY *Herald Tribune Book Review*, August 17, 1958, p. 5.

Bassett, James, "Banned Novel to Raise Stir," Los Angeles *Mirror News*, August 25, 1958, Part I, p. 6.

Bauer, Malcolm, "Nabokov's 'Lolita' Tagged as Controversial," Portland *Oregonian*, August 31, 1958, Sec. 1, p. 11.

Berkeley *Daily Gazette*, September 10, 1958, p. 20.

Blackford, Frank, "An Aging European Roue and His Strange Passion," *Virginian-Pilot* and Portsmouth *Star* (Norfolk-Portsmouth, Va.), August 17, 1958, p. 6F.

Boroff, David, "Lolita: A New Kind of Love," NY *Post*, August 17, 1958, p. M11.

Bradley, John L., "Satire Does Not Come Off," Worcester *Sunday Telegram*, September 7, 1958, Sec. D, p. 11.

Brewer, Anita, "Abnormal the Norm for Artists?" Austin (Texas) *American-Statesman*, September 7, 1958, p. F-3.

Buchan, Bliss S., "Touchy Subject Treated With Freshness, Humor," New Orleans *Times-Picayune*, August 24, 1958, Sec. 2, p. 5.

Burlington (Vt.) *Free Press*, August 20, 1958, p. 7.

College English, XXI (October 1959), 69.

Collins, Arthur, "L'Affaire Lolita," Albany (NY) *Times-Union*, August 17, 1958, Sec. E, p. 11.

"Controversial Book Appears in U.S. Edition," Savannah *Morning News*, August 24, 1958, Magazine Section, p. 13.

Coogler, Edith Hills, "Hard to Put Down—You'll Find Humor in This Murder Tale," Atlanta *Journal and Constitution*, August 17, 1958, p. 2-E.

Creecy, John, "Is Best Seller Lolita Trash or Fine Novel?" Detroit *Sunday Times*, October 26, 1958, Sec. C, p. 5.

Culligan, Glendy, "Lolita Or As You Like It," Washington *Post*, August 17, 1958, p. E6.

Cuneo, Paul K., *The Critic*, XVII (December 1958-January 1959), 62–63.

Current Medical Digest, XXV (November 1958), 34.

Dame, Lawrence, "Lolita Reaches New Level of Daring," Sarasota *Herald-Tribune*, October 26, 1958, p. 34.

Derleth, August, "The Lolita Novel By Vladimir Nabokov—Book Lauded, Flayed," *Capital Times* (Madison, Wis.), August 28, 1958, p. 15.

Dettmer, Roger, Chicago *American*, November 23, 1958, pp. 37, 39.

Dusheck, George, "Beneath the Scandal, Real Literary Value," San Francisco *News*, August 23, 1958, TV Section, p. 10.

Fraser, Hugh Russell, "As I See It," San Francisco *Daily Commercial News*, November 17, 1958, p. 4.

Frost, Derland, "Serious Sex or a Spoof of American Romance?" Houston *Post*, August 24, 1958, Houston Now Section, p. 10.

G., E.W., "Nabokov's Lolita," *Cross Currents*, VIII (Fall 1958), 380.

G., W., "Controversial," Binghamton (NY) *Sunday Press*, August 24, 1958, p. 12-B.

Grabowski, Z.A., "Apropos 'Lolita,' " *Time and Tide*, XL (November 21, 1959), 1275.

Green, Peter, "Recent Fiction—Why Orchids For Lolita?" London *Daily Telegraph and Morning Post*, November 6, 1959, p. 17.

Hanscom, Leslie, "Exotic Distillation of Grotesque Love," NY *World-Telegram and Sun*, August 18, 1958, p. 19.

Hartley, Anthony, "Through the Taste Barrier," Manchester *Guardian*, November 6, 1959, p. 8.

H[artmann], F[rederick], Wilmington (Del.) *Morning News*, August 18, 1958, p. 8.

H[ass], V[ictor] P., "Erotica That Got Past U.S. Customs Officials," Omaha *Sunday World-Herald*, September 14, 1958, Magazine Section, p. 31.

Hatch, Robert, *The Nation*, CLXXXVII (August 30, 1958), 97.

Hazo, Samuel J., "Taxing But Rewarding," Pittsburgh *Press*, September 21, 1958, Sec. 5, p. 12.

Heth, Edward Harris, "Lolita's Shocking Case," Milwaukee *Journal*, August 24, 1958, Part 5, p. 4.

*Hicks, Granville, " 'Lolita' and Her Problems," *Saturday Review*, XLI (August 16, 1958), 12, 38.

Hogan, Thomas, "Off Limits?" *Irish Times* (Dublin), December 12, 1959, p. 8.

Hollander, John, "The Perilous Magic of Nymphets," *Partisan Review*, XXIII (Fall 1956), 557–560.

Houston *Press*, August 15, 1958, p. 10.

Hughes, Riley, "Lolita," *Catholic World*, CLXXXVIII (October 1958), 72.

Janeway, Elizabeth, "The Tragedy of Man Driven By Desire," NY *Times Book Review*, August 17, 1958, pp. 5, 25.

Jones, Tom, " 'Lolita' Called Lewd Kind of Pornography," Charleston (S.C.) *News and Courier*, September 21, 1958, p. 11-C.

Joysmith, Toby, "Concerning Nymphets. . . . At Last You Can Read the Novel You Could Not Buy!" *Mexico City News*, September 28, 1958, p. 8-A.

Keister, Don A., "Bit Boring, Says Critic of Novel Paris Banned," Cleveland *Plain Dealer*, August 31, 1958, p. 16-B.

Kennedy, Gerald, *Together*, III (February 1959), 56.

Kincheloe, H.G., " 'Lolita'—A Book to Disillusion and Dismay," Raleigh *News and Observer*, August 24, 1958, Sec. III, p. 5.

Kirk, Irene, "The Critic's Review of Current Books," Honolulu *Star-Bulletin*, January 31, 1959, p. 20.

Kirsch, Robert R., "Esthetic Bliss in Satirical Novel," Los Angeles *Times*, August 31, 1958, Part V, p. 6.

"L'Affair Lolita Bursts Into a Literary Flame," Washington (D.C.) *Sunday Star*, August 24, 1958, p. E-7.

La Fleche, Duane, "Beware! Here's *Lolita*," Albany (NY) *Knickerbocker News*, September 20, 1958, p. 11-B.

Lauter, Paul, "The Nymphet's Tale," New Leader, XLI (September 8, 1958), 22–23.

[Leathem, Leonard], Books of the Month (London), LXXIV (December 1959), 21.

" 'Lolita' and Its Critics," Manchester Guardian, January 23, 1959, p. 6.

Lynch, Mary, "Three Books You'll Hear About," Pittsburgh Press, September 14, 1958, Sec. 5, p. 12.

McLaughlin, Richard, "All That Anticipation, for What?" Boston Sunday Globe, August 24, 1958, p. 75.

McManis, John, "2 New Novels Pose Question," Detroit News, August 17, 1958, p. E-19.

M[ahony], [Esther R.], "Book Sensation," Montgomery Advertiser-Alabama Journal, October 5, 1958, Sec. H, p. 2.

Malcolm, Donald, "Lo, the Poor Nymphet," New Yorker, XXXIV (November 8, 1958), 195–196.

Mechling, Portia A.P., "Sensuality, Satire," Tulsa Sunday World, September 7, 1958, Magazine Section, p. 22.

*Meyer, Frank S., "The Strange Fate of 'Lolita'—A Lance Into Cotton Wool," National Review, VI (November 22, 1958), 340–341.

Minot, G., "Literate, Shocking," Boston Sunday Herald, August 17, 1958, Sec. III, p. 15.

Molnar, Thomas, "Matter-of-Fact Confession of a Non-Penitent," Commonweal, LXIX (October 28, 1958), 102.

Moore, John Rees, "My Sin, My Soul . . . New Novel By Nabokov," Roanoke Times, August 31, 1958, p. C-6.

"Nabokov's 'Lolita,' " The Scotsman (Edinburgh), November 7, 1959, p. 6.

*Nemerov, Howard, "The Morality of Art," Kenyon Review, XIX (Spring 1957), 313–314, 316–321.

"New Fiction," London Times, November 12, 1959, p. 15.

"New Novels—The Book of the Case," Glasgow Herald, November 5, 1959, p. 9.

Nichols, Luther, " 'Lolita'—Obscenity or Art?" San Francisco Examiner, August 18, 1958, Sec. II, p. 3.

Oakland Tribune, September 14, 1958, p. C-11.

O'Neill, Frank, "Nabokov's Hell-bent Anti-hero," Cleveland News, August 18, 1958, p. 13.

Owen, Theodore C., William Allen White Library Book Reviews (Emporia, Kan.), 4th Series (1960), 28.

Parker, Dorothy, "Sex—Without the Asterisks," Esquire, L (October 1958), 102–103 [103].

Peckham, Stanton, "Revolting or Ironically Amusing," Denver Post, August 17, 1958, Roundup Magazine, p. 28.

Pickrel, Paul, Harper's, CCXVII (September 1958), 96–97.

Playboy, V (September 1958), 20–21.

Prescott, Orville, "Books of The Times," NY Times, August 18, 1958, p. 17.

Price, Emerson, "Ignoble Theme," Cleveland Press, September 9, 1958, p. 14.

Reichert, Philip, M.D., Sexology, XXV (June 1959), 745.

Rennert, Leo, "A Superb Writer Fashions Work of Art on a Questionable Theme," Sacramento *Bee*, August 23, 1958, p. L-22.

R[ogers], W.G., "Much Ado About 'Lolita': Brilliant Game of Mind," Jackson (Miss.) *Clarion-Ledger and Daily News*, August 17, 1958, Sec. D, p. 7. See also Pasadena (Cal.) *Independent Star-News*, August 17, 1958, *Scene Magazine*, p. 10; Durham (N.C.) *Morning Herald*, September 28, 1958; Knoxville *News Sentinel*, September 7, 1958, p. E-2; Indianapolis *News*, November 15, 1958; Rochester (NY) *Democrat-Chronicle*, August 31, 1958.

Rolo, Charles, *Atlantic*, CCII (September 1958), 78.

Root, William, "This One Is at the Top of the Lists of Best-Sellers," *People's World* (San Francisco), October 18, 1958, p. 7.

Rovit, Earl H., *Books Abroad*, XXXIII (Spring 1959), 160.

"Russian Author Writes Shocker of Strange Love," Miami *Herald*, August 24, 1958, p. 6-H.

*Schickel, Richard, "Nabokov's Artistry," *The Progressive*, XXII (November 1958), 46, 48–49.

————, "A Review of a Novel You Can't Buy," *The Reporter*, XVII (November 28, 1957), 45–47.

Schoch, Russ, "Witty and Expert Writer," Des Moines *Sunday Register*, November 9, 1958, p. 15-G.

Schorr, Burt, "Lolita, at 12, Makes Scarlett O'Hara Turn Forever Amber," *Houston Press*, September 24, 1958, p. 11.

Schroetter, Hilda N., "Fine European Work," Richmond (Va.) *Times-Dispatch*, August 24, 1958, p. L-7.

Seldon, E.S., "Lolita and Justine," *Evergreen Review*, II (Autumn 1958), 156–159.

"A Sense of the Absurd," *Times Literary Supplement*, November 13, 1959, p. 657.

Shapiro, Charles, "It's Shocking . . . It's Funny . . . It's 'Lolita,'" Louisville *Courier-Journal*, August 24, 1958, Sec. 4, p. 8.

Sherman, John K., "'Lolita' May Give You the Creeps," Minneapolis *Sunday Tribune*, August 17, 1958, Editorial Section, p. 6.

Tallmer, Jerry, "*Lolita*," *Village Voice*, September 3, 1958, p. 5.

T[errell], L.D., *Chattanooga Times*, October 5, 1958, p. 18.

Tinkle, Lon, "Virtuosic Defense of Self-Indulgence," Dallas *Morning News*, August 17, 1958, Sec. 5, p. 10.

"To the End of Night," *Time*, LXXII (September 1, 1958), 62, 64.

Toynbee, Philip, "In Love With Language," London *Observer*, November 8, 1959, p. 22.

"Tremendous or Trivial?" Charlotte *News*, August 23, 1958, p. 5A.

Troy, George, "The Corruption of Lolita," Providence *Sunday Journal*, August 24, 1958, p. W-16.

Virginia Quarterly Review, XXXV (Winter 1959), x.

Vogler, Lewis, "'Lolita' Shocks With Superb Diabolical Wit," San Francisco *Chronicle*, August 24, 1958, *This World* Magazine, p. 26.

Walbridge, Earl F., *Library Journal*, LXXXIII (August 1958), 2183.

Walsh, John, "Sex Novel Has Power to Shock," Louisville Times, August 27, 1958, Sec. 1, p. 10.

W[eissblatt], H[arry] A., "Unique Novel," Trenton Sunday Times-Advertiser, September 14, 1958.

*West, Rebecca, " 'Lolita': A Tragic Book With a Sly Grimace," London Sunday Times, November 8, 1959, p. 16.

Windhorn, Stan, "The Clinical Cult," Sarasota Herald-Tribune, October 23, 1958, p. 6.

Winfrey, Lee, "French Novel Judged a Stout Dose," Nashville Tennessean, September 7, 1958, p. 10-G.

Wisconsin Library Bulletin, LIV (September-October 1958), 436.

Wolff, Anthony, "View & Preview," Daily Tar Heel (Univ. of N. Carolina, Chapel Hill), October 10, 1958, p. 2.

Yeiser, Frederick, "Some Recent Fiction," Cincinnati Enquirer, August 24, 1958, p. 11K.

PNIN. NY: Doubleday, 1957; London: William Heinemann, 1957; NY: Avon, 1957; London: Penguin, 1960; NY: Atheneum, 1964.

Ames, Alfred C., "Comedy, Satire, Tragedy," Chicago Sunday Tribune Magazine of Books, March 10, 1957, p. 12.

Amis, Kingsley, "Russian Salad," The Spectator, No. 6744 (September 27, 1957), 403.

Baisier, Leon, Best Sellers, XVII (April 1, 1957), 8.

Barefoot, Carl, Jr., "Novel Features Russian Mr. Peepers," Richmond (Va.) Times-Dispatch, April 14, 1957, p. 10-L.

Barnett, Steven R., "Vladimir Nabokov's Pnin: Tale of an Emigre Scholar," Harvard Crimson, April 27, 1957, pp. 3, 6.

Barrington, Kay, "Eccentric's Saga, Funny and Pathetic," Columbus (Ohio) Dispatch, March 31, 1957, TAB Section, p. 10.

Becket, Roger, "Heartbreaking Farce," National Review, III (April 6, 1957), 338.

Bishop, Dorothy, Ottawa Journal, April 6, 1957, p. 46.

Booklist, LIII (April 1, 1957), 404.

Bookmark (NY State Library, Albany), XVI (April 1957), 160.

Brady, Charles A., "3 New Novels Make Fiction Seem Real, Are a Delight to Read," Buffalo Evening News, March 23, 1957, Magazine Section, p. 6.

Bruccoli, M[atthew] J., "Pathetic Figure Dominates Tragicomedy," Richmond (Va.) *News Leader*, June 4, 1957, p. 11.

Burns, A.J., *Library Journal*, LXXXII (March 1, 1957), 673.

[Burton, Hal], "A Russian, Real Gone," *Newsday* (Garden City, NY), March 9, 1957, p. 27.

[Cassell, Harriet, and Richard Cassell], Mitchell (S. Dak.) *Daily Republic*, March 9, 1957, p. 4.

The Cresset (Valparaiso, Ind.), May 1957, p. 25.

Daugherty, Julia, " 'Pnin' Battles World in Comic Tale," Indianapolis *Star*, March 17, 1957, Sec. 8, p. 4.

Des Moines *Sunday Register*, April 28, 1957, p. 19-G.

Digges, Dudley, "Hilarious, Touching Life of Mr. Pnin," Baltimore *Sun*, March 31, 1957, Sec. A, p. 6.

Elliott, George P., *Hudson Review*, X (Summer 1957), 289–291.

Friedman, Robert, "Sadness in This Humor," St. Louis *Sunday Post-Dispatch*, May 12, 1957, p. 4C.

Green, C. Sylvester, "Complications Grow to Provide a Story," Durham (N.C.) *Morning Herald*, April 28, 1957, p. 5.

H., C.G., St. Paul *Sunday Pioneer Press*, March 24, 1957, TAB Section, p. 8.

Hanscom, Leslie, "Pnin a Lovable Creation," Gary *Post-Tribune*, April 7, 1957, *Panorama* Section, p. 10.

Havighurst, Walter, "Po Amerikanski," *Saturday Review*, XL (March 9, 1957), 14.

Hicks, Granville, "Chaplin With a Russian Accent," NY *Times Book Review*, March 10, 1957, p. 4.

Hutchens, John K., "Book Review," NY *Herald Tribune*, March 15, 1957, p. 17.

Johnson, Pamela Hansford, "New Novels," *New Statesman*, LIV (September 21, 1957), 361–362 [361].

Kirk, Irene, Honolulu *Star-Bulletin*, June 7, 1958, p. 17.

Kirsch, Robert R., "The Book Report," Los Angeles *Times*, March 12, 1957, Part III, p. 5.

La Farge, John, *America*, XCVII (April 27, 1957), 144.

Lange, Victor, "A Saint of the Comic," *New Republic*, CXXXVI (May 6, 1957), 16.

Latham, Robert M., "The Adventures of a Professor," Chattanooga *Times*, May 26, 1957, p. 18.

Laughlin, Ruth, "Fiction By an Italian and a Russian Emigre," Greensboro (N.C.) *Daily News*, April 7, 1957, Feature Section, p. 3.

L[aycock], E[dward] A., Boston *Sunday Globe*, March 24, 1957, p. B-7.

Lerman, Leo, *Mademoiselle*, XLV (July 1957), 50.

"Lightly Go," *Times Literary Supplement*, October 4, 1957, p. 598.

L[ong], H.S., "Man of Misery," Columbia *Missourian*, June 11, 1957, p. 4.

Longstreet, Steven, "Off the Bookshelf," Los Angeles *Free Press*, March 14, 1957, p. 2.

Macon *News*, March 14, 1957, p. 31.

Maddocks, Melvin, "Respecting the Rule to 'Write About What You

Know,'" *Christian Science Monitor*, March 7, 1957, p. 5.

Maslin, Marsh, "Introducing Unique Timofey Pnin," *San Francisco Call-Bulletin*, March 27, 1957, p. 26.

Mattingly, G.Q., *Grail*, August 1957, p. 53.

Means, Marianne, "Square Peg in Round Hole," Lincoln (Neb.) *Sunday Journal and Star*, March 17, 1957, Sec. D, p. 3.

*Nemerov, Howard, "The Morality of Art," *Kenyon Review*, XIX (Spring 1957), 313–314, 316–321 [314].

"New Leases of Life?" *Times Literary Supplement*, September 2, 1960, p. 562.

Nichols, Luther, "The Book Corner—A Mirror of Our Foibles," *San Francisco Examiner*, March 7, 1957, Sec. III, p. 3.

Parker, Dorothy, "Best Fiction of 1957," *Esquire*, XLVIII (December 1957), 60, 62, 64, 66 [62].

"Pathetic Professor Pnin Battling With Progress," *Berkeley Daily Gazette*, June 15, 1957, Vista Section, p. 6.

Paulding, Gouverneur, "A Moment of Passion on the Croquet Court," *The Reporter*, XVI (March 21, 1957), 48.

Peterson, Virgilia, "Prof. Pnin Is Wonderful," *NY Herald Tribune Book Review*, March 10, 1957, p. 5.

Pickrel, Paul, *Harper's*, CCXIV (April 1957), 90.

*"Pnin & Pan," *Time*, LXIX (March 18, 1957), 108, 110.

Poore, Charles, "Books of The Times," *NY Times*, March 7, 1957, p. 27.

Popkin, George, "The Defenestration of Pnin," *Providence Sunday Journal*, March 24, 1957, Sec. VI, p. 8.

The Progressive, XXI (June 1957), 38.

Redfield, Malissa, "Humorous, Tender Tale of a Tragicomic Russian," *Virginian-Pilot* and *Portsmouth Star* (Norfolk-Portsmouth, Va.), March 10, 1957, p. 6-C.

Rodgers, James P., "A Russian in America," *Pittsburgh Press*, March 10, 1957, Sec, 3, p. 10.

Rose, Ruth Goodman, *The Scrantonian* (Scranton, Pa.), March 17, 1957, p. 19.

S., E.M., "Eccentric Teacher Wistfully Funny," *Hartford Times*, June 1, 1957, p. 18.

S., H.M., Wilmington (Del.) *News*, March 18, 1957, p. 15.

"Sad Sack With Russian Accent," *Savannah Morning News*, April 21, 1957, p. 47.

Simmons, Fern, "Transplanting Of a Russian," *Springfield (Mo.) Sunday News and Leader*, June 30, 1957, p. B5.

Smith, Alice Waddell, "Reader Can't Laugh Aloud at Poor Pnin," *Fort Wayne News-Sentinel*, March 23, 1957, p. 3.

*Stern, Richard G., "Pnin and the Dust-Jacket," *Prairie Schooner*, XXXI (Summer 1957), 161–164.

Stull, Carolyn, "Odd Adventures of Russian Emigre on College Campus," *Oakland Tribune*, April 14, 1957, p. 14-C.

Sweet, Joy, "A Beautiful Short Novel," *Louisville Courier-Journal*, March 17, 1957, Sec. 4, p. 7.

Turner, Decherd, "Fantasy, Irony, and History Too," Dallas *Times Herald*, April 14, 1957, *Roundup* Section, p. 12.

Vogler, Lewis, "The Emigre Professor Suffered From Noise, Fools and Squirrels," San Francisco *Chronicle*, March 17, 1957, *This World* Magazine, p. 23.

W., L., "Appealing Character," Boston *Sunday Herald*, March 17, 1957.

Warshaw, Steven, "Meet Pnin, Loveable Flop," San Francisco *News*, March 16, 1957, p. 16T.

Washington Post and Times Herald, March 10, 1957, p. E7.

W[eissblatt], H[arry] A., "Professor," Trenton (N.J.) *Sunday Times-Advertiser*, April 14, 1957, Part Four, p. 12.

W[ellner], J[essica], Auburn (NY) *Citizen-Advertizer*, March 23, 1957, p. 4.

"White Russian World," Ogden *Standard-Examiner*, March 23, 1957, p. 11-B.

Williams, David, "New Novels," Manchester *Guardian*, September 10, 1957, p. 4.

NABOKOV'S DOZEN: A COLLECTION OF THIRTEEN STORIES. NY: Doubleday, 1958; Toronto: Doubleday, Canada, 1959; London: William Heinemann, 1959; NY: Popular Library, 1959; London: Penguin, 1960.

Alpert, Hollis, "The Timelessness of Now," *Saturday Review*, XLI (October 25, 1958), 30.

Beckett, Roger, "Nabokov As a Storyteller," *NY Herald Tribune Book Review*, September 28, 1958, p. 6.

Berkman, Sylvia, "Smothered Voices," *NY Times Book Review*, September 21, 1958, pp. 5, 45.

Buchan, Bliss, "Linguistic Trick-Shots in Stories," *New Orleans Times-Picayune*, May 17, 1959, Section Two, p. 4.

Hogan, William, "A Bookman's Notebook—Stories By Nabokov and Other New Collections," San Francisco *Chronicle*, September 30, 1958, p. 29.

Lewis, Naomi, "New Short Stories," *New Statesman*, LVII (March 21, 1959), 420.

"Mixed Fiction," *Time*, LXXII (September 22, 1958), 88.

Nemerov, Howard, "The Ills From Missing Dates," *Venture*, III (Nos. 1 & 2, 1959), 66–69.

"New Fiction," London *Times*, March 19, 1959, p. 15.

"New Leases of Life?" *Times Literary Supplement*, September 2, 1960, p. 562.

Oboler, E.M., *Library Journal*, LXXXIII (September 1, 1958), 2322.

O'Dell, Scott, "Nabokov Exudes Vulgarity Again," Los Angeles *Mirror News*, September 22, 1958, Part 2, p. 2.

Shapiro, Charles, "13 Short Ones By Nabokov," Louisville *Courier-Journal*, November 16, 1958, Sec. 4, p. 7.

"Short, But Not Always Sweet," *Times Literary Supplement*, March 27, 1959, p. 173.

Sullivan, Richard, "Thirteen Engaging and Nicely Balanced Stories," *Chicago Sunday Tribune Magazine of Books*, September 28, 1958, p. 3.

Towne, Jane H., *The Pilot* (Southern Pines, N.C.), February 4, 1960, Sec. 1, p. 3.

Wilson, Angus, "Nabokov's Basement," *The Spectator*, No. 6821 (March 20, 1959), 412.

POEMS. NY: Doubleday, 1959; Toronto: Doubleday, Canada, 1959; London: George Weidenfeld & Nicolson, 1961.

Bergonzi, Bernard, "New Notes in English," Manchester *Guardian*, April 14, 1961, p. 6.

Booklist, LVI (October 1, 1959), 72.

Booth, Philip, "Voices That Speak in Verse," NY *Times Book Review*, September 6, 1959, p. 6.

Bruccoli, M[atthew] J., "Poetry: Nabokov's Verse Shows Rare Wit," Richmond (Va.) *News Leader*, September 16, 1959, p. 13.

Buchanan, Leigh M., "Early Nabokov Novel Describes Dim-Lit World of Artists' Soul," *Cornell Daily Sun* (Ithaca, NY), January 20, 1960, p. 9.

[Carnahan, Ken], Berkeley *Gazette*, August 22, 1959, Vista Section, p. 12.

Churchill, Kay, "Author of *Lolita* Fails to Hit Mark in His Poems," Kingsport (Tenn.) *Times-News*, September 6, 1959, p. 5-B.

Clarke, Austin, "At Home and Abroad," *Irish Times* (Dublin), April 15, 1961, p. 10.

Coogler, Edith Hills, *Atlanta Journal and Constitution*, August 16, 1959, p. 2-E.

Deschner, Don, "Nabokov, From 'Lolita' to 'Poems,'" Los Angeles *Herald Express*, August 31, 1959, p. C-3.

Dickinson, Peter, "Native Wood-Notes Tame," *Punch*, CCXL (April 12, 1961), 589.

Dudek, Louis, "The Fireworks of Nabokov's Poetry Are Brief and Cool," *Montreal Star*, February 6, 1960, p. 30.

Greacen, Robert, "Poetry Selection," London *Daily Telegraph and Morning Post*, July 21, 1961, p. 16.

Hartmann, Frederick, Wilmington (Del.) *News*, August 31, 1959, p. 9.

Hecht, Anthony, "The Anguish of the Spirit and the Letter," *Hudson Review*, XII (Winter 1959–1960), 593–603 [593].

Hoffman, Daniel G., "Arrivals and Rebirths," *Sewanee Review*, LXVIII (January-March 1960), 118–137 [123–124].

Holley, Fred S., "Poetry Today—Frost's Influence Apparent," *Virginian-Pilot and Portsmouth Star* (Norfolk-Portsmouth, Va.), August 28, 1960, p. 6-F.

Jacobsen, Josephine, Baltimore *Evening Sun*, November 18, 1959, p. 40.

Kahn, Hannah, "Novelists Weave Glowing Poetry," *Miami Herald*, November 22, 1959, p. 23-E.

Kohler, Dayton, "Nabokov As a Poet," Louisville *Courier-Journal*, October 11, 1959, Sec. 4, p. 7.

Morse, Samuel F., "Sample of Each," *Hartford Courant*, September 6, 1959, Magazine Section, p. 13.

"Nabokov Poems," San Antonio *Express and News*, September 13, 1959, *Relax* Section, p. 14.

"New Sidelights On a Lepidopterist," *Times Literary Supplement*, April 7, 1961, p. 218.

Norris, Hoke, "Nabokov Spins Profound Magic in Two Works," Chicago *Sun-Times*, September 6, 1959, Section Three, p. 4.

Peel, J.H.B., "Poetry, Like Peppermint," *John O'London's*, V (August 10, 1961), 183.

Robie, B.A., *Library Journal*, LXXIV (July 1959), 2190.

"Russian Poet," Sacramento *Union*, September 13, 1959, p. 7A.

Schott, Webster, "Obscure Symbolism Is 'Out' in the Offerings of Many Poets of Today," *Kansas City Star*, October 15, 1959, p. 42.

Stuart, Francis, "Nabokov in Verse," *Irish Press* (Dublin), May 27, 1961, p. 4.

Thwaite, Anthony, "Several Accomplishments," *The Spectator*, No. 6935 (May 26, 1961), 770.

Tomlinson, Charles, "Last of Lands," *New Statesman*, LXI (April 28, 1961), 674.

Walsh, Chad, "Nabokov, Poet," *NY Herald Tribune Book Review*, January 31, 1960, p. 4.

W[edgewood], M[aurice], "The Nabokov Collection," *Northern Echo* (Darlington), April 14, 1961.

Wright, James, "A Poetry Chronicle," *Poetry*, XCV (March 1960), 373–378 [378].

Young, Douglas, "New Verse—Some Younger Voices," *Glasgow Herald*, June 8, 1961, p. 6.

INVITATION TO A BEHEADING. NY: G.P. Putnam's, 1959; London: George Weidenfeld & Nicolson, 1960; Toronto: Longman's Green, 1960.

Amis, Kingsley, "More or Less Familiar," London Observer, June 5, 1960, p. 18.

Bryden, Ronald, "I, Cincinnatus," The Spectator, No. 6884 (June 3, 1960), 810.

Crane, Milton, "Grim Story of Our Era in Nabokov," Chicago Sunday Tribune Magazine of Books, November 8, 1959, p. 10.

Davenport, Dorrie, " 'Lolita' Really Came From the Steppes," Washington Post, November 1, 1959, p. E7.

DeMott, Benjamin, "Monge and Other Destinations," Hudson Review, XII (Winter 1960), 618–626 [620–621].

Dill, Marshall, Jr., "Two Earlier Novels By Lolita's Author," Oakland Tribune, December 6, 1959, p. C-9.

"The Dream of Cincinnatus C," Time, LXXIV (October 26, 1959), 109.

"An Early Nabokov Novel," The Press (Christchurch, N.Z.), August 27, 1960, p. 3.

Forster, Peter, "Another Nabokov and This Time He Lets Slip the Secret of His Strange Talent," London Daily Express, June 2, 1960, p. 6.

Gobi, Nunzio, "The Magician's Rope," Brunonia Book Review (Brown University), Winter 1960, pp. 24–26.

Green, Peter, "Recent Fiction—A Whip for English Colonials," London Daily Telegraph and Morning Post, June 3, 1960, p. 16.

Kippax, H.G., "Early Tale By Author of 'Lolita,' " Sydney Morning Herald, September 17, 1960, p. 14.

Kops, Bernard, "Under the Tyrants," Jewish Chronicle (London), August 26, 1960, p. 18.

McLaughlin, Richard, "Highly Poetic Novel By Vladimir Nabokov," Springfield (Mass.) Sunday Republican, December 20, 1959, p. 5D.

MacPherson, H.I., "Strange Fantasy," New Zealand Weekly News (Auckland), October 5, 1960, p. 38.

Millard, John, "New Novels," London Evening News, June 9, 1960.

"New Novels—Murder in the Village," Glasgow Herald, June 9, 1960, p. 5.

"New Novels: Nabokov's Nightmare," The Scotsman (Edinburgh), June 18, 1960, p. 6.

New Yorker, XXXV (November 28, 1959), 240–241.

NY Herald Tribune Book Review, July 9, 1961, p. 12.

Oboler, E.M., Library Journal, LXXXIV (October 1, 1959), 3057.

Peerman, Dean, Christian Century, LXXVII (February 3, 1960), 141.

Perkin, Robert L., "Wry Sort of Allegory, or Is It?" Rocky Mountain News (Denver), October 25, 1959, p. 6A.

Peterson, Virgilia, "In Front of Reason He Waves a Red Cape," Saturday Review, XLII (October 24, 1959), 35.

Phelps, Robert, "The Unique Vision of Vladimir Nabokov," NY Herald

Tribune Book Review, November 22, 1959, p. 10.

Pickrel, Paul, "Vintage Nabokov," *Harper's*, CCXIX (November 1959), 104, 106 [104].

Price, R.G.G., "New Novels," *Punch*, CCXXXVIII (June 15, 1960), 854.

Richardson, Maurice, "New Novels," *New Statesman*, LIX (June 4, 1960), 832–834 [832–833].

Rolo, Charles, "Basic Illegality," *Atlantic*, CCIV (December 1959), 171.

——, "Duped By a Nightmare," *NY Times Book Review*, October 25, 1959, pp. 4, 69.

"Romantic Rascal," *Birmingham Mail*, June 8, 1960, p. 3.

"Ruffling Thin Hair," *Times Literary Supplement*, January 10, 1960, p. 365.

Scott, J.D., "Freedom & Love," *London Sunday Times*, June 5, 1960, p. 18.

Singer, Burns, "Utopia and Reality," *Encounter*, XIV (January 1961), 77–79 [77].

Stringfellow, Olga, "Masquerade of Parasites," *John O'London's*, II (June 23, 1960), 752.

Vogler, Lewis, "'Lolita' Produced a Haul of Nabokov," San Francisco *Sunday Chronicle*, December 13, 1959, *This World* Magazine, p. 36.

*Wain, John, "Nabokov's Beheading," *New Republic*, CXLI (December 21, 1959), 17–19.

Webb, W.L., "Invitation to the Danse Macabre," *Manchester Guardian*, June 10, 1960, p. 8.

Williams, Owen, "Nabokov Presents a Weird Allegorical Nightmare," *Cape Times* (Cape Town), June 29, 1960, p. 10.

THE SONG OF IGOR'S CAMPAIGN (tr. by Nabokov). NY: Vintage, 1960; London: George Weidenfeld & Nicolson, 1961.

Bowra, C.M., "Song of the Steppes," *London Sunday Telegraph*, April 16, 1961, p. 7.

Christian, R.F., "Nabokov's Version," *Birmingham Post*, March 28, 1961, p. 4.

Costello, D.P., "In Defence of Igor," *Manchester Guardian*, March 24, 1961, p. 17.

Cross, Gustav, "Fine Poetry From Russia," *Sydney Morning Herald*, August 26, 1961, p. 14.

Greacen, Robert, "Poetry Selection," *London Daily Telegraph and Morn-*

ing Post, July 21, 1961, p. 16.
"Igor Fights Again," London *Times,* June 15, 1961, p. 17.
"New Sidelights on a Lepidopterist," *Times Literary Supplement,* April 7, 1961, p. 218.
W[edgewood], M[aurice], "The Nabokov Collection," *Northern Echo* (Darlington), April 14, 1961.

PALE FIRE. NY: G.P. Putnam's, 1962; London: George Weidenfeld & Nicolson, 1962; NY: Lancer Books, 1963.

A., R., "Another Fancy Failure By the Author of 'Lolita,'" *Peoples World* (San Francisco), October 13, 1962, p. 7.
Adams, Robert M., "Fiction Chronicle," *Hudson Review,* XV (Autumn 1962), 420–430 [420–423].
Alexander, Holmes, "Author Dissects 'Lolita' Critics the Hard Way," *Tampa Tribune,* June 3, 1962, p. 11-D.
Allsop, Kenneth, "After *Lolita* Is This Nabokov Just Pulling Our Legs?" London *Daily Mail,* November 8, 1962, p. 12.
Altshuler, Thelma, "'Lolita's' Back in New Version," *Miami News,* June 17, 1962, p. 6B.
Ashford, Gerald, "Nabokov Has a New One, But . . . What Does It Mean?" San Antonio *Express and News,* May 27, 1962, p. 2-G.
B., V.A., "Still Has His Secret," Trenton (N.J.) *Sunday Times-Advertiser,* July 29, 1962, Part Four, p. 14.
Barkham, John, "A Fantastic New Novel By the Author of 'Lolita,'" NY *World-Telegram and Sun,* May 25, 1962, p. 27. See also Gary *Post-Tribune,* June 3, 1962, p. D-17; St. Petersburg *Times,* May 27, 1962, p. 18.
Barley, Rex, "Two Novels Out of Routine Rut," *Arizona Republic* (Phoenix), June 3, 1962, p. 16-B.
Barrett, William, *Atlantic,* CCIX (June 1962), 108.
Benedictus, David, London *Daily Express,* November 8, 1962, p. 14.
"The Best Charlotte Russe," *Newark News,* June 24, 1962, Sec. 8, p. A4.
Best Sellers, XXII (June 1, 1962), 107–108.
Booklist, LVIII (July 15, 1962), 786.
Bradbury, Malcolm, "New Novels," *Punch,* CCXLIII (December 12, 1962), 875–876.
Bradley, Van Allen, "Author's 'Secret' Is Not Worth the Search," Columbus (Ohio) *Dispatch,* July 1, 1962, TAB Section, p. 10. See also

Chicago *Daily News*, May 28, 1962.

Brady, Charles A., "Author of 'Lolita' Displays Disturbing Side of His Fancy," Buffalo *Evening News*, May 26, 1962, p. B-8.

Broderick, John, "Appearance and Reality," *Irish Times* (Dublin), December 1, 1962, p. 8.

Brooks, Gwendolyn, " 'Lolita's' Author Lampoons Poets," Chicago *Sun-Times*, June 3, 1962, Section Three, p. 2.

Brown, Alexander C., "Scholastic Trappings Serve to Tell Story in 'Lolita' Author's New Novel," Newport News *Daily Press*, June 10, 1962, Sec. D, p. 4.

Bruckman, Pat, *Canadian Forum*, XLII (January 1963), 227–228.

Buchan, Bliss S., "Nabokov Talent Shines in Novel With Odd Plot," New Orleans *Times-Picayune*, June 17, 1962, Section Two, p. 6.

Burgess, Anthony, "Nabokov Masquerade," *Yorkshire Post* (Leeds), November 15, 1962, p. 4.

Butler, Rupert, "Pale Fires," *John O'London's*, VII (December 6, 1962), 524–525.

Cannell, Kathleen, " 'Pale Fire' Satire Extraordinary," Providence *Sunday Journal*, May 27, 1962, p. W-20.

Chamberlain, John, "Reading for Pleasure—Coffee Made of Acorns," *Wall Street Journal*, June 7, 1962, p. 14.

*Chester, Alfred, "Nabokov's Anti-Novel," *Commentary*, XXXIV (November 1962), 449–451.

Church, Richard, "New Books—Language of Wit and Bravura," *Country Life* (London), CXXXIII (January 17, 1963), 133, 135 [133].

Cloyne, George, "Jesting Footnotes Tell a Story," *NY Times Book Review*, May 27, 1962, pp. 1, 18.

Coffey, Jerry, "Book Jacket Correct—'Lolita' Author's New Book Defies Description," Fort Worth *Star-Telegram*, June 10, 1962, Sec. 2, p. 14.

Coleman, John, "Books," *Queen*, CCXXI (November 13, 1962), 21.

Colton, Larry, "Nabokov's Latest No 'Lolita,' " Portland (Me.) *Sunday Telegram*, June 24, 1962, p. 2C.

*Connolly, Cyril, "Nabokov's High Fantasy," London *Sunday Times*, November 11, 1962, p. 31.

Costello, Carl, " 'Pale Fire' Greeted By Fusillade," Duluth *Sunday News-Tribune*, July 1, 1962, *Cosmopolitan* Section. p. 2.

Dennis, Nigel, "It's Hard to Name This Butterfly!" London *Sunday Telegraph*, November 11, 1962, p. 6.

Doar, Harriet, "Nabokov's Book Leaves One Uneasy," *Charlotte Observer*, May 27, 1962, p. 9-C.

Driver, Morley, "The Fire Is Not Pale," Detroit *Free Press*, June 3, 1962, Sec. B, p. 5.

Dwight, Ogden G., "You Read New Nabokov Like an Insane Anagram," Des Moines *Sunday Register*, June 17, 1962, p. 15-G.

Engle, Paul, "An Immense Fantasy of Glittering Brilliance," Chicago *Sunday Tribune Magazine of Books*, June 10, 1962, p. 3.

E[vans], E[ric], "The Nabokov Enigma," *Oxford Times*, November 23, 1962, p. 28.

Faulconbridge, Faith, "New Novels—Hall of Mirrors," Glasgow *Herald*, November 15, 1962, p. 11.

Feinstein, George W., "Vladimir Nabokov's Newest Novel Described as Elaborate Leg-Pull," Pasadena *Independent Star-News*, May 27, 1962, Scene Section, p. 12.

Fiedler, Leslie A., "The Persistence of Babel," Manchester *Guardian*, November 9, 1962, p. 14. See also Manchester *Guardian Weekly*, LXXXVII (November 15, 1962), 10.

Foley, Charles, "Lolita's Creator as Spoofer," Savannah *Morning News*, June 3, 1962, Magazine Section, p. 8.

Forrest, Alan, "Bookshelf," London *Sunday Citizen*, December 2, 1962, p. 24.

Freedley, George, "Nabokov's New Novel: 'Pale Fire,'" NY *Morning Telegraph*, May 26, 1962, p. 2.

Garner, Edward, "Pale Novel," Raleigh *News and Observer*, February 17, 1963, Sec. III, p. 5.

Goldsborough, Diana, *Tamarack Review*, Autumn 1962, pp. 110–111.

Goodspeed, John, "Nabokov's Latest Less Shocking," Baltimore *Evening Sun*, June 14, 1962, p. A18.

G[reet], D[onald] P., "Books," Ithaca *Journal*, June 8, 1962, p. 5.

Harvey, Elizabeth, "A Great Comic Writer," Birmingham *Post*, November 13, 1962, p. 4.

H[ayes], E. N[elson], "Spectacular New Nabokov Novel Reflects Reader, Not the World," New Haven *Register*, May 27, 1962, Sec. 4, p. 7.

*Highet, Gilbert, "To the Sound of Hollow Laughter," *Horizon*, IV (July 1962), 89–91.

Hinson, Betsy, "Genius Scores Another Victory," Charlotte *News*, June 23, 1962, p. 18-C.

Holley, Fred S., "Nabokov's Tour de Force—Satiric Joke on Man and His Foibles," Norfolk *Virginian-Pilot*, May 27, 1962, p. F-6.

Holloway, David, "Recent Fiction—A Joke on the Academics," London *Daily Telegraph and Morning Post*, November 9, 1962, p. 17.

Hutchens, John K., "'Pale Fire,'" NY *Herald Tribune*, May 28, 1962, p. 27.

Idema, Jim, "Nabokov's New Novel Is in Tricky Form," Denver *Sunday Post*, May 20, 1962, Roundup Section, p. 11.

Irish Press (Dublin), February 2, 1963, p. 6.

Jack, W.T., "Nabokov's Spoofing Novel—A Blind Man Plays 3 Dimensional Chess," Dallas *Times Herald*, May 27, 1962, Sec. E, p. 8.

Jaffee, Dan, "Unfortunately, the Parody Lost Its Punch," Kansas City *Star*, May 26, 1962, p. 16.

Johnson, Eva, "A Non-Novel By Nabokov Revolving Around a Poem," San Francisco *Examiner*, May 27, 1962, Highlight Section, p. 3.

Keese, Parton C., "Olympian Horsing Around," Worcester *Sunday Telegram*, May 27, 1962, Sec. E, p. 12.

*Keir, Walter, "Nabokov's Score," *New Saltire*, No. 6 (December 1962), 77–81.

*Kermode, Frank, "Zemblances," *New Statesman*, LXIV (November 9, 1962), 671–672.

Kirsch, Robert R., "The Full Range of Drollery," Los Angeles *Times*, June 3, 1962, *Calendar* Section, p. 14.

Langguth, Jack, "Author of *Lolita*—'Pale Fire' Brilliant," North Hollywood (Cal.) *Valley Times*, August 3, 1962, *Today* Section, p. 10.

L[aycock], E[dward] A., "Even Index Worth Reading," Boston *Sunday Globe*, May 27, 1962, p. 50.

Le Clair, Edward E., Jr., "Nabokov Has New Book," Albany (NY) *Times-Union*, June 3, 1962, Sec. F, p. 6.

Lerner, Laurence, "Nabokov's Cryptogram," *The Listener*, LXVIII (November 29, 1962), 931.

Lister, Richard, "The New Nabokov—A Mixture of Poetry and Puzzles," London *Evening Standard*, November 13, 1962, p. 9.

M.,G., "How to Be Taken and Like It," South Bend *Tribune*, July 1, 1962, Sec. 1, p. 12.

*McCarthy, Mary, "A Bolt From the Blue," *New Republic*, CXLVI (June 4, 1962), 21–27. See also *Encounter*, XIX (October 1962), 71–72, 74, 76–78, 80–82, 84.

*Macdonald, Dwight, "Virtuosity Rewarded or Dr. Kinbote's Revenge," *Partisan Review*, XXIX (Summer 1962), 437–442.

McLaughlin, Richard, "Nabokov the Virtuoso," *Commonweal*, LXXVI (July 6, 1962), 380.

——, " 'Pale Fire,' " Springfield (Mass.) *Republican*, June 17, 1962, p. 4D.

Malin, Irving, *Wisconsin Studies in Contemporary Literature*, IV (Spring-Summer 1963), 252–255.

*Maloff, Saul, "The World of Rococo," *The Nation*, CXCIV (June 16, 1962), 541–542.

Mercier, Jeanne, "A New Nabokov Firework," Milwaukee *Journal*, August 5, 1962, Part 5, p. 4.

Mims, Catherine, " 'Pale Fire' a Fusion of Image and Music," Nashville *Tennessean*, June 3, 1962, p. 12-F.

Moon, Eric, *Library Journal*, LXXXVII (May 15, 1962), 1916–1917.

Moore, Harry T., "Another First-Rate Spoof—Author of 'Lolita' Does It Again," St. Louis *Post-Dispatch*, June 3, 1962, p. 4B.

Morgan, T.J., "Death Halts Poet at Line 999—King's Exploits in 'Pale Fire,' " Hartford *Times*, May 26, 1962, p. 32.

"Multivalence," *Times Literary Supplement*, November 16, 1962, p. 869.

*Murray, Michele, "Aesthetic Delight—The Author-Created Confusion Is Deliberate," *Catholic Reporter* (Kansas City, Mo.), July 6, 1962, p. 11.

Nesbitt, W.J., "Nabokov's Tour de Force," *Northern Echo* (Darlington), November 16, 1962.

"New Fiction," London *Times*, November 15, 1962, p. 16.

"New Idea in Novel Writing," *East Anglian Daily News* (Ipswich), January 25, 1963, p. 7.

Newquist, Roy, "Novel By Nabokov Is Off Beat and Fiery," Chicago *Heights Star*, May 27, 1962, p. 6.

Nichols, Alan, "Nabokov Writes a Witty Satire," *The Age* (Melbourne), March 2, 1963, p. 19.

Nordell, Roderick, "Nabokov: Parody, Pedantry, and Waste," *Christian Science Monitor*, May 31, 1962, p. 7.

Nye, Robert, "Nabokov's Blue Magic," *The Scotsman* (Edinburgh), December 1, 1962, Week-end Magazine, p. 2.

O'Brien, E.D., "Literary Lounger," *Illustrated London News*, CCXLI (November 24, 1962), 852.

O'Brien, John H., " 'Betern Lolita Somwat'—Belles-Lettres Uniquely Done," *Detroit News*, June 24, 1962, p. 3-G.

Owen, B. Evan, "On the Fringe of Sanity," *Oxford Mail*, November 8, 1962, p. 8.

Pagones, Dorrie, "Nabokov Needles the Novel," *Washington Post*, May 27, 1962, p. E6.

[Pasley, Virginia], "Not Pale at All But a Brilliant Exhibition," *Newsday* (Garden City, NY), May 26, 1962, p. 35.

Peden, William, "Inverted Commentary on Four Cantos," *Saturday Review*, XLV (May 26, 1962), 30.

Peterson, Virgilia, "Novel About Poet Caught Between Two Lunatics Is Wild, Funny and Original," *Toledo Blade*, June 10, 1962, Sec. 2, p. 6. See also *NY Herald Tribune Books*, May 27, 1962, p. 7.

Pickrel, Paul, "A Strange One," *Harper's*, CCXXIV (June 1962), 92, 94.

Playboy, IX (July 1962), 27.

Prescott, Orville, "Books of The Times," *NY Times*, May 28, 1962, p. 27.

Price, Emerson, "Cynical Tale," *Cleveland Press*, May 29, 1962 p. A 8.

"Problem-piece By Nabokov," *Nottingham Guardian Journal*, November 15, 1962, p. 4.

Raven, Simon, "Nabokov's Blueprint," *The Spectator*, No. 7014 (November 30, 1962), 864–865.

"The Russian Box Trick," *Time*, LXXIX (June 1, 1962), 84.

S[cott], W[infield] T[ownley], "After Lolita, What?" *Santa Fe Sunday New Mexican*, June 10, 1962, Pasatiempo Section, p. 7.

Show, II (June 1962), 104.

Shroyer, Frederick, "World of Books," *Los Angeles Herald Examiner*, July 1, 1962, p. B-2.

Slavitt, D.R., *Book-of-the-Month-Club News*, June 1962, p. 8.

Smith, Miles A., "Dazzling Mixture," *Omaha World-Herald*, June 3, 1962, Magazine Section, p. 30. See also *Bridgeport Sunday Post*, May 27, 1962; *El Paso Times*, June 17, 1962; *Durham (N.C.) Morning Herald*, June 24, 1962; *St. Petersburg Independent*, June 6, 1962.

Southern, Terry, "When Film Gets Good," *The Nation*, CXCV (November 17, 1962), 331.

Spearman, Walter, "The Literary Lantern," *Greensboro Record*, May 26, 1962, Sec. A, p. 4.

Steiner, George, "Lament for Language Lost," *The Reporter*, XXVI (June 7, 1962), 40, 42, 44–45.

Stern, Jerome, "No Curio But a Search for Reality," *Raleigh News and Observer*, July 15, 1962, Sec. III, p. 5.

Sutton, Carol, "Nabokov Still Shines Without Lolita," Louisville *Times*, June 28, 1962, Sec. 1, p. 15.

Thorpe, Day, "Lolita's Nabokov Now Does a Novel in Verse," Washington (D.C.) *Sunday Star*, May 27, 1962, p. B-5.

Toynbee, Philip, "Nabokov's Conundrum," London *Observer*, November 11, 1962, p. 24.

Trotter, Margaret, "Baffling After 'Lolita'—Nabokov's 'Pale Fire' Glows for the Persistent," Atlanta *Journal and Constitution*, June 17, 1962, p. 12-D.

Virginia Quarterly Review, XXXVIII (Autumn 1962), civ.

Vogler, Lewis, "Nabokov's Tour de Force Warms Your Risibilities," San Francisco *Sunday Chronicle*, June 3, 1962, *This World Magazine*, p. 30.

Wade, Gerald, "Self-Glorification Is Egotist's Goal In Poem Critique," Beaumont *Journal*, June 8, 1962, p. 24.

Ward, May Williams, "Books," Wellington (Kan.) *Daily News*, July 28, 1962, p. 3.

Weir, Sybil, "Nabokov's 'Pale Fire' Is Significant Work," Oakland *Tribune*, May 27, 1962, p. 2-EL.

Whitworth, Walter, "Nabokov's 'Pale Fire' Is Jibe at University Folk," Indianapolis *News*, June 23, 1962, p. 2.

Williams, Bethea, "Nabokov's 'Pale Fire' Lauded," Charleston (S.C.) *News and Courier*, June 10, 1962, p. 11-C.

Williams, Vera, " 'Lolita' Author Treads New Path," Long Beach (Cal.) *Independent Press-Telegram*, June 10, 1962.

Wright, John F., " 'Lolita's' Author Rides On Name," Memphis *Commercial Appeal*, June 10, 1962, Sec. IV, p. 10.

Y., H.W., "Nabokov Has Good Time At Expense of Reader," Columbus (Ohio) *Citizen-Journal*, June 9, 1962, p. 13.

Yeiser, Frederick, "Nabokov Has His Little Jokes in His New Novel, 'Pale Fire,' " Cincinnati *Enquirer*, May 26, 1962, p. 12.

Zeiger, Arthur, "A Bifocal Novel With One Lens Distorted," Louisville *Courier-Journal*, June 17, 1962, Sec. 4, p. 7.

THE GIFT. NY: G.P. Putnam's, 1963; Ontario: Longman's, Canada, 1963; London: George Weidenfeld & Nicolson, 1963.

Abram, Lynwood, "Strangest Prose-Poet Russia Ever Produced," Houston *Chronicle*, June 2, 1963, *Zest Magazine*, p. 10.

Allsop, Kenneth, "Nabokov . . . Long Before Lolita," London Daily Mail, November 7, 1963, p. 16.

B., A.G., "Nabokov Novel Not Up to Par," Charleston (S.C.) News and Courier, July 28, 1963, p. 11-C.

Barrett, William, "Dream of Russia," Atlantic, CCXI (May 1963), 135.

Benedictus, David, "Before Lolita," London Sunday Telegraph, November 10, 1963, p. 17.

B[rady], C[harles] A., "Brilliant Novel By Nabokov Has Limited Appeal," Buffalo Evening News, May 25, 1963, p. B-10.

Brown, Alexander C., "Early Nabokov Novel Charms But Befuddles," Newport News Daily Press, July 7, 1963, Magazine Section, p. 9.

Brown, Leonard, " 'Lolita' Nabokov Offers The Gift," Pasadena Independent Star News, June 23, 1963, Scene Section, p. 9.

Butler, Henry, "Russia's Not What It Used to Be." Indianapolis Times, May 26, 1963, p. 31.

Coffey, Jerry, "Translation Shows Younger Nabokov," Fort Worth Star-Telegram, June 2, 1963, Sec. 2, p. 13.

Cook, Bruce, The Critic, XXII (August-September 1963), 74–75.

Cook, Eric, "Nabokov's 'Gift,' " Time & Tide and John O'London's, XLIV (28 November-4 December 1963), 24–25.

Corke, Hilary, "Nabokov: Old News From Old Prospero," New Republic, CXLIX (July 6, 1963), 25, 27.

Crane, Milton, "Intricate Tale With Russian Literature As the Heroine," Chicago Sunday Tribune Magazine of Books, June 2, 1963, p. 5.

Culligan, Glendy, "Nabokov's Early Gift," Washington Post, May 26, 1963, p. G8. See also San Francisco Chronicle, May 31, 1963, p. 37.

Daily Worker (London), December 19, 1963, p. 2.

Dance, Jim, "The Creator of Lolita Bares Writer's Soul," Detroit Free Press, June 2, 1963, Sec. B, p. 5.

Darack, Arthur, "Nabokov's Newest Novel Is a Russian Translation," Cincinnati Enquirer, May 25, 1963, p. 10.

Davie, Donald, "Reader in the Dock," Manchester Guardian, November 8, 1963, p. 8.

Dwight, Ogden G., "Difficult But Absorbing Is Early Nabokov Novel," Des Moines Sunday Register, July 28, 1963, p. 5-F.

Feinstein, Elaine, "Fiction," Cambridge Review, LXXXV (November 23, 1963), 152.

Forsyth, Malcolm, "Old Nabokov Work Put Into English," New Orleans Times-Picayune, June 9, 1963, Section Three, p. 7.

Fuller, Edmund, "Reading for Pleasure—Studies in Character," Wall Street Journal, June 17, 1963, p. 10.

Gilmore, Jane L., "Early Nabokov Novel Paradoxical Wonder," Omaha Sunday World-Herald, July 14, 1963, Sec. G., p. 25.

Griffin, Lloyd W., Library Journal, LXXXVII (April 15, 1963), 1688.

Gustafson, R.F., America, CIX (July 27, 1963), 99.

Gutwillig, Robert, "The Russian Finale of V. Nabokov," NY Herald Tribune Books, May 26, 1963, p. 7.

Hayes, E. Nelson, "A Nabokov Definition: 'Genius Is an African Who

Dreams Up Snow,' " New Haven *Register*, June 23, 1963, Part 4, p. 6.

Hayes, Mary Anne, "Suggestion For a Plot—Literature Is the Heroine of Early Nabokov Novel," Houston *Post*, June 2, 1963, *Perspective* Section, p. 7.

Hern, Anthony, "Clever Stuff From Nabokov," London *Evening Standard*, November 12, 1963, p. 19.

Hicks, Granville, "The Birth of the Bard," *Saturday Review*, XLVI (June 1, 1963), 17, 48.

Hilgenstuhler, Ted, "From Lolita's Author," Los Angeles *Herald-Examiner*, June 16, 1963, p. K-5.

Hinde, Thomas, "Waugh's Oxford," *The Spectator*, No. 7063 (November 8, 1963), 605.

Holley, Fred S., "Man's Self-Deception," Norfolk *Virginian-Pilot*, June 16, 1963, p. B-6.

H[unter], A[nna] C., "Autobiography Mystic Maze of Truth Whim and Fiction," Savannah *Morning News*, June 9, 1963, *Magazine* Section, p. 8.

Hutchens, John K., "A Novel—But a Memoir, Too," NY *Herald Tribune*, May 27, 1963, p. 28. See also Minneapolis *Sunday Tribune*, June 23, 1963, p. E-6; Miami *News*, June 2, 1963.

*Hyman, Stanley Edgar, "Nabokov's Gift," *New Leader*, XLVI (October 14, 1963), 21.

Idema, Jim, "Russian Exiles in Berlin," Denver *Post*, May 26, 1963, *Roundup* Section, p. 10.

Iglehart, L.T., Jr., "Served By Vladimir Nabokov—A Rich, Slavic Pudding," St. Louis *Globe-Democrat*, June 1-2, 1963, p. 4F.

Iremonger, Lucille, *Housewife* (London), January 1964, p. 17.

Keane, F.J., "Recent Fiction: From Russia and Ireland," *Irish Independent*, LXXII (November 30, 1963), 12.

Kirsch, Robert R., "Four Newcomers: A Study in Extremes," Los Angeles *Times*, June 16, 1963, *Calendar* Section, p. 12.

Kostelanetz, Richard, "The Gift," *Village Voice*, June 13, 1963, pp. 7–8.

Laycock, Edward A., "Nabokov's Best Russian—A New Experience," Boston *Sunday Globe*, May 12, 1963, p. 73.

Levine, Paul, "Easterns and Westerns," *Hudson Review*, XVI (Autumn 1963), 455–462 [462].

London *Sunday Citizen*, November 24, 1963, p. 23.

"Lord of Language," *Time*, LXXXI (June 14, 1963), 102.

MacGillirray, Arthur, S.J., *Best Sellers*, XXIII (July 1, 1963), 123–124.

McLaughlin, Richard, "Nabokov's Many Talents Shown Clearly in 'Gift,' " Springfield (Mass.) *Sunday Republican*, July 7, 1963, p. 4D.

*Malcolm, Donald, "A Retrospect," *New Yorker*, XL (April 25, 1964), 198, 201, 202–205.

Malin, Irving, "Anti-Heroic Novel," Louisville *Courier-Journal*, June 2, 1963, Sec. 4, p. 5.

Mercier, Jeanne, "Samovars in Berlin," Milwaukee *Journal*, June 30, 1963, Part 5, p. 4.

Mitchell, Julian, "Dazzling Energy," London *Sunday Times*, November 10, 1963, p. 38.

Moore, Harry T., "Early Novel of Nabokov Is Fine Fun," Boston *Sunday Herald*, June 2, 1963, Sec. 1, p. 10.

Murray, Michele, "Gift From Nabokov Deserves Gratitude," *Catholic Reporter* (Kansas City, Mo.), June 28, 1963, p. 5.

"Nabokov Makes Dialogue Sparkle," Duluth *Sunday News-Tribune*, July 21, 1963, *Cosmopolitan* Section, p. 2.

"Nabokov Makes It Difficult," Nottingham *Guardian Journal*, November 14, 1963, p. 4.

[Nesbitt, W.J.], "Nabokov: And an Irish Epic," *Northern Echo* (Darlington), November 29, 1963.

"New Fiction," London *Times*, November 14, 1963, p. 17.

Newquist, Roy, "Another Rich Novel By Nabokov," Chicago Heights *Star*, June 6, 1963, p. 14.

Nordell, Roderick, "Nabokov: Straining for the Faraway," *Christian Science Monitor*, May 29, 1963, p. 11.

Norris, Hoke, Chicago *Sun-Times*, June 9, 1963, Sec. 3, p. 2.

O'Donnell, John, "Nabokov's New Old Novel," Baltimore *Sun*, May 26, 1963, Sec. A, p. 5.

O'Hara, Robert C., "A Vladimir Nabokov of Solid Stature," Tampa *Tribune*, June 16, 1963, p. 6-G.

Page, James F., "A Professor Pure, Puzzled and Put Out," Memphis *Press Scimitar*, July 26, 1963, p. 6.

Pasley, Virginia, *Newsday* (Garden City, NY), May 4, 1963, p. 33.

Perlberg, Mark M., "A Novel of the Pursuit of Excellence—Eccentric, Hilarious, Splendid and Beautiful," Chicago *Daily News*, June 8, 1963, *Panorama* Section, p. 10.

Perley, Maie E., "The Book Scene—A Glowing Work By Nabokov," Louisville *Times*, July 29, 1963, Sec. 1, p. 7.

Pollock, Venetia, "New Fiction," *Punch*, CCXLV (December 4, 1963), 828–829 [829].

Portland *Sunday Oregonian*, June 9, 1963, p. A7.

Pusey, William W., III, "Two Offbeat Works By Russian Writers," Roanoke *Times*, September 15, 1963, p. B-8.

Rogers, Leona, "Nabokov Tale Pleases Admirer," Fort Wayne *News-Sentinel*, August 10, 1963, p. 4A.

Rogers, W.G., "Nabokov Novel Not a *Lolita*," Gary *Post-Tribune*, May 26, 1963, Sec. D, p. 9. See also Dallas *Morning News*, May 26, 1963, Sec. 5, p. 10; Hartford *Times*, May 25, 1963.

Rollow, Jack W., "Nabokov's Merry Pranks Hard to Follow in 'Gift,' " Charlotte *Observer*, June 2, 1963, p. 5-C.

Ross, Maggie, "New Novels," *The Listener*, LXX (November 21, 1963), 852–853 [852].

Rowe, Percy, "Even the Mighty Can Fall," Toronto *Telegram*, October 5, 1963, p. 16.

"Russian Romp," *Times Literary Supplement*, November 7, 1963, p. 901.

Sanders, Nicholas, "New Nabokov Novel Is Literary Event," Nashville *Banner*, June 7, 1963, p. 32.

Sandrof, Nancy, "Work of Uncanny Lucidity," Worcester *Telegram*, May 26, 1963, p. 16E.

"Scarey Sophistication," *Newsweek*, LXI (June 3, 1963), 86.

Segal, David I., "Stretching the Novel," *Commonweal*, LXXVIII (July 12, 1963), 431.

Share, Bernard, "The Moth and the Candle," *Irish Times* (Dublin), November 16, 1963, p. 10.

Sherman, Thomas B., "Reading & Writing—Nabokov Nets Another Mixed Literary Bag," St. Louis *Sunday Post-Dispatch*, September 22, 1963, p. 4C.

Smith, Miles, "Early Nabokov Tale Wordy, Confusing," Toledo *Blade*, May 26, 1963, Sec. 2, p. 6. See also Berkeley *Daily Gazette*, June 8, 1963; Utica *Observer*, July 7, 1963.

Snyder, Mary Rennels, Gary *Post-Tribune*, May 19, 1963, p. D-22.

"Soviet Writer Remembers Berlin Life," Miami *Herald*, June 2, 1963, p. 7-J.

"A Sparkling Vladimir Nabokov," Santa Barbara *News-Press*, June 23, 1963, p. C8.

Spender, Stephen, "A Poet's Invented and Demolished Truth," *NY Times Book Review*, May 26, 1963, pp. 4–5.

The Sphere, CCLV (November 30, 1963), 346–347.

Stanley, Donald, "A Bizarre Tale By Lolita's Creator," San Francisco *Examiner*, May 26, 1963, *Highlight* Section, p. 18.

Sylvester, William, "Magnificent 'Gift'—Nabokov's Talent Shines Again," Cleveland *Plain Dealer*, June 2, 1963, p. 8-F.

Taubman, Robert, "Near Zero," *New Statesman*, LXVI (November 8, 1963), 653–654 [654].

Thorpe, Day, "Earlier Nabokov From the Russian," Washington (D.C.) *Sunday Star*, May 26, 1963, p. B-5.

Tucker, Martin, "Nabokov's Latest Novelty," *NY Post*, July 7, 1963, *Magazine* Section, p. 13.

W., C.E.S., Kitchener-Waterloo *Record*, July 27, 1963, p. 6.

Watkins, Sue, "On Russia," Austin (Texas) *American-Statesman*, June 16, 1963, *Show World* Section, p. 21.

Weir, Sybil, "Nabokov's 'The Gift' Reveals An Artist's Direction," Oakland *Tribune*, June 9, 1963, p. EL-2.

W[eissblatt], H[arry] A., "The Poet In Exile," Trenton (N.J.) *Sunday Times-Advertiser*, June 23, 1963, Part Two, p. 14.

Williams, Vera, Long Beach (Cal.) *Independent Press-Telegram*, June 13, 1963, pp. P-17, P-25.

Wolff, Renate C., "Early Nabokov Novel—'The Gift' Not Up to 'Lolita,' " Atlanta *Journal and Constitution*, September 22, 1963, p. 9-D.

EUGENE ONEGIN (tr. by Nabokov). NY: Pantheon, 1964.

Adams, Phoebe, *Atlantic*, CCXIV (October 1964), 150.

Bowra, C.M., "Two Translations of *Eugene Onegin*," *Sewanee Review*, LXXIII (Spring 1965), 330.

Burgess, Anthony, "Pushkin & Kinbote," *Encounter*, XXIV (May 1965), 74.

Choice, II (June 1965), 232–233.

Conquest, Robert, "Nabokov's *Eugene Onegin*," *Poetry*, CVI (June 1965), 236–238.

Daniels, Guy, "Pushkin and the Lepidopterist," *New Republic*, CLII (April 3, 1965), 19.

"Great Performance," *Time*, LXXXIV (July 31, 1964), 64.

Hingley, Ronald, "Pushkin's Monument," *The Spectator*, (January 1, 1965), 19.

Kublin, Hyman, *Library Journal*, LXXXIX (October 1, 1964), 3754.

Monas, Sidney, "Where Are You, Pushkin?" *Hudson Review*, XVII (Winter 1964–65), 597–608 [598–602].

"Pushkin, Nabokov and Eugene Onegin," *Times Literary Supplement*, January 28, 1965, p. 68.

Rayford, Julian Lee, "Hosannahs on His Name!" *American Book Collector*, XV (April 1965), 4.

Ricks, Christopher, "Nabokov's Pushkin," *New Statesman*, LXVII (December 25, 1964), 995.

Rosen, Nathan, "Variations on Russian Verse," *Saturday Review*, XLVII (November 28, 1964), 25.

Salisbury, Harrison, "End Papers," *NY Times*, July 6, 1964, p. 27.

*Simmons, Ernest J., "A Nabokov Guide Through the World of Alexander Pushkin," *NY Times Book Review*, June 28, 1964, pp. 4–5.

Slater, Lydia Pasternak, "Letter-perfect May Not Be Flawless," *Book Week* (NY *Herald Tribune*, Washington *Post*, San Francisco *Examiner*), July 19, 1964, pp. 4, 16.

Strong, R.L., Jr., *Books Abroad*, XXXIX (Winter 1965), 89.

*Wilson, Edmund, "The Strange Case of Pushkin and Nabokov," *NY Review of Books*, July 15, 1965, pp. 3–6.

THE DEFENSE (THE DEFENCE). NY: G.P. Putnam's, 1964; London: George Weidenfeld & Nicolson, 1964.

Adams, J.R., "His Dream World Faces Checkmate," *Rocky Mountain News* (Denver), September 13, 1964, p. 16A.

*Adams, Robert M., "Nabokov's Game," *NY Review of Books*, January 14, 1965, pp. 18–19.

Allen, Morse, "*The Defense*," Hartford *Courant*, December 13, 1964, Magazine Section, p. 22.

Ancrum, Calhoun, "Vladimir Nabokov Centers Novel Around Chess Game," Charleston (S.C.) *News and Courier*, September 27, 1964, p. 5-C.

Aronow, Judith, "Nabokov's Early Novel Is Translated, Is Perceptive," Beaumont *Journal*, February 26, 1965, p. 18.

Bainhart, Marjorie, "Nabokov Writes of Chess Genius in *The Defense*," Fort Wayne *News-Sentinel*, September 26, 1964, p. 4A.

Baldwin, Helene, "A Losing Game," *Georgetown Spectator* (Georgetown University, Washington, D.C.), November 4, 1964, pp. 5, 7.

Barrett, William, "Checkmate," *Atlantic*, CCXIV (November 1964), 197.

Beichman, Arnold, "Nabokov Checkmated," *Christian Science Monitor*, October 1, 1964, p. 11.

Berridge, Elizabeth, "Recent Fiction—Dissection of a New Town," London *Daily Telegraph and Morning Post*, November 12, 1964, p. 21.

Best Sellers, XXIV (October 1, 1964), 261.

Bischoff, Barbara, *Oregon Journal* (Portland), October 17, 1964, p. 7.

Blake, Robert G., "Case Against Art For Art's Sake," Charleston (W. Va.) *Sunday Gazette-Mail*, February 28, 1965, p. 22m.

Booklist, LXI (December 15, 1964), 382.

Bowman, Harry, "Life Seen as Game of Chess," Dallas *Morning News*, October 4, 1964, Sec. 6, p. 10.

Bradbury, Malcolm, "Grand Master," *The Spectator*, No. 7116 (November 13, 1964), 643–644.

Brady, Charles A., "What Became of Novels? Three Latest Examples," Buffalo *Evening News*, September 26, 1964, p. B-12.

Brogan, Colm, "Gobbledegook in Oxford," *Yorkshire Post* (Leeds), November 26, 1964, p. 4.

Butler, Henry, Indianapolis *Times*, September 27, 1964, p. 27.

Cevasio, George, *The Sign* (Union City, N.J.), XLIV (December 1964), 64–65.

Chmelev, G., *Books Abroad*, XXXIX (Spring 1965), 218.

Choice, II (March 1965), 27–28.

Clements, Robert J., "Life Was Like a Chessboard," *Saturday Review*, XLVII (September 26, 1964), 45–46.

Clute, John, "Another Attempt to Catch the Moth," *Varsity* (University of Toronto), LXXXIV (October 30, 1964), 7.

Cope, Tom, Fort Pierce (Fla.) *News Tribune*, May 22, 1964, Roundup Section, p. 1.

Coppard, Kit, "Serious Relationships," London *Tribune*, January 1, 1965, p. 12.

Davenport, Guy, "Turn the Other Face," *National Review*, XVI (November 3, 1964), 978–979 [979].

Davis, Jeff, "Insane Genius," Los Angeles *Herald-Examiner*, October 11, 1964, p. D-7.

Dekom, Otto, "Early Nabokov," Wilmington (Del.) *Morning News*, January 20, 1965, p. 19.

Dennis, Nigel, "Sacrifices of a Grandmaster," *NY Times Book Review*, September 27, 1964, p. 4.

Derleth, August, "An Early Nabokov Novel," *Capital Times* (Madison, Wis.), October 1, 1964, p. 17.

"The Devil's Tongue," *Newsweek*, LXIV (September 28, 1964), 98, 99A.

Diehl, Suzanne, "New Nabokov Character," San Antonio *Express and News*, October 4, 1964, p. 8-H.

"Faded Snapshot," *Time*, LXXXIV (October 2, 1964), 137, 139.

*Field, Andrew, "The View From Above," *New Leader*, XLVII (October 26, 1964), 22–23.

Forbes, Anthony, "New Translation Shows Russian Author at Best," Nashville *Banner*, January 15, 1965, p. 21.

Freshwater, Phillip C., "Early Nabokov Double Game Hides Parable in Chess," Sacramento *Bee*, October 25, 1964, p. L20.

Fuller, Edmund, "Destiny From a Game of Chess," *Chicago Sunday Tribune Books Today*, October 4, 1964, p. 4.

Furbank, P.N., "Chess and Jigsaw," *Encounter*, XXIV (January 1965), 83–86.

Garrett, James, "Four New Books Provide Variety," Cleveland *Press*, October 16, 1964, *Showtime* Section, p. 12.

Griffin, Lloyd W., *Library Journal*, LXXXIX (October 15, 1964), 3973.

Hall, Barbara Hodge, "Nabokov's *Defense* Brilliant," Anniston (Ala.) *Star*, October 4, 1964, p. 6C.

*Hampshire, Stuart, "Among the Barbarians," *New Statesman*, LXVIII (November 6, 1964), 702–703.

Harvey, Elizabeth, "A Set of Tragic Comedies," Birmingham *Post*, November 27, 1964, Christmas Books Supplement, p. VII.

Hayes, E. Nelson, "A Life Devoted to the Game," Worcester *Sunday Telegram*, September 20, 1964, p. E20.

Heppenstall, Rayner, "Gambit Accepted," London *Sunday Telegraph*, November 8, 1964, p. 21.

Herman, Jerry, "Another Brilliant Tale From Nabokov's Pen," Oakland *Tribune*, October 20, 1964, p. D-19.

Hobby, Diana, "A Pattern on Squares," Houston *Post*, November 1, 1964, '64 Section, p. 6.

Hogan, William, "Nabokov's Chess . . . A Grand Passion," San Francisco *Chronicle*, October 1, 1964, p. 47.

Holder, Laurie, Jr., "All the Pieces Fit Into Place," Raleigh *News and Observer*, October 18, 1964, Sec. III, p. 5.

Hoyt, Charles Alva, "Vladimir Nabokov: A Pretty Good Novel," Louisville

Courier-Journal, November 22, 1964, Sec. 4, p. 5.

Keenan, Joseph T., *Extension*, LIX (January 1965), 11.

Kennedy, Maurice, "Of Chess and Checkmates," *Irish Times* (Dublin), November 28, 1964, p. 10.

Kermode, Frank, "Squares in Front of His Eyes," *Book Week* (NY Herald *Tribune*, Washington *Post*, San Francisco *Examiner*), September 27, 1964, pp. 3, 17.

Koziar, Theodore, "The Chess Genius," Newark *Sunday News*, November 15, 1964, p. E10.

L., B.L., "Nabokov Still Deft," Kitchener-Waterloo *Record*, December 19, 1964, p. 8.

Legate, David M., "Pawns and People," Montreal *Star*, October 24, 1964, Entertainments Section, p. 7.

Library Journal, LXXXIX (September 15, 1964), 3509.

Mercier, Jeanne, "A Master of Chess in Check," Milwaukee *Journal*, September 27, 1964, Part 5, p. 4.

Miller, Anne, "Life's Chess Game Makes Weird Plot," Fort Worth *Star-Telegram*, November 1, 1964, Sec. 5, p. 10.

Moore, Harry T., St. Louis *Sunday Post-Dispatch*, October 18, 1964, p. 4C.

[Nesbitt, W.J.], *Northern Echo* (Darlington), November 20, 1964, p. 14.

"New Fiction," London *Times*, November 19, 1964, p. 16.

Newquist, Roy, "And Hilarity Reigns Supreme," Chicago Heights *Star*, September 27, 1964, p. 10.

Newsweek, LXIV (December 21, 1964), 82.

Norris, Hoke, "Again, The Brilliance of Nabokov," Chicago *Sun-Times*, September 27, 1964, Section Three, p. 2.

Nottingham *Guardian Journal*, November 18, 1964, p. 8.

"Novel, Hero Both Suffer 'Breakdown,' " Augusta (Ga.) *Chronicle-Herald*, September 27, 1964, p. 14-E.

O'Donnell, John B., "Life As a Game of Chess," Baltimore *Sun*, October 4, 1964, Sec. D, p. 5.

Perlberg, Mark, "Rise and Fall of a Chess Master," Chicago *Daily News*, September 26, 1964, *Panorama* Section, p. 7.

Phillips, Jerry J., "Superior Writer on Love Views Youth's Awakening," Chattanooga *Times*, October 25, 1964, p. 20.

Pineo, Mari, "About Books," Vancouver *Sun*, October 23, 1964, *Leisure* Section.

Poore, Charles, "Vladimir Nabokov's Novel of Life as a Game of Chess," NY *Times*, September 24, 1964, p. 39.

Price, R.G.G., "New Fiction," *Punch*, CCXLVII (December 9, 1964), 901.

Pryce-Jones, Alan, "Life Through Prisms," NY *Herald Tribune*, October 6, 1964, p. 27.

Ratcliffe, Michael, "Grandmaster on the Run," London *Sunday Times*, November 8, 1964, p. 48.

Ravitz, Abe C., "Chess Sets Slower Pace Than 'Lolita,' " Cleveland *Plain Dealer*, September 20, 1964, p. 8-H.

Rogers, W.G., "*Lolita* Man Turns to Chess," Eugene (Ore.) *Register-Guard*, October 4, 1964, *Emerald Empire* Section, p. 6.

Rowe, Percy, "Masters and Madness in Book of the Week," Toronto *Telegram*, October 17, 1964, *Showcase* Supplement, p. 23.

Sale, Roger, "Provincial Champions and Grandmasters," *Hudson Review*, XVII (Winter 1964–65), 608–618 [611–612].

Scratch, Patty, Van Nuys (Cal.) *News*, January 22, 1965, p. 24.

Seward, William W., Jr., "The Hero-Masochists," Norfolk *Virginian-Pilot*, September 27, 1964, p. B-6.

Smith, Miles A., "Nabokov Again Plays Games With Readers," Columbus (Ohio) *Dispatch*, October 11, 1964, TAB Section, p. 17.

Sokolsky, Anatole A., "Unreality Is Price of Originality," Tampa *Tribune*, October 11, 1964, p. 6-F.

Spearman, Walter, "Protestantism in the South," Chapel Hill (N.C.) *Weekly*, October 11, 1964, Sec. 2, p. 3.

"Strange Mating," *Times Literary Supplement*, November 19, 1964, p. 1033.

T., M., "Grandmaster in Check," Glasgow *Herald*, December 5, 1964, Christmas Books Section, p. IV.

Taylor, Robin, "A Game of Chess," Winnipeg *Free Press*, November 21, 1964, *Modern Living and Leisure* Section, p. 5.

*Thorpe, Day, "A Master Chess Player Loses in Game of Life," Washington (D.C.) *Sunday Star*, September 27, 1964, p. C-5.

*Updike, John, "Grandmaster Nabokov," *New Republic*, CLI (September 26, 1964), 15–18.

Urquhart, Fred, "Ribald Morality," Oxford *Mail*, November 12, 1964, p. 8.

Wall, Stephen, "New Novels," *The Listener*, LXXII (November 19, 1964), 806.

Wardle, Irving, "Nabokov's Golden Touch," London *Observer*, November 8, 1964, p. 27.

Webb, W.L., "Nabokov's Chess Man," Manchester *Guardian*, November 6, 1964, p. 8.

Weiss, Lawrence G., "Nabokov's Virtuosity Shines in 'The Defense,'" Denver *Post*, October 11, 1964, *Roundup* Section, p. 38.

W[ellner], J[essica], Auburn (NY) *Citizen-Advertizer*, October 3, 1964, p. 4.

White, Edward M., "'The Defense' Swells Nabokov's Reputation," Boston *Globe*, September 24, 1964, p. 63.

SELECTED BIBLIOGRAPHY
OF NABOKOV'S WORK*

Originally in Russian

Novels:
Mashenka (1926)
Korol dama valet (*King Queen Knave*, 1928)
Zashchita Luzhina (*The Defense*, 1930)
Soglyadatay (*The Eye*, 1930)
Camera Obscura (1932)
Podvig (*The Exploit*, 1932)
Otchayanie (*Despair*, 1936)
Dar (*The Gift*, 1937)
Priglashenie na kazn' (*Invitation to a Beheading*, 1938)

Short Story Collections:
Vozvrashchenie Chorba (*The Return of Chorb*, 1930)
Soglyadatay (*The Eye*, 1938)
Vesna v Fialte (*Spring in Fialta*, 1956)

Poems:
Stichotvorenia (*1929–1951*) (*Poems 1929–1951*, 1952)

Originally in English

Novels:
The Real Life of Sebastian Knight (1941)
Bend Sinister (1947)
Lolita (1955)

* This Selected Bibliography is in part based upon the extensive bibliography of Nabokov's published writings by Dieter E. Zimmer, Vladimir Nabokov, Bibliographie des Gesamtwerks (Reinbek bei Hamburg, 1964)—Donald Sheehan.

Pnin (1957)
Pale Fire (1962)

Other Works:
Nabokov's Dozen (1958), a collection of short stories
Nikolai Gogol (1944 and 1959), literary criticism
Conclusive Evidence (1951) or Speak, Memory (1960; rev. 1966), a memoir
Poems (1959)

Translations

Three Russian Poets, Selections from Pushkin, Lermontov and Tyutchev (1944), verse translations from Russian
The Song of Igor's Campaign (1960), anonymous, translated from Old Russian
Eugene Onegin (1964), Alexander Pushkin, translated with commentary

Russian Novels translated into English

Despair (1936; rev. 1966)
Camera Obscura (1936) or Laughter in the Dark (1938 and 1960)
Invitation to a Beheading (1959)
The Gift (1963)
The Defense (1964)
The Eye (1965)

Drama

Smerti (Death, 1923)
Dedushka (The Grandfather, 1923)
Polius (The [North] Pole, 1924)
Tragedia gospodina Morna (The Tragedy of Mr. Morn, 1924/25?)
Tshelovek is SSSR (The Man from the U.S.S.R., 1927)
Sobytie (The Event, 1938)
Izobretenie Val'sa (The Waltz Invention, 1938; rev. 1960)

INDEX